Rural Republican Realignment
in the Modern South

Rural Republican Realignment in the Modern South

THE UNTOLD STORY

M.V. Hood III and Seth C. McKee

THE UNIVERSITY OF
SOUTH CAROLINA PRESS

© 2022 University of South Carolina

Published by the University of South Carolina Press
Columbia, South Carolina 29208

www.uscpress.com

Manufactured in the United States of America

31 30 29 28 27 26 25 24 23 22
10 9 8 7 6 5 4 3 2 1

Library of Congress Cataloging-in-Publication Data
can be found at http://catalog.loc.gov/.

ISBN: 978-1-64336-301-1 (hardcover)
ISBN: 978-1-64336-302-8 (paperback)
ISBN: 978-1-64336-303-5 (ebook)

To Chuck, Earl, and Merle; you will never know how much y'all taught us about Southern Politics.

Contents

Acknowledgments

You only get to write so many books in this amazing journey called life, and this book is one of which we are admittedly rather proud. To be sure, it takes the assistance of others to get the job done, so we want to thank some people. First, as dutiful husbands and fathers, we are exceedingly grateful that our respective wives and children tolerate the incessant political science research we have collaborated on, dating back to a fateful conversation at the *Citadel Symposium on Southern Politics* cocktail hour in March of 2006. To Esther, Jesse, and Andrew McKee and Ashley, Madison, McKinley, Maitland, Austin, and Addie Grace Hood, a heartfelt thanks for letting us pursue this scholarly passion that we know all of you could hardly care less about!

Next, we are thankful that Ehren Foley at the University of South Carolina Press conveyed such strong support in bringing our project to the attention of his colleagues and assuring us that this was just the kind of book he saw as deserving of an advance contract. Hopefully, we have not disappointed.

With respect to financial support, we thank Professor Emeritus of Political Science and Philip H. Alston Jr. Distinguished Chair Emeritus Keith T. Poole at the University of Georgia and the Department of Political Science at Texas Tech University for underwriting the costs associated with the 2020 survey we conducted, which served as the foundation for the discussion and analysis located in chapter ten. Trey first presented many of the results from our survey as the keynote speaker at the 2020 biennial *Citadel Symposium on Southern Politics*. Thanks to Scott Buchanan, now at Georgia College (and the Symposium director at the time) for selecting Trey for this opportunity.

Regarding some of the data presented in the book, we appreciate Clark Bensen at POLIDATA (for US House of Representatives data), Sean Evans at Union University (for Tennessee polling data), and Lia Merivaki and Steve Shaffer at Mississippi State University (for Mississippi Poll data).

For some old academic citations on rural migration patterns, we thank the indefatigable Jim Gimpel at the University of Maryland. A timely thank you to Keith Dougherty at the University of Georgia for asking Seth if he was interested in presenting a paper at the 2021 American Political History Conference. There is no question that chapter seven, on US House elections, got done a lot faster because of our participation in this conference. We also thank our discussant Kate Krimmel at Barnard College for directing some pointed and important questions to us. We also thank our colleagues Chuck Bullock at the University of Georgia and Irwin Morris at North Carolina State University.

Their latest work on southern politics is greatly appreciated and cited in the pages that follow.

Finally, we want to thank our parents for the opportunities they provided us growing up in various parts of the southern United States. Neither of us would identify as country boys. We are products of the amalgam of the New South, having lived predominantly in suburban communities, but with easy access to rural and urban settings and, hence, having acquired a comfortable familiarity with both. Indeed, we have lived in and traveled extensively throughout the region, from Far West Texas to Key West, Florida, and to just about every area of the South in between. And given our ages, we have also lived through the remarkable partisan transformation of Dixie from a predominantly Democratic milieu to a two-party competitive environment, to a Republican stronghold that is, depending on the area, becoming more competitive again. Among all these changes, the shift of rural white southerners to the Grand Old Party appears the most pronounced and enduring, and yet, at least in academic writing, this development has not received nearly enough attention. Hence, we do not stoop to hyperbole by characterizing our account of this realignment as the untold story. It is no more.

M.V. (Trey) Hood III, Oconee County, Georgia
Seth C. McKee, Stillwater, Oklahoma

Introduction

Texas: Thirty Years Apart

It has been more than a quarter century since the last Democrat represented the Lone Star State in the US Senate. In 1988, current Houstonian and erstwhile transplanted Connecticut Yankee George H. W. Bush handily defeated Massachusetts Governor Michael Dukakis to become America's forty-first president. Bush's win made it three consecutive Republican presidential victories. Among the eleven ex-Confederate states,[1] only Georgia awarded its Electoral College votes to a Democrat, dating back to 1980, when it remained loyal to its embattled native son, President Jimmy Carter. Meanwhile, as Bush easily dispatched Dukakis in Texas with fifty-six percent of the two-party vote, veteran Democratic Senator Lloyd Bentsen defeated his Republican challenger by amassing just under sixty percent.[2]

Texas has 254 counties, far more than any other state (Georgia is the runner-up, with 159). In 1988, of the 223 counties that delivered a majority of their votes to Democratic Senator Bentsen (i.e., 87.7% of Texas's counties favored the Democrat for US Senate), fully 138 (61.8%) of these same counties also delivered majority support to Grand Old Party (GOP) presidential nominee George Bush. Put somewhat differently, consider that Bush garnered a popular presidential vote majority in 169 Texas counties (66.5%), with 138 of these backing Bentsen (81.6%). In other words, ticket-splitting for a Democratic senator and a Republican presidential candidate was rampant among Texans in 1988. However, lest the reader thinking about contemporary American politics consider these election results in Texas in 1988 to be remarkable—or at least aberrant—at the time, it was actually the normal state of affairs and had been in the Lone Star State and its southern neighbors for roughly the previous twenty years.

As explained by identical twins Earl and Merle Black, southern politics savants who grew up in the small east Texas town of Sulphur Springs,[3] "[s]plit-level realignment . . . accurately describes the different central tendencies of partisan officeholding in the South" (1987, p. 259). That is, by the late 1980s, the GOP had dominated Dixie's presidential contests since 1968, whereas Democrats maintained an albeit waning but still pronounced electoral advantage in congressional elections that reached all the way back to the 1880s (Black and Black, 2002). For instance, on the basis of responses to the 1988 American National Election Study (ANES), "more than half of white southerners (fifty-two percent) who voted Republican for President cast Democratic House ballots" (McKee, 2019, p. 89).

Senator Bentsen is best remembered for his famous retort leveled at Indiana Senator Dan Quayle in their 1988 vice presidential debate when he averred: "Senator, I served with Jack Kennedy, I knew Jack Kennedy, Jack Kennedy was a friend of mine. Senator, you are no Jack Kennedy" (National Public Radio [NPR], 2006). Prompting Bentsen's zinger was moderator Tom Brokaw's question of what made the Indiana Senator qualified if thrust into the role of president, and Quayle stated that he had "as much experience in the Congress as Jack Kennedy did when he sought the presidency" (NPR, 2006).[4]

After the 1988 Dukakis–Bentsen Democratic ticket succumbed to the GOP pairing of Bush–Quayle, Senator Bentsen remained in the US Senate until 1993, when the victorious 1992 Democratic presidential nominee Bill Clinton picked him to serve as treasury secretary. In the special Texas Senate election to fill Bentsen's vacancy, Republican Kay Bailey Hutchison became the first woman to represent the Lone Star State in the nation's upper congressional chamber.

Given the long-term partisan changes across the South, including Texas, with the Republican Party inarguably ascendant by the mid-1990s, political observers can be forgiven for assuming that even the controversial and highly polarizing GOP Senator Ted Cruz would face feeble Democratic opposition in his first bid for reelection in 2018. However, in the thirty years since the last Texas Democrat breezed to his Senate reelection, the political landscape had transformed. The demographically diverse megacities of the state (e.g., Houston, San Antonio, Dallas, Austin, and Fort Worth) were undergoing a steady march in the Democratic direction. Conversely, no longer did the rural and small-town communities found throughout the state look electorally favorable to Democrats of any ilk, especially in settings disproportionally populated by Anglo (non-Hispanic white) residents.

Throughout Dixie, deep into the second decade of the current millennium, many of the region's cities have become blue Democratic enclaves surrounded by crimson suburbs and burgundy rural communities staunchly aligned with the GOP. This aptly characterizes Texas's political geography (Myers, 2013). Accordingly, Republican strength has generally increased as the number of residents in a locality declines and their density of settlement lessens (Teigen, Shaw, and McKee, 2017). Whereas, historically, the backbone of the southern Democracy was principally located in rural counties and especially those located within the Black Belts of the Deep South states of

Alabama, Georgia, Louisiana, Mississippi, and South Carolina, where whites were often outnumbered by their African American neighbors (Key, 1949), now rural counties are the bulwark of modern southern Republicanism.

Therefore, in this political milieu, it must have been more than a little surprising that first-term Republican Senator Ted Cruz, a Tea Party political outsider of Cuban descent, drew an Anglo Democratic challenger with a catchy Spanish nickname who, for three terms (2012–2016), represented his hometown majority-Latino city of El Paso in the US House of Representatives (District Sixteen). Perhaps even more curious was that this Democrat, former Congressman Robert Francis "Beto" O'Rourke, decided upon a campaign strategy for 254 counties. Yes, much more impressive than a presidential hopeful visiting all ninety-nine Iowa counties—in 2018, O'Rourke decided to stump in all 254 of Texas's. Keep in mind that several of the Lone Star State's counties have more livestock than people. No matter—O'Rourke was hellbent on bringing his message to the entire Texas electorate, not just the folks who agreed with him or those who might be persuaded (Tilove, 2018).

Among Texas's many rural counties, King County is as good an example as any in highlighting the futility of O'Rourke paying it a campaign visit in the 2018 Senate contest. Situated three square-shaped counties due east and about one hundred miles from Lubbock (the city and county), King County last preferred a Democratic presidential candidate in 1976. Yet it was twelve years after Carter that the last Democratic senatorial nominee carried King County: in 1988, Democratic Senator Bentsen managed 51.4% of the votes in this entirely rural outpost. If a forty-year presidential drought for Democrats wasn't enough, starting with the historic election of Barack Obama in 2008, King County has delivered over ninety percent of its two-party vote to the Republican opposition. In 2016, Democrat Hillary Clinton pried five votes from King County, whereas Republican Donald Trump took the remaining 154 cast for the major parties (ninety-seven percent). In 2018, O'Rourke bested Clinton in King County by wrangling six votes in a place that literally wrangles. Cruz was the beneficiary of the remaining 124 major party votes cast (ninety-five percent) in this sparsely populated ranching community.

Nonetheless, and despite his lack of traction in the rural sections of the state—particularly those in West Texas (Dotray, 2016), where Anglos are notably more participatory than Latinos—O'Rourke still came frighteningly close to ending the Texas GOP's twenty-year monopoly on statewide office-holding (Hood and McKee, 2017b). When all of the two-party votes had been tallied, Cruz captured 51.3% to O'Rourke's 48.7%—a paltry 2.6-percentage-point victory margin for the Republican incumbent. Putting aside Cruz's substantial likability deficit and the fact that national political conditions favored the Democratic Party (Jacobson, 2019), what primarily accounts for the highly competitive 2018 Texas Senate election is the latest manifestation of the political dynamics undergirding American politics, particularly those prevailing in Dixie.

Simply put, there has been and continues to be a wholesale geographic partisan sorting of the American electorate (Bishop and Cushing, 2008; McKee and Teigen, 2009). The densest sections of America are now decidedly and increasingly Democratic, the neighboring suburbs are becoming more competitive (meaning less Republican in most southern localities), whereas most rural communities have slowly constructed GOP fortresses. In the case of O'Rourke, he almost finished first in 2018 because of the historic mobilization of city dwellers who strongly backed his candidacy over Cruz. Texas has a proud tradition of early voting; in its thirty most populous counties, early voting in 2018, at 39.9%, doubled that in the previous 2014 midterm (18.8%) and even surpassed the early turnout in these counties for the 2012 presidential election (39.2%; see Wang, Cameron, and Essig, 2018). In 2014, there were almost 3.4 million Democratic and Republican Senate votes cast in these counties, and the Democratic nominee took 40.6% against the GOP incumbent John Cornyn. Four years later, these counties registered over 6.5 million major party votes for the Senate (a ninety-two percent increase over 2014), and O'Rourke won 54.8% of them; 6.1 points higher than his statewide vote share of 48.7%.

In 2018, O'Rourke sure as heck didn't campaign as a Dixiecrat or as a Boll Weevil Democrat like Texas Congressman Phil Gramm did in the 1980s before he switched to the GOP; nor did O'Rourke run as a moderate Blue Dog Democrat. No, O'Rourke ran in Texas as a national Democrat, espousing and advocating his party's generally liberal policy agenda. O'Rourke's uncompromising positioning as a national Democrat provides, in stark relief, a picture of the present and future state of Texas and southern politics writ large.

Consider Table I1a, which displays the county-level matchup of the Republican majority (Democratic majority) Senate vote for 1988 with the corresponding Republican majority (Democratic majority) presidential vote cast in 1988. As mentioned earlier, in 1988, most counties (fifty-four percent) favored the Democrat for the Senate and the Republican for president. Also, a third of Texas counties registered a consistent Democratic majority for both the Senate and president. It is still quite surprising that, in 1988, only twelve percent of Texas counties were consistent in voting majority Republican for the Senate and president. Finally, not one Texas county went majority Republican for the Senate while favoring the Democratic presidential candidate.

Table I1b provides a similar comparison between Texas counties for the 2016 presidential race and the 2018 US Senate contest. Because of the enduring electoral pattern of presidential Republicanism and down-ballot Democratic voting since the late 1960s, during this later time period, there is only

Table I1a. Partisan Voting in Texas Counties,
Presidential and US Senate Elections, 1988

Republican presidential majority (%)	Republican Senate majority (%)	
	YES	NO
Yes	12	54
No	0	33

one county that went majority Republican for the Senate and majority Democratic for president. By 2016, the partisan sort across elective offices, or what one might characterize as the nationalization of American politics (Jacobson and Carson, 2020; Sievert and McKee, 2019), is essentially complete in the Lone Star State's presidential and senatorial contests. Of Texas's 254 counties, just seven (less than three percent) delivered a split partisan majority for these offices in 2016 (president) and 2018 (Senate). Instead, what is patently evident now is that the lion's share of counties registering a partisan majority for president also deliver the same partisan majority for the Senate. Further, because the Texas GOP remains electorally dominant for now, eighty-seven percent of Texas counties (221 of 254) favored Republicans Trump in 2016 and Cruz in 2018. Likewise, almost all of the remaining counties, albeit only ten percent of the total (26 of 254), backed Democrats Clinton in 2016 and O'Rourke in 2018.

To be sure, many factors are responsible for the modern alignment of partisan politics in Texas, in which voters are expressing a common preference for one political party regardless of the office (so far only demonstrated in elections for president and the Senate). And yes, we are admittedly making

Table I1b. Partisan Sorting in Texas Counties, Presidential
and US Senate Elections, 2016–2018

Republican presidential majority (%)	Republican Senate majority (%)	
	YES	NO
Yes	87	2
No	<1	10

Note. Cell entries for the given election sequence sum to one hundred percent (with rounding error) and are based on the denominator of 254 total Texas counties. For example, in 2018, Republican Senator Ted Cruz won a majority vote in 221 Texas counties that also registered a majority vote for Republican presidential nominee Donald Trump in 2016, which results in the 87% entry shown above.

this inference on the basis of county-level election returns in the second most populous state, which also happens to harbor the largest number of counties. Nevertheless, as we move through the book, it comes as no revelation that individual-level voting behavior closely jibes with the aggregate-level findings presented here. Additionally, because our emphasis is firmly placed on the question of how party politics has transformed in geographic space, this is the element of the contemporary southern Republican realignment (SRR) that we focus on.

Observers of southern politics often simplify investigations of the SRR by recognizing that the stalwart attachment of Blacks to the Democratic Party since the consequential 1964 presidential election (Carmines and Stimson, 1989), distills most of the explanation for modern GOP ascendancy henceforth to the political behavior of southern whites (e.g., Hood, 2016; Lupton and McKee, 2020). We shall do the same. Specifically, we are interested in what we argue is an overlooked subgroup in the GOP's southern advance: rural whites. Historically, the scions of this population were, for better or worse, the keepers of the Democratic Solid South (Key, 1949). Their rural progeny, however, have been overlooked in terms of their contribution to the SRR, because urban whites were initially at the forefront of the South's partisan transformation (Bartley and Graham, 1975; Strong, 1960). Indeed, rural whites have been the obvious laggards in their embrace of the modern southern Republican Party (McKee, 2008). Nonetheless, we are certain that, despite being the last to realign to the GOP, rural southern whites will remain affiliated the longest, as they have now ironically become the most loyal and fervent Republicans.

One last demonstration from Texas should drive home the point as to how important rural residents are to the modern realignment of the South to the Republican Party. Figure I1 maps the results of the 1988 and 2018 US Senate elections at the county level. Counties are classified into four categories based on geography and electoral outcome: Democratic majority/small town; Democratic majority/urban; Republican majority/urban; and Republican majority/small town.[5]

The map on the left side of Figure I1 details the results of the 1988 Senate contest with the bulk of Texas's counties shaded black, indicating that Democratic Senator Bentsen carried the majority of rural residents' votes. Conversely, the second map plotting the 2018 Senate contest reveals that Republican Senator Cruz's most electorally fertile areas in 2018 were also the lion's share of small-town counties (shaded white)—the same counties Bentsen dominated thirty years earlier. Put another way, of the counties delivering a majority vote to the Democrat Bentsen in 1988, seventy-four percent of them were of the small-town variety. In practically a mirror image, three decades later, seventy-eight percent of Republican Cruz's majority-vote counties

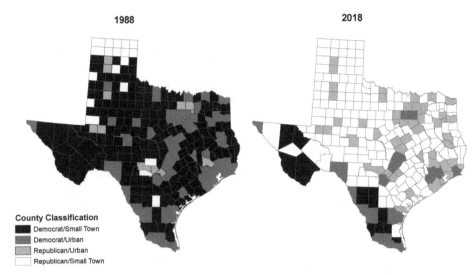

Figure I1. Texas Senate Elections, 1988 and 2018

were classified as small town. In comparison, in 2018, O'Rourke became the first Democratic Senate candidate since Bentsen to win the half-dozen counties containing Texas's largest cities.[6,7]

As we will show, the Texas political transformation is far from unique. Although Texas has been the second most urban southern state as far back as 1940 (behind Florida; Key, 1949, p. 85), and despite having the smallest percentage of Blacks and the highest share of Latinos, partisan changes in the Lone Star State in varying degrees of magnitude exist throughout Dixie. And just as demographic changes portend a Democratic comeback emanating from the region's largest cities and other high-growth localities, regardless of their size (Morris, 2021)—especially those in Texas (see chapter nine; Hood and McKee, 2021)—this recent revival of two-party competition will be slowest to take hold in the countryside, where rural white southerners are now the staunchest Republican supporters. We have no doubt that a growing number of scholars will shift their attention to the return of Democratic electoral viability originating in, and spreading outward from, the urban South (Bullock, 2021; Bullock et al., 2019; Morris, 2021). For now, however, we believe that the story of the long and deep realignment of rural southern whites to the GOP should finally be told in a detailed and exhaustive book-length account.

1 America's Longest and Deepest Realignment

Moribund. That was the state of the Republican Party in the American South from the 1880s into the 1950s. With exceptions—such as the Civil War resistance enclaves of mountain Republicanism found across eastern Tennessee, western North Carolina, southwestern Virginia, and smaller swaths in the highlands of Alabama and Georgia—the GOP might as well have been an apparition with respect to its impact on southern politics (Heard, 1952). The GOP's pathetic post-Reconstruction status in southern elections was due to decades of legal and extralegal machinations spearheaded by a select group of southerners: the whites of the rural Black Belt counties (Key, 1949; Kousser, 1974) located disproportionally in the five states comprising the Deep South: Alabama, Georgia, Louisiana, Mississippi, and South Carolina. The record of southern Republican electoral success, or lack thereof, prompted numerous political observers to reflect on this singular region of the United States where a two-party system was a veritable figment of the imagination and better conceived of as a wishful aspiration.

Consider some of the sweeping evidence of GOP futility in contests for elective office among Dixie's eleven ex-Confederate states.[1] Since the closely contested 1880 presidential election featuring the victorious Republican James Garfield against the Democrat Winfield Hancock and up through Franklin Delano Roosevelt's fourth and final win in 1944, the eleven southern states favored the Democratic nominee in 181 of 187 (ninety-seven percent) of these contests. The six aberrant Republican triumphs in southern states spanning these seventeen presidential elections and sixty-four years were concentrated in 1928, when the Catholic antiprohibitionist Democrat Al Smith of New York turned off a majority of voters outside of Arkansas and the five Deep South states, so that Republican Herbert Hoover prevailed in Florida, North Carolina, Tennessee, Texas, and Virginia. The remaining additional Republican presidential victory occurred eight years prior in 1920 in Tennessee, where Warren Harding bested the Democrat James Cox by three percentage points.

Below the presidential line, southern Democrats owned congressional elections for a century and twenty more years, from 1874 until 1994 (Black and Black, 2002). Not a single southern Republican in the latter half of the twentieth century could claim a US Senate seat until John Tower won the 1961 special election to replace the Democrat Lyndon B. Johnson, whom President John F. Kennedy selected as his vice president because Texas and the rest of Dixie was still America's most Democratic region. For many of their numerous decades in the electoral wilderness, the entire southern Republican US House delegation did not extend much beyond the two reliably GOP seats in east Tennessee (McKee, 2019)—an outpost of formidable Republican resistance dating back to the "War Between the States" (Key, 1949). Gubernatorial elections were also repeated Republican lessons in failure. However, unlike in House contests, at least more often than not, a GOP candidate would run for governor, even if before the 1960s (Black and Black, 1987) it must have been extremely disheartening to know that Democratic primary participation usually exceeded general election turnout in which the lion's share of Republican nominees were sacrificial lambs. Indeed, one southern state, Georgia, managed to get through the entire twentieth century without placing a Republican in the governor's mansion (Hayes and McKee, 2004).

For most of its history, the American South was overwhelmingly rural, severely lagging behind the industrialization in the latter half of the 1800s, which permeated many northern states and led to the creation of large and densely packed urban cities reliant on cheap and heavily immigrant labor to run the factories (Key, 1955, 1959). As shown in Figure 1.1, the disparity in rurality between the South and North was palpable for most of the 1900s. In

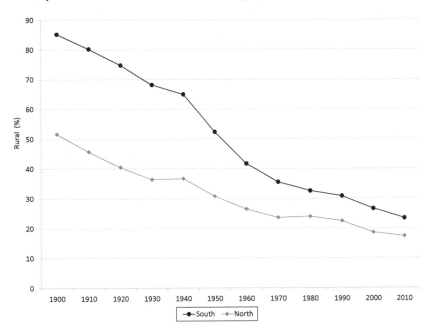

Figure 1.1. Rural Percentage of Northern and Southern Populations, 1900–2010

1900, more than eighty-five percent of the South was rural, whereas only a slight majority of the North (fifty-two percent) was rural. This was the last US Census year in which a majority of northerners resided in rural settings, but it was not until after the 1950 census that a majority of southerners finally resided in urban areas. By the 2010 census, the sectional difference in ruralism had reached its lowest margin, with just six percentage points separating the South (twenty-three percent rural) from the North (seventeen percent rural).

The dominance of rural settlement in the South over many decades helps explain why Democratic powerbrokers in the region were located in small towns where severely malapportioned district-level elections (e.g., congressional and state legislative contests) effectively stymied urban political advancement (Bullock, 2010; Key, 1949; Nixon, 1948). By rigging political boundaries in their favor throughout most of the South, more often than not, for the first half of the twentieth century, the rulers of the county courthouse gangs ran state and local politics. To no surprise, it necessarily followed that the landmark Supreme Court decisions ushering in the "one person, one vote" reapportionment revolution (Ansolabehere and Snyder, 2008; Cox and Katz, 2002) of the 1960s primarily originated from southern disputes (Ladewig and McKee, 2014).[2] In fact, we are confident that no lesser an authority than V. O. Key, author of the still relevant *Southern Politics in State and Nation* (1949), would not quibble with the notion that, with few exceptions (e.g., "Boss" E. H. Crump in Memphis), southern politics in the first half of the 1900s essentially amounted to rural politics. That was where the locus of authority made its home in most southern states.

Dixiecrat Revolt and the Urban Republican Breakthrough

Eric Schickler's (2016) masterful work on how civil rights realigned the major parties in the North and South from the late 1930s to mid-1960s, gives us a fresh account of how changes in the political system were unfolding for years at the state and local levels and often separately from the guidance, demands, and desires of many leading national politicians (e.g., presidential nominees). In the North, the Democratic Party, especially in large cities with sizable Black electorates as a consequence of the Great Migration (Wilkerson, 2010), was moving for years in a liberal direction on civil rights, and this was reflected in the positions written down in party platforms (Feinstein and Schickler, 2008). In contrast, northern Republicans, despite being notably more conservative on economic issues, were gradually distancing themselves from the GOP's historic defense of civil rights, particularly outside of the Northeast where it was more politically precarious to ignore or, even worse, disavow the cause of Black equality, since Blacks in this region were an important coalition of the increasingly formidable Democratic opposition.

The powershifting victory of Franklin Delano Roosevelt and the Democratic Party in 1932 meant that the largest segment of the party's majority New Deal Coalition—white southerners—had been politically pulled in two untenable directions: a liberal stance on economics coupled with a vehement resistance to the rights of Blacks. However, it was not many years into Roosevelt's reign that many southern Democrats holding positions of power in Congress and at the state and local levels abandoned the national Democrats' liberal economic agenda, because it was an obvious gateway for the embrace of Black civil rights through unionization and other means of workplace regulation serving to equalize the employment playing field (Caughey, 2018; Jewell, 2017; Schickler, 2016).

Indeed, the impending divorce from the northern wing of the Democratic Party was evident as early as the 1938 midterm elections, when President Roosevelt went on the warpath in a generally failed attempt to purge his party of conservative congressional Democrats, most of whom naturally resided in places below the Mason-Dixon Line. Roosevelt's botched effort at removing conservative congressional (and primarily southern) anti-New Deal Democratic malcontents pushed these members toward northern Republicans, resulting in the genesis of the long-running conservative coalition of southern Democrats and northern Republicans, who coalesced around a shared philosophy of resistance to national/northern Democrats' liberal policies (Shafer, 2016).

Hence, decades before the permanent national split by the major parties on the issue of Black civil rights was consummated in the 1964 presidential election (Carmines and Stimson, 1989), the fissures and cleavages leading to this outcome were discernible in the North and South, in Congress, and in state and local politics (Schickler, 2016). In fact, two elections twenty years apart offer several clues as to why the 1960s civil rights movement would ensure the collapse of the Democratic Solid South, a one-party bulwark that was always propped up by the outsized power of rural politicians. In *Southern Politics in State and Nation* (1949), Key's fifteenth chapter was titled "Hoovercrats and Dixiecrats." He was examining southern whites' political behavior in the 1928 and 1948 presidential elections, referring to the former contest as "The Bolt of 1928" and the latter race as "The Revolt of 1948."

The 1928 election was intriguing because southern whites in the Rim South states of Florida, North Carolina, Tennessee, Texas, and Virginia expressed a closer cultural affinity to the Republican Herbert Hoover, who was socially and economically conservative and, by all accounts, an upstanding prohibitionist Protestant. Further, county-level returns indicated that even at this early date, Democratic defections to the GOP presidential nominee were more evident in urban areas. To be sure, race was the principal factor correlating with the presidential vote. As Key put it in the acceptable language of the times: "Minute examination of the relation between the distribution of the Al Smith vote and Negro population amply sustains the major thesis: that the diehard Democratic strength in 1928 centered in counties with high proportions of Negroes" (1949, p. 328). Nevertheless, in the absence of survey data, Key's scrutiny of various southern counties showed that urban ones typically were more Republican than what was expected on the basis of their percentage of Blacks. This pattern contributed to Hoover's success in Peripheral South states such as Texas, where the Republican carried Dallas, Harris (Houston), and Tarrant (Fort Worth) counties (Key, 1949, p. 321). Likewise, even in Deep South states such as Georgia, where Hoover was shut out, he did better than recent history might suggest, because "in a few instances, urbanism apparently outweighed racial restraints" (Key, 1949, p. 326).

The 1928 contest is important to mention, because it was the first presidential election to cleave the American South after it became solidly Democratic in 1880. Interestingly, at this early date, the significance of place was notable because the more urban/metropolitan counties displayed a greater tendency to support the Republican Hoover. In contrast, the core of Dixie—its Black Belt counties primarily located in Deep South states with the highest African American populations and least dense settlement patterns—remained stalwart in their support of the Democrat Al Smith; "rum and Romanism" be damned.[3] Finally, for the next twenty years, the 1928 contest appeared to be a one-off aberration, mainly because the Democrat Roosevelt dominated the South in presidential politics from 1932 through 1944. In 1928, the issue of race was arguably indirect in its influence on southern whites' preferences, since neither major party nominee had broached Black civil rights, and the expectation that Jim Crow would be undermined was a pipe dream. Two decades hence, the possibility of Black emancipation from a segregated South took on an urgency reflected in the battles erupting throughout the 1948 presidential campaign. Unlike in 1928, the ramifications of the 1948 contest were not ephemeral, but instead permanent, and responsible for the death knell of the Democratic Solid South.

In the 1944 *Smith v. Allwright* case (originating in Texas), the US Supreme Court struck down as unconstitutional the South's most effective means for disenfranchising Black voters, the white Democratic primary.[4] Because winning the Democratic primary almost always led to winning that particular elective office in the general election, excluding Black participation in most localities removed the possibility of even meager Black influence over the selection of southern officeholders. The *Smith* decision, although historic, only amounted to around one in five Blacks being listed on the southern voter registration rolls by the time the Republican Dwight D. Eisenhower terminated southern Democrats' monopoly on presidential elections in 1952

(Black and Black, 1987). In other words, in the 1948 presidential election, white votes would once again rule the day.

Disconcerting to a substantial portion of southern whites, however, was that by the late 1940s, Black votes had become critical in determining outcomes in several northern battleground states such as Illinois. Eminently aware of this, the former Ku Kluxer and "Man from Missouri" (Salts, 1916), Democratic President Harry S. Truman decided to make a strong push for northern Black votes while taking the risk of inciting a southern white Democratic rebellion. This Truman did, in the course of forming a Committee on Civil Rights in 1947, desegregating the military by means of executive order the following year and finally standing behind what would be the most liberal civil rights platform the Democratic Party had ever endorsed at their national convention in Philadelphia, Pennsylvania (Frederickson, 2001). At the Democratic National Convention, the entire Mississippi delegation walked out, as did half of Alabama's (Key, 1949). As Key makes clear, the rhetoric of southern white elites disgruntled by President Truman's civil rights overtures was hyperbolic and had the effect of getting the most reactionary white supremacists to hastily organize a homegrown insurgent Democratic opposition in the form of the States' Rights Democratic Party, more commonly known and referred to as the Dixiecrats.

Befitting the foremost objective of defending the Jim Crow South, the two southern states with the highest share of Blacks also delivered the Dixiecrat nominations for president and vice president: Governor J. Strom Thurmond of South Carolina and Governor Fielding H. Wright of Mississippi. Throughout the South, there were heated intraparty Democratic skirmishes over whether the national party under Truman or Thurmond's Dixiecrats would get the preferred official recognition of the Democratic Party on the 1948 presidential ballot. In Peripheral South states where the GOP had an electoral presence (e.g., North Carolina, Tennessee, and Virginia) or where the share of white supremacist alarmists was relatively smaller (e.g., Arkansas, Florida, and Texas), Truman secured official Democratic placement on the ballot. In contrast, with the exception of Georgia, in the Deep South states where Truman's actions met the harshest rebuke, the Dixiecrat ticket was granted preferential status; in Alabama, Truman's name didn't even don the ballot. The Republican Thomas Dewey failed to win a southern state, and Thurmond wrested four from Truman, those where he was designated the official Democratic nominee: Alabama, Louisiana, Mississippi, and South Carolina.[5]

Remarking upon southern voters in 1948, Key noted that "their behavior was generally the reverse of that in 1928. Thurmond usually polled his heaviest vote in those counties with the highest proportions of Negroes while the white counties remained most loyal to the national ticket" (1949, p. 342). This conclusion closely tracks the racist vitriol of the most vocal Dixiecrats[6] and the formal language laid down in their party platform, which included the following passages: "We stand for the segregation of the races. . . . We oppose the elimination of segregation, the repeal of miscegenation statutes. . . . We oppose and condemn the action of the Democratic Convention in sponsoring a civil rights program calling for the elimination of segregation."

Dixiecrats' fervent defense of white supremacy perhaps unwittingly eclipsed the importance that these insurgent southern Democrats placed on a conservative/laissez-faire capitalist/free-market economic philosophy. Indeed, several statements in the Dixiecrat Party platform espoused economic liberty. Consider these passages: "We stand for . . . the constitutional right to . . . accept private employment without governmental interference, and to earn one's living in any lawful way. . . . We oppose . . . control of private employment by Federal bureaucrats called for by the misnamed civil rights program. . . . We oppose . . . regulations of private employment practices."[7]

It is worth stressing the Dixiecrats' emphasis on free-market economics because conservative southern Democrats' initial alignment with northern Republicans in Congress was based on their mutual opposition to Roosevelt's New Deal policies (Schickler, 2016).[8] However, the Dixiecrats' economic stance ran counter to the rather humble station of the majority of rank-and-file rural white southerners who were the principal beneficiaries of federal redistributionist New Deal policies (Black and Black, 2002). Hence, as long as most southern Democrats placed the race issue above the economic issue, most rural white southerners remained loyal to the party. This dynamic is telling because, as fate would have it, national Republican opposition to Democratic economic liberalism meant that the most likely southern converts to the GOP were urban whites. Whereas, in the case of rural white southerners, alignment with the Democratic Party was historically rooted in the defense of white supremacy, urban white southerners never possessed a commensurate fervor in defending Jim Crow. So, in the decades before the 1960s civil rights movement, the economic cleavage had become a more compelling means for moving urban white southerners into the Republican Party (Shafer and Johnston, 2006).

In the first presidential election after the 1948 intrasquad southern Democratic scrimmage in which the GOP candidate Dewey garnered zero electoral votes, the Republican Eisenhower downplayed the race issue and concentrated his appeals on the burgeoning postwar South's white urban middle class (Seagull, 1975). In 1952, this strategy yielded the GOP nominee the electoral votes of four Peripheral South states (Florida, Tennessee, Texas, and Virginia) and, in so doing, marked the end of the one-party Democratic South in presidential elections (Black and Black, 1992). According to the 1950 census, Eisenhower was victorious in the two most urban southern states, Florida and Texas, respectively, and also the fourth (Virginia) and sixth (Tennessee) most urban states in the region. In Eisenhower's successful 1956 reelection campaign, he added the Deep South state of Louisiana to his win column; at that time, the Pelican State was Dixie's third most urban.

In the two 1950s presidential elections, which witnessed the same major party nominees, neither candidate addressed the race issue. In eluding the cause of Black equality, the two-time Democratic loser Adlai Stevenson prevailed in seven southern states in 1952 and six in 1956. There is no question that Stevenson was most popular in those areas of the region inhabited by rural whites possessing the strongest lineage to the old southern Democracy. By comparison, a "solid majority of upper-income urban southern whites had voted for Eisenhower, and the president believed that he could win over more moderate southern Democratic supporters" (Schickler, 2016, p. 253). Additionally, data from the American National Election Studies (ANES) placed Eisenhower's vote among urban white southerners at fifty-seven percent, compared with forty-four percent of rural white southerners (a significant difference at $p < .05$).[9]

The urban movement toward Eisenhower can also be depicted graphically: Figure 1.2 plots the urban percentage of southern counties (1950 census data) on the horizontal axis against the Republican two-party percentage of the 1956 presidential vote on the vertical axis. Also, the figure uses circles of various sizes so that more populated counties are represented by larger circles. Not only is there a positive relationship between the 1956 GOP presidential

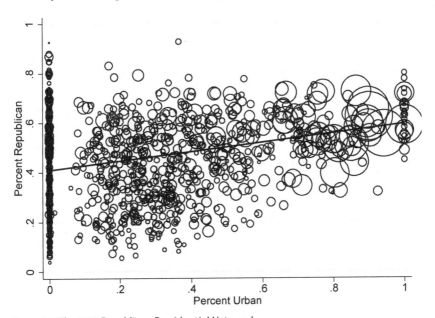

Figure 1.2. The 1956 Republican Presidential Vote and Urban Percentage in Southern Counties

vote and the urban percentage in a county, but also this correlation is notable among several of the more populous southern counties (e.g., Pinellas, FL, at seventy-three percent Republican; Orleans Parish, LA, at fifty-nine percent; Knox, TN, at sixty-one percent; Harris, TX, at sixty-two percent; and Richmond City, VA, with a GOP vote of seventy-two percent).[10]

The 1950s southern breakthrough in presidential politics probably speaks more to the triumph of personality over issues (e.g., "I like Ike"), because Stevenson was no match against the former supreme commander of the Allied forces in Europe. Nevertheless, it is also undeniable that Eisenhower's appeal among urban whites was due to an emphasis on economics as opposed to race. According to the ANES data, in Eisenhower's two successful presidential runs, forty-five percent of urban white southerners voted for the five-star general while also voting Democratic for the US House of Representatives. In contrast, only twenty-seven percent of rural white southerners exhibited this same ticket-splitting pattern in 1952 and 1956.[11]

The 1960s Upheaval and the Stunted Republican Realignment of Rural Whites

In the 1950 midterm, the last one before Eisenhower's first presidential election victory, the 105-member southern House delegation was ninety-eight percent Democratic, including just the two Republican members from the First (B. Carroll Reece) and Second (Howard H. Baker) Districts in east Tennessee.[12] The newly elected Republican president had short coattails, but from such a pathetic 1950 baseline, the Republican House delegation tripled in size with the election of one member from North Carolina and three from Virginia. The 1954 midterm saw the election of a Republican in Florida and another in Texas. It is important to note that this small contingent of newly elected GOP congressmen were pioneers in establishing the beachhead for the advancement of urban Republicanism in the South. For instance, Republican Charles Raper Jonas (representing North Carolina's Ninth Congressional District) was elected in 1952 to a Charlotte-area district he represented for two decades (Black and Black, 2002), and it has (albeit with permutations by means of redistricting) remained in GOP hands to this day. In 1954, the Republican Bruce Alger was victorious in the Dallas-based Fifth District, which he held for a decade. Finally, Republican Bill Cramer was the first GOP member from Florida since Reconstruction, winning a St. Petersburg district in 1954 and running unopposed in his final contest in 1968. C. W. "Bill" Young represented roughly the same congressional boundaries from 1970 until his passing in 2013.

Although their numbers were small, the expansion of the southern GOP delegation to the US House of Representatives in the 1950s was an accurate reflection of the fairly moderate urban Republicanism that Eisenhower stood for. During his tenure, President Eisenhower made an investment in growing the southern wing of the GOP, most notably with his undertaking of Operation Dixie, a grassroots effort at local party building and candidate recruitment. In the words of Schickler (2016, p. 253), "Eisenhower's vision for Operation Dixie was that it would create a Republican Party based primarily in the growing urban areas of the South, appealing to upper middle-class professionals rather than traditional segregationists. . . . In most cases, the candidates recruited by the Southern Division during the Eisenhower years did not emphasize segregation as an issue and instead highlighted their economic conservatism."

However, the ground was swiftly shifting beneath Eisenhower and national Republicans hailing from the Northeast (think Rockefeller Republicans), who were losing their grip on the GOP to more conservative politicos in the Midwest (led by Senator Robert Taft of Ohio) and West (Senator Barry Goldwater of Arizona). By the time Eisenhower exited the political scene, his Operation Dixie had become a vessel for more racially conservative, anti-civil rights activists who intended to steer the southern GOP away from its urban roots in favor of a naked appeal to the racial prejudices of rural whites (Maxwell and Shields, 2019).

The historically close 1960 open-seat contest between the Democrat John F. Kennedy and Dwight Eisenhower's vice president, Republican Richard Nixon, amounted to a "me-too" debate over civil rights, with both candidates professing to champion the cause.[13] Kennedy prevailed with a national two-party popular vote of 50.1% (rounded up). In a pattern reminiscent of his old boss Eisenhower in 1952, Nixon carried Florida, Tennessee, and Virginia. Kennedy naturally won in Texas, because Johnson was his running mate. Kennedy also won the remaining southern states' popular votes over Nixon, although, in Mississippi, a plurality of popular votes (thirty-nine percent) actually went to unpledged electors. In spite of his considerable efforts at mollifying civil rights leaders, President Kennedy was perceived as not moving fast enough in the eyes of Martin Luther King, Jr. (see his 1963 "Letter from Birmingham Jail"). By the late spring and early summer of 1963, the gripping unrest in Birmingham, Alabama, had moved civil rights into the top spot for the nation's most important problem when Gallup polled Americans (Black and Black, 1987, p. 110).

Kennedy rose to the moment in his national address on June 11, 1963, essentially laying out the broad parameters for what would become the first signature achievement of the slain president's successor, when Johnson managed to get Congress to pass the 1964 Civil Rights Act the following summer. These salient actions on the race issue, which finally took center stage in American national politics, unsurprisingly resulted in an immediate short-term southern white backlash to the leaders of the Democratic Party. Southern whites' approval of President Kennedy took a nosedive in the spring and summer of 1963, as he responded to the mass protests and violence engulfing Birmingham (Kuziemko and Washington, 2018, p. 2851). Then the so-called critical moment (see Stimson, 2004) occurred when Republican Senator Goldwater voted against the 1964 Civil Rights Act and subsequently represented the GOP as the presidential nominee in opposition to President Johnson.

Carmines and Stimson (1989) are rightly credited with being the first to recognize the long-term significance of the 1964 presidential election and crafting a theory of issue evolution around this event. Nevertheless, as realignment scholars know, the concept of a critical election introduced by Key (1955) was later disavowed by Key (1959) not long after, because pivotal electoral moments are preceded by the culmination of changes that foretell and enable punctuated political shifts. As Schickler (2016) contended, much had taken place in terms of jockeying by the major parties in the North and South below the presidential level (from the late 1930s into the 1960s) that ultimately manifested with the permanent switch in the Democratic and Republican national positioning on Black civil rights in 1964. In other words, the actions of party activists, congressional leaders, and state and local politicians made the events of the 1964 election understandable—and perhaps anticipated—even if, nevertheless, still groundbreaking in their effects and consequences.

By disavowing federal intervention to dismantle the Jim Crow South, Goldwater was the originator of the GOP's "Southern Strategy" (Aistrup, 1996) of driving a wedge between white Democrats on the race issue (Hillygus and Shields, 2009). Nevertheless, because of the roots put down by the GOP in the urban South in the 1950s, even a hard turn on the race issue, by itself, was not enough to get rural whites to surrender wholesale to a party that heretofore was aggressively catering to their more financially endowed white urban neighbors. Albeit the sample sizes are small, according to the ANES data on the 1964 presidential election, fifty-eight percent of white southerners backed the Democrat Johnson. More relevant for our purposes, on the basis of location, sixty-three percent of urban whites voted for the Republican Goldwater, whereas sixty-nine percent of rural whites favored Johnson.[14]

Of course, there is considerable state-level variation in the southern vote in the historic 1964 contest, which would be the last time a majority of southern whites voted for the Democratic presidential nominee in a two-party matchup (Black and Black, 1992). For example, at sixty-two percent rural (1960 census), Mississippi had the highest rural population among the southern states, and with an almost entirely white electorate, it cast eighty-seven percent of its ballots for Goldwater. However, the race issue, then and even now, consumes most white Mississippians (Parker, 1990; Silver, 2012) in the South's most rural state.[15] In contrast, in the relatively less race-conscious state of

North Carolina, which happened to have the second highest rural population at sixty percent, fifty-six percent of Tar Heels voted for Johnson, the Democrat's second-best southern performance, only topped by the sixty-three percent support Johnson received from his fellow Texans.

It is also true that the percentage of Blacks voting in the Deep South states, all of which Goldwater carried, was markedly smaller than the more enfranchised Black electorate in the Rim South states that Johnson won (Bullock and Gaddie, 2009; McKee, 2017). Furthermore, in 1960 (according to the US Census) the Deep South was forty-eight percent rural, whereas the Peripheral South was thirty-eight percent rural. Thus, one can make a compelling argument that rural whites in the Deep South exhibited considerably higher support for Goldwater (see Cosman, 1966), notwithstanding the admittedly deficient ANES data to the contrary. Up to this point, the evidence of a sustainable inroad for the GOP in the South had tracked a decidedly urban path. The 1964 election was a watershed event because, with the exception of Louisiana (again, the most urban Deep South state at this time), its more rural Deep South neighbors finally broke from the Democratic Party in presidential contests. Specifically, South Carolina last backed a GOP presidential nominee in the disputed 1876 contest, which ended Reconstruction. The sister states of Alabama and Mississippi last voted Republican for Abraham Lincoln's greatest Civil War general, Ulysses S. Grant in 1872. Finally, Georgia, which did not comply with northern-led oversight of military Reconstruction and had to twice be readmitted to the Union (McKee, 2019), never supported a Republican presidential contender before 1964.

There are palpable parallels to the 1948 and 1964 presidential elections. Although, in the former contest, the Republican Dewey was shut out of Dixie, States' Rights Democrat Thurmond was the defender of the Jim Crow South. Sixteen years later, Lyndon B. Johnson's greatest early presidential achievement was inarguably his heroic effort (Whalen and Whalen, 1985) to have Congress pass the 1964 Civil Rights Act, landmark legislation that hardly any southern congressional Democrats voted for. The Republican Goldwater, who was aligned with the small minority of Republican senators voting against the Civil Rights Act,[16] sent a loud signal reverberating throughout the South that the ducks he was hunting for in the upcoming presidential contest were conservative whites (Murphy and Gulliver, 1971), a disproportionate share of whom resided in the rural Deep South (Bartley and Graham, 1975; Cosman, 1966).

Figure 1.3 displays scatterplots that juxtapose the county-level votes for Goldwater on the vertical axis with the county-level votes for Thurmond on the horizontal axis. The first scatterplot indicates the percentage of these county-level presidential votes for Georgia, Louisiana, Mississippi, and South Carolina (fifty-eight percent rural in the 1950 census and forty-nine percent

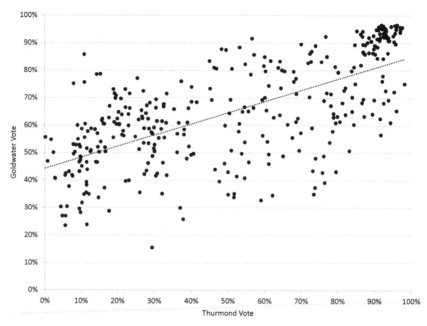

Figure 1.3.1. County Vote for Goldwater (1964) and Thurmond (1948) in Deep South States

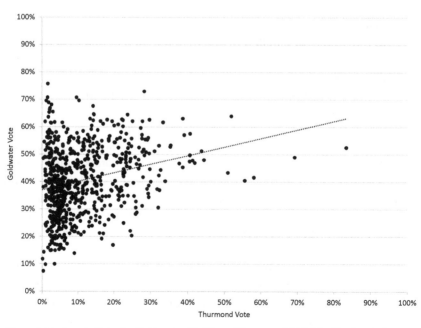

Figure 1.3.2. County Vote for Goldwater (1964) and Thurmond (1948) in Rim South States.

rural in the 1960 census). Alabama data are omitted because, in 1948, Truman did not make it onto the ballot, and in 1964, neither did Johnson.[17] A decade and six years apart, in these four states with large rural populations and only a small share of enfranchised Blacks, the correlation between the Goldwater and Thurmond vote is an impressive .672 ($p < .001$, $n = 351$ counties). By comparison, the six Peripheral South states of Arkansas, Florida, North Carolina, Tennessee, Texas, and Virginia (forty-nine percent rural in the 1950 census and thirty-eight percent rural in the 1960 census) yield a correlation of .255 ($p < .001$, $n = 711$ counties).[18] Not only is the correlation more than two and half times larger in the four Deep South states, but also the clustering of counties below the fifty-percent mark on the x axis in the Rim South shows how unpalatable the Dixiecrat Thurmond was outside the segregationist stronghold of the Deep South.

An even better opportunity to unmoor rural southern whites from their ancestral Democratic Party took place in the 1968 presidential election, which featured the return of Republican Richard Nixon (McGinniss, 1969), Lyndon B. Johnson's Democratic Vice President Hubert Humphrey, and former Alabama Democratic Governor George Wallace running under the American Independent Party banner. With Humphrey as a civil rights liberal, Nixon knew that his "Law and Order" and "Silent Majority" campaign slogans would not be parroted by the Minnesota Democrat. Instead, Nixon viewed the Alabamian as a much greater threat to his presidential chances (Nelson, 2014), because Wallace would command the loyalties of legions of unreconstructed white southern Democrats motivated by his race-baiting rhetoric and staunch resistance to Black equality during his tenure as Alabama governor (1962–1966) at the height of the civil rights movement. Further, unlike Goldwater and Nixon, who were both economic conservatives, Wallace combined his raw racist appeals with a distinct brand of populist demagoguery (Carter, 1995). In other words, in eschewing the GOP's conservative economic outlook, Wallace was a more suitable choice for substantial numbers of downscale rural white southerners.

For Wallace, like Thurmond twenty years prior versus Truman, the hope was to siphon off enough votes from Nixon to throw the contest into the Electoral College, where important political concessions could be made. Nixon's popular vote margin over Humphrey was extremely narrow, yet he enjoyed a comfortable Electoral College victory (301 to 191 votes).[19] In Dixie, with a big assist from Lyndon B. Johnson, Humphrey only won Texas. Wallace took over thirteen percent of the national popular vote and the remaining forty-six votes in the Electoral College. Not surprisingly, given his stronger appeal in his native region, Wallace was only victorious in the South, winning the most popular votes in Arkansas, Alabama, Georgia, Louisiana, and Mississippi. He also was the beneficiary of one electoral vote cast by a faithless elector in North Carolina, where Nixon was the plurality vote winner. Wallace was denied South Carolina primarily because the popular Senator Thurmond, who switched to the GOP in the 1964 Goldwater campaign, fervently backed Nixon.

The ANES data for the 1968 election are revealing of Nixon's and Wallace's success among white southerners. Once again, we must caution that these are small samples. Nonetheless, the combined white southern presidential vote for Nixon and Wallace was seventy-four percent. Nixon captured forty-three percent, and Wallace captured thirty-one percent of the southern white vote, leaving Humphrey with twenty-six percent. Urban whites voted thirty percent for Humphrey, twenty-two percent for Wallace, and forty-eight percent for Nixon. By comparison, rural whites voted twenty-four percent for Humphrey, thirty-five percent for Wallace, and forty-one percent for Nixon. The rural/urban white difference in the Wallace vote is significant at $p < .10$, even with such a small sample ($n = 67$ urban whites and $n = 116$ rural whites). Because the ANES put the rural southern white vote for Goldwater at thirty-one percent, in the three-candidate race in 1968, the third-party contender Wallace outperformed Goldwater among rural whites. Conversely, in juxtaposition to the liberal Texan President Johnson who went all-in on civil rights while still capturing sixty-nine percent of the rural southern white vote (based on the ANES data), the Minnesotan Humphrey four years later unquestionably registered a new low for his party with his paltry twenty-four percent showing among rural white southerners.

In *The Emerging Republican Majority* (1969), Kevin Phillips was prescient in his vision of a GOP coalition that could take over American national politics once white southerners joined the party. This eventually came to pass, but perhaps inordinately slowly in the minds of Republican strategists. Of course, at the presidential level, the 1968 election was the first of a half dozen in which only one Democrat would win: former Georgia Governor and peanut farmer Jimmy Carter. The GOP's southern strategy of peeling off white southerners, by initially overt and then more often covert messages priming southern whites' racial prejudices (Haney-López, 2014; Lamis, 1988; Mendelberg, 2001), was unquestionably a winning approach in presidential elections. Indeed, Black and Black (1987) assiduously documented the grassroots county-level takeover of the GOP in southern presidential contests, which had solidified by 1968, despite Wallace's third-party bid and, later, the deviant case of Carter in 1976. Below the top of the ticket, however, Republican electoral success in the other elections we examine in this book (governor, US senator, and US representative), was underwhelming, as southern Democrats retained the upper hand for decades after the 1960s.

It was rural white southerners who offered the greatest resistance to fully aligning with the Republican Party. For one, it only made sense to back the racially conservative presidential nominee, who was, with the exception of Gerald Ford in 1976, always the Republican from 1964 forward (Stimson, 2004). However, the persistence of a split-level alignment of southern presidential Republicanism starting in the late 1960s and the enduring Democratic dominance in all other elective offices until the 1990s (Lublin, 2004) are principally due to rural state and local Democratic officeholders' positioning on the issues of concern to their white constituents. In short, these politicians were slow to embrace the liberalism of the national/northern wing of the party. In fact, the racial liberalism of national Democrats, championed by President Johnson, was first met by large-scale resistance on the part of southern congressional Democrats. As Black and Black (2002, p. 390) have shown, for the entire decade of the 1970s, the most prominent members of the southern US House delegation, according to their roll-call voting behavior in Congress, were conservative Democrats.

To be sure, in 1964, Goldwater had congressional coattails, but they were closely tied to a handful of southern states where he registered some of his strongest performances (in Alabama, Georgia, and Mississippi).[20] Likewise, in 1968, Nixon helped bring in some congressional Republicans, but the Wallace distraction was probably detrimental to the GOP's cause. In percentage terms, between 1962 and 1964, the southern Republican US House delegation went from ten percent to almost sixteen percent; and between 1966 and 1968, the share of Republicans increased from twenty-one percent to twenty-five percent (see McKee, 2019, p. 88). These are respectable gains, but most of this southern GOP advancement was not registered in the more rural congressional districts where the pull of incumbency was stronger (see chapter three) and local Democrats continued to represent the sentiments of their culturally conservative constituents (Fenno, 2000).

The 1970s decade was one of dealignment more than partisan realignment (Abramson, 1976, 1979; Beck, 1977), with over forty percent of rural white southerners voting Republican for president and Democratic for US House (up from eighteen percent in the 1960s). Interestingly, however, during this decade of peak split-ticket voting exhibited by rural white southerners, compared with their urban white counterparts, more of the former group identified as Republicans (see chapters three and eight). This greater shift by rural whites to the GOP in the 1970s would appear to reflect their heightened concern over the massive influx of re-enfranchised Black southerners in the wake of the 1965 Voting Rights Act (VRA). With the benefit of scholarly hindsight, rural whites' greater affiliation with the Republican Party in the 1970s appears to be an outward demonstration of a countermobilization to the large numbers of Blacks registering to vote (McKee, 2017), particularly in rural Deep South settings where their greater presence constituted a genuine threat to traditional white Democratic hegemony (Hood, Kidd, and Morris, 2014).

However, from the 1980s into the new millennium, urban white southerners, compared with rural white southerners, were more aligned with the GOP.

Voter preferences are a leading indicator of long-term political changes, whereas party identification is a lagging indicator (Black and Black, 2002; Fiorina, 1981). With the exception of US House contests, rural and urban white southerners showed roughly similar levels of Republican support in presidential, senatorial, and gubernatorial elections from the 1960s through the 1980s. Nonetheless, we contend that the Republican realignment of rural white southerners is the longest and deepest, because it is not until the 1990s when they finally show a growing and increasingly consistent proclivity to vote for Republicans, regardless of the office. And, it is not until the 2010s when rural white southerners identify with the GOP at higher rates than those of urban whites, depending on the data source and metric for rurality. Therefore, despite southern Republicans taking control at the presidential level in the late 1960s, their work was far from done in capturing the allegiance of most rural whites, who proved to be the staunchest holdouts to GOP overtures.

From Wallace to Trump

Whereas Dixiecrat Strom Thurmond was the harbinger to the Republican Barry Goldwater's southern strategy of attracting racially conservative white Democratic votes, and Ronald Reagan was the patron saint of culturally conservative modern southern Republicanism that resonated more with country-club urban whites (Black and Black, 1987), Donald Trump's latest brand of Republicanism is the closest in both style and substance to a politician who never actually joined the GOP: Alabamian George Wallace. In the 2016 presidential election, Trump may have borrowed his principal campaign themes directly from Wallace's opponent Richard Nixon in 1968 by repeating his slogans "Law and Order" and "Silent Majority," but there is no question that Trump's kindred political spirit was the four-time Alabama governor.

In spite of the mortal hindrance associated with attempting to win a presidential election sans a major party label, Wallace was an enormously consequential politician in both southern and national politics (Carter, 1995, 1996). His influence spanned the civil rights and post-civil rights eras of massive electoral change. As a racist demagogue (before his mea culpa in the 1970s regarding his opposition to the civil rights movement; McKee, 2019) and an economic populist, Wallace was ideally positioned to attract rural white support.[21] In the latter half of the 1970s, and most clearly in his last successful gubernatorial term in the 1980s (1982–1986), Wallace had morphed into a New South Democratic politician dependent on the votes of a biracial coalition (Lamis, 1988). Before his transformation, however, Wallace embodied a mix of political positions and a style of demagoguery that closely resembled the Democrat-turned-Republican real estate mogul, reality TV star, and political amateur who shocked the world when he won the 2016 presidential election. Donald Trump is eerily reminiscent of George Wallace, when the latter was a militant segregationist (Black, 1976) in the 1960s. Unlike the string of Republican presidents from Nixon to George W. Bush, Trump had a rhetorical embrace of economic populism that made him a better fit among rural white southerners than any of these previous presidents who also benefited greatly from this same group's support.

We expect that because of impressive gains in Black registration after passage of the 1965 VRA and before the 1968 presidential election (especially in Mississippi, Alabama, and Louisiana; see Timpone, 1995), the county-level vote for Wallace in 1968 tracks Trump's 2016 support in the five states where the former Alabama governor was victorious: Alabama, Arkansas, Georgia, Louisiana, and Mississippi. Wallace did not win South Carolina (as mentioned earlier), but it was closely fought. In fact, Wallace performed better in Tennessee than in South Carolina, but for the following demonstration, we will keep the Palmetto State with its Deep South neighbors and Arkansas.

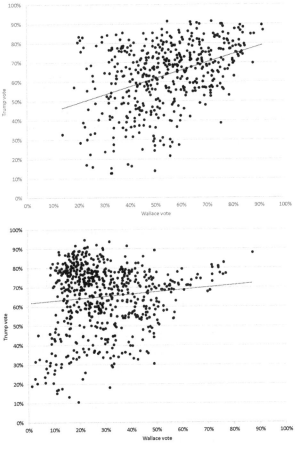

Figure 1.4 displays scatterplots of the county-level 2016 Trump vote on the vertical axis and the 1968 Wallace vote on the horizontal axis. The scatterplot on top shows the returns for Trump and Wallace in the aforementioned half-dozen states (Alabama, Arkansas, Georgia, Louisiana, and Mississippi, and South Carolina), whereas the scatterplot on the bottom shows similar returns for Trump and Wallace in Florida, North

Figure 1.4. County Vote for Trump (2016) and Wallace (1968) in Southern States

Carolina, Tennessee, Texas, and Virginia. The linkage between Trump and Wallace is much clearer in the scatterplot for the Deep South states plus Arkansas. For two presidential contests occurring almost a half-century apart, and comparing the votes for a Republican with a third-party candidate, the correlation is .432 ($p < .001$; $n = 493$ counties). In contrast, for the remaining five Peripheral South states, the correlation is four times smaller at .103, although still significant at $p < .01$ ($n = 646$ counties).[22]

The wiregrass region of southeastern Alabama (specifically, Barbour County: sixty-eight percent rural in the 2010 census)[23] and the borough of Queens, New York, may have very little in common, but they produced two of the most influential political demagogues in American history. And it is this unvarnished demagoguery with respect to style, and no matter the political issue, that unites Wallace and Trump and explains their rabid appeal among large segments of rural white southerners. Until Wallace's plea for forgiveness as a New South Democrat, he and Trump were never ones to apologize for their incendiary rhetoric (on Wallace, see Carter, 1995; and Frady, 1996; on Trump, see Muravchik and Shields, 2020). Both politicians also aired long lists of grievances and slights to gin up their voters, even if the narcissistic Trump leveled them with a more personalized focus. Neither figure harbored any elaborate ideological philosophy but rather promoted populist positions that perfectly meshed with their white working-class base. Finally, despite both politicians' lack of moral probity (both thrice-married adulterers), neither Wallace nor Trump was stopped from embracing a social conservatism that combined racist pronouncements with endorsements of religious piety. This was especially true for Trump, since the religious right was firmly aligned with the GOP by the time he arrived on the political scene, something that was not true in the late 1960s (see Layman, 2001).[24]

A Synopsis of the Southern Rural Republican Realignment

Instead of switching to the GOP, like so many of his contemporaries did (Canon and Sousa, 1992), Wallace instead abandoned the Old South Democratic Party's anti-Black foundation in favor of the New South version of the party that relied on biracial coalitions to win most elections except that for president. Wallace began this transition in the mid-1970s when it was becoming increasingly apparent that the expansive re-enfranchisement of southern Black voters as Democratic loyalists ensured the persistence of the party's electoral dominance, despite the notable ongoing movement of conservative whites into the Republican Party (Campbell, 1977). It is hard to question Wallace's strategy, since he was reelected as Alabama governor in 1974 and then won his final term in 1982. However, Wallace was one of those rare politicians who exerted an outsized impact on southern politics, specifically the balance of party politics in his state, much like Thurmond in South Carolina and Bill

Clinton in Arkansas. Indeed, once Wallace left the scene in 1986, a Republican (Guy Hunt), won the Alabama governorship, marking the first time since Reconstruction that a Republican had held that office in the state. Whereas the party switcher Thurmond accelerated GOP advancement in South Carolina, like the Democrat Bill Clinton in Arkansas, Wallace was primarily responsible for slowing Republican ascendancy in Alabama.

Thus far, the bulk of this chapter has laid out a historical political narrative of the dynamics at play in southern politics from the mid-twentieth century through the 1970s, and how these events affected the political behavior of urban and rural whites. Henceforth, this story of the Republican realignment of rural white southerners can be told more succinctly because of what we know about broad patterns of change that do not hinge on such detailed historical explanations. This is possible thanks to the work of several scholars contributing to our insight on party system change in the South, as well as nationally.

A fundamental reason why it took decades for rural white southerners to become the base of the GOP in the American South is rooted in the importance of party identification. The old southern Democracy was built upon white supremacy and defending the post-Reconstruction Jim Crow South, both from opponents within (notably, the civil rights movement) and against enemies from the outside (principally federal attempts to enforce civil rights legislation, whether it was initiated first by Republicans or years later by Democrats). As Key (1949, p. 10) tellingly put it, "Attachments to partisan labels live long beyond events that gave them birth." Such a profound statement could not ring truer for rural southern whites. It may have appeared contradictory for most rural whites to consistently vote Republican for president in the late 1960s while still backing Democrats in other contests well into the 1980s, but as long as Democrats in these down-ballot contests pushed a conservative agenda, this voting behavior entailed hardly any political compromise.

Given the enduring attachment to a political party, it is no wonder that Green, Palmquist, and Schickler (2002) estimated that approximately half of the realignment of white southerners to the GOP is due to generational change. Examining this issue with panel data on southern white high school seniors and their parents in 1965, and then in subsequent years (1973 and 1982, and also in 1997 for the high school cohort), McKee (2010) found that the parents exhibited hardly any long-term movement to the GOP, whereas their majority-Democratic offspring in 1965 had become majority-Republican by 1997 (the last interview year). McKee (2019) also found that over time, up until the mid-1990s to the turn of the twenty-first century, no matter the cohort, all southern whites have gradually shifted in favor of affiliating with the Republican Party.

Because older voters are not as likely to change their party identification (Green, Palmquist, and Schickler, 2002), the secular realignment of rural whites to the GOP in the South at some point must have displayed a period when this group was markedly younger than their Democratic counterparts. The ANES data show this dynamic. For instance, from the 1950s to the 1970s, the median age of white rural Republicans was forty-six versus forty-eight for white rural Democrats; essentially no difference. However, from the 1980s to 2000, when the southern GOP made its deepest electoral inroads (Black and Black, 2002), the median age of rural white Republicans was thirty-seven years old, ten years younger than the median age of rural white Democrats (forty-seven years old) during this twenty-year span. Finally, with the rural Republican realignment (RRR) reaching a mature stage in the most recent years, the 2019 ANES Pilot Study data put the median age of rural white Republican southerners at sixty years of age compared with fifty-eight years old for urban white Democratic southerners.

The RRR is, of course, just one particular kind of realignment that has been running its course in contemporary American politics. As Bartels (2000), Hetherington (2001), and later Levendusky (2009) demonstrated, the national electorate has undergone partisan sorting dating back to the 1980s. This sorting process fundamentally involves the alignment of party with ideology, so that most Democrats are now liberals and the vast majority of Republicans are conservatives. In the South, Black and Black (1987) found that, around the mid-1980s, white conservatives were the first to constitute a majority of Republican identifiers. Likewise, with the use of ANES panel studies, Abramowitz and Saunders (1998) discovered that, although most of the parents of white southerners in the 1970s were Democrats, by the 1990s, their children, most of whom were conservatives, had become Republicans.

Over the long run, this partisan sorting dynamic, which involves a heavy dose of generational change, has persisted because partisan elites continue to polarize over the most salient political issues (Fleisher and Bond, 2004; Hetherington, 2001; Theriault, 2008). Rural whites in the South eventually became even more aligned with the GOP than urban whites, because, in this ongoing partisan polarization, the Republican Party has submerged economic issues while ramping up their emphasis on social issues (Prysby, 2020; Rodden, 2019). This is a departure from the Reagan years in the 1980s (Black and Black, 1987), when the two-term president advocated a conservatism that encompassed practically every major issue domain (e.g., race, religion, economics, and national defense; see Abramowitz, 1994). By stressing culturally conservative values while downplaying free-market capitalism, even welcoming protectionist trade policies and a more expansive economic populism—the political and policy agenda led by President Trump—this latest incarnation of the Republican Party better reflects the profile of its base of rural white southerners. The upshot is a recursive relationship so that as more rural whites have realigned to the GOP, more elected Republicans are cognizant of the imperative to represent these core constituents' views.

Modern-Day Descendants of the Old Southern Democracy

Without a close examination of the evidence, we suspect that most political observers would not be aware of the recency of southern rural whites' embrace of Republicanism. The sample of evidence that follows will make this apparent. Furthermore, because of the extent to which rural white southerners now affiliate with the GOP, we contend that they, although several generations removed, are the most legitimate heirs and descendants of the Old South Democratic Party. Stated somewhat differently, with the outsized presence and influence of rural whites, and hence the attention paid to representing these constituents' interests, the old southern Democracy bears the closest resemblance to the latest version of the modern southern Republican Party. Quoting Black and Black (2002, p. 119), in *The Unsolid South*, Devin Caughey (2018, p. 173) posed the question, "Has the voting rights revolution empowered black voters, or has the South merely undergone a '*shift from conservative Democrats elected by whites to conservative Republicans still elected by whites*[?]'"[25] It is important to note that Caughey's citation to Black and Black is actually a quote that was specific to US Senate elections in Mississippi and not the broader state of southern politics. Regardless, we will answer the aforementioned question: The white rural takeover of the Republican Party has led to the latter condition quoted above, in most, but not all, of the modern South.

In 1960, the ANES recorded twenty percent of rural white southerners affiliating with the GOP (including independent leaners) compared with thirty-five percent of urban whites doing the same (a significant difference at $p < .05$). In 2000, fifty-six percent of urban white southerners identified as Republicans versus thirty-nine percent of their rural white neighbors (a significant difference at $p < .05$). Almost two decades later, according to the 2019 ANES Pilot Study, forty-six percent of urban white southerners affiliated with the GOP, whereas now, fifty-seven percent of rural white southerners identified as Republicans (a significant difference at $p < .05$). Perhaps even more remarkable than the ten-point contemporary advantage in Republican affiliation among rural white southerners, is the flip side, the share of white southern Democrats. In 2019, the percentage of urban white southern Democrats was forty-one percent compared with twenty-nine percent of rural white southerners (a significant difference at $p < .01$). Hence, over the past twenty years, the percentage of urban white Republicans has declined by ten points, whereas the share of rural white Republicans has increased by eighteen points. Conversely, urban white Democrats are now much more plentiful than rural white Democrats.

Obviously, the evidence indicates that large-scale changes in party affiliation among rural and urban white southerners are very recent. Again, this dynamic speaks to how party identification lags vote choice. Nonetheless, since the modern Republican Party is overwhelmingly reliant on a coalition of white supporters (more than ninety percent white in the South; McKee, 2019), it should be noted that the GOP was still firmly at an electoral disadvantage vis-à-vis southern Democrats at the beginning of the 1990s. In the three subpresidential offices that we examine, McKee and Yoshinaka (2015, p. 958) pointed out that, after the 1990 elections, southern Republicans occupied thirty-six percent of governorships, thirty-two percent of Senate seats, and thirty-four percent of the House delegation. Thus, at the start of what would be a historic decade of Republican gains below the presidential level, the first election cycle was not terribly auspicious.

Another eye-opening example of the humble roots of the southern GOP comes from South Carolina. Figure 1.5 displays the percentage of the state's white electorate participating in state-level Republican primaries (not presidential primaries, which are usually held on a different date and, of course, only every four years) from 1984 to 2020 in midterm and presidential cycles.

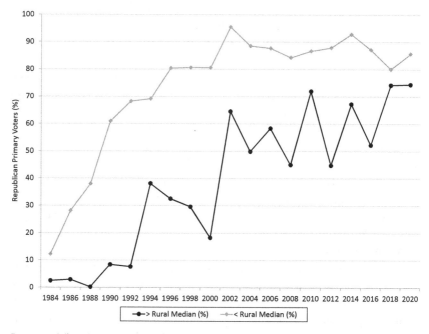

Figure 1.5. White Participation in South Carolina Republican State Primaries, 1984–2020

The two lines in the figure distinguish white voters who reside in counties that are either above or below the median percent rural based on the 2010 census: over 60.8% rural or under 60.8% rural. South Carolina has forty-six counties, and cutting the data this way allows us to account for white South Carolinians who reside in counties that are generally rural (twenty-three counties that are seventy-five percent rural, on average) or generally urban (twenty-three counties that are thirty-five percent rural, on average). First, most surprising is perhaps just how meager white participation was in the Palmetto State's Republican primaries at the start of the time series in the 1980s. Indeed, whites from more rural counties are practically absent in 1980s GOP primaries. Second, whites in more urban counties are much quicker in switching their participation in favor of Republican primaries, and for decades, they have remained exceedingly more prevalent in this regard than their more rural counterparts. However, by the time of the past two election cycles in 2018 and 2020, the Republican primary participation margins between more and less rural white voters narrowed to their lowest differences.

To make sense of recent primary participation patterns in presidential contests, it is necessary to focus on those elections in which the seat is open, because otherwise a sitting president seeking reelection usually (but not always) has only token intraparty competition, and, therefore, these contests naturally draw low participation (McKee and Hayes, 2009, 2010). Hence, most recently, the elections to consider would be in 2008, when President Bush was term limited, and in 2016, when President Obama was term limited. Because of its availability of data on the participation of white voters, South Carolina is once again an illuminating example of the impressive shift in rural whites to the GOP. Sticking with the same metric used earlier, sixty-two percent of whites in above-the-median rural counties participated in the 2008 Republican presidential primary in the Palmetto State. By comparison, sixty-six percent of whites in below-the-median rural counties also voted in South Carolina's 2008 GOP presidential primary. Eight years later, in the next open-seat presidential contest, white participation in the 2016 South Carolina GOP presidential primary among voters in counties above the rural median was ninety percent. In contrast, eighty-four percent of white voters in counties below the rural median participated in the 2016 South Carolina Republican presidential primary.

It is, perhaps, a universal condition in modern industrialized democratic nations that migratory patterns indicate that urban population centers are magnets for resettlement, whereas the countryside/rural settings are the places from which most people depart (Greenwood, 1975; Hitt, 1956; Taeuber, 1941). And even though the general migratory pattern dating back to the 1970s is one of growing in-migration to the American South (Wright, 2013), within the region most of these newcomers have chosen to reside in metropolitan/

urban centers (Morris, 2021). This means that the more rooted and native population of white southerners consists of rural stock.

Data from the Southern Focus Poll (SFP) administered in the fall of 1994, yield insight on differences in the rootedness and southern identity of whites according to whether they live in urban or rural places.[26] Consider the following significant differences between rural and urban white southerners based on these 1994 data: (1) Respondent's community is in the South: ninety-eight percent of rural whites versus ninety-five percent of urban whites ($p < .05$); (2) respondent has lived in the South their entire life: seventy-one percent of rural whites versus fifty-nine percent of urban whites ($p < .01$); (3) respondent considers self a southerner: eighty-five percent of rural whites versus seventy-two percent of urban whites ($p < .001$). SFP respondents were also asked if they had ancestors living in the United States in 1860 (on the eve of the Civil War), and eighty-four percent of rural whites said yes, compared with seventy-six percent of urban whites (difference significant at $p < .05$). Last, and certainly a cultural nugget of political relevance, was an entry in which, without asking the respondent, the survey interviewer recorded whether the respondent (1) had a strong southern accent, (2) a detectable southern accent, or (3) no southern accent. These data are highly revealing of town and country differences in southern speech patterns. The SFP interviewers classified forty-two percent of rural whites as having a strong southern accent as compared with twenty-five percent of urban whites falling into this category (the difference is significant at $p < .001$). Recent experimental research has found that, controlling for other political factors, subjects perceived hypothetical candidates with southern accents to be Republicans and conservatives, and were generally less inclined to support such candidates (Ash et al., 2020). We consider these findings as evidence of the general perception of a southern rural white takeover of the modern GOP.

Continuing with the expectation that contemporary rural white southerners are the most likely posterity of the Old South Democratic electorate, the ANES data are once again illuminating. The top half of Table 1.1 displays the recollected party identification of white southerners' parents from 1952 to 1992. There is no significant difference in terms of the rate of Republican identification among rural and urban whites' parents (and the same goes for the share of independents); but a higher percentage of rural whites' parents recalled to have been Democrats (difference was significant at $p < .001$). The bottom half of the table considers southern nativism with respect to the share of whites who grew up in the South. The ANES data are partitioned into three periods: (1) 1952–1966, (2) 1968–2000, and (3) for 2004 and 2016. The first two periods come from the ANES Cumulative Data File (CDF), but after the 2000 election, the ANES CDF does not make respondent location available, and thereafter, the question of where a respondent grew up is only available along

Table 1.1. Parents' Party Identification and Southern Upbringing

% Recollection of father and mother's party identification, 1952–1992

	DEMOCRAT	INDEPENDENT	REPUBLICAN	OTHER
Rural	68	6	21	5
Urban	63	9	21	8
Diff.	5*	−3	0	−3

% Rural and urban white southerners who grew up in the South

	1952–1966	1968–2000	2004 & 2016	OVERALL
Rural	82[a]	82[a]	86[b]	82
Urban	61[a]	70[a]	69[b]	69
Diff.	11[a],*	12[a],*	17[b],*	13*

Note. ANES data are from the Cumulative Data File (CDF) for the top half of the table. ANES CDF data up to 2000 for the bottom half of the table (denoted with [a]), and individual ANES times series data for 2004 and 2016 (denoted with [b]). Diff. = difference.

*$p < .001$ (two-tailed).

with respondent location in the 2004 and 2016 ANES time series studies. All this said, regardless of the time period, rural whites are markedly more likely to have grown up in the South, and the disparity is greatest (seventeen points) in the most recent years (2004 and 2016).

It is one thing to demonstrate that rural white southerners are, indeed, more rooted in their region and more tied to it than urban whites, but to cement the case that the former group constitutes the greatest contingent of Republicans who are descendants of the old southern Democracy requires a comparison of selected characteristics of rural and urban whites who identify as Republicans. This can be determined with the 2016 Cooperative Election Study (CES) survey, as it contains very large samples (see chapter two for further discussion of data sources and their sample sizes). Table 1.2 presents a battery of CES survey questions asked of respondents in 2016. We selected questions with an eye toward demography (education, income, religiosity) and political attitudes (ideology and opinions on racial, cultural, and social issues). The data in the table are limited to white southerners whom we classify as small-town South (STS) or urban (see chapter two for coding) and self-identify as Republicans (including independents who lean toward the GOP).[27]

As noted in the table, of the thirteen comparisons, in only one instance, there is not a significant difference between small-town South (STS) and urban white Republicans; a slight majority of both groups (fifty-two percent) see the Republican Party as either conservative or very conservative. In the

**Table 1.2. Some Characteristics of Small-Town South (STS)
and Urban White Republicans**

Features and Views of southern white Republicans	Small-town South	Urban
Education and income		
% College graduates	16**	26
% Below median family income	68**	57
Ideology		
% Conservative/very conservative (self-placement)	67**	59
% View Republican Party as conservative/very conservative	52	52
% View Democratic Party as liberal/very liberal	90*	87
Questions on race		
% Agree with being angry that racism exists	64*	67
% Strongly disagree that white people in the United States have advantages because of the color of their skin	68**	59
Religiosity		
% Born again	67**	53
% Attend church once a week or more	45**	38
Cultural/social issues		
% Oppose banning assault rifles	67**	58
% Oppose allowing gays and lesbians to marry legally	77**	63
% Support making abortions illegal in all circumstances	30**	24

Note. All data were calculated by the authors from the 2016 CES (Cooperative Election Study). Differences between rural and urban white Republicans on a given answer are: $*p < .05$; $**p < .001$ (two-tailed). In 2016, the southern white median family income was $57,455 (Source: 2016 American Community Survey, US Census Bureau).

other dozen matchups, STS white Republicans exhibit differences from their urban white counterparts in ways that we would expect. First of all, STS white Republicans have a lower educational attainment, and more of them reside in households below the southern white median family income in 2016. Regarding ideology, compared with urban white Republicans, STS white Republicans considered themselves to be more conservative, and they also viewed the Democratic Party as more liberal. With respect to religiosity, a greater percentage of STS white Republicans profess a born-again experience and are more frequent church attendees. On two questions dealing with race, STS white Republicans were not as angry that racism exists, and they were substantially more likely to disavow white privilege (advantages due to white skin color). Finally, as expected, on cultural/social issues, STS white Republicans are considerably more conservative than urban white Republicans. By six points, the former group is more likely to favor banning all abortions; by nine points, they are more opposed to banning assault rifles; and by fourteen points, STS white Republicans are more opposed to the legalization of gay marriage.

Two other pieces of data from the CES drive home the notable movement of downscale/low socioeconomic (SES)-status rural white southerners to the Republican Party. First, however, we present a brief and necessary historical discussion to contextualize what we are about to show. By the 1950s, northern white adherents of the Democratic and Republican parties had sorted on the economic cleavage, so that white Democrats were generally of a lower income than white Republicans. In the 1950s South, this relationship was reversed; the staunchest white Democrats in the South were also located in the highest income brackets (Nadeau and Stanley, 1993). Thus, in the American South, the New Deal realignment of the major parties on the basis of class took much longer to get underway and then proceed to run its course. In the subsequent decades after the 1950s, however, the positive relationship between income and Republicanism among white voters had become more pronounced in the South than in the North (Gelman et al., 2008; Nadeau et al., 2004; Stonecash, 2000; Stonecash, Brewer, and Mariani, 2003). Furthermore, by the 1980s, it was apparent that not just higher income southern whites, but those of higher education (often one and the same), who were college educated and resided in more urban settings, were the most powerful engine of GOP growth (Black and Black, 1987; see also Lublin, 2004; and Shafer and Johnston, 2006).

Since the mid-2000s, the influx of southern rural whites to the GOP has altered and attenuated the longstanding positive relationship between whites of a higher SES and Republican affiliation (Prysby, 2020). On this point, data from the CES are informative. Figure 1.6 presents the share of Republican identifiers (leaners included) according to family income parceled into thirds (low, middle, and high) for STS whites and urban whites in the South from 2006 through 2018. At the start of the time series in 2006, the old pattern of a much stronger linkage between Republican identification and higher income registers for both STS whites and urban whites. In 2006, the GOP affiliation gap for high- versus low-income STS whites is a chasm of thirty-six percentage points and half this amount (eighteen points) for high- versus low-income urban whites. Interestingly, though, as this relationship waned among middle- and high-income whites, reaching nadirs in 2012 for STS whites

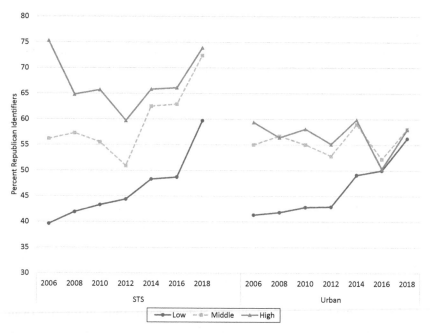

Figure 1.6. Party by Place and Income, 2006–2018

and 2016 for urban whites, the relationship only continues to strengthen for low-income whites, and particularly for STS whites. After 2012, among STS whites, Republican affiliation increases for all three income groups. Likewise, there is an across-the-board increase in GOP identification among urban whites from 2016 to 2018. By 2018, the share of Republican urban whites does not show discernible variation on the basis of income category. For STS whites in 2018, the Republican identification gap between high- and low-income groups reached its smallest difference (fourteen points), and there is essentially no GOP affiliation disparity with respect to high- and middle-income STS whites (a paltry 1.5 points). However, looking across the groups of STS and urban whites, most remarkable in 2018 is that the percentage of low-income Republican STS whites is higher than the share of Republican urban whites, regardless of the latter group's income category.

   In the past three election cycles (2016, 2018, and 2020), the media and scholarly commentary appears to place greater emphasis on education as opposed to income, with respect to a minimalist and, hence, imprecise approach to identifying white working-class voters. This might simply be due to the fact that, in these recent elections, a simple bifurcation of college graduate versus no college degree has revealed massive differences in the preferences of white voters. Assessing the 2016 presidential contest, Sides, Tesler, and Vavreck (2017, p. 42) contended that, "The education divide among whites provided Trump with a narrow path to victory." As Rodden (2019, p. 79) noted, "The share of college graduates in the population has grown everywhere over the subsequent forty years, but the growth has been far stronger in metropolitan counties. The gap between rural and metropolitan counties was around 10 percentage points in 1970, but by 2010, it had grown to over 20 percentage points." Indeed, *CNN* even allows one to filter the 2020 exit poll crosstabs based on white voters with or without a college degree. For our purposes, this binary distinction is useful because rural white southerners do not possess the same level of educational attainment as urban white southerners (in the case of Republicans, refer to Table 1.2). Additionally, it is indisputable that the Republican Donald Trump cultivated support from lesser educated white voters who constituted a large component of his coalition (Hicks, McKee, and Smith, 2021).

Figure 1.7 shows CES data from 2006 to 2018, with percent Republican identification on the vertical axis and plotted lines for STS (left side) and urban (right side) white southerners with and without a college degree. For college-educated whites, STS and urban, Republican identification patterns are marked by considerable movement; first downward (from 2006 to 2012), then back up in 2014, back down in 2016, and then an upward spike in 2018. The notable volatility in college-educated whites' Republican affiliation is not shared by non-college-educated whites.

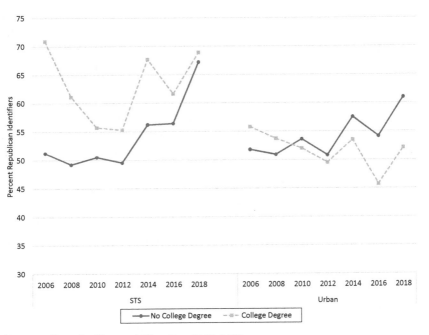

Figure 1.7. Party by Place and Education, 2006–2018

To be sure, there is a repetitive down-and-up pattern for most of the time series for whites lacking a college degree, but this movement is not substantial until the upward spike in 2014. After 2014, GOP identification patterns for STS and urban white southerners are different. A decline in GOP affiliation among urban whites in 2016 is followed by a shift back upward in 2018. By comparison, STS whites' Republican identification is steady between 2014 and 2016 and then surges in 2018; going from fifty-six percent Republican in 2016 to sixty-seven percent Republican in 2018. In the urban South, non-college-educated white Republicanism has exceeded that of college-educated whites since 2010, and the difference (nine percentage points) is largest in the 2018 election cycle. In the small-town South, a massive twenty-point Republican identification gap in 2006 separating college-educated and non-college-educated whites is nearly closed by 2018 (a 1.7-point difference). Now, STS non-college-educated whites are more Republican than urban whites with or without a college degree. From 2006 to 2018, whether the variable of interest is income (Figure 1.6) or education (Figure 1.7), the largest gains by far in GOP identification over this period are found among STS whites with lower incomes and less education.[28]

The Rural White Republican South and a Brief Overview of the Book

When V. O. Key (1959) revised his conception of critical elections to better reflect a realignment process more gradual in its alteration of long-term changes to voting behavior, the slow but generally unremitting movement of rural white southerners to the GOP was in its nascent stages.[29] Now, looking back, the rural Republican realignment of southern whites is not only the longest in duration in America's historical record but also perhaps the deepest with respect to the extent to which this group is now affiliated with the GOP and no longer wedded to their ancestral Democratic Party. We emphasize rural white southerners' ties to the old southern Democracy (the post-Reconstruction but pre-civil rights white electorate) because, as demonstrated earlier, these modern-day Republicans are clearly the most connected to it in terms of genealogy, demography, and political attitudes.

This political reality has obvious and important implications for southern and national politics. For one, it means that cultural conservatism has played a bigger role in the policy agenda and political posturing of Republican officeholders. This, in turn, has led to a deemphasis on economic issues and the embrace of an economic populism unheard of during President Reagan's tenure. Tilting the fulcrum on the economic issue so that Republicans are now more protectionist than Democrats (Miller and Schofield, 2008) and also the primary defenders of the old economy (e.g., manufacturing, agriculture, and extraction [gas and coal mining]), while promoting culture war battles, has provided an opening for urban white southerners to reconsider aligning with the Democratic Party. Slowly, as more rural white southerners have joined the ranks of the GOP and their urban white counterparts have sought refuge in the Democratic opposition, the modern Republican Party is morphing into a coalition ill suited to capture the votes of an increasingly urbanizing, growing, and demographically diversifying region (Bullock et al., 2019; Morris, 2021). Also, it is finally the case that the youngest generations of white southerners are no longer as Republican as their elders (McKee, 2019), a key warning sign for the GOP as rural residents are typically older than urban dwellers (especially urban Democrats). In the final chapter, we further detail and evaluate important demographic changes to the southern electorate and explain how these developments—most significantly, the rural takeover of the GOP—affect the balance of power in southern and national politics.

In meticulously detailing the origins of America's urban–rural political divide, Rodden (2019) first points out that the groundwork for an ascendant Democratic New Deal majority coalition was tied to industrialization occurring in the late 1800s and into the early twentieth century. It was at the railheads where manufacturing industries took root and created densely populated cities of various sizes that Democratic strongholds emerged under the leadership of President Roosevelt in the 1930s. Advocacy of workers' rights and economic relief in the midst of a Great Depression cemented the allegiance of a preponderantly urban, northern working class to the Democratic Party. Meanwhile, down South, a generally rural and overwhelmingly white enfranchised electorate remained faithful to a Democratic Party that heretofore avoided meddling with Dixie's Jim Crow system of race relations. Interestingly, as the North's party politics came to reflect the urban–rural divisions found in democratic countries most similar to the United States (e.g., Canada, most of Europe, Great Britain and its former colonies of Australia and New Zealand; see Rodden, 2019), the South was an aberration in which the more conservative Republican Party had become electorally formidable in urban settings. This curious twist of fate, where the southern GOP initially gained electoral traction in metropolitan areas and then solidified these gains, has taken decades to unravel and reverse. But now, finally, southern population density patterns have come to reflect the most typical pattern of a culturally liberal (Democratic) party dominating in the cities, whereas the culturally conservative (Republican) party rules the countryside.

Chapter two outlines the various ways we measure place to examine differences in the political behavior of rural and urban white southerners from the 1950s to current times. We suspect that there is no detriment to the reader in skipping this chapter if the details involved in residential density metrics are less than captivating. Nonetheless, what should give anyone confidence in our assessment of changing patterns in political behavior is the reliance on numerous data sources and different measures of place to show that the

Republican realignment of rural white southerners is an undeniable modern reality. We lean heavily on ANES data to document voting behavior from the 1950s through the 1980s, the long era in which the manifestation of southern Republican presidential dominance was slow to materialize in down-ballot offices. The next four chapters commence in the early 1990s and proceed into the 2010s to examine the increasing success of the southern GOP among rural whites in presidential, senatorial, gubernatorial, and House elections.

Whereas chapters three through seven emphasize voter preferences, in chapters eight and nine, we focus on party identification. Chapter eight takes a Southwide approach to looking at long-term changes in the party affiliation of rural white southerners in comparison with urban whites. Chapter nine then highlights patterns of party identification in four southern states (Arkansas, Mississippi, Tennessee, and Texas) with different shares of rural white populations and, not surprisingly, different rates of Republican advancement. In both of the aforementioned chapters, to capture changes in party affiliation, we lean on survey data sources with lengthy time series. Chapter ten evaluates differences between rural and urban whites, with recent survey data to point out the various and politically important distinctions between these two groups that constitute the vast majority of Republican adherents in the South. We reserve our evaluation of the 2020 elections for chapter eleven. As fortune would have it, the southern state of Georgia decided which party would control the US Senate, and we make use of voter registration data to examine the political behavior of rural whites in these two pivotal runoff contests. Additionally, we offer a broad pronouncement of the significance of the 2020 election cycle, which included the defeat of an incumbent president who benefited from a fiercely loyal following, especially among rural white southerners. In chapter twelve, we conclude by emphasizing the historical importance and future political implications of the rural Republican realignment of southern whites.

2 Measuring Place and the Data Associated with It

In this chapter, we present a general overview of the various methods and data sources we will utilize throughout the book to study the rural Republican realignment of southern whites. The key variable for any analysis presented in this text is that of *place*. Here, we differentiate between rural and small-town areas from urban locales. As described later, there are a number of methods we utilize to accomplish this goal, depending on the type and source of data being relied on to present summary results and make statistical inferences. The first part of this chapter discusses the measurement of place, and the second half outlines the various types and general sources of data utilized throughout the book.[1]

Measuring Place

In this book, we rely on three major definitions of *place*: urban and rural, as defined by the US Census Bureau; a new measure that we have developed and use, termed *small-town South* (STS); and population density.[2] This section devotes some detail to describing and explaining these three place-based measures.

Urban and Rural

One could say that, starting with the first census in 1790, keeping track of where Americans live has been a paramount concern for a variety of reasons (especially congressional apportionment). Therefore, any work that examines where Americans live must start with the US Census and its definitions for rural and urban.[3] Beginning with the 1910 census, population and territory have been classified as rural and urban (Ratcliffe, 2016). The definitions used by the US Census Bureau have changed over time, with major alterations occurring as late as the 2000 census.[4]

Technically, multiple criteria are used by the US Census Bureau to classify a geographic area and the population of an area as urban and, as such, not rural. Ratcliffe et al. (2016, p. 3) indicate that the Census Bureau uses "total population thresholds, density, land use, and distance" as criteria for classifying blocks (the smallest geographic unit used by the Census) as urban.[5]

Moving away from a purely technical discussion, in the next few paragraphs, we present a high-level overview of urban and rural areas in the United States.

As the bulk of our empirical analyses occur from 1990 through 2020, we will limit our discussion of urban and rural under the Census Bureau's definition to that period of time as well.[6] In 1990, the Census Bureau defined an urbanized area as containing a population of fifty thousand or more. Census-designated places containing equal to or more than twenty-five hundred persons up to fifty thousand persons were also defined as urban. Any area outside these two types of urban settings were, by default, classified as rural.

Beginning with the 2000 census, the Census Bureau reconfigured its definition scheme to create two types of urban-related components: urbanized areas and urban clusters. Urbanized areas contain fifty thousand or more persons, and urban clusters range from between 2,500 to 50,000 residents. Although it may appear that census-designated places (for 1990) and urban clusters (for 2000 and 2010) are analogous, the criteria used to delineate these units did significantly differ, especially the incorporation of a density-based approach post-1990.[7] The total urban population combines individuals living in urban areas with those living in urban clusters. Population segments outside of urban areas or urban clusters are, by definition and default, rural.[8]

For reference, Table 2.1 details the Census Bureau's urban/rural population breakdown by southern state from 1990 through 2010, as well as region-wide totals. In 2010, the most urbanized state, at ninety-one percent, was Florida. The least urbanized state—and hence, by definition, the most rural—was Mississippi. At just over fifty percent rural, Mississippi is now the only southern state in the latest census count with a majority of its population living in rural areas. For the region as a whole, the South was split approximately one-quarter rural (23.4%) and three-quarters urban (76.6%) in 2010.

We believe that the US Census Bureau's definition of what constitutes a rural area, although foundational, is too restrictive for our purposes. There is little doubt that a rural area, as defined by the census, is rural, but what is needed is a geographic-based measure that includes residents of both rural areas along with those living in smaller towns throughout the region. For example, in 2010, the Census Bureau classified Crisp County, Georgia (population, 23,439) as fifty-three percent urban. Crisp County's urban residents are all located in the city of Cordele. The county seat, Cordele, contained 12,416 residents, which would make it an urban area under the Census Bureau definition. Would anyone visiting Cordele (or Crisp County, for that matter)—famous for its Watermelon Festival, popularized by the country music star Tracy Byrd in his song "Watermelon Crawl"—equate this place with the urban behemoth of Atlanta? Although both Cordele and Atlanta are *urban* according to the Census Bureau definition, most would recognize that the characteristics of these two areas are distinctively different.

Table 2.1. Percentage of State Population Classified as Urban and Rural, 1990–2010

| | 1990 | | 2000 | | 2010 | |
State	URBAN	RURAL	URBAN	RURAL	URBAN	RURAL
AL	60.4	39.6	55.4	44.6	59.0	41.0
AR	53.5	46.5	52.5	47.5	56.2	43.8
FL	84.8	15.2	89.3	10.7	91.2	8.8
GA	63.2	36.8	71.6	28.4	75.1	24.9
LA	68.1	31.9	72.6	27.4	73.2	26.8
MS	47.1	52.9	48.8	51.2	49.4	50.6
NC	50.4	49.6	60.2	39.8	66.1	33.9
SC	54.6	45.4	60.5	39.5	66.3	33.7
TN	60.9	39.1	63.6	36.4	66.4	33.6
TX	80.3	19.7	82.5	17.5	84.7	15.3
VA	69.4	30.6	73.0	27.0	75.5	24.5
South	69.2	30.8	73.5	26.5	76.6	23.4

% State population in:

Source: US Census.

Across the South, there are many areas that are synonymous with the Crisp County example. To provide a more inclusive measure of place, we build on official definitions to create a new measure that we term *small-town South* (STS). Our purpose with this measure is to more adequately capture both rural and small-town areas at the exclusion of urban areas.

The STS measure is based on differentiating between midsized urban units, defined by the Census Bureau as urban clusters. Again, urban clusters are a geographic unit that contains between twenty-five hundred and fifty thousand individuals. This is in contrast to urban areas, which are geographic units that contain more than fifty thousand people. For our purposes, urban areas are considered strictly urban.

We differentiate between urban clusters on the basis of the population contained therein. Any county containing an urban cluster with a population of twenty thousand or less, which is not geographically contiguous to an urban area, is denoted as small town. Conversely, any urban cluster with a population larger than twenty thousand is considered urban. For each county, we combine the populations residing in rural areas and urban clusters that meet the criteria of our definition and divide by the total county population. The resulting percentage is our measure of STS. It follows that any population within a county not considered STS is urban. Therefore, if a county is forty-three percent STS, it is fifty-seven percent urban.

Our STS measure can be used as both a percentage measure ranging from zero to one hundred percent or as a binary indicator. In the case of a binary indicator, we define any county with an STS population of ninety-five percent or higher as STS. The Census Bureau only undertakes rural/urban calculations, a block-level activity, every ten years with the compilation of the decennial census. For the purpose of statistical inferences offered in this book, we calculate our STS measure for 1990, 2000, and 2010.[9] The 1990 measure is used for the years 1990–1999, the 2000 measure is used for 2000–2009, and the 2010 measure is used for 2010–2019. A detailed description of our STS measure is available in the Appendix located at the end of this chapter.[10]

For the reader's reference, we provide a summary of our STS measure by state and for the South from 1990 through 2010. The percentage of a state's population classified as STS in 2010 ranges from a low of 10.9% in Florida to a high of 62.2% in Mississippi. These figures can also be compared to the urban/rural calculations for the southern states located in Table 2.1. As our STS measure is designed to be a more inclusive measure of what constitutes a rural area, it is no surprise that the percentage of southerners living in STS areas constitutes a larger share of the population than those who live in rural areas (as defined by the Census Bureau). For example, in 2010, 43.8% of Arkansas's population lived in rural areas, compared with 57.6% of the Natural State's population found in STS areas—a notable difference of 13.8 percentage points.

Tables 2.1 and 2.2 reveal another point that should be made regarding the South. As a region, and as is true throughout the United States, Dixie continues to become more urbanized over time. This is the case whether one uses the Census Bureau's definition of rural or our STS measure. At the regional level, the STS population shrank from 38.1% in 1990 to 33.0% in 2000, to 29.3% in 2010—a drop of 8.8 percentage points over twenty years. Because STS and urban classifications are mutually exclusive, a shrinking STS population therefore means a growing urban population. Most of the analyses in this book are devoted to studying the political differences between whites in the South based on *place*; however, chapter twelve will also examine the electoral effects and implications of the changing STS-urban population distribution at the state level and Southwide.

Figure 2.1 displays the spatial distribution of STS counties in 2010 across the eleven-state South. STS counties are shaded black, and urban counties are shaded white.[11] The South contains a total of 1,142 counties and parishes.[12] In 2010, 714 counties, or 62.5%, were classified as STS. Conversely, the 428 urban counties constituted 37.5% of the total. STS counties account for 64.3% of the region's land area but only 14.9% of the South's overall population. Urban counties constituted over a third (35.7%) of the South's land mass but contained 85.1% of Dixie's population.[13]

Table 2.2. Percentage of State Population Classified as Small-Town South (STS), 1990–2010

State	1990	2000	2010
AL	49.2	54.1	48.1
AR	61.9	62.7	57.6
FL	17.8	13.5	10.9
GA	46.2	35.4	31.2
LA	39.9	37.1	36.0
MS	67.3	65.3	62.2
NC	57.5	46.4	39.4
SC	54.2	47.4	40.0
TN	46.9	44.8	41.0
TX	26.9	25.5	21.7
VA	36.1	31.2	28.9
South	38.1	33.0	29.3

Source: US Census.

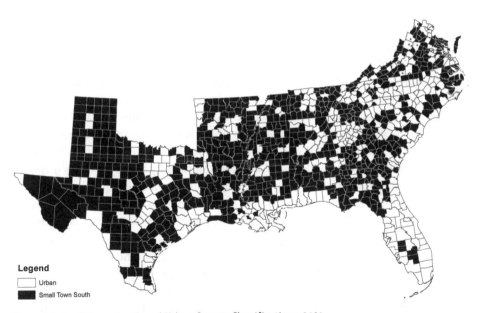

Legend

☐ Urban

■ Small Town South

Figure 2.1. Small-Town South and Urban County Classifications, 2010

Population Density

Another method for measuring rurality is to calculate the population density of a given geographic area. Geographies with higher levels of density can be said to be more urban and low-density areas, more rural. We calculate density for a particular geographic unit as:

natural log [population/area in square miles].[14]

For example, a county that is one thousand square miles with a population of two thousand would have a population density of two persons per square mile (0.3 in logged terms). The population density of the same geographically sized county with a population of a million would be one thousand persons per square mile (or three in logged terms). So, the latter county can be seen to have a greater population density and, therefore, is also more urban than the former. Although population density is easy to obtain, calculate, and compare, one drawback is a difficulty in the establishment of an exact threshold for what constitutes an urban versus a rural area. In other words, it is obvious that the greater the density of an area, the more urban, but a value or cut point where an area would be classified as urban as opposed to rural is difficult to define. Despite this issue, density is an intuitive means to compare the degree of urbanization among geographic areas. In addition, population density can be readily included as an explanatory factor (independent variable) in statistical models to study its relationship to various political concepts and actions, including partisanship and voting behavior.

For a concrete demonstration of population density in a southern setting, we will compare Brewster County, Texas, to Dallas County, Texas. Located in the Big Bend region of the Lone Star State, at 6,192 square miles, Brewster County is Texas's largest in terms of land area.[15] The estimated population of the county based on the 2018 American Community Survey (ACS) is 9,216, producing a population density measure of 1.49 persons per square miles (or 0.17 in logged terms). By comparison, Dallas County is 2,966 square miles in land area. The 2018 ACS population estimate for Dallas County (home to the city of Dallas) was 2,586,552, producing a population density value of 872.06 persons per square mile (2.94 in logged terms). In 2010, the Census Bureau classified Brewster County as two-thirds urban (65.1%), compared with 99.3% for Dallas County.[16] Thus, this example from Texas highlights why population density is a better approximation of urbanization than the urban categorization as defined by the Census Bureau.[17]

For comparative purposes, we examine the relationship between our place-based measures using the Pearson correlation coefficient, which ranges from −1.0 to 1.0. A −1.0 or 1.0 would indicate a perfect correlation between the two variables of interest or that x is an exact predictor of y. In graphical terms, the points on an *x, y* scatterplot would all perfectly appear on a straight line. The closer the Pearson correlation statistic is to −1.0 or 1.0, the stronger the relationship. A score of zero would indicate that there is no relationship between the two variables of interest.

In 2010, the correlation between the county-level percent STS and population density is a very robust −.76. This indicates that these two measures are, indeed, tapping into the same construct: the level of rurality. The negative sign in this context simply means that density is inversely related to the STS measure, which makes intuitive sense; as a county becomes more urbanized (higher density), it should correspondingly score lower on the STS measure. The correlation between percent rural and density, at −.68, although also high, indicates that it is not as strongly associated with density as is the STS measure. The percent STS and population density are, therefore, better substitutes for one another than are the percent rural and population density.

Data Types and General Sources

To study the Republican realignment of rural white southerners, we use various types of data from a wide range of sources. This section provides a general overview with specific references to data sources by chapter, which are available in Appendix A (online).

Survey Data

One of the central data sources we utilize are survey data in which the individual is the unit of analysis. A number of surveys are available to study rural white southerners longitudinally and over time. In addition, these surveys provide the ability to locate respondents spatially, either through internal coding (in the survey) or through the presence of geographic identifiers such as the county of residence. Respondents can be further sorted by factors such as race, party identification, and vote choice for various elective offices.

Key survey data series used throughout this work include the American National Election Studies (ANES); the Cooperative Election Study (CES); the news consortium election exit polls; state-specific surveys; and a survey that we commissioned for this book. Having been administered continuously for every presidential election cycle since 1948, the ANES is the longest running political survey of the US electorate. Until fairly recently, the ANES was the only detailed longitudinal survey available to study American politics. The ANES has also consistently provided place-based variables for respondents over time.

In 2006, the CES made its debut, filling a large void for studying midterm political behavior, since the ANES terminated midterm surveys after 2002. Starting in 2006, the CES has been continuously administered to the American public in midterm and presidential cycles. Compared with the ANES, the

CES contains a substantially larger number of cases, providing a representative sample of the American electorate in every state. This data source also contains key geographic identifiers including state, county, and congressional district for each respondent. Using these identifiers, we can merge geographic-related information to locate respondents within specific place-based settings. For example, knowing the county where each respondent lives allows us to append information on the context of respondents, such as the characterization of their county of residence in terms of the percent STS or population density.

Exit polls conducted by news organizations during each federal election cycle (midterm and presidential) also provide important longitudinal data for assessing political changes to rural white southern voters. These surveys offer representative southern state samples of voters (although not all southern states are surveyed individually in every election cycle), along with a national exit poll. It is possible to subset the national exit poll in each year to denote the eleven-state South. However, it was not until 1984 that the exit polls made available a state indicator; therefore, our use of exit poll data commences with this year. Although these surveys are limited in terms of variables and states included in a given year, they have consistently incorporated a variable indicating the size of place for surveyed voters. We make use of this size of place variable to classify exit poll respondents into rural/STS and urban areas for analyses presented throughout the book.

We were also able to locate a number of longitudinal state-specific surveys conducted by various universities covering four southern states: Arkansas, Mississippi, Tennessee, and Texas. These surveys all contained a consistent measure of *place* over time, which allowed us to make a more detailed examination of political change in these four states. The Arkansas Poll is conducted by the University of Arkansas and includes yearly data from 1999 through 2020. The Mississippi Poll, conducted by Mississippi State University, is a biennial state poll spanning the time period from 1984 through 2014.[18] For Tennessee, we relied on two surveys conducted at different points in time. The first, conducted by the University of Tennessee, covers 1990 through 1996. We also make use of another poll on the Volunteer State, conducted by Vanderbilt University, which provides data for a more recent time period: 2012–2018. With respect to the Lone Star State, we have procured annual data derived from the University of Texas/Texas Tribune Survey, which spans thirteen years, from 2008 to 2020.

Last, we have administered our own survey, which was in the field during the winter of 2020 and completed before the onset of the COVID-19 pandemic. We surveyed an online panel of respondents made available from the national polling firm Dynata. In this survey, described in greater detail in chapter ten, we polled approximately three thousand non-Hispanic white southerners, half residing in STS counties and the other half living in urban counties. With an oversample of STS respondents, we are able to adequately compare this group with their urban counterparts on a wide variety of topics, including demographic traits, cultural distinctions, racial attitudes, policy opinions, and political dispositions.

Aggregate-Level Data

Outside of individuals, we also use several geographically based aggregate units of analysis, such as counties and congressional districts. As implied, *aggregate* in this context simply means a composite measurement of a particular element. For example, the number of whites of voting age in a particular county would be an aggregate-level unit. For these aggregate-level analyses, we use various place-based measures, including the percent rural, STS, and population density. We couple these measures with election returns for president, US Senator, governor, and US House, along with select demographic data available for these geographic units.

Any population-related data, including detailed information on race and ethnicity, are from either the decennial censuses or from various years of the ACS, which are large-scale surveys also produced by the US Census Bureau. Data on rural/urban composition by various geographic units are available from the Census Bureau in either tabulations or at the block level, which one can then aggregate to the desired level of geography (e.g., congressional districts). Population density measures and our STS measure are also derived from data available from the Census Bureau. Election data at the county, congressional, and state levels, were collected from either *Dave Leip's Atlas of U.S. Presidential Elections* or Congressional Quarterly's online *Voting and Elections Collection*.

The Importance of Time

Most of the analyses presented in this book are designed to detect and evaluate the Republican realignment of rural white southerners in the context of high-profile elections, including the bulk of the empirical material found in chapters four through seven and in chapters nine, eleven, and twelve, which covers the three-decade period from 1990 to 2020. Chapter three provides historical background (spanning 1952 to 1988) leading up to the principal time period under analysis (1990s-2010s). Chapter eight highlights the long-term Southwide changes in rural and urban white party affiliation from the 1950s into the 2010s. Chapter nine is best characterized as four detailed case studies of the rural white realignment to the GOP in four southern states. Chapters ten and eleven are more recent, covering opinions and attitudes from 2020 and the results of the 2020 election cycle, respectively. The concluding chapter twelve takes a more reflective view of the rural realignment of white southerners to the GOP in terms of its historical significance and future implications regarding the status of party politics in the region.

A Final Note on the Presentation of Our Findings

In the academic spirit of preeminent southern politics scholars Earl Black and Merle Black, a fundamental goal of this book is to provide a straightforward and accessible exploration, accounting, and assessment of political change in the South through the documentation of long-term general patterns. Although empirical data are used to buttress this investigation, we have endeavored to present our findings in easily digestible portions. To accomplish this, we rely on tables, figures, and maps (these are also labeled and referred to as figures) to help summarize and display patterns. Many of the figures presented are simply percentage-based measures. At times, it is necessary to use multivariate statistical modeling to derive estimates for specific quantities of interest (e.g., the percentage of white STS residents voting Republican for president in 2016). These models are based on well-tested and widely accepted social science techniques, such as ordinary least squares (OLS) regression and probit analysis. In the text, we translate the findings from such statistical models into easy-to-read tables and figures. For those seeking more information, the detailed results of these models are reported online in Appendix B.

Chapter 2 Appendix

Detailed Definition of Small-Town South

This definition examines Urban Clusters (UC) and reclassifies these areas as *Small-Town* or *Urban*. Urban Areas (UA) remain classified as *Urban*.

For 2000 and 2010:

1. Use counties as building blocks.
2. For each county, identify all Urban Clusters (UC).
3. Count any Urban Cluster
   a.) with a population of 20,000 or less[1,2]
   b.) which is not contiguous to an Urban Area[3]
   as *Small-Town*.
4. Combine rural and small-town (as defined in Condition 3) and divide by the total county population. This computation will yield the percentage of each county labeled *small-town South*.
5. By definition, any geography not classified as small-town is *urban*.

For 1990:

Using IPUMS data[4] it is possible to closely approximate the STS definition above. Prior to the 2000 census, UCs were not used by the U.S. Census Bureau. The key difference for these pre-2000 data is a lack of detailed information for persons falling into the category: *living outside of Urban Area*. The total number of persons living outside of UAs within a county is available. However, the 1990 calculation cannot account for counties that, in a subsequent time period, may have more than one UC, at least one of which might fall below the 20,000-person threshold.[5] The procedure to calculate STS for 1990 is modified as follows:

1. Use counties as building blocks.
2. For each county, use total population residing outside of UAs (that is not defined as rural).
3. Count non-UA population of 20,000 or less as *Small-Town*.
4. Combine rural and small-town (as defined in Condition 3) and divide by the total county population. This will yield the percentage of each of county labeled *small-town South*.
5. By definition, any geography not classified as small-town is *urban*.

3 Presidential Republicanism and Democratic Darn Near Everything Else

Despite a clear historical departure from the major parties' positions on Black civil rights, which solidified in the 1964 presidential election (Carmines and Stimson, 1989), between 1952 and 1988, a long period of split-level alignment took hold in southern politics. To be sure, the electoral evidence indicates movement in favor of the GOP, but it was slow enough in most contexts throughout Dixie to stand by the pronouncement that Republicans were prohibitive favorites for the White House while Democrats were the same for all remaining offices.

In the span of three and a half decades, southern Democrats managed to maintain their electoral advantage in subpresidential politics because of two fundamental factors. Most important was the distribution of Democratic and Republican supporters. Key (1949, p. 10) was prescient when he stated back in the late 1940s that "[a]ttachments to partisan labels live long beyond events that gave them birth." In short, not until the mid-1980s did Republican affiliation among white southerners finally reach parity with their corresponding rate of Democratic identification (Black and Black, 1987). Also, given the significance of the incumbency advantage prevailing from the 1960s through the 1980s (Cover, 1977; Cox and Katz, 1996; Jacobson, 2015; Mayhew, 1974), by dint of being the majority party since the end of Reconstruction, southern Democrats held the bulk of congressional and gubernatorial seats.

The 1965 Voting Rights Act (VRA) infused the southern electorate with an unprecedented number of Black voters overwhelmingly aligned with the Democratic Party because of the national (northern) party's championing of Black equality. So, just as the events of the 1960s civil rights era compelled racially conservative whites to exit the Democratic Party, their ranks were filled by Blacks who, along with a declining but still substantial plurality of white Democrats, created biracial coalitions typically large enough to deliver Democratic victories in most congressional and gubernatorial contests from the late 1960s through the 1980s (Lamis, 1988).

So where did rural white southerners find themselves in this remarkably fluid time of coalitional change (Petrocik, 1981) and yet, perhaps ironically, very gradual Republican advancement? Put differently, were they among the leading contributors to the persistence of a split-level alignment? There are strong reasons to think that the answer is yes. First, as mentioned previously (see chapter one), the backbone of the post-Reconstruction Democratic Solid South were the legions of rural whites aligned with the party upholding and staunchly defending white supremacy because such a stance was imperative in the Black Belts where Blacks often outnumbered whites (Key, 1949). Second, the early growth of the southern GOP was most notable in metropolitan centers where an increasing number of upwardly mobile urban whites were aligning with the party mainly because of economic issue congruence (Bartley and Graham, 1975; Strong, 1960) and not necessarily based on racial antagonism (Black and Black, 1987; Cosman, 1966; Shafer and Johnston, 2006). Third, the crystallization of differences among the major party presidential nominees post-1968 was not met with the same clarity of positioning in down-ballot races for the Senate, governorship, and House (Black and Black, 2002). That is, a rural southerner could easily support the typically more racially and culturally conservative Republican for president and, for similar reasons, vote for the Democratic candidate in all down-ballot offices (more often than not, the incumbent seeking another term). Last, because of the persistent Democratic advantage in rural areas (except those pockets of mountain Republicanism most prominently found in places like east Tennessee and western North Carolina), these geographic contexts were laggards in attracting viable Republican contenders for our one district-based office of analytical interest: US House elections.

This chapter takes a detailed look at southern election results from 1952 to 1988 and then focuses on the role of rural whites. We begin with an overview of electoral patterns by means of the display of descriptive data to highlight the aforementioned split-level alignment. Then we home in on the political behavior of rural whites. To emphasize possible differences in voting preferences across political offices, elections are often assessed for presidential years. For instance, split-ticket voting behavior is examined (Burden and Kimball, 2002), but with respect to voting for president and the Senate, or president and the House, because after 1984, only North Carolina chooses its governor in presidential years. Our evaluation of rural white political behavior, with surveys from the American National Election Studies (ANES) and exit polls, provides us with a much better understanding of this key constituency's contribution to a persistent split-level alignment that, by the late 1980s, was reaching the verge of collapse.

Overview of the Split-Level Alignment

The historic breakthrough of the Republican Eisenhower's two successful presidential runs in 1952 and 1956 opened up a chasm in GOP voting between the top of the ballot and all other contests in Dixie. Indeed, the general pattern of Republican growth was aptly dubbed "top-down advancement" (Aistrup,

1996), because white support for the GOP, beginning in the mid-twentieth century, was so clearly skewed in favor of presidential nominees. Figure 3.1 shows the top-down pattern in rather stark relief by presenting the GOP percentage of the (two-party) popular presidential vote (in dotted black) along with David's Index (David, 1972) of Republican strength, which is a simple composite index of the Republican share of the vote cast in equal parts (thirds) for the US Senate, governorship, and US House. The index is displayed in both its raw form for each year (in gray) and also in smoothed form by means of a ten-year moving average (in solid black). Below the presidential level, Republican electoral viability was under twenty percent until 1966, and thereafter, GOP gains rose to over thirty percent in the 1970s and peaked at just over forty percent in 1988, which is the terminal year of investigation for this chapter. Despite the growth of subpresidential Republicanism, even in the late 1980s, it is evident that the party remained considerably more formidable in presidential contests at a time when President Reagan made the GOP historically popular among the white southern electorate (Black and Black, 1987).

In 2016, the final year in the time series displayed in Figure 3.1, the consolidation of southern Republicanism has come to fruition—a development arguably completed in the 2000s. In this book, we seek to understand the role of rural whites in the realignment of the most Democratic region of the United

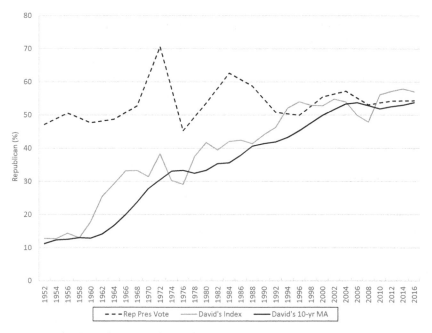

Figure 3.1. The General Pattern of Republican
Advancement in Southern Politics, 1952–2016

States to the GOP. At least from the early 1950s to 1988, it appears incontrovertible that the American South featured a split-level electoral alignment in which Republicanism was gradually increasing in subpresidential offices. Table 3.1 presents additional evidence of the long-term trend in Republicanism from 1952 to 1988, with data limited to presidential years. Although the GOP won a respectable and competitive forty-seven percent of the popular presidential vote in 1952, in this year, Dixie had not one Republican senator or governor, and Republicans constituted a meager six percent of the South's House delegation.

Averaging the GOP presence across the US Senate, governorship, and US House (SGH) amounts to four percent in 1952; thus, the gap between presidential Republicanism and GOP representation in these three subpresidential offices (P-SGH = 47−4) was an astounding forty-three percentage points. Not until the 1960s does a Republican contender notch a victory in an election for the Senate or governorship. Nonetheless, from this decade forward, Republican advancement is fairly steady, and by 1988, the party accounts for about a third (Senate and House) to forty-five percent (governorship) of these subpresidential offices. By the late 1980s, the GOP had made impressive electoral gains below the presidential level, but still the gap in support for president versus the remaining offices remained a notable twenty-five percentage points in 1988 (fifty-nine percent for president minus thirty-four percent for SGH equals twenty-five points). Hence, the South's split-level electoral alignment is characterized by an unusually long period of waning but undeniably persistent Democratic hegemony in subpresidential officeholding.

Emphasis on Senate and House Contests

Recognizing the palpable shift in white southerners' support for presidential Republicanism in the wake of the 1948 "Dixiecrat Revolt" (Frederickson, 2001), and especially after the pivotal Johnson versus Goldwater matchup in 1964 (Black and Black, 1992; Carmines and Stimson, 1989; Phillips, 1969), Democrats in several southern states found it prudent to move their gubernatorial contests to off-year/midterm cycles. Republican presidential coattails may affect US Senate and House voting, but thanks to federalism, Democratic legislators could at least keep the race for governor less exposed to "the conservative contagion of national politics" (Black and Black, 1987, p. 283). In 1952, five southern states already held their gubernatorial elections outside of presidential years (Alabama, Georgia, Mississippi, South Carolina, and Virginia), and 1952 was the last year Tennessee would choose its governor in a presidential cycle. In contrast, the last gubernatorial election held in a presidential year was 1964 for Florida, 1972 for Louisiana and Texas, and 1984 for Arkansas. Since 1988, North Carolina is the only southern state whose gubernatorial contest coincides with the presidential election.[1] Additionally, recognizing

Table 3.1. Republican Popular Presidential Vote and Percent Republican Seats for the Senate, Governorship, and House

% in year:

Office	1952	1956	1960	1964	1968	1972	1976	1980	1984	1988	'88–'52
President	47	51	48	49	53	71	45	54	63	59	12
Senate	0	0	0	9	18	32	23	45	45	32	32
Governor	0	0	0	0	18	27	18	45	18	45	45
House	6	7	7	15	25	31	25	36	37	34	28
SGH	4	5	5	13	23	31	24	38	37	34	30
P-SGH	43	46	43	36	30	40	21	16	26	25	–18
N	(139)	(139)	(139)	(139)	(139)	(141)	(141)	(141)	(149)	(149)	10

Note. Entries show the percentage of the Republican (two-party) popular presidential vote along with the Republican percentage of seats for the Senate, governorship, and House for the corresponding presidential election year. S = Senate; G = governorship; H = House; SGH = the combined Republican share of seats for these three offices. P-SGH shows the difference between the GOP popular presidential (P) vote and the GOP share of seats from the three aforementioned offices. N represents the total number of seats in each year for the Senate (twenty-two) plus the governorship (eleven) plus the House (this varies according to reapportionment allocations depending on the decade). '88–'52 indicates the difference in the entry for 1988 compared with that for 1952 (e.g., the GOP presidential vote was fifty-nine percent in 1988 versus forty-seven percent in 1952, so '88–'52 equals twelve percentage points).

the powerful electoral deterrent of incumbency, "[b]etween 1966 and 1984 nine southern states revised their constitutions to permit governors to serve a second consecutive four-year term" (Black and Black, 1987, p. 285).

Thus, given the infrequency of gubernatorial elections taking place alongside presidential contests, in the context of a split-level alignment, there is more analytical purchase in evaluating GOP support in Senate and House races. Henceforth, more emphasis is placed on these federal elections to compare Republican voting that occurs simultaneously with the opportunity to select a president. This said, gubernatorial voting is not wholly ignored, because there is still value in looking at voting patterns that may or may not involve the presidential cycle.

Regarding Senate elections, Table 3.2 summarizes the performance of southern Republicans in presidential years. The table highlights the percentage of Senate elections that Republicans contested, their total percentage of wins (for all contests held in the cycle), and the percent difference in votes cast for president and the Senate in contested races (Democrat versus Republican). Speaking to Democratic dominance over these ten election cycles spanning thirty-six years, not once did a Republican nominee run for a Senate seat without facing Democratic opposition.

Although Texan John Tower was the first Republican to win a Senate contest in the modern South (a 1961 special election for the seat vacated by Vice President Lyndon Johnson), the first GOP Senate victory in a *presidential* year happened in 1968.[2] After 1968, the aberrant 1976 election in which Georgian Democrat Jimmy Carter won the White House while carrying every southern state except Virginia, was the only election year when GOP candidates did not contest every Senate race. As for the disparity in voting Republican for president versus voting Republican for the Senate in the context of contested Senate races, there is considerable variation depending on the year: a minimum difference of two percentage points in 1964 and a maximum difference of twenty-eight points in 1952. Nevertheless, there appears to be no trend in differences for Republican voting across these offices outside of the unsurprising reality that GOP support is always higher for president. In fact, the seventeen-point gap in 1988 is the widest margin since the twenty-one-point difference registered during Republican President Nixon's 1972 landslide victory over Democrat George McGovern. In sum, Table 3.2 chronicles Republican growth in Senate elections coinciding with presidential years, starting at a time when the GOP was completely shut out in the 1950s up to the 1980s, when Republicans challenged every seat and won forty to fifty-seven percent of the Senate races held in this decade's three presidential cycles.

Perhaps the most remarked-upon feature of the long-running split-level alignment was the abundance of southern congressional districts carried by Republican presidential nominees but frequently won by Democratic House

Table 3.2. Senate Elections Coinciding with Presidential Contests

Category	1952	1956	1960	1964	1968	1972	1976	1980	1984	1988	'52-'88
Contested	25	38	60	83	86	100	60	100	100	100	77.8
Rep Wins	0	0	0	0	14	50	0	57	50	40	23.6
Pres.-Sen.	28	20	13	2	15	21	6	8	13	17	13.0
N	4	8	10	6	7	10	5	7	10	5	72

Note. Data entries are percentages rounded up to the nearest whole number. For example, in 1952, one Republican ran for the Senate out of a total of four contests (Contested = twenty-five percent). Republican victories (Rep Wins) are out of the total number of Senate contests; therefore, in 1968, Rep Wins = fourteen percent, because one Republican candidate was victorious out of seven total contests. Pres.-Sen. denotes the percentage point difference in the total Republican presidential vote cast versus the total Republican Senate vote cast for only the two-party contested elections in a given year. For instance, in 1976, there were three contested Senate elections, the percentage of the Republican presidential vote was 47.2 percent, and the corresponding Republican Senate vote was 41.5 percent, so $47.2 - 41.5 = 5.7$, which rounds up to six percentage points. The final column ('52–'88) is a summary of all these Senate contests held in the presidential years from 1952 to 1988.

candidates (Stonecash, 2008). Among several factors, not the least being that a Senate seat is more sought after than a House seat and, therefore, attracts more competition (Sides et al., 2018), the much-lauded incumbency advantage in the latter office (for House) was historically robust from the years after World War II up through the 1980s (Jacobson, 2015). The relatively greater electoral isolation and more geographically limited scope of congressional districts provided a unique localized environment to effectively ward off challenges leveled by an upstart southern Republican Party. And on the basis of decades of weak party centralization (Wattenberg, 1998), southern Democrats were ideally situated to cultivate their incumbency advantage in a manner that sustained majority voter coalitions even as white southerners found themselves increasingly attracted to the GOP's political philosophy (Bass and De Vries, 1995; Black and Black, 2002).

Table 3.3 presents the distribution of southern congressional districts in presidential years (1952–1988) according to four possibilities: (1) same-RR: majority Republican for president and House; (2) Split-RD: majority Republican for president and majority Democratic for House; (3) same-DD: majority Democratic for president and House; and (4) split-DR: majority Democratic for president and majority Republican for House. Including all contests (opposed and unopposed), this amounts to 1,086 elections held in presidential years from the first election of President Eisenhower in 1952 to the election of President Bush in 1988.

Overall (every contest), the share of commonly recognized Split-RD districts is 38.7%, which totals 420, whereas the most common type of district, Same-DD, is barely more prevalent (N = 422, 38.9%). When parceling districts according to contested and uncontested, those of the Split-RD variety are a plurality of the former type (37.2%). Among uncontested districts (those with only one major party contender), almost half (49.7%) are of the Same-DD variety. This brings up a remarkable feature of the milieu in southern congressional politics for this long interlude of gradual Republican growth amidst a declining Democratic advantage. Of *all* Democratic victories for this timespan captured in the table, fifty-one percent were secured without GOP opposition. In contrast, Republican winners enjoyed a free ride in nineteen percent of their elections.

Given the history of a Democratic Solid South, perhaps it isn't surprising that hardly any districts deliver a Democratic presidential vote majority while also electing a Republican to the House (Split-DR seats). These Split-DR districts are truly exotic, constituting a mere 2.5% of the total for the entirety of this period. Whereas Republicans let legions of US House Democrats win their seats without GOP opposition, districts that appear to favor the Democratic Party (based on the presidential vote) are almost always contested and won by Democrats. Hence, the lion's share of Republicans win in House districts

Table 3.3. Distribution of US House Seats According to Majority Vote Cast for President and House

Election	1952	1956	1960	1964	1968	1972	1976	1980	1984	1988	Total
All contests	(106)	(106)	(106)	(106)	(106)	(108)	(108)	(108)	(116)	(116)	(1,086)
Same-RR	6	7	7	11	20	32	14	32	37	33	20.0
Split-RD	31	43	28	30	32	67	14	30	57	52	38.7
Same-DD	63	50	65	55	43	2	61	34	6	15	38.9
Split-DR	0	0	0	4	5	0	11	5	0	1	2.5
Contested	(32)	(41)	(39)	(72)	(67)	(70)	(75)	(72)	(69)	(74)	(611)
Same-RR	19	15	13	17	27	44	16	31	48	37	28.2
Split-RD	31	61	36	14	34	54	13	31	49	55	37.2
Same-DD	50	24	51	64	31	1	56	32	3	7	30.4
Split-DR	0	0	0	6	8	0	15	7	0	1	4.3
Uncontested	(74)	(65)	(67)	(34)	(39)	(38)	(33)	(36)	(47)	(42)	(475)
Same-RR	0	2	3	0	8	8	9	33	21	26	9.5
Split-RD	31	32	24	65	28	90	15	28	68	45	40.6
Same-DD	69	66	73	35	64	3	73	39	11	29	49.7
Split-DR	0	0	0	0	0	0	3	0	0	0	0.2

Note. Number of districts are shown in parentheses. All other numbers indicate the percentage of districts in a category. The four categories are: majority Republican for president and House (Same-RR), majority Republican for president and majority Democratic for House (Split-RD), majority Democratic for president and House (Same-DD), and majority Democratic for president and majority Republican for House (Split-DR). Contested indicates that a Democrat and Republican faced off in the general election for the House seat. Percentages are rounded to nearest whole number; hence, summation in a category might be slightly under/over one hundred percent.

that are also carried by the Republican presidential candidate. In contrast, Democrats thrived in districts carried by either major party and, in the last two elections (1984 and 1988), were substantially more prominent in Split-RD districts (fifty-four percent) than in Same-DD seats (ten percent). The distinctive nature of southern House elections sheds considerable light on the political behavior of rural white southerners during this lengthy split-level alignment.

Rural Respondents in the American National Election Studies (ANES)

The ANES is a valuable resource for getting a holistic view of possible alterations to the political behavior of rural whites and how this unfolds in juxtaposition to their urban white counterparts. Fortunately, the ANES has classified survey respondents according to urbanism for the duration of the split-level alignment. Specifically, we make use of the ANES Cumulative Data File (CDF), which provides a variable for urbanism with the following three categories: (1) central cities; (2) suburban areas; and (3) rural areas, small towns, and outlying and adjacent areas. We collapse the categories one and two to denote urban respondents and maintain the category three for rural respondents.

The major drawback to the ANES data is squarely due to sample size. Unlike the Cooperative Election Study (CES), which came about in the 2006 midterm and has several thousand southerners per survey, the ANES samples are markedly smaller, typically containing roughly three hundred southerners (regardless of race) for a given election year. This means that we necessarily pool white southerners across multiple years, and the most intuitive way is by decade, so that in the ensuing analyses, we show findings for the 1950s, 1960s, 1970s, and 1980s. Further, with respect to House data, the ANES did not make available definitive classifications for the type of House contest until the 1980s; therefore, a greater emphasis will be placed on this decade of elections.[3] Despite these issues, we believe that there remains a requisite richness to the ANES that allows us to tell a convincing story of how rural white political behavior has evolved in southern politics from the 1950s to the 1980s.

We start with summary statistics of voter preferences and party affiliation and then proceed to a separate examination of House elections (in the next section) because of their particular significance in distinguishing the political profiles of rural and urban white southerners. Table 3.4 shows the distribution of the Republican share (two party) of the vote reported by rural and urban white southerners by decade for president, the Senate, governor, and the House. Scanning across the results for each decade provides additional evidence of the split-level nature of southern white voting behavior; much higher support for Republican presidential nominees vis-à-vis GOP nominees for the remaining three lower offices. As expected, this vote disparity is most pronounced in the 1950s, when both rural and urban respondents reported

Table 3.4. Republican Vote by Location and Decade

% Republican vote

Office	1950s			1960s			1970s			1980s		
	RURAL	URBAN	R-U	RURAL	URBAN	R-U	RURAL	URBAN	R-U	RURAL	URBAN	R-U
President	45	57	-12	42	64	-22	68	63	5	66	69	-3
N			(379)			(586)			(568)			(648)
Senate	15	14	1	25	42	-17	43	42	1	45	44	1
N			(263)			(474)			(705)			(568)
Governor	7	5	2	28	45	-17	39	31	8	41	49	-8
N			(151)			(274)			(607)			(287)
House	14	11	3	21	40	-19	30	35	-5	33	49	-16
N			(452)			(801)			(961)			(892)

Note. Entries for rural and urban respondents show the percentages of respondents voting Republican (two party). There are no controls for whether a subpresidential election was contested by both major parties (Democrat vs. Republican). Numbers in parentheses indicate cases for each office by decade (rural plus urban respondents). Data are confined to white southerners. The place variable for determining urban location is "central cities" and "suburban areas," and the place variable for determining rural location is "rural areas, small towns, and outlying and adjacent areas." R-U indicates the rural percentage in the category minus the urban percentage in the category. Data span 1952 to 1988.

single-digit support for GOP gubernatorial candidates. More important, the table reveals the emergence of a stronger connection between presidential Republicanism and urbanism. The difference between rural and urban support for GOP presidential candidates goes from –12 points in the 1950s (Table 3.4, see "R-U" columns) to a gaping –22 points in the following decade.

The differences in Republican voting among rural and urban respondents in the 1950s and 1960s reinforces the findings in previous studies that stressed an initially stronger relationship between white urban populations and top-down GOP advancement (see Cosman, 1966; Strong, 1960). Interestingly, however, the 1970s paints a somewhat murky picture of rural and urban voting behavior. In this decade, white southerners of all stripes were repelled by the liberal Democrat McGovern's 1972 presidential bid, which prompted massive white Democratic defections to Nixon (McKee, 2019); but then the native southerner and Democrat Jimmy Carter was able to win back many white southerners in 1976 (though not a majority; see Black and Black, 1992). Rural GOP support at the top of the ticket exceeded urban support by five points and rural respondents were eight points more Republican in their vote for governor, too.

In the 1980s, the rural-urban gap in presidential voting had narrowed to three points, with urban respondents now reporting more Republican support. As was the case in 1970s' Senate contests, in the 1980s, there was no distinction between rural and urban voter preferences for this office. By comparison, an eight-point rural Republican voting advantage in 1970s' gubernatorial contests flipped to an eight-point urban Republican edge in the 1980s. Finally, the substantial rural-urban division in Republican House voting that arose in the 1960s (Table 3.4, "R-U" = –19), but was subsequently reduced to –5 points in the 1970s, widened again to –16 points in the 1980s. It is in House contests where the rural-urban divide is most persistent, as locational distinctions essentially disappear in Senate elections and decline to single digits in races for president and governor.

Voting behavior is generally a leading indicator of partisan change, whereas party affiliation lags behind, because attachments to political parties are more enduring than decisions concerning whom to vote for in any given election (Campbell et al., 1960). For instance, the hyperliberalism of McGovern in 1972 led a whopping eighty percent of white southerners to back Nixon (McKee, 2019), yet most remained affiliated with the Democratic Party until President Reagan's second term in the mid-1980s (Black and Black, 1987). Table 3.5 shows the distribution of party identification (PID) among rural and urban white southerners by decade. As is common practice, because the voting preferences of independents who lean toward a party are more similar to that of partisans than pure independents (Keith et al., 1992), these leaners are classified as partisans on the basis of the party to which they report being closer.

Table 3.5. Party Affiliation by Location and Decade

% Party affiliation as:

Decade	Democrat			Independent			Republican			N
	RURAL	URBAN	R-U	RURAL	URBAN	R-U	RURAL	URBAN	R-U	
1950s	76	77	−1	5	6	−1	19	17	2	1,004
1960s	69	56	13	10	14	−4	22	30	−8	1,521
1970s	52	55	−3	16	21	−5	31	25	6	2,518
1980s	50	46	4	16	12	4	34	42	−8	1,941
'80s–'50s (diff.)	−26	−31		11	6		15	25		

Note. Data are compiled by authors from the American National Election Studies (ANES) Cumulative Data File. Entries for party identification are given in percentages, and independent leaners are folded into the appropriate partisan category. Data are confined to white southerners. The place variables for determining urban location are "central cities" and "suburban areas," and the place variable for determining rural location is "rural areas, small towns, and outlying and adjacent areas." R-U = the rural percentage in the category minus the urban percentage in the category. Data span from 1952 to 1988.

In other words, based on the ANES seven-point PID scale, Democrats include strong Democrats, weak (i.e., "not so strong" in ANES survey parlance) Democrats, and independent-leaning Democrats; Republicans include strong Republicans, weak Republicans, and independent-leaning Republicans. Thus, independents are pure independents, and this accounts for their relatively smaller share of the ANES sample.

As shown in Table 3.5, the 1950s was the last decade reflecting the "Old South" Democracy, with over three quarters of rural and urban whites identifying with the party. This stasis is shattered in the 1960s, as the GOP realignment finally gets underway. In concert with the emergence of Republican presidential voting in the white metropolitan South, the initial decline in Democratic affiliation and corresponding increase in GOP identification is much greater among urban whites (as shown in the 1960s data). Further dealignment from Democratic identification proceeds in the 1970s, with fifty-two percent and fifty-five percent of rural and urban whites, respectively, still aligned with the party. Concomitantly, the proportion of rural and urban independents peaks at sixteen percent and twenty-one percent, respectively. This development is expected because the height of white dealignment in national and southern politics occurred in the 1970s (Abramson, 1976; Bartels, 2000; Beck, 1977).

Somewhat surprising is that, in the 1970s, by a six-point margin, rural Republicans exceeded urban Republicans ("R-U" in Table 3.5). This pattern does coincide with voting patterns in the 1970s (see Table 3.4), but it is short-lived because, in the 1980s, rural whites once again lagged behind urban whites in their shift toward GOP affiliation. As noted by Black and Black (1987), the ANES data tend to understate movement in favor of Republican identification among white southerners in the mid-1980s. They demonstrated this by presenting data from other surveys taken on or around the same time as the 1984 ANES. According to Black and Black (1987, p. 240): "The Republican surge in the early 1980s, the sharpest ever observed among white southerners, doubtless reflected the success of the Reagan presidency in changing the image of the Republican party to conform to values and beliefs held by majorities of white southerners." We have no reason to dispute this statement but would add that, with respect to rural and urban whites, the latter group was apparently much more receptive to the Reagan brand of Republicanism. From the 1970s to the 1980s, the share of rural Republicans increased three points (thirty-one percent to thirty-four percent). By comparison, in the 1970s, twenty-five percent of urban whites affiliated with the GOP, and their proportion of Republican identifiers vaulted to forty-two percent in the 1980s. Conversely, half of rural whites remained Democrats in the 1980s, whereas less than a majority (forty-six percent) of urban whites claimed the same partisan allegiance. It would appear that, at least in the 1980s, the ascending GOP held more appeal to the interests of a growing southern urban middle class (Black and Black, 1987) than to the values and interests of their rural neighbors.

We conclude this section with a presentation of bivariate correlations between rural location (1 = rural, 0 = urban) and PID (seven-point scale: strong Democrat to strong Republican), and between rural location and Republican voting for president, US Senate, governor, and US House from the 1950s to 1980s. In short, Table 3.6 is an efficient way to summarize whether there is a statistically significant relationship between place of residence and the political behavior of white southerners. In the 1950s, there is no correlation between rural location and PID, but the emergence of urban presidential Republicanism shows up as rural respondents are significantly *less* supportive of Eisenhower in 1952 and 1956. The 1960s indicate the across-the-board urban shift toward the GOP in terms of party affiliation and voter preferences in all four offices. Once again, the 1970s reveal a complicated transitional period in which rural respondents are marginally more Republican in party identification while also being somewhat more inclined to vote Republican in gubernatorial contests.

By the 1980s, Table 3.6 shows that urban whites are notably more Republican in terms of party affiliation, but with regard to voting behavior, the only remaining rural-urban division manifests in US House elections. The marked

Table 3.6. Correlations for Rural Location and Its Relationship with Party Affiliation and Voting

PID and office	1950s	1960s	1970s	1980s	1952–88
PID	0.03	−0.13***	0.03*	−0.07***	−0.05***
President	−0.12**	−0.21***	0.06	−0.04	−0.09***
Senate	0.02	−0.17***	0.01	0.01	−0.05**
Governor	0.04	−0.16***	0.08*	−0.07	−0.04
House	0.05	−0.20***	−0.05	−0.17***	−0.14***

Note. PID = party identification. Here, PID is based on a seven-point scale on which 1 = strong Democrat, 2 = weak Democrat, 3 = independent-leaning Democrat, 4 = Independent, 5 = independent-leaning Republican, 6 = weak Republican, and 7 = strong Republican). For respondent location, 1 = rural and 0 = urban; for votes, 1 = Republican vote (for president, Senate, governor, House) and 0 = Democratic vote. Data are confined to white southerners. The number of cases for each correlation between rural location and the corresponding office by decade can be found in Table 3.5. Likewise, the number of cases for each correlation between rural location and PID by decade can be found in Table 3.4. Likewise, the number of cases for each correlation between rural location and PID by decade can be found in Table 3.5 (*N* for 1952–88 = 6,984).

*p < .10; **p < .05; ***p < .01 (two-tailed).

difference in House voting deserves greater attention, because it is substantial and, we suspect, due to notable variation in the local political contexts of rural and urban whites.

The Rural-Urban Division in House Elections

In *The Rise of Southern Republicans* (2002), Earl and Merle Black exquisitely dissect the panoply of factors contributing to the prolonged success of southern congressional Democrats decades after the civil rights movement. They also posed this overriding question: "Why did it take decades for southern Republicans to become a competitive force in House and Senate elections? . . . [Their] exceedingly slow rise cannot be understood without appreciating the tenacity, resilience, and profound transformations of their Democratic opponents" (Black and Black, 2002, p. 38). As Black and Black made clear, in painstaking detail, the incumbency advantage of southern congressional Democrats served as a bulwark for slowing the Republican advance up until the 1990s.

With the passage of the 1965 Voting Rights Act (VRA), there followed a surge in Black registration in Deep South states such as Mississippi, Alabama, and Louisiana (Bullock and Gaddie, 2009; McKee, 2017; Timpone, 1995). However, gains in Black enfranchisement were more than offset by accompanying white registration, particularly where Black mobilization was greatest (Black and Black, 1987; McKee, 2017). Hence, in the short term, southern congressional Democrats actually held firm to their "unreconstructed" views on Black civil rights, thereby thwarting Republican electoral threats arising from the racially conservative right. As time passed and an increasing share of whites exited the Democratic Party, southern Democrats deftly pivoted by cultivating biracial coalitions that proved a winning formula into the late 1970s and throughout the 1980s (Black and Black, 2002; Lamis, 1988).

Not given enough attention, however, in the explanation for enduring southern Democratic success in congressional elections—and specifically House contests—is the context in which most rural whites found themselves. Indeed, given a very different localized geographic setting, it is likely that rural whites would otherwise have been as supportive of Republican House candidates, as were their urban neighbors. Simply put, a disproportionate number of rural southern whites were located in House districts represented by Democrats, and these voters proved highly susceptible to the incumbency advantage, as reflected in their lopsided Democratic voting preferences.

We narrow our scope to 1980s House elections for two principal reasons. First, in this decade, the ANES provides reliable data on the type of contest: Republican incumbent, open seat, or Democratic incumbent. Second, the 1980s is the last decade firmly tied to the split-level alignment, when rural whites are decidedly less Republican in their House voting preferences. Table 3.7 shows Republican voting in House contests for the 1980s by location and

Table 3.7. Republican Voting in 1980s House
Elections by Location and Seat Status

Contests	Rural	Urban	R-U	N
All contests				
Rep incumbent	84	82	2	278
Open seat	77	56	21*	83
Dem incumbent	14	18	−4	531
All districts	33	49	−16**	892
Contested only				
Rep incumbent	82	81	1	244
Dem incumbent	24	29	−5	313
All districts	40	59	−19**	557

Note. Entries for rural and urban respondents show the percentage of respondents voting Republican (two party). Total respondents for each type of House contest are listed in the *N* column (e.g., 244 total respondents in districts with a Republican incumbent running for reelection with a Democratic challenger [contested-only races]). R-U = the rural percentage in the category minus the urban percentage in the category; Rep = Republican; Dem = Democrat. Data span 1980 to 1988. Data are confined to white southerners. Every open seat in the dataset was contested; hence, that is why the category is absent among the Contested-only House seats. Difference in Republican voting is significant at: *$p < .05$; **$p < .001$ (two-tailed).

congressional district type (Republican incumbent, open seat, or Democratic incumbent) and subdivided for all contests and only those with two-party competition (contested only). There is no row entry for open-seat races among contested elections, because every open seat drew two-party competition (their inclusion in the top half of the table suffices).

Starting with all US House races (contested and uncontested), rural and urban support for Republican incumbents is overwhelming and commensurate, at eighty-four percent and eighty-two percent, respectively. Notice, however, that in open-seat contests, all of which were contested, rural whites are decidedly more Republican, seventy-seven percent versus fifty-six percent, a twenty-one-point gap based on location. However, in districts with a Democratic incumbent seeking reelection, only fourteen percent of rural whites voted for the GOP challenger, compared with only a slightly higher eighteen percent of urban whites who did the same. Overall, a third of rural whites voted Republican for House candidates in the 1980s, whereas almost half (forty-nine percent) of urban whites voted Republican in these elections.

Examining only contested House races once again shows equivalency in rural and urban support for Republican incumbents; eighty-two percent and eighty-one percent GOP votes, respectively. Naturally, Republican voting is relatively higher when Democratic incumbents face Republican opposition, but again it is in this context—a Democratic incumbent running for reelection— where rural whites are less Republican in their House voting vis-à-vis urban whites: twenty-four percent versus twenty-nine percent Republican. What is perhaps most interesting from the entirety of the data displayed in Table 3.7 is that in limiting the voting comparison according to district type, the only *significant* difference emerges in the case of open seats, and in this condition, rural whites are actually more Republican in their voting behavior. Nevertheless, in summing all of the contests together, regardless of the specific type of district (Republican incumbent, open seat, or Democratic incumbent), rural voting for Republican candidates is significantly lower in all contests (Table 3.7, R-U = −16), and in just those limited to two-party competition (Table 3.7, R-U = −19).

It would seem, then, that on the basis of the data presented in Table 3.7, rural whites are more Democratic in their House voting because of structural factors and not necessarily because they remain more favorably inclined toward the Democratic Party. Additional evidence supports this contention. First, because of the importance of the incumbency advantage in attracting voter support (Cox and Katz, 1996), rural voters should be notably more prevalent in districts represented by Democratic incumbents. Sure enough, the ANES data reveal that forty-seven percent of urban whites, versus seventy-five percent of rural whites, reside in districts with a Democratic incumbent.[4] Second, on the basis of the discussion of the data found in Table 3.3, rural whites should be disproportionally located in uncontested districts, as so many more of these voters are represented by Democratic incumbents. This expectation is also confirmed, with twenty-five percent of urban whites as compared with forty-five percent of rural whites situated in uncontested House races. Although the bulk of uncontested House races belong to Democratic incumbents, the difference in the distribution of rural and urban whites is also significant: Eighty-nine percent of rural whites versus eighty-three percent of urban whites are located in districts where an unopposed Democratic incumbent sought another term. Last, with respect to contested districts, rural whites are also overrepresented in those held by Democratic incumbents. Close to two thirds (sixty-four percent) of rural whites, versus thirty-five percent of urban whites, lived in districts with an opposed Democratic incumbent. All of these comparisons are displayed in Figure 3.2.

We conclude this section with a brief examination of split-ticket voting for president and the House in the 1980s. The ANES poses the question of the combination of voting for president and the House with four possibilities (if a respondent made a selection for both offices): (1) straight Republican: Republican votes for president and House; (2) straight Democratic: Democratic

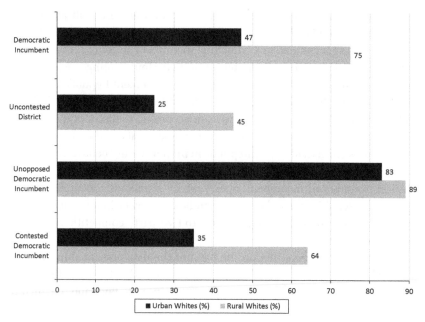

Figure 3.2. Different Congressional District Contexts for
Rural and Urban Whites, 1980s

votes for president and House; (3) split ticket: Republican vote for president
and Democratic vote for House; and (4) split ticket: Democratic vote for president and Republican vote for House. Before proceeding with the findings, it
is worth pointing out that there is no discernible variation in urban and rural
ticket splitting with regard to voting for president and the Senate, and this
should be expected because the ANES data show no distinction in Republican
voting for the Senate on the basis of location (see Table 3.4).

According to the distribution of congressional districts shown in Table
3.3, it should come as no surprise that hardly any rural and urban whites in
the 1980s (under ten percent for both groups) claimed to have voted Democratic for president and Republican for the House (a Split-DR ticket). In contrast, a sizable share of respondents reported splitting their tickets in favor of
the GOP for president and Democratic for the House. Also, despite small overall sample sizes of 258 urban whites and 291 rural whites across four response
options (two straight-ticket options and two split-ticket possibilities), statistical significance was obtained in the case of Split-RD voting in all House
elections (contested and uncontested). In all House contests, thirty-four percent of rural whites and twenty-six percent of urban whites reported voting Republican for president and Democratic for the House. If the data are

circumscribed to contested House races, then the rural-urban division in Split-RD voting narrows to three percentage points, with twenty-five percent of rural whites and twenty-two percent of urban whites splitting their tickets in this fashion (not a significant difference).

Finally, it should be the case that the largest observable difference in rural versus urban split-ticket voting of the Split-RD variety occurs in uncontested House races because the lion's share of these elections involve Democratic incumbents, and rural whites are more likely to reside in these districts (thus lacking the opportunity to vote for a Republican House candidate). The ANES data reflect this expectation as fifty-four percent of rural whites and forty percent of urban whites reported voting a Split-RD ticket in uncontested House races (not a significant difference). Split-ticket voting behavior is revisited in the next section, as the sample sizes from the exit polls are more suitable (large enough and more representative) to consider testing for statistical significance among rural and urban white voters.

Rural Voters in the 1984, 1986, and 1988 Exit Polls

In 1984, the national exit polls finally added a state indicator. Before this election year, the national exit polls only provided a region variable, which lumped Kentucky and Oklahoma in with the eleven ex-Confederate states to constitute the "South" region. Rather than explain away possible differences because of the inclusion of two Border South states, we assess the political behavior of rural white southerners in 1984, 1986, and 1988, because this allows us to stick with our preferred "eleven ex-Confederate–state South" definition. The exit polls include substantially larger samples than the ANES (especially in presidential years), but these data have always been a black box with respect to sample collection, because precinct locations within reported areas of higher aggregation (e.g., a congressional district) are never released. Further, the classification of voters in terms of place is more detailed than the ANES. For example, the 1988 exit poll included an "Urbanity Code" with six categories: (1) over five hundred thousand; (2) two hundred fifty thousand to less than five hundred thousand; (3) fifty thousand to less than two hundred fifty thousand; (4) suburbs; (5) ten thousand to less than fifty thousand; and (6) rural. For all three exit polls (1984–88), we collapsed the first through fourth categories into "Urban" and collapsed the fifth and sixth categories into "Rural/ Small-Town South (STS)." We view voters in cities of 10,000–49,999 residents as small towns that have more in common with rural locations than larger urban areas. This demarcation is suitable and happens to be quite similar to the classification scheme we use for distinguishing rural and urban populations on the basis of county data in later chapters.[5]

Similar to our assessment of ANES data, we examine possible differences in the political behavior of rural/STS and urban white southerners in the mid- to late-1980s. Once again, we emphasize voter preferences across the same set of offices and then go into more detail with regard to House elections. Because these data have larger and more representative sample sizes and closely overlap the 1980s ANES coverage, it is anticipated that the findings reinforce the story already unfolding. Starting with Republican voting, Table 3.8 partitions the GOP vote percentages for rural/STS and urban white southerners by election year and office for 1984 through 1988. In presidential years (1984 and 1988), to no surprise, there is more support for presidential nominees than for contenders for the Senate and House. Subtracting the difference in the House vote from the vote for president (P-H, for 1984 and 1988 combined) reveals a sizable gap according to location: a twenty-point difference among rural/STS whites versus a ten-point difference for urban whites. Rural/STS and urban differences in Republican voting for president in 1984 and 1988 are minimal and insignificant. In contrast, the patterns for Senate voting vary considerably depending on the election, and this is not necessarily surprising in the absence of controls for the type of contest (i.e., Republican incumbent, open seat, and Democratic incumbent) and given the fact that there are notable differences in terms of which states are holding Senate contests in each election cycle.[6] Whereas rural/STS whites were more supportive of Republican Senate candidates in presidential years (Table 3.8, by 9 points in 1984 and 6 points in 1988), this was definitely not the case in the 1986 midterm elections. In all seven Senate contests held in 1986, the Republican candidate lost (McKee, 2019), and evidently, rural/STS white southerners assisted in their downfall (forty-eight percent Republican), whereas urban whites were much more supportive (sixty-one percent Republican).

The inconsistency in Republican voting for Senate according to location is interesting, but it is more attributable to the type of contest and which state is holding an election as opposed to differences necessarily tied to whether a respondent is a rural/STS or urban voter. Stated differently, by the 1980s, controlling for most factors, the general propensity of voting Republican for Senate was not much different on the basis of location. By comparison, it remains the case that greater differentiation in the political contexts of rural/STS and urban voters (the congressional districts they inhabit) affects their Republican voting in House elections. There is no question that the lack of differentiation in the House vote registered by rural/STS and urban whites in 1986 is curious; notice also that in the two presidential years when rural/STS voters are less likely to vote Republican for House, they are markedly more likely (than urban voters) to vote Republican for Senate.

Rather than dismiss an indistinguishable difference in rural/STS and urban voting for Republican House candidates in the 1986 midterm, we instead summarize House voting behavior for all three election cycles in Table 3.9. In other words, despite the anomalous midterm findings, it is expected that

Table 3.8. Republican Vote by Location
in the 1984, 1986, and 1988 Exit Polls

Office	% Rural	% Urban	% R-U	N
1984				
President	76	73	3	1,883
Senate	67	58	9**	1,491
House	60	65	−5*	1,689
P-H	16	8		
1986				
Senate	48	61	−13**	443
House	55	54	1	678
S-H	−7	8		
1988				
President	68	69	−1	2,290
Senate	54	48	6*	1,334
House	42	59	−17**	1,897
P-H	26	10		
1984–88				
President	72	71	1	4,173
Senate	60	54	6**	3,268
House	52	60	−8**	4,264
P-H	20	10		

Note. Data are confined to white southerners in the national exit polls conducted for the 1984, 1986, and 1988 general elections. All data are weighted. R-U = the rural percentage in the category minus the urban percentage in the category (e.g., 76 − 73 = 3 for the rural and urban Republican presidential votes cast in 1984); S-H = the Republican percentage of the vote cast for the Senate minus the Republican percentage of the vote cast for the House; P-H = the Republican percentage of the vote cast for president minus the Republican percentage of the vote cast for the House; N = the total respondents for a given row (rural plus urban). Computed differences can appear slightly off in rounding to whole numbers. Percentage point difference for R-U is statistically significant at: *p < .10; **p < .01 (two-tailed).

rural/STS whites are generally less supportive of Republican House candidates for the same contextual reasons divulged with the ANES data in Figure 3.2. In this vein, Table 3.9 is set up just like Table 3.7. The only notable difference in Table 3.9 is that the national exit poll data include voters who resided in uncontested open seats. Compared with the ANES data presented in Table 3.7, the exit poll data in Table 3.9 reveal a very similar dynamic. In all contests, it is, again, the case that rural/STS whites vote more Republican in open seats (Table 3.9, R-U = 11). However, in the case of all contests (opposed and

Table 3.9. Republican Voting in House Elections
by Location and Seat Status, 1984–88

Contests	Rural	Urban	R-U	N
All contests				
Rep incumbent	71	74	−3	1,743
Open seat	75	64	11*	559
Dem incumbent	35	43	−8**	1,963
All districts	52	60	−8**	4,265
Contested only				
Rep incumbent	72	72	0	1,447
Open seat	63	65	−2	522
Dem incumbent	44	48	−4	1,300
All districts	57	62	−5*	3,269

Note. Data are confined to white southerners in the national exit polls conducted for the 1984, 1986, and 1988 general elections. All data are weighted. R-U = the rural percentage in the category minus the urban percentage in the category (e.g., $71 - 74 = -3$ for the rural and urban Republican House votes cast in all contests from 1984 to 1988); N = the total respondents indicated in parentheses for a given row (rural plus urban); Rep = Republican; Dem = Democrat. Percentage point difference for R-U is statistically significant at: $^*p < .01$; $^{**}p < .001$ (two-tailed).

unopposed) with a Democratic incumbent seeking reelection, compared with urban whites, rural/STS whites are significantly less likely to vote Republican (Table 3.9, R-U = −8). With regard to contested elections, the same pattern found in the ANES data shows up: in each type of House election (i.e., Republican incumbent, open seat, and Democratic incumbent), there is no significant difference in Republican voting between rural/STS and urban whites, but after aggregating all of these votes across contested House races, rural/STS whites are significantly less supportive of Republican candidates (Table 3.9, R-U = −5).

Although there is reason to be skeptical of the ANES data, because the principal investigators of the survey make it explicit that there is no representativeness of the American electorate down to the level of the congressional district (as elaborated upon in endnote 3), the national exit polls have much larger samples that are more representative of the population of House voters. We emphasize this point because despite differences with respect to sampling and the urbanism classification, the national exit poll data (1984–88) wholly reinforce the ANES findings regarding the expectations that rural/STS whites are less Republican in their House voting because of where they are situated among the population of southern congressional districts. On all four counts examined previously with ANES data, the same pattern holds with the exit poll data in comparisons between rural/STS and urban white voters: (1) Rural/STS voters are more prevalent in districts with a Democratic incumbent running for reelection (fifty-three percent vs. forty-two percent); (2) rural/STS voters constitute a greater portion of voters residing in uncontested districts (forty-four percent vs. twenty-one percent); (3) rural/STS voters are more plentiful in uncontested districts with a Democratic incumbent seeking another term (seventy-four percent vs. fifty-eight percent); and (4) rural/STS voters constitute a greater percentage of residents in contested districts represented by Democratic incumbents (forty-four percent vs. thirty-eight percent).[7] All of these differences between rural/STS and urban whites are statistically significant and displayed in Figure 3.3.

In addition, we can reconsider the propensity of split-ticket voting for president and the US House with the national exit poll data combined for 1984 and 1988. With this larger sample, we expect that, compared with urban whites, rural/STS whites should be more likely to vote Republican for president and Democratic for the House (Split-RD). As shown in Figure 3.4, this is the case regardless of whether we consider all contests (Split-RD = twenty-two percent for rural/STS whites and fourteen percent for urban whites), contested-only elections (Split-RD = eighteen percent for rural/STS whites and thirteen percent for urban whites), or uncontested races (Split-RD = twenty-nine

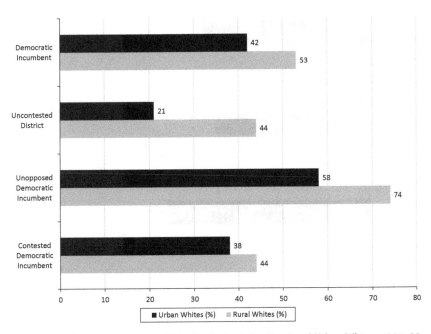

Figure 3.3. Different Congressional District Contexts for Rural and Urban Whites, 1984–88

percent for rural/STS whites and seventeen percent for urban whites). Once again, the finding that the greatest difference in split-ticket voting among rural/STS whites and urban whites occurs in uncontested House elections (R-U = 12; Figure 3.4) is plausible and intuitive, because we know that rural/STS whites are disproportionally located in House districts where Democratic incumbents do not face Republican challengers (Figure 3.3). In other words, the local context is more likely to deny rural/STS whites the opportunity to choose between a Democrat and Republican for the House (i.e., a greater likelihood that only a Democrat runs for the House), and hence, by default, these conditions foster a greater inclination to vote Democratic for the House and Republican for president.[8]

We conclude this assessment of House elections with a brief discussion of Figure 3.5, which provides a visual presentation of southern congressional districts within the context of partisan representation and voting behavior across the South in 1988. Turning back to the data shown in Table 3.3, Figure 3.5 maps these data in 1988 for all southern congressional districts according to the four classifications: Same-RR (thirty-eight districts), Split-RD (sixty districts), Same-DD (seventeen districts), and Split-DR (one district).

At fifty-two percent of the total, Split-RD districts (denoted in gray in Figure 3.5) are found throughout Dixie. Same-RR districts (denoted in black)

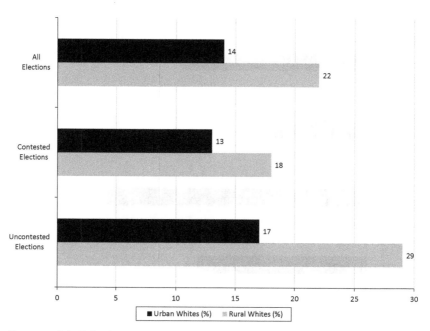

Figure 3.4. Split-Ticket Voting: Republican for
President and Democratic for House, 1984–88

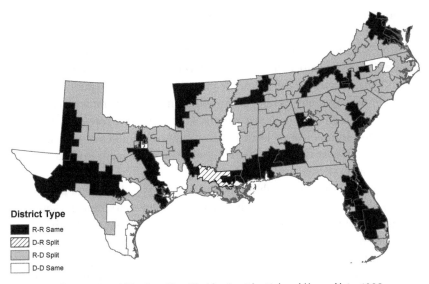

Figure 3.5. Congressional Districts Classified by Presidential and House Vote, 1988

are the next most prominent (thirty-three percent), but it would appear that these constituencies, which voted majority Republican for president and US House in 1988, tend to be more urban than the Split-RD districts. As for the fifteen percent of districts that are Same-DD (denoted in white), they generally appear to be of two types: located in highly urban centers with large minority populations (e.g., Atlanta, Dallas, Houston, and Memphis) or rural settings with large minority populations (e.g., south and east Texas and the Mississippi Delta).

In fact, regarding the rurality of southern congressional districts in 1988, the data comport with the naked eye. On the basis of the average district percent rural, Split-RD seats lead the way at forty percent. By comparison, Same-RR districts are twenty-seven percent rural, and Same-DD districts are the least rural at fifteen percent. The only Split-DR district (Louisiana's Eighth District, denoted by a cross-hatch pattern in Figure 3.5) is fifty-three percent rural. It is reassuring to know that the macro-level pattern in Figure 3.5 closely coincides with the political behavior of rural white southerners as documented in the ANES and exit poll surveys.[9]

Discussion and Conclusion

In 1980, Ronald Reagan kicked off his presidential campaign at the Neshoba County Fair located in the small town of Philadelphia, Mississippi. In the Mississippi "Freedom Summer" of 1964, Neshoba County made national news when the bodies of three murdered civil rights workers were discovered (Woodward, 2002, p. 183). It is indisputable that Reagan, like Nixon and Goldwater before him (Hillygus and Shields, 2009), chose Philadelphia, Mississippi, as his initial campaign stop to broadcast and perpetuate the GOP's highly successful "southern strategy" of attracting the votes of racially conservative whites (Phillips, 1969). In hindsight, however, it seems that Reagan was ahead of his time, because in the 1980s, the growth of southern Republicanism was stronger among a burgeoning urban white middle class rather than among the backroads and in the small towns where most white residents still found reasons to continue voting Democratic in subpresidential contests, and especially in US House elections where Republicans were loath to challenge seasoned Democratic incumbents.

Characterizing the Republican brand in the 1980s, Black and Black (1987, p. 313) wrote: "Though its mass base includes some working-class southerners, in terms of real influence and control the GOP is preeminently the vehicle of upper-middle-class, well-educated, conservative whites. Southern Republicanism is the party of *Southern Living,* if that magazine could be imagined to possess an explicit political philosophy." To be sure, in the 1980s, presidential Republicanism still reigned supreme (top-down advancement persisted), but there were typically no longer clear distinctions in the support that rural and urban whites registered for GOP candidates seeking the presidency, the governor's mansion, or a seat in the US Senate. What, however, did continue to distinguish rural and urban white southerners was the extent to which they identified with the Democratic and Republican parties, as well as the degree to which each group voted Republican in House contests.

Compared with our current era of polarized politics (Abramowitz, 2010), in the 1980s, the white southern electorate was woefully under-sorted with respect to the alignment of party with ideology (Levendusky, 2009). Nevertheless, as Table 3.10 shows, between the 1970s and 1980s, the joining of ideology with the appropriate party was underway. Regarding urban whites, between the 1970s and 1980s, there was a substantial decline in conservative Democrats (from thirty-eight percent to twenty-five percent) and a tremendous rise in conservative Republicans (from forty-eight percent to sixty-seven percent). The percentage of independents dropped in each ideological category, but curiously, the percentage of liberal Republicans actually increased from eight percent in the 1970s to twenty-five percent in the 1980s. Likewise, the share of moderate Republicans grew from seventeen percent to thirty-three percent. The data seem to suggest that, for urban white southerners, the GOP had become the more attractive, perhaps even trendy brand in the 1980s.

By comparison, alterations in the marriage between ideology and partisanship were relatively smaller but appeared more evident of deliberative action on the part of rural whites. Notice that the shifts among ideological and partisan categories are more reflective of a true partisan sort, absent a bandwagon effect (which seems evident in the case of some urban whites).

Table 3.10. Ideology and Party Affiliation by Location in the 1970s and 1980s

Location and ideology	Democrats		Independents		Republicans	
	1972–78	1980–88	1972–78	1980–88	1972–78	1980–88
Rural						
Liberals	65	71	10	12	25	17
Moderates	54	56	16	19	30	25
Conservatives	44	35	13	11	43	54
N	419	305	114	89	295	244
Urban						
Liberals	78	72	14	2	8	25
Moderates	61	52	22	16	17	33
Conservatives	38	25	14	8	48	67
N	312	275	95	59	164	303

Note. Data are from the ANES CDF; partisans include leaners. Ideology is coded as follows: 1 = extremely liberal, liberal, and somewhat liberal (Liberals); 2 = moderate/middle-of-the-road (Moderates); and 3 = extremely conservative, conservative, somewhat conservative (Conservatives). Data are confined to white southerners.

Between the 1970s and 1980s, the portion of conservative Democrats declined nine points (from forty-four percent to thirty-five percent), whereas the share of conservative Republicans increased eleven points (from forty-three percent to fifty-four percent). Similarly, liberal Democrats increased six points (from sixty-five percent to seventy-one percent), whereas liberal Republicans declined eight points (from twenty-five percent to seventeen percent). Hence, even though the shift toward Republican identification was notably higher among urban as opposed to rural conservatives, the general pattern of partisan sorting across the three ideological categories foretold a more credible and lasting movement of rural whites in favor of the inarguably more conservative contemporary southern GOP.

Without question, Black and Black (1987) were spot on in likening the principal coalition of white southern Republican adherents to those who would subscribe to *Southern Living*. It was a party in Dixie that had greater affinity for the country club crowd than the boys confabbing at the local bar (McKee, 2019). However, just as white dealignment from the Democratic Party initially overshadowed realignment in favor of the Republican Party (Petrocik, 1987; Stanley, 1988), the slower but steadier movement of rural white southerners to the GOP was masked by the comparatively more impressive shift in the same direction among urban whites who also were the first group to embrace presidential Republicanism dating back to the 1950s. Eventually though, Reagan

Republicanism, which had more appeal among metropolitan, middle-class, economically conservative whites, would yield to a more downscale, lower-class, and decidedly more culturally conservative and native rural white electorate.[10] In the realm of southern Republicanism, *Southern Living* subscribers were going to be eclipsed by aficionados of *Field & Stream*.

4 Voting for the Biggest Prize

Presidential Elections

In the 1980s, the GOP reigned supreme in southern presidential elections. With the one exception of Georgia sticking with its native son, incumbent Democratic President Jimmy Carter in 1980, the popular vote was carried by the GOP nominee in every state in every contest in 1980, 1984, and 1988. In short, over these three presidential election years Republicans compiled a record of thirty-two out of thirty-three (ninety-seven percent) popular vote victories in the South's eleven ex-Confederate states. In terms of the percentage breakdown in the Southwide popular presidential vote (two-party), the GOP took a lopsided 58.6%. Translated into the Electoral College, the combined number of southern votes that Republican Presidents Ronald Reagan and George H. W. Bush amassed vis-à-vis their hapless Democratic opponents was 394 to 12 (ninety-seven percent GOP votes cast by southern electors from 1980 to 1988).

As noted in the previous chapter, by the 1980s, there was no longer evidence of a significant difference in the presidential preferences of rural and urban white southerners. Both groups were equally Republican in their support for the top of the ticket. However, the 1990s would cast a notably different dynamic in elections for America's biggest prize. Whereas Republicans were blessed by the presence of back-to-back northern liberal Democratic opponents in 1984 (Carter's Vice President Walter Mondale of Minnesota) and 1988 (Massachusetts Governor Michael Dukakis), in the 1990s, a centrist southern Democrat emerged to notch substantial inroads into Dixie's recently all-Republican presidential map.

Shortly before the 1992 Democratic ticket of Arkansan Bill Clinton and Tennessean Al Gore wrested away four southern states from the GOP, Earl and Merle Black (1992) cogently argued in their book *The Vital South: How Presidents Are Elected* that Dixie was pivotal for winning the presidency because bloc voting for one party in America's largest region gave presidential nominees a prohibitive advantage in the Electoral College. Thus, for Democrats, it was critical to pick off some southern states to assist with stronger performances outside Dixie. For Republicans, southern sweeps would strongly offset weaker performances in the North. Indeed, as Black and Black (1992) demonstrated, in the 1980s, pathetic southern performances made it impossible for Democrats to win the Electoral College; but the 1990s was a decade of transition in presidential politics. Some regions outside the South were moving strongly in favor of the Democratic Party, especially the Northeast (McKee and Teigen, 2016; Reiter and Stonecash, 2011) and Pacific Coast (Black and Black, 2007); hence, Clinton could have ceded the entire South in 1992 while still prevailing in the Electoral College (Stanley, 2006).

To be sure, in post-1980 presidential politics the South remained vital but principally for Republicans and not Democrats because of the latter party's growing reach outside the region. In fact, given the more recent success of Democratic nominees by means of robust northern electoral performances, one scholar made the case for Democrats "Whistling Past Dixie" (Schaller, 2008), since the party could win the presidency sans southern electoral votes. Nonetheless, it would be premature to write off whole sections of the country in campaigns for the most prized political office, because battleground states are scattered throughout the nation, with Florida constituting the most coveted swing state in presidential elections since 1992 (Choi and McKee, 2009; McKee and Craig, 2017–2018). In more contemporary times, the fluidity of presidential politics in a changing South has found Virginia the only state in the region that favors Democrats (McKee, 2019), whereas North Carolina has joined Florida as the latest to appear perennially purple. Certainly, the unique circumstances surrounding the 2020 presidential election would give anyone pause before writing off additional newly competitive states (e.g., Georgia and Texas) in America's most vote-rich region (more on this is presented in chapters eleven and twelve).

In this chapter, we examine patterns in presidential voting preferences over the past three decades. Specifically, in reflecting on the strength of the Republican Party in the South, which realigned at the presidential level arguably as early as 1968 (Black and Black, 1987), the two groups responsible for this development are urban whites and rural whites. Of course, the latter group is our primary focus; therefore, we emphasize variation in rural white support for GOP presidential nominees from 1992 to 2016. Similar to the last chapter, we often find it useful to present analyses according to decade (1992–1996, 2000–2008, 2012–2016). This provides us with two elections in the 1990s, three in the 2000s, and two more in the 2010s. Unlike in chapter three, however, here we greatly expand our evaluation of voting behavior by drawing upon multiple data sources available at the aggregate and individual levels.

As outlined in chapter two, there are many ways to assess rurality. At the heart of our enterprise is the intent to document and analyze the reasons propelling rural white southerners to the GOP and eventually at a degree of partisan attachment unrivaled by any other group in Dixie. In this regard, the core argument is that those whites residing in less densely populated locales throughout the region came to acquire an affinity for the GOP because the party stands for a set of principles better aligned with the sentiments, values, and beliefs of this constituency. With respect to the empirical evidence of this development, we believe that a variety of data that essentially measures the same phenomena, but with different metrics, only serves to bolster the support for our expectations. Hence, the chapter makes use of data at the county level measured in terms of population density and on the basis of residential inhabitant patterns we classify in relative magnitudes of urban or small-town South (STS). Additionally, we use survey data from three different sources that utilize different measures of rurality: the American National Election Studies (ANES for 1990–2000), the Cooperative Election Studies (CES for 2008–2016), and national and state exit polls (1990s–2010s).

We start our evaluation of presidential voting from 1992 to 2016 with county-level data spanning the entirety of this period. Obviously, there is an element of inferential proclamation, as counties are acting as stand-ins for the behavior of individuals (hence, susceptibility to the ecological inference fallacy). However, because of the bevy of data we have for analysis, including plenty at the individual level, our main concern is to trace out a general pattern of voting behavior that is corroborated over time and across datasets and sources. Next, we turn to ANES survey data. For our purposes, these data are unfortunately fairly limited because they terminate in 2000. After the 2000 presidential election, the ANES blocked the place indicator from public access for confidentiality concerns. To reiterate (see our brief discussion on this in chapter three), the ANES survey samples are markedly smaller and less representative than those found in the CES and exit polls, which made it imperative to pool these data by decade in chapter three. Next, we turn to an evaluation of presidential voting preferences with the CES data. Last, we examine vote choice with exit polls, using the national data to assess Southwide presidential preferences and data on individual states when and where they are available.

County-Level Patterns

With some minor alterations, mainly in Virginia, which classifies independent cities as county-equivalent territories, Dixie consists of 1,142 counties in our analysis of presidential voting behavior from 1992 to 2016. In this section, we present the results of county-level models designed to explicate presidential voting patterns in the South by decade: 1990s (1992 and 1996), 2000s (2000, 2004, and 2008), and 2010s (2012 and 2016). As mentioned, these models rely on aggregate-level data to make inferences about individual-level voter preferences. As such, some caution should be urged in not overstating these findings. Nevertheless, these models do offer full data for 1,142 counties across seven presidential election cycles and make it possible to hold the effects of time, race, and other factors constant to make a determination concerning the role of place in presidential voting in the South.[1]

The first model uses our STS indicator to study the role of place in presidential voting patterns among white southerners. It is expected that Republican presidential voting increases over time in STS counties. The model results are displayed in Figure 4.1, which plots white presidential voting for the GOP according to place and decade (1990s, 2000s, and 2010s). The general trend finds a clearly positive trajectory for Republican presidential voting across the time period analyzed. In the 1990s, Republican presidential support in urban counties exceeded that for STS counties by thirteen points, seventy-one percent versus fifty-eight percent. However, in the 2000s, this gap was essentially erased, as STS GOP voting rose to seventy-five percent, compared with seventy-six percent white Republican voting in urban counties. Finally, in the latest decade, 2010s GOP presidential support in STS counties exceeded that in urban counties by nine points, eighty-nine percent versus eighty percent.

We complement the findings in Figure 4.1 with Figure 4.2, which uses county density (as opposed to our STS/urban classification scheme) to examine once again the relationship between rurality and Republican presidential voting among white southerners. Estimated Republican presidential support

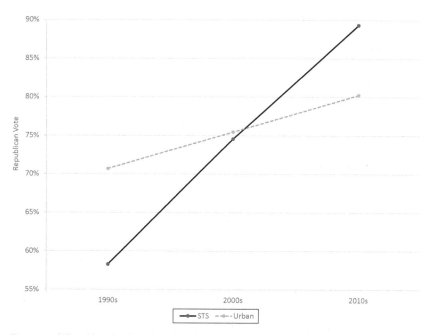

Figure 4.1. White Vote for President by Place and Decade

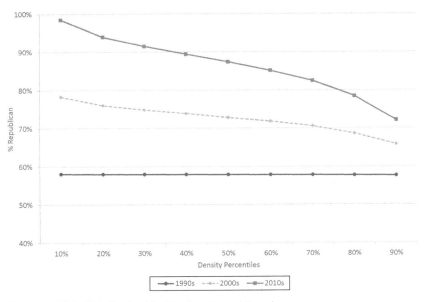

Figure 4.2. White Vote for President by Density and Decade

levels are plotted across values of population density by decade. County population density is shown along the horizontal axis, ranging from the tenth
percentile to the ninetieth percentile. For instance, in 2016, Mitchell County,
North Carolina (a population of 15,107), was located in the tenth percentile for population density, whereas Tarrant County, Texas (a population of
1,967,241), was located in the ninetieth percentile.[2] Of course, density should
be inversely related to the level of GOP presidential support. In other words,
the more population located in closer proximity, the lesser the propensity to
cast Republican presidential votes (McKee and Teigen, 2009).

Figure 4.2 reveals an interesting and obviously notable changing pattern
in Republican presidential voting by decade and county-level population density. First, there is essentially no relationship between density and the GOP
presidential vote for elections held in the 1990s, as evidenced by the horizontal line for this decade. In essence, white presidential voting behavior in
heavily urban counties in the 1990s was no different from white voter preferences for president in highly rural counties. The absence of a relationship
between density and Republican presidential voting changes a good deal in
the 2000s. In this more recent decade, the white GOP presidential vote in a
county in the ninetieth percentile for population density is estimated to be
sixty-six percent, as compared with seventy-eight percent Republican for a
county in the tenth percentile (a twelve-percentage-point voting disparity).
By the 2010s, the relationship between density and GOP presidential support

becomes most pronounced. In this latest decade, there is a twenty-six-point gap in Republican presidential voting, comparing the ninetieth population-density percentile (seventy-two percent Republican) to the tenth (98.5% Republican). Finally, we should emphasize that, in addition to the rising positive relationship between rurality (declining population density) and GOP presidential voting over the past three decades, it is the case that GOP presidential voting levels increased in both high- and low-density areas across the time period analyzed, but this trend is markedly more evident in the most sparsely settled counties.

ANES Data for 1992–2000

In our first individual-level assessment of southern white presidential voting for president since the 1980s, we present evidence based on ANES data for the 1992, 1996, and 2000 elections. Again, the data terminate in 2000 because the ANES blocked public access to the place variable after this year. To be clear, it is possible to request access to this variable for more recent elections, but given issues of representativeness and the markedly smaller ANES samples of white southerners vis-à-vis the CES and exit polls, there is only marginal added value to examining ANES vote choice data post-2000 (hence, in this chapter, we don't).[3] Nonetheless, it is useful to show southern whites' presidential voting preferences in the 1990s and 2000, because we can refer back to the preferences of this electorate in the 1980s (as documented in chapter three).

Table 4.1 shows the Republican (two-party) percentage of the presidential vote cast by rural and urban white southerners for the 1992, 1996, and 2000 elections, and these data are pooled for all three contests combined. We are, of course, cognizant of Texas billionaire H. Ross Perot's back-to-back presidential runs in 1992 and 1996, but we discount their political significance, because in neither cycle did this independent (in 1992)-turned third-party contender (Reform Party in 1996) garner a single electoral vote.[4] As displayed in Table 4.1, there is little difference in GOP presidential voting among rural (fifty-three percent) and urban (fifty-six percent) white southerners in 1992 (not statistically significant), and in 1996, these two groups voted the same, at fifty-six percent Republican. In contrast to the 1990s presidential contests, there is a palpable jump in GOP voting in 2000, especially among urban white southerners at eighty percent, versus sixty-six percent in the case of their rural white neighbors. Still, because of the small samples for these voters (fifty-seven rural white southerners and sixty-five urban white southerners), this fourteen-point gap in GOP presidential support by location in 2000 is not statistically significant ($p = .08$, two-tailed). Finally, the last column in Table 4.1 shows the Republican share of the presidential vote when all three elections

Table 4.1. Republican Presidential Vote by Location, 1992–2000

Location	% Republican presidential vote			
	1992	1996	2000	1992–2000
Rural	53	56	66	56
Urban	56	56	80	61
Difference	−3	0	−14	−5
Rural cases	119	98	57	274
Urban cases	127	135	65	327

Note. Data computed from the ANES Cumulative Data File (CDF). Republican share of the two-party vote is displayed in table. Data are confined to southern whites residing in rural or urban locations. Data are weighted.

are pooled (1992–2000). Over this span of three elections, fifty-six percent of rural white southerners favored the Republican presidential nominee, as did sixty-one percent of urban white southerners, a five-point difference that is not statistically significant.

Perhaps most telling about the data in Table 4.1 is how it compares with Republican voting in the 1980s. As shown previously (see Table 3.4 in the last chapter), in the 1980s, rural white southerners voted sixty-six percent Republican for president, and their urban counterparts voted at a sixty-nine percent GOP clip. In short, in the 1990s, Democrat Bill Clinton had considerable success in attracting the votes of white southerners, regardless of location. After Clinton's two terms, as Table 4.1 shows, there is an impressive rise in support for Texas Republican George W. Bush over Clinton's Vice President and Tennessean Al Gore. An underappreciated and rarely acknowledged fact of the Clinton Presidency is that this Arkansas Democrat's performance in the South is not commensurate with the number of states he carried in his two successful campaigns: four in 1992 (Arkansas, Georgia, Louisiana, and Tennessee) and four in 1996 (Arkansas, Florida, Louisiana, and Tennessee). Indeed, despite only carrying four southern states in 1996, Clinton actually won a popular-vote plurality over Republican Bob Dole when accounting for all votes cast in the region (Lamis, 1999; McKee, 2019). Put another way, the forty-four percent Democratic presidential vote that white southerners delivered to Clinton (based on the ANES data in Table 4.1) in 1996 was impressive. Support for Democratic presidential candidates among white southerners, however, massively declined in more recent contests, which has already been made evident with the county-level results. This trend will be amplified with additional survey data in the following sections of this chapter.

CES Data: 2008–2016

The CES is a more recent survey featuring large state-level samples, which began with the 2006 midterm cycle. For our purposes in this chapter on presidential voting patterns, we have data for the 2008, 2012, and 2016 elections. Unlike exit poll data, an advantage of the CES is that each respondent can be located in their county of residence. Using this information, we added specific contextual data, including STS and population density indicators for each individual in the dataset. Thus, we can place each respondent in their own particular residential context and use this localized geography to examine their presidential voting behavior.

Confining the CES samples to non-Hispanic whites living in the South, we specify models for the 2008, 2012, and 2016 elections where the dependent variable presents a binary choice for presidential vote. A value of one represents a vote for the Republican presidential nominee, and a value of zero denotes a vote for the Democratic contender. One set of models uses the STS indicator as the independent variable of interest for evaluating presidential vote choice, whereas a second model relies on population density as the variable of interest for assessing southern white voter preferences on the basis of location.[5]

The following figures generated from our models are interpreted by translating the results into predicted vote probabilities (Hanmer and Kalkan, 2013), where the scale ranges from zero to one.[6] Figure 4.3 provides the likelihood that a white southerner votes Republican for president in each election (2008, 2012, and 2016) according to the county percent STS. Of course, our expectation is that the probability of voting Republican will be positively associated with a higher county percent STS. This is the case. For all three elections analyzed, the likelihood of voting for the Republican presidential nominee rises with the county percent STS. For example, looking at the 2008 election data plotted in Figure 4.3, a white respondent residing in a zero percent STS county (stated differently, a one hundred percent urban county) has a 0.59 probability of voting for the GOP presidential nominee, which compares with a 0.73 probability for a respondent living in a one hundred percent STS county. This fourteen-point difference in the probability a white southerner votes Republican for president according to the county percent STS constitutes a substantial change on a zero-to-one scale.

It is also evident from Figure 4.3 that there is an increasing probability of Republican presidential voting associated with higher levels of STS in all three elections. The 2016 contest reveals heightened levels of GOP support, with respondents residing in one hundred percent STS counties having a 0.79 probability of voting for the Republican Donald Trump, compared with a 0.58 probability for a respondent living in a one hundred percent urban county.

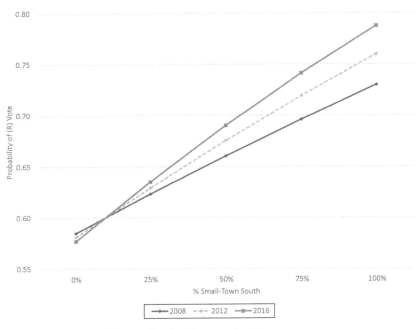

Figure 4.3. White Vote for President by Place, 2008–2016

Not surprisingly, this twenty-one-point GOP presidential vote probability disparity on the basis of STS is statistically significant.

The results from the second set of models using county population density as the key variable are presented in Figure 4.4. Unlike the previous models using the STS indicator (showing a positive relationship between STS and GOP voting), for these, we expect Republican presidential voting to be inversely related to population density: Greater density should reduce the likelihood of a GOP vote (see Teigen, Shaw, and McKee, 2017). Figure 4.4 shows the probability of voting for the Republican presidential nominee plotted across values of county population density ranging from the tenth through ninetieth percentiles.[7]

The association between place and voting based on the STS indicator is also confirmed in the case of county population density. White respondents living in lower density counties are more likely to vote for the GOP presidential candidate than are whites living in counties with higher population densities. Consider the findings from 2012; a respondent living in a county in the tenth percentile for population density had an estimated 0.73 probability of voting Republican, whereas the GOP vote probability for a respondent living in a county in the ninetieth population density percentile was 0.53—a significant difference of 0.20. The inverse pattern between population density and the probability of voting Republican manifested in 2008 and 2016. As with the

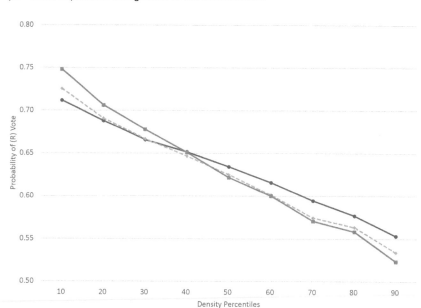

Figure 4.4. White Vote for President by Density, 2008–2016

previous models using the STS variable, the 2016 GOP vote disparity between white respondents in rural versus urban areas is a notable and significant difference of 0.23. Specifically, respondents living in counties in the tenth percentile for population density were predicted to have a 0.75 probability of voting for Republican Trump, compared with a 0.52 GOP presidential vote probability among voters living in a county at the ninetieth population density percentile.

Exit Poll Data: 1990s–2010s

Finally, we turn to one last data source to explore white southerners' presidential voting patterns: exit polls conducted by various news media outlets from 1992 through 2016. We examine both the national exit polls and individual state exit polls when and where available. Similar to the CES surveys, exit polls contain large and highly representative samples of white southerners. In addition, exit polls typically include a location variable that makes it possible to categorize respondents on the basis of the "size of place" associated with their residence.[8] In keeping with the classification scheme introduced in chapter three, rural/STS voters comprise residents in the designated rural category and also those living in cities with a total population ranging from ten thousand to less than fifty thousand. All other respondents are classified as urban voters (see chapter three).

Figure 4.5 displays the white Republican presidential vote percentage (two-party) by location from 1992 to 2016, with data from the national exit polls.[9] The figure contains two lines of data on white southerners, one for urban voters and another for rural/STS voters. The longitudinal trend for both of these groups is generally positive, with the exception of a notable drop in Republican presidential support in 2008. Across this quarter century, however, the exit polls always indicate higher levels of Republican presidential voting among rural/STS residents as compared with their urban counterparts. As early as 1992, there was a ten-point gap between these two groups, with sixty-five percent of rural/STS respondents voting for President Bush, compared with fifty-five percent of urban voters. By the end of the time series, seventy-eight percent of rural/STS residents, versus seventy percent of urban residents, reported voting for Republican presidential nominee Donald Trump. Thus, although levels of GOP voting increased across this time period, in 2016, there remained a considerable eight-point difference in Republican presidential voting according to voter location.

Compared with the ANES data displayed in Table 4.1, the national exit poll data tell a somewhat different story regarding the level of Republican presidential voting exhibited by white southerners on the basis of location. Again, it is worth noting that the ANES samples are substantially smaller and less geographically representative of the white electorate in part because of the

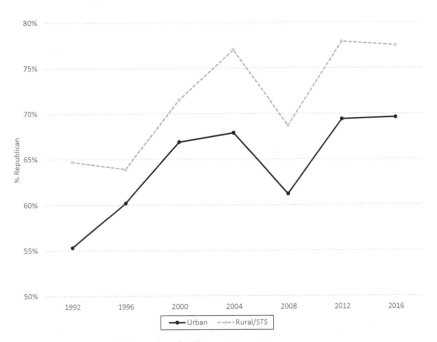

Figure 4.5. White Vote for President by Place, 1992–2016

sampling method (Maxwell and Shields, 2019). On the other hand, even though the exit polls contain a size of place variable, a voter's county location is never disclosed.[10] Ultimately, however, what matters is that both surveys reveal the long-term ascendant relationship between rurality and southern presidential Republicanism (McKee, 2007, 2008).

For some inexplicable reason (as we see it!), in the 1990s, none of the individual state exit polls contained the size of place indicator. Therefore, to track white southerners' presidential voting preferences with state-specific exit polls, we have to start in the 2000s. Table 4.2 records the results by location for the individual state exit polls from 2000 through 2016.[11] Among these data, there is a lot of variability between states. For example, in 2008, Republican presidential voting among whites in urban areas ranged from fifty-six percent in Florida to ninety percent in Alabama. For rural/STS voters in the same election, GOP support ranged from sixty-two percent in Tennessee to ninety-one percent in Louisiana.

As a general pattern, however, compared with urban voters, rural/STS voters have a higher propensity to vote Republican for president. There are thirty-six state data points (with urban vs. rural/STS dyads) presented in Table 4.2 across five presidential election years. For twenty-nine of these cases, or eighty-one percent of the time, rural/STS GOP presidential voting exceeded that of urban residents. Also, in the bottom row of Table 4.2, we calculate the mean Republican presidential vote by location and election year. In 2016, the average Republican vote among rural/STS voters was seventy-seven percent compared with sixty-eight percent for urban voters—a substantial and significant nine-percentage-point difference. Further, with the important caveat that the included southern states are not always the same across election years, it is *always* true that the average rural/STS Republican presidential vote is higher than the corresponding urban mean. These findings are part of a larger pattern of data presented in this chapter that show rural/STS whites now routinely register the highest levels of Republican presidential support found among residents living in the eleven southern states.

Conclusion

In the decades after the GOP's southern and national dominance of 1980s presidential politics, the alignment of rural voters with the Republican Party has become much more evident (McKee, 2008). Coalitional politics has altered substantially. Historically, and contrary to the typically positive relationship between population density and support for the Democratic Party (Rodden, 2019), in Dixie, the GOP's postwar (World War II) inroads proceeded faster and farther by cultivating an appeal among whites residing in growing urban areas (Bartley and Graham, 1975). As demonstrated in this chapter, the electoral dynamics underway in the 1990s finally reached a point at which

Table 4.2. Republican Presidential Vote by State and Location, 2000–2016

% Republican share of presidential vote

State	2000		2004		2008		2012		2016	
	URBAN	RURAL/STS	URBAN	RURAL/STS	URBAN	RURAL/STS	URBAN	RURAL/STS	URBAN	RURAL/STS
AL			81	81	90	89	83	89		
AR			62	64	63	77				
FL	58	68	56	68	56	65	60	72	64	73
GA	72	78	75	78	78	75			73	90
LA			73	83	84	91				
MS			87	85	82	90	86	92		
NC			71	76	61	69	64	76	64	73
SC			74	84	77	70			75	66
TN			65	66	55	62				
TX			74	77	72	87			71	87
VA	63	60	68	70	57	70	62	64	60	72
M	64	69	71	75	70	77	71	79	68	77

Note. Entries show the two-party vote for the Republican presidential nominee cast by southern white respondents living in urban or rural/STS places. Mean represents the mean Republican presidential vote by location and election year. Source: Exit poll data calculated by authors. *M* = mean.

rural whites are now unquestionably more Republican in their presidential voting preferences compared with their urban white neighbors.

In the 1980s, Black and Black (1987) utilized a county-level analysis of southern presidential vote returns to drive home the ascendant status of the GOP. Dividing presidential contests in a before (1952–1964)-and-after (1968–1980) fashion, they discovered that, in the latter period, there was a dramatic collapse in the number of counties that typically registered Democratic presidential vote majorities. In their words, "Even before the Reagan administration began, the Republicans . . . had established a marked superiority over the Democrats in the scope and vitality of their grassroots political bases" (Black and Black, 1987, p. 266). They concluded by averring that, "The breadth of the Democratic collapse is staggering. It would be difficult to find comparable instances in American political history of such a rapid and comprehensive desertion of an established majority party by an entire region" (1987, pp. 266 and 268). Notable to us is that, in describing the three primary geographic sources of the GOP's southern presidential strength—mountain Republicanism, urban Republicanism, and interstate Republicanism—Black and Black (1987, p. 268) emphasized that, "Urban Republicanism, rooted in the rapidly expanding white middle class, remains the key to Republican success." What was true in the 1980s is no longer true now.

In post-1980s politics, there is an interesting progression of presidents, starting with the Democrat Bill Clinton in 1992.[12] He came into office with Democratic congressional majorities, which were subsequently wiped out in the 1994 midterm. Nevertheless, in spite of persistent divided government, Clinton served two terms. He holds the distinction of being the last southern Democratic president, and in this capacity, he was adept at peeling off substantial GOP-leaning constituencies—primarily because of his centrist political positioning (Black and Black, 2002) coupled with a felicity for retail-style campaigning that is highly attractive to rural whites (Fenno, 1996).

In contrast to Clinton, his Republican successor, George W. Bush, wrested back legions of rural and urban whites who still found reasons to vote Democratic in the 1990s. Bush's southern electoral prowess was palpable simply because he swept the popular presidential vote in Dixie's eleven states in 2000 and 2004. As a conservative Texan, Bush held tremendous cultural and regional appeal among rural whites. Additionally, as an openly devout Christian, Bush's religious faith made for a hard-to-overstate political commodity. In short, as Black and Black (2002) would contend, Bush basically checked all the boxes in terms of what southern whites demanded and valued in a political leader. Of course, despite serving two terms, with some of his tenure under divided government, the twin burdens of an unpopular war and a historic economic collapse doomed Bush's presidential legacy (Jacobson, 2007).

Nonetheless, Bush's electoral dominance in southern presidential politics had solidified rural white allegiance to the GOP and meant that the path to the presidency for a Democratic contender would have to be based on a very different coalition than the one Clinton assembled. Indeed, as much as President Bush attracted rural white southerners to the GOP, it is likely President Barack Obama proved just as repelling and repulsive a force in dissuading them from seeking political refuge within the Democratic opposition. The twice victorious President Obama assembled a political coalition noticeably absent of white rural voters, yet he managed to carry three southern states (Florida, North Carolina, and Virginia) in 2008 and two more (Florida and Virginia) in 2012. Like Clinton and Bush before him, Obama came in with copartisan congressional majorities that he subsequently lost handily (the House in 2010 and the Senate in 2014), despite serving two terms. As shown in Figure 4.5, the national tide in favor of the Democratic Party did reduce white southerners' support for the GOP in 2008, but sixty-nine percent of rural voters still backed the Republican John McCain; and after four years of President Obama, rural white southerners' support for his 2012 Republican opponent Mitt Romney vaulted to seventy-eight percent.

In his two presidential runs, Democrat Bill Clinton won 49.6% of the South's popular vote (two-party), and Republican George W. Bush won 56.5% of Dixie's popular vote in his back-to-back southern sweeps, whereas Democrat Barack Obama was held to 46.3% of the region's popular vote in his two successful presidential campaigns. Undoubtedly, the relatively substantial size of the South's rural white electorate, and its increasing alignment with the GOP, was principally responsible for limiting the electoral success of the Obama coalition in Dixie.

In the lead up to his bid for the 2016 Republican presidential nomination, Donald Trump made noise by vociferously casting doubt on whether President Obama was born in the United States. "Birtherism," as this conspiracy came to be known, held considerable appeal among Republicans, and particularly among the Tea Party movement (Gervais and Morris, 2018) that fueled the Democrats' sixty-three-seat midterm loss in the 2010 House elections (Jacobson, 2011). Despite possessing no cultural connection to the South and being devoid of piety (Bullock et al., 2019), Trump spoke a language of conservative populism and fanned the flames of political resentment (Cramer, 2016) in a demagogic manner that strongly resonated with rural white southerners. On his way to a comfortable Electoral College victory, despite losing the national popular vote (as Bush had in 2000), rural white southerners contributed mightily to Trump's success in Dixie (see the data displayed in Figures 4.3, 4.4, and 4.5), where he won 54.4% of the popular vote, carried ten of eleven states, and garnered one hundred forty-five electoral votes to Democrat Hillary Clinton's thirteen (all from Virginia).[13]

We conclude with a county-level comparison of the Southwide presidential vote registered in 1992 and 2016, the elections that bookend this chapter. Figure 4.6 displays the presidential vote cast at the county level in 1992, and Figure 4.7 presents the same data for the 2016 election. The data shown in these two figures fall into four possible categories: (1) Democratic vote majority in an STS county (Democrat/STS), (2) Democrat/urban county, (3) Republican/urban county, and (4) Republican/STS county.[14] We are, of course, interested in the changes across the four county categories between 1992 and 2016. As evident in Figure 4.6, in 1992, the southern ticket of Democrats Clinton and Gore did very well in securing the votes of rural southerners on their way to winning four states in the region and defeating the Republican incumbent ticket of President George H. W. Bush and Vice President Dan Quayle. In terms of the share of the presidential vote cast by county type, in 1992, it was as follows: thirty-eight percent Democrat/STS, twelve percent Democrat/urban, twenty-one percent Republican/urban, and twenty-eight percent Republican/STS. Hence, not only did the Democrat Clinton amass the lion's share of his vote majorities in STS counties, but this category also comprised a plurality of southern counties in the 1992 election.

The data in Figure 4.7 tell a very different story. In the mid-1980s, Black and Black (1987) chronicled the county-level "grassroots Democratic collapse" in southern presidential politics; Figure 4.7 presents data on the ascendance of rural presidential Republicanism. In the 2016 open-seat contest against Bill

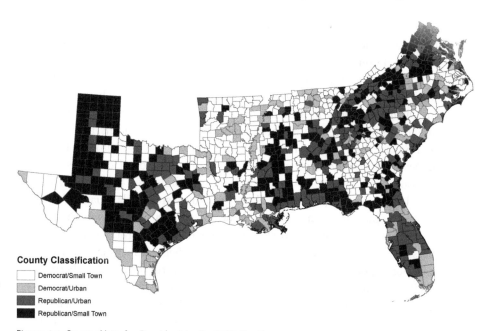

County Classification
☐ Democrat/Small Town
▨ Democrat/Urban
▦ Republican/Urban
■ Republican/Small Town

Figure 4.6. County Vote for President in the 1992 Election

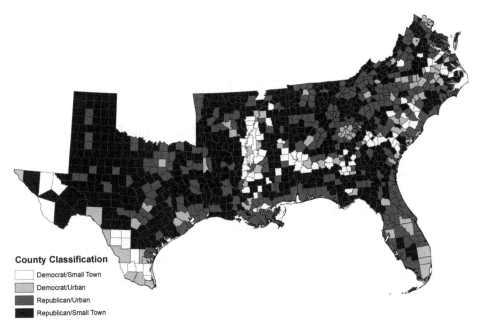

County Classification

- Democrat/Small Town
- Democrat/Urban
- Republican/Urban
- Republican/Small Town

Figure 4.7. County Vote for President in the 2016 Election

Clinton's wife, the Republican Trump was carried by rural votes. With respect to the percentage breakdown of the presidential vote cast by county type, in 2016 it was: eight percent Democrat/STS, ten percent Democrat/urban, twenty-eight percent Republican/urban, and fifty-four percent Republican/STS. In 2016, the Democrat/STS category contained the smallest share of counties, whereas it was the largest in 1992.[15] The Republican/STS category contained the second greatest share of counties in 1992, at twenty-eight percent, but in 2016, it accounted for fully fifty-four percent of Dixie's counties. To be sure, in 2016, it was critical that Trump scaled the "blue wall" of Michigan, Pennsylvania, and Wisconsin on his way to winning the presidency. The South, however, was also vital to Trump's Electoral College victory, and more than any other constituency, it was the overwhelming support from Dixie's rural whites that made his improbable presidential win a reality.

5 US Senate Elections

Republicans' Most-Promising and Attainable Seats

In Texas's 1961 US Senate special election to fill the recent vacancy of newly seated Democratic Vice President Lyndon B. Johnson, Republican John Tower became the first in his party to represent a southern state in the nation's upper chamber since the end of Reconstruction. Regarding the offices below the presidency, because of its tight alignment with respect to issues and its federal context (Black and Black, 1987), southern Republican success has been quickest and most sustained in US Senate contests. This dynamic has proven enduring, especially as the major parties continue to polarize, and nationalization—an increasing consistency in partisan voting for the White House down to the bottom of the ticket—grows in strength (Hopkins, 2018). Senator Tower was originally the beneficiary of a rift that split open in the much larger and more powerful Texas Democratic Party. Because the eventual Democratic nominee at the runoff stage, William Blakley, was considered to be even more conservative than Republican John Tower, enough Democrats defected to make Tower the narrow victor.[1] Nonetheless, despite there being far more Texas Democratic voters than Texas Republicans, Senator Tower was able to hold his seat until he voluntarily retired in 1984.

The high profile of a Senate seat makes it harder to separate oneself from the national image of the officeholder's party and because of scarcity (just one hundred senators) and the tremendous political clout that goes with the position, Senate elections often draw formidable competition. Hence, all else equal, it is typically harder to hold onto a Senate seat compared with a governorship (more insulated from national politics) or a House position (incumbency tends to be worth more at the ballot box and most congressional districts are drawn to clearly favor one party). Nonetheless, what has for decades advantaged southern Republicans is the fact that their conservative branding is in closer proximity to the views of their states' majority white constituents. Further, the wholehearted embrace of socially conservative positions makes Republican Senate contenders very attractive to the most culturally conservative segment of the southern electorate: rural whites.

Before turning specifically to longitudinal changes in southern white support of the GOP in Senate elections according to location, Table 5.1 displays the Republican percentage of the two-party vote cast in these contests by

Table 5.1. Republican Vote in Elections for Senate, 1990s–2010s

Decade	All contests	% Republican share of Senate vote Republican	Open	Democratic
1990s	48 (39)	60 (15)	54 (7)	36 (17)
2000s	53 (37)	60 (16)	51 (14)	41 (7)
2010s	58 (36)	61 (20)	56 (8)	51 (8)

Note. There were a handful of uncontested Senate elections (eight total), and these cases are omitted from the data displayed in the table. Data presented in the table show the Republican share of the two-party vote in contested elections, and the number of cases by category appear in parentheses. Republican = a Republican incumbent sought reelection; Open = no major party incumbent sought reelection; Democratic = a Democratic incumbent sought reelection. Senate data include all of the special elections held from 1990 to 2018 (Texas in 1993, Tennessee in 1994, Georgia in 2000, Mississippi in 2008, South Carolina in 2014, Alabama in 2017, and Mississippi in 2018).

decade and type of race. Admittedly, the trend in favor of the GOP may not be as pronounced as one would anticipate, but it is important to note that even in the 1980s, southern Republicans had already notched considerable success in Senate elections (Black and Black, 1987). Still, the GOP tilt is evident, as the party's share of the two-party vote in contested elections (Democrat vs. Republican) increased from less than fifty percent in the 1990s to fifty-eight percent in the 2010s. GOP dominance in seats with Republican incumbents seeking reelection has remained nearly constant at sixty to sixty-one percent of the vote for the past three decades. GOP performance in open-seat contests went from fifty-four percent of the vote in the 1990s down to fifty-one percent in the 2000s and then to a high of fifty-six percent of the vote in the 2010s. Finally, Republicans have registered their most notable gains in elections with a Democratic senator running for another term. In the 1990s, Republicans captured thirty-six percent of the vote in these seats and then increased their vote share to forty-one percent a decade later. In the 2010s, it is remarkable that even in contests with incumbent Democrats, their Republican challengers captured fifty-one percent of the vote.

Figure 5.1 shows how the increase in the Republican share of the vote in contested southern Senate elections has translated into seat gains from the 1990s to the 2010s. Even in the 1990s, the GOP controlled a slight majority of Senate seats (fifty-three percent) in contested elections. However, in the following two decades, Republican growth has been tremendous, vaulting to seventy percent of the South's Senate delegation in the 2000s and then up to eighty-six percent in the 2010s, which amounts to just under nineteen of

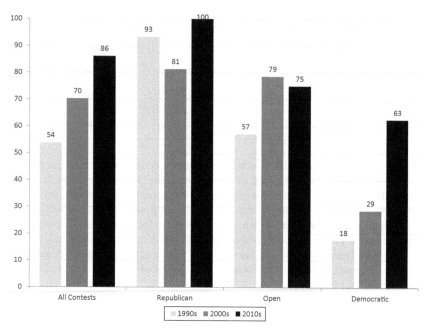

Figure 5.1. Percentage of Republican Seats in Senate Elections, 1990s–2010s

the twenty-two seats in the eleven ex-Confederate states. Once again, most of the growth in Republican seat gains in Senate contests has been at the direct expense of Democratic incumbents. In the 1990s, the GOP only captured eighteen percent of seats with Democratic incumbents running for reelection. Republican success in these most difficult contests increased to twenty-nine percent in the 2000s and then up to an extraordinary sixty-three percent in the 2010s. Similarly, but with more success, the GOP increased its share of wins in open-seat races from fifty-seven percent in the 1990s to seventy-five percent or higher in the 2000s (seventy-nine percent) and 2010s (seventy-five percent). Last, in the the 2010s, not one Republican incumbent lost to a Democratic challenger, a resounding statement of how powerful incumbency has been in recent contests for GOP senators.

County-Level Patterns

Similar to presidential elections (see chapter four), with the passage of time, increasingly more rural counties in the South have shifted Republican, regardless of the type of political office being contested. Alabama in 1992 versus 2016, provides a useful and interesting anecdote that also happens to be typical of the general movement of rural counties in favor of GOP Senate candidates. Richard Shelby of Alabama was first elected to the US Senate in 1986 and still serves in this capacity, winning his most recent reelection bid in 2016.

Interestingly, Senator Shelby, like so many southern Democrats of his generation (Canon and Sousa, 1992; Yoshinaka, 2016), switched to the Republican Party. The 1994 midterm was a historically successful cycle for southern Republicans, who, for the first time since 1874, picked up majorities in Dixie's US House and US Senate delegations (Black and Black, 2002). Fittingly, given the severity of Democratic losses, the day after the 1994 elections, Senator Shelby publicly professed his new allegiance to the GOP (Barone and Ujifusa, 1995, p. 6).

Figure 5.2 shows the county-level results for the 1992 (left side) and 2016 (right side) Alabama Senate elections that Senator Shelby won. Alabama has sixty-seven counties, and the figure indicates the type of county in terms of four exclusive categories: (1) Democrat/small-town South (STS), (2) Democrat/urban, (3) Republican/urban, and (4) Republican/STS. Simply put, the party designation corresponds to which party won the most votes in the county, whereas the place designation indicates whether the county is classified as urban or rural/STS. In 1992, when Senator Shelby was a Democrat, he only lost one Alabama county, which coincidentally happened to be his namesake:

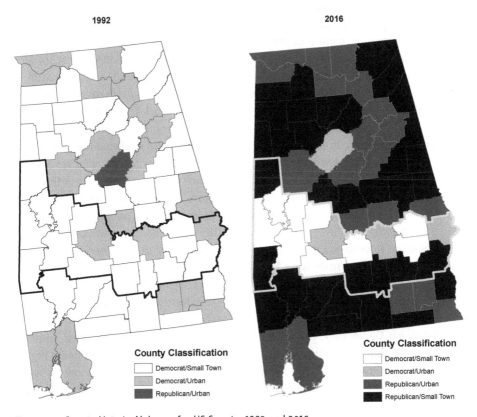

Figure 5.2. County Vote in Alabama for US Senate, 1992 and 2016

urban Shelby County, located in the middle of the state and directly below Jefferson County, where Alabama's largest city of Birmingham is located. It is important to note that, because the only county Shelby's Republican opponent carried was urban, the category Republican/STS did not appear in 1992. With respect to percentages, in the 1992 Alabama Senate election, 67.2% of counties were Democrat/STS, 31.3% were Democrat/urban, and 1.5% (one county) were Republican/urban.

Like most southern states, especially its counterparts in the Deep South (Georgia, Louisiana, Mississippi, and South Carolina), Alabama contains a large territory of Black Belt counties. Specifically, there are a total of eighteen Black Belt counties in Alabama, and, as is true throughout the South, these Black Belt counties contain the highest percentage of Black residents because the largest proportion of enslaved people lived in these areas before the Civil War (Key, 1949).[2] Before passage of the 1965 Voting Rights Act (VRA), when the vast majority of Blacks were disfranchised in the Black Belt counties, the rural whites in these localities were the most staunchly Democratic, because the party was foremost a bulwark in defense of white supremacy (Kousser, 1974). The white scions of planters/plantation owners in the Black Belt were the most politically influential from the end of Reconstruction until the 1960s civil rights movement undermined Jim Crow segregation. Particularly in Alabama, tremendous wealth was generated by the slave economy whose locus resided within the Black Belt counties (Acharya, Blackwell, and Sen, 2018). However, after the 1965 VRA led to the massive re-enfranchisement of Black Alabamians who constitute a large percentage of Black Belt residents and are overwhelmingly aligned with the Democratic Party, this region became the most Democratic in the South. Figure 5.2 outlines the Alabama Black Belt in 1992 with a black border. In 1992, Democratic Senator Shelby won seventy-seven percent of the vote in Alabama's Black Belt counties, with a low of 70.3% in urban Russell County and a high of 91.8% in rural Greene County.

Almost a quarter century later, as an entrenched Republican senator in 2016, Shelby won over eighty percent (fifty-four) of Alabama's sixty-seven counties. Revealing a sea change in voting patterns, in the 2016 Senate election, 50.7% of counties were Republican/STS, 29.9% were Republican/urban, 13.4% were Democrat/STS, and six percent were Democrat/urban. As expected, because the Black Belt is currently the most Democratic part of Alabama—not due to the many rural whites who can trace their ancestry back to the old southern Democracy, but rather because of the large share of Black voters who are almost all affiliated with the modern Democratic Party—Shelby registered his lowest support here (on the 2016 map, the Black Belt is now shown with a gray border). Unlike in 1992, when Shelby was a Democrat and won every Black Belt county by a landslide (seventy percent or higher), as a Republican in 2016, Shelby only won a third (six) of these eighteen counties.

Jefferson County was the only one outside the Black Belt that Shelby lost. Overall, in 2016, Shelby won 41.8% of the vote in the Alabama Black Belt, ranging from a low of 17.3% in rural Macon County to a high of 71.7% in rural Crenshaw County. Viewed another way, in 1992, Shelby's Republican opponent won twenty-three percent of the vote in Alabama's Black Belt, whereas in 2016, Republican Senator Shelby did 18.8 percentage points better. As southern Blacks have been Democratic stalwarts since 1964 (Carmines and Stimson, 1989), it would seem that the considerable increase in the GOP Senate vote in the heavily rural Alabama Black Belt is principally due to a boost in white support.

We move beyond the case of Alabama and now turn to a Southwide county-level examination of Senate voting on the basis of location. Similar to the county-level results shown in chapter four for the presidential vote, Figure 5.3 displays the Republican share of the Senate vote according to decade (1990s, 2000s, and 2010s) and whether a southern county is urban or STS. Further, because the plotted data are extracted from a parsimonious model (see Appendix B for more details regarding the construction of the model that Figure 5.3 is based on), we are also able to control for the racial composition of each county and the type of Senate contest.[3]

On the basis of the aforementioned stipulations, at the county level in the 1990s, white urban support for the GOP in Senate contests (70.1%) exceeded

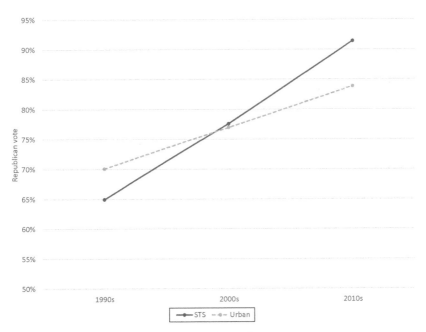

Figure 5.3. White Vote for Senate by Place and Decade

the rate registered by rural whites (64.9%). In the 2000s, however, parity was achieved, with 77.6% of the rural white county vote and seventy-seven percent of the urban white county vote going to Republican Senate candidates. In the most recent decade of the 2010s, rural white county support for Republican Senate candidates has continued to increase to an impressive 91.4%. Urban white county support for GOP Senate contenders has also gone up (83.9%), but it is now 7.5 points below that of rural white county residents.

Figure 5.4 shows the county-level percentage of the vote cast for Republican Senate candidates according to decade and on the basis of population density. Once again, contests are set to the open-seat condition and the county racial composition is one hundred percent white. On the horizontal axis, county population density is displayed in percentiles, from the tenth percentile (the lowest density shown in the figure) up to the ninetieth percentile (the highest density shown in the figure). In the 1990s, there has already appeared a distinction in the Republican percentage of the Senate vote according to county density: sixty-four percent Republican in the least dense counties versus 52.4% Republican in the densest counties. The rural/urban divide on the basis of county population density truly rears its head in the next two decades. In the 2000s, the disparity in the Republican Senate vote is a notable nineteen points: 79.5% Republican for a county in the tenth percentile versus 60.2% Republican for a county in the ninetieth percentile. In the 2010s, for a

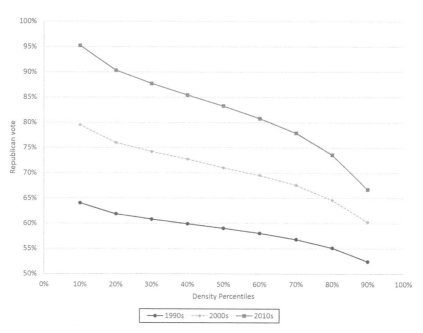

Figure 5.4. White Vote for Senate by Density and Decade

county in the tenth percentile for density, the GOP candidate is predicted to win 95.2% of the vote. By comparison, for a county at the ninetieth percentile for density, the vote for the Republican Senate candidate in the 2010s is reduced to 66.7%. The twenty-nine-point Republican Senate vote chasm that emerges in the 2010s when comparing rural counties (tenth percentile density) to urban counties (ninetieth percentile density) is a testament to how much the modern Republican Party in the South is reliant on the support of rural whites.

Cooperative Election Study (CES) Data

The CES, first administered for the 2006 midterm elections, allows us to examine the voting behavior of southern white respondents according to location. Figure 5.5 shows the percentage of southern whites voting for Republican Senate candidates based on the county percent STS in twenty-five-percent increments while setting the election type to open seat. Additionally, the plotted data for the GOP Senate vote is partitioned into two time periods: the 2000s (2006 and 2008) and the 2010s (2010–2018) (please see Appendix B for further modeling details).[4] Both lines in the figure show a clear upward trend in the Republican Senate vote going from zero percent STS to one hundred percent STS. Further, support for GOP Senate candidates is markedly higher, regardless of the percent STS in the latter period for the 2010s. For instance,

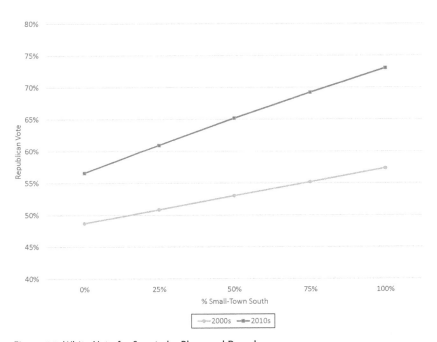

Figure 5.5. White Vote for Senate by Place and Decade

in the 2000s, at fifty percent STS, the GOP Senate vote was fifty-three percent, whereas at fifty percent STS in the 2010s, the Republican Senate vote was 65.2%. Finally, the slope is steeper for the 2010s line, meaning that the rate of increasing support among whites in more rural counties has accelerated versus that in the 2000s. Specifically, the difference in the GOP Senate vote for one hundred percent STS versus zero percent STS in the 2000s equals 8.6 percentage points (57.3%–48.7%), whereas the difference in the GOP Senate vote for one hundred percent STS versus zero percent STS in the 2010s is 16.4 percentage points (73%–56.6%).

Figure 5.6 plots the Republican Senate vote cast by white southerners with respect to county density, ranging from the tenth percentile to the ninetieth percentile. The downward slopes in the GOP Senate vote as county density increases are palpable. Compared with the 2000s, the downward slope is higher and declines more precipitously in the 2010s. At the fiftieth percentile for density in the 2000s, the white vote for GOP Senate candidates is 52.5%. In contrast, at the same density level (fiftieth percentile) in the 2010s, the white Republican Senate vote is 62.5%. The difference in white southerners' support for Republican Senate contenders is greatest across time periods for those respondents residing in the most rural counties (tenth percentile density). In the 2000s, the white GOP Senate vote in these areas is 57.8%, and in the 2010s white support increased to 72.3%. In sum, the most pronounced shift

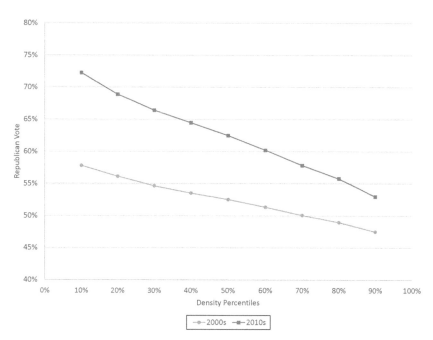

Figure 5.6. White Vote for Senate by Density and Decade

in favor of Republican Senate candidates is due to the increasing GOP support registered by rural whites.

Exit Poll Data

Exit polls are also instructive of the long-term changes in white southerners' support for Republican Senate candidates on the basis of location. Exit polls are conducted nationally and also for individual states. Unfortunately, in the 1990s, 1990 was the only election in which exit polls were administered for individual southern states. Starting in 2000, however, there are state exit polls for every election cycle except 2002. Designating the exit poll categories for rural and cities with fewer than fifty thousand residents as rural/STS, and every other place classification as urban, Table 5.2 displays the percentage of the Republican Senate vote cast by urban and rural/STS white voters in the eleven southern states from 1990 to 2018. The entries are confined to contested Senate elections, but obviously not all of these elections are accounted for, because the exit polls were not conducted for every state in every election cycle (as just one example, voters were not surveyed for the 2012 Texas Senate election featuring Republican Ted Cruz vs. Democrat Paul Sadler).

Nevertheless, even with a somewhat spotty record of coverage, a general pattern emerges by simply computing the mean Republican Senate vote of white southerners across states in each election cycle according to location. Most important for our purposes, after the 2000 election, rural/STS white southerners' Republican vote either matches that of their urban white counterparts or exceeds it. The 2010 midterm was historically poor for the Democratic Party, and this is reflected in the eighty-two percent Republican Senate vote registered by urban and rural/STS white southerners. After 2010 and up through 2018, the average rural/STS white support for GOP Senate candidates has always been higher than the Republican Senate vote cast by urban whites. In 2018, southern voters were surveyed in five states (Florida, Mississippi, Tennessee, Texas, and Virginia) holding a total of six Senate elections (Mississippi had a special election in addition to a regularly scheduled contest), and only in Virginia did the white urban Republican vote (fifty-six percent) exceed the white rural/STS Republican vote (fifty-five percent), albeit by just one percentage point. Overall, in 2018, the mean percentage of the Republican Senate vote cast by rural/STS whites was seventy-six percent versus sixty-eight percent in the case of urban whites.

Finally, the South can be extracted from the national exit polls to track the Republican Senate vote for the entire region from 1990 to 2018. Over this period, national exit poll data are only excluded for 2004 and 2008.[5] Also, the advantage of using the national exit polls is that although the state sample sizes vary (considerably, in some cases, on the basis of the population of the state; e.g., Arkansas samples are much smaller than Texas samples), there

Table 5.2. Republican Senate Vote by State and Location, 1990–2018

Election year and place	% Republican share of Senate vote											
	AL	AR	FL	GA	LA	MS	NC	SC	TN	TX	VA	M
1990												
Urban	59						59	80	34	71		61
Rural/STS	43						68	80	33	70		59
2000												
Urban		53	55								59	59
Rural/STS		65	46								62	58
2004												
Urban	84	47	52	77	70		69	68				67
Rural/STS	86	53	65	80	65		71	76				71
2006												
Urban			42						63	67	56	57
Rural/STS			52						55	75	61	61
2008												
Urban	91			73	66	88, 80	57	76	66	72	42	71
Rural/STS	86			73	68	93, 82	62	72	69	80	46	73
2010												
Urban		68	91		77			90				82
Rural/STS		68	90		77			91				82
2012												
Urban			50			78					60	63
Rural/STS			92			93					62	82
2014												
Urban		65		74	80	90	63	80, 84		76	61	75
Rural/STS		70		84	81	81	72	78, 77		85	65	77
2016												
Urban			64	76			66	78				71
Rural/STS			74	91			72	76				78
2018												
Urban			59			82, 83			61	67	56	68
Rural/STS			71			89, 86			71	82	55	76

Note. Entries show the two-party vote for the Republican Senate nominee cast by southern white respondents living in urban or rural places. Data for special elections are underlined (Mississippi in 2008 and 2018 and South Carolina in 2014). Source: Exit poll data calculated by authors. *M* = Mean.

are samples of voters from all eleven southern states. Of course, in any given election year, only a subset of southern states will have Senate elections.

Similar to Table 5.2, we distinguish between urban and rural/STS white voters and then plot the Republican share of the Senate vote cast by these two groups in Figure 5.7. It is interesting to note a general saw-toothed pattern with large variation in GOP Senate support across election years (incumbency and national conditions most likely contribute to this). Also, the gap in Republican Senate voting between rural/STS and urban voters tends to be more pronounced in presidential elections; and, although in the last two elections (2016 and 2018) the GOP Senate vote declines, if a line were placed over the entire time period (1990–2018), it would show an upward trend.

Across these thirteen elections displayed in Figure 5.7, only twice is the white urban vote cast for Republican Senate candidates higher than the white rural/STS vote: a difference of one percentage point in 2002 and three percentage points in 2006. Otherwise, rural/STS whites are consistently more supportive of GOP Senate candidates than are urban whites. Corroborating the data shown in Table 5.2, there is no discernible difference in the 2010 Republican Senate vote cast by rural/STS and urban white southerners in this midterm, but in the next four election cycles (2012–2018), there is a pronounced gap with rural/STS whites decidedly more supportive of GOP Senate nominees. Despite a dip in the GOP Senate vote in the 2018 midterm—a

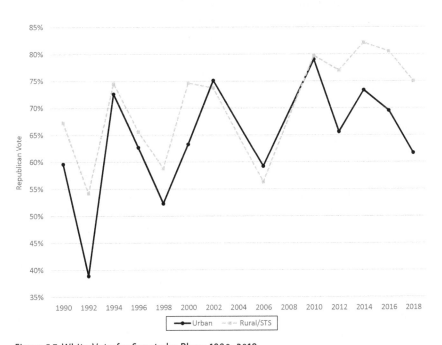

Figure 5.7. White Vote for Senate by Place, 1990–2018

very favorable cycle for Democrats nationally—the thirteen-percentage-point difference in Republican support among rural/STS whites (seventy-five percent) versus urban whites (sixty-two percent) is the second largest for the entire twenty-eight-year period (only higher in 1992, with a gap of fifteen points).

Conclusion

Writing in the 1980s, Earl and Merle Black (1987, p. 285) observed an interesting irony in their examination of southern Senate and gubernatorial elections, which they stated as follows:

> [T]he setting most conducive to Republican gains has appeared more often in the office that is comparatively isolated from national political influences, while the office that is more susceptible to pro-Republican national influences has frequently been immunized through Democratic incumbency.

The former office mentioned in this quote is for governor, and the latter office is for senator. By the 1980s, most gubernatorial elections had been moved to off-years (midterms or odd years); therefore, Republican hopefuls could not reap the electoral benefits of GOP presidential coattails. Also, with respect to Senate elections, the absence of term limits made it very difficult to unseat Democratic incumbents, even in presidential years.

Things have changed considerably since the 1980s. In more recent decades, the GOP has made impressive gains across the board in Senate elections, including contests with Democratic incumbents seeking another term (see Table 5.1 and Figure 5.1). White support for Republican Senate nominees has generally increased among both rural and urban dwellers, but especially in the case of the former group, which historically constituted the backbone of the old southern Democracy (McKee, 2008). In the 1980s Black and Black (1987, p. 290) noted that, particularly in the Deep South states, for Republican contenders to prevail in elections for governor and senator, they had to "depend more on Democratic mistakes, miscalculations, malfeasance, and factionalism than on anything they can do for themselves." This erstwhile bleak electoral picture is now downright rosy for southern Republicans, especially those running for the Senate in Deep South states (the 2021 Georgia Senate runoff contests notwithstanding).

Indeed, the tables have completely turned; now, Deep South Democrats have to hope for Republican errors and good fortune to win Senate contests. This explains how Democrat Doug Jones managed to eke out a victory in Alabama's 2017 special Senate election to replace Republican Jeff Sessions, who vacated his seat to join the Trump administration as US Attorney General.

Doug Jones's Republican opponent was Roy Moore, a twice-removed Alabama Supreme Court justice who was widely reported to have sought out the romantic attention of teenaged girls when he was in his thirties. Still, when all the votes were counted, Jones won the two-party vote by less than 1.7 percentage points! Massive margins run up in the Alabama Black Belt contributed mightily to Jones's win.[6] However, Jones was not as lucky in 2020, when he ran against scandal-free Republican and former Auburn University head football coach Tommy Tuberville (see chapter eleven).

We conclude this chapter with a brief discussion of Table 5.3. The table puts in stark relief how much the southern Senate delegation has changed between the 1990 and 2018 elections. The tight alignment between presidential outcomes and the composition of the contemporary southern Senate is on full display. As mentioned at the outset of this chapter, the nationalization of American politics (Jacobson and Carson, 2020) makes it increasingly rare to witness southern politicians elected to statewide offices who are aligned with the party opposite the winner of that state's most recent presidential contest. However, as shown in Table 5.3, nationalization was far less powerful in 1990. Consider that, prior to 1990, Republican President George H. W. Bush won all eleven southern states in the 1988 election. However, after the 1990 midterm, five southern states had split Senate delegations (Florida,

Table 5.3. The Nationalized Southern US Senate Delegation, 1990 versus 2018

State	Party of delegation in:	
	1990	2018
AL	2 D	Split (1 D, 1 R)
AR	2 D	2 R
FL	Split (1 D, 1 R)	2 R
GA	2 D	2 R
LA	2 D	2 R
MS	2 R	2 R
NC	Split (1 D, 1 R)	2 R
SC	Split (1 D, 1 R)	2 R
TN	2 D	2 R
TX	Split (1 D, 1 R)	2 R
VA	Split (1 D, 1 R)	2 D
South	5 split, 5 unified D, 1 unified R	1 Split, 9 unified R, 1 unified D

Note. The partisan composition of southern US Senate delegations is presented according to the results of the 1990 and 2018 elections (or the outcome of the 2017 special Senate contest in Alabama). D = Democrat; R = Republican.

North Carolina, South Carolina, Texas, and Virginia), five others had unified Democratic delegations (Alabama, Arkansas, Georgia, Louisiana, and Tennessee), and one state had a unified Republican delegation (Mississippi).

In contrast, in 2016, Republican Donald Trump won every southern state but Virginia, and the composition of the South's Senate delegation two years later was almost a perfect reflection of the 2016 presidential results. The exception to a state's Senate delegation in 2018 reflecting the partisan outcome of the last presidential contest was in Alabama where, as discussed, Democrat Doug Jones was the beneficiary of running against a tainted Republican opponent in the 2017 special Senate election.

It would appear that, at least for now, split Senate delegations in the South are less likely because of the lower odds of electorates splitting the partisan vote for president and senator. Nevertheless, if the current trend in favor of greater competitiveness in several southern states persists (e.g., Florida, Georgia, North Carolina, and Texas), more split Senate delegations may return in the near future. Chapter six examines elections for governor, an office more insulated from the pull of national politics (Black and Black, 1987) because of the scheduling of these contests and, more important, because of the nature of the position (Sievert and McKee, 2019). This said, as highlighted by the case of Alabama senatorial contests in this chapter, southern gubernatorial elections have also become notably more hospitable to GOP contenders, and primarily because of the strong shift of rural whites in favor of the Republican Party.

6 The Rural Transformation in Southern Gubernatorial Elections

There is no question that southern Republicans had to make up a lot more ground in contests for governor versus their level of success in Senate elections. Because it is a federal office, campaigns for the Senate have focused more on national issues dividing the major parties. In addition, compared with gubernatorial races, it will always be more convincing when campaigns tie Senate candidates to the positions associated with their national parties (Black and Black, 1987).[1] Southern Democrats, even as their electoral fortunes have waned, still maintain a puncher's chance in contests for governor, because state issues often separate themselves from the polarized politics currently saturating the national environment (Sievert and McKee, 2019).

Another interesting dynamic in southern gubernatorial elections, which likely delayed Republican ascendancy, was the variability of the positions GOP contenders promoted in the wake of the 1960s civil rights movement. For instance, the first Republican to occupy Arkansas's governorship was a northern transplant from one of America's wealthiest dynasties: Winthrop Rockefeller. Rockefeller won his first term in 1966, just a year after passage of the landmark Voting Rights Act (VRA). True to the philosophy of so-called northern "Rockefeller Republicans," Winthrop was a liberal with respect to racial issues, and he cobbled together a winning coalition highly dependent on African American support. Across the other side of Dixie, three years later in Virginia, Republican Linwood Holton also won the gubernatorial contest, and he, too, presented himself as a liberal regarding race relations.

In the immediate aftermath of the civil rights movement, the South was in a state of flux, because so many whites were still Democrats while substantial Black re-enfranchisement also contributed to a surge in Democratic affiliates. By embracing racial equality, at least two of the first southern Republican governors since the days of Reconstruction managed to win office by appealing to Blacks. Hence, in the mid-1960s and 1970s, like many Democrats, some Republicans running for governor also experienced success by constructing biracial coalitions (Bass and De Vries, 1995). This was possible because, in many states, the dominant but slowly declining southern Democracy comprised a complicated and increasingly fractious assemblage of racially conservative rural white populations with a growing segment of Black voters.

Similar to the eventual demise of the national New Deal Coalition (Petrocik, 1981), this Democratic confederation of rural conservative white voters and Blacks in the South could not persist over the long haul (Hood, Kidd, and Morris, 2014). But in the short term, however, some Republican gubernatorial hopefuls were victorious by drawing on the votes of a burgeoning white urban electorate (Bartley and Graham, 1975) that was less threatened by the presence of Black supporters, many of whom still recognized (if increasingly faintly) the receding halo effect of a GOP whose great leader during the Civil War decreed the emancipation of their enslaved ancestors.

By the 1990s, however, the Republican Party no longer had any bankable Black vote to rely on (Black and Black, 2002). And in the case of the GOP's overwhelmingly white base of supporters, rural denizens were gradually becoming the most ardent backers of the party of Lincoln, often surpassing the rate at which urban whites voted Republican in gubernatorial contests. Table 6.1 offers an overview of the Republican share of the two-party vote in races for governor by decade and type of contest, starting in the 1990s. In all gubernatorial contests from 1990 through 2009, the GOP share of the vote held steady with a mean of fifty-two percent. In the past decade, from 2010 to 2019, the Republican percentage of the vote increased to an impressive fifty-six percent. Unlike in Senate elections, where the GOP's strongest boost in vote share came at the expense of Democratic incumbents (see chapter five), in races for governor, the long-term increase in the Republican vote is due to growing support in open seats (a high of fifty-four percent in the 2010s) and contests with a Republican incumbent (a high of sixty percent in the 2010s). Although there were only two contests in the 2010s in which a Democratic incumbent governor sought reelection, the Republican share of the vote was a modest forty-one percent, notably lower than the GOP percentage of the vote in these races in the 2000s (forty-seven percent) and 1990s (forty-six percent).

Table 6.1. Republican Vote in Elections for Governor, 1990s–2010s

Type of race	% Republican share of vote			
	All contests	Republican	Open	Democratic
1990s	52 (31)	58 (10)	51 (12)	46 (9)
2000s	52 (24)	57 (8)	50 (10)	47 (6)
2010s	56 (31)	60 (13)	54 (16)	41 (2)

Note. Data presented in the table show the Republican share of the two-party vote in contested elections; the number of cases by category appears in parentheses. Republican = a Republican incumbent sought reelection; Open = no major party incumbent sought reelection; Democratic = a Democratic incumbent sought reelection.

Translated into seats, there is no question that the southern GOP has become the dominant party in contemporary gubernatorial elections. As Figure 6.1 shows, the percentage of the South's eleven governorships won by Republicans was fifty-two percent in the 1990s, sixty-three percent in the 2000s, and eighty-one percent in the 2010s, which amounts to just under an average of nine offices occupied by GOP affiliates in the most recent decade. The importance of Republican incumbency is evident as GOP governors have accrued considerably more success by decade in comparison with their Republican counterparts contesting open seats or running against Democratic incumbents. Nevertheless, in the 2010s, the most important contests for southern Republicans have taken place in open seats. In contrast to the 2000s, when GOP gubernatorial candidates won only thirty percent of these races, their rate of success in open seats vaulted to eighty-one percent in the 2010s.

In the 2010s, Republicans were shut out in elections with Democratic incumbents, which comports with the fact that their average share of the vote was forty-one percent in these two contests (as mentioned in Table 6.1). In the 2000s, GOP governors boasted a perfect record of winning reelection. In the 2010s, as nationalization continued to creep into contests for governor, North Carolina Republican Governor Pat McCrory most likely had become too ardent in his support of some of the more controversial culture war positions of his party—particularly his vocal backing of the so-called bathroom bill, which

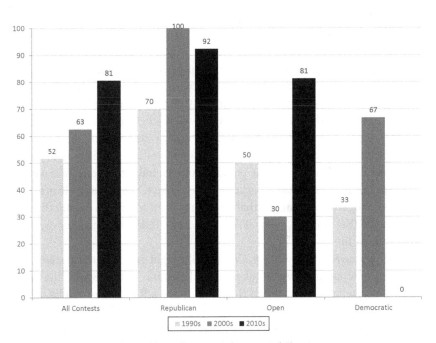

Figure 6.1. Percentage of Republican Seats in Gubernatorial Elections, 1990s–2010s

mandated individuals use the public bathroom matching the sex listed on their birth certificate. In 2016, while Republican Donald Trump won North Carolina's critical fifteen electoral votes by beating Democrat Hillary Clinton with fifty-two percent of the two-party vote, the Democratic Attorney General Roy Cooper won the governorship with a 0.2% margin of victory over Republican incumbent Pat McCrory (Cohen and Barnes, 2017).[2]

County-Level Patterns

We take a dip into Georgia politics to highlight the extent and breadth of the realignment of rural white voters in favor of Republican gubernatorial candidates in the modern South. Of all the southern states, in V. O. Key's (1949) masterful assessment of their political dynamics, Georgia stood out for exhibiting the most pronounced Democratic factionalism tied to a rural-urban division. Out of this geographic split emerged a clear bifactionalism within the Georgia Democratic Party. The political machine with the upper hand was run by Eugene Talmadge.[3] The Talmadge-led faction had the strong backing of rural whites, and this usually was enough to defeat Democratic primary rivals who did not so much stand for a decidedly different agenda, but foremost as an anti-Talmadge coalition.

The more urban anti-Talmadge faction was placed at an acute electoral disadvantage by a unique feature of Georgia Democrats' primary apparatus. In most contests, including for governor, the Democrats utilized a county-unit system (Buchanan, 1997; Key, 1949) similar to the Electoral College. Under this system, the least populated and most rural counties exercised a disproportionate influence because their number of county unit votes were enough to overcome those assigned to more urban and populous counties. In the words of Key (1949, pp. 118–119), "The candidate with the greatest following in the rural areas is almost certainly the winner. Great is the incentive to incite antagonism toward the cities." In the twenty years before the time Key wrote *Southern Politics in State and Nation* (1949, p. 120), no fewer than four Democratic primary candidates for various statewide offices carried county unit-vote majorities while losing the popular vote, including Eugene Talmadge in the 1946 Democratic gubernatorial primary. Hence, there was a clear reason why Talmadge "often bragged that he did not want to carry a county that had a streetcar" (Key, 1949, p. 116) and also why Key subtitled his chapter on Georgia, "Rule of the Rustics."

At the time Key was writing, Georgia, like eight other southern states, had last seen a Republican win a gubernatorial election in the 1870s.[4] The Peach State was also, by far, the last in the South to see a Republican candidate win the governorship in modern times: not until 2002, which was a full decade after runner-up Mississippi opted for Republican Kirk Fordice in 1991. Interestingly, however, in the first post-VRA election of 1966, Republican Howard

"Bo" Callaway came as close as any GOP candidate to winning Georgia's governorship, until Republican Sonny Perdue finally triumphed in 2002 (Bullock and Hood, 2015).[5] The Peach State had a simple popular vote majority provision to win the election. So, despite Callaway winning most of the popular vote in 1966, in addition to his segregationist Democratic opponent Lester Maddox, the presence of former governor Ellis Arnall was enough to deny Callaway a popular vote majority. Short of a majority, under Georgia law, the state legislature voted to determine the winner of the gubernatorial election; not surprisingly, given its overwhelmingly Democratic composition, Lester Maddox was chosen.[6]

Georgia's 1966 gubernatorial election was another instance that pointed to the reality that, in those days, the GOP was much stronger in urban areas. Two years prior, Callaway was one of several Republican Deep South House candidates who benefited from Barry Goldwater's coattails in the 1964 presidential election. Callaway won a congressional seat in the Atlanta area and was widely viewed as a "country club Republican." In the 1960s and 1970s, especially in Georgia, urban upscale country club Republicans were much more prevalent than Republicans residing in the countryside. In the long run, if the Georgia GOP was going to have a breakthrough in gubernatorial elections, then they would have to vastly improve on their performance among the rural white electorate. That is exactly what happened when Republican Sonny Perdue made history in his upset win over Democratic Governor Roy Barnes. In hindsight, the once widely popular Governor Barnes made two costly missteps in his run-up to the 2002 election: (1) He got into hot water with education reforms that rankled Georgia's teachers, and (2) he had the Confederate emblem removed from the state flag. This latter action was a flashpoint for rural white voters, and Barnes suffered his greatest losses in rural sections of the state (Hayes and McKee, 2004). Democrats have been in the electoral wilderness since Perdue reclaimed Georgia's highest office for Republicans in 2002. The current strength of the Georgia GOP in gubernatorial contests is clearly due to the heightened support from rural whites.

A comparison of the 1998 and 2018 Georgia gubernatorial elections puts in stark relief how much stronger rural support for the GOP has become over this twenty-year period. Democrat Roy Barnes comfortably defeated socially conservative Republican Guy Millner in 1998 (fifty-four percent to forty-six percent of the two-party vote). In another open-seat contest twenty years later, Republican Georgia Secretary of State Brian Kemp narrowly defeated former Democratic Georgia House Minority Leader Stacey Abrams (fifty-one percent to forty-nine percent of the two-party vote). Figure 6.2 displays the county-level results of the 1998 race in the map on the left and the 2018 results in the map on the right. As usual, we have classified election

1998   **2018**

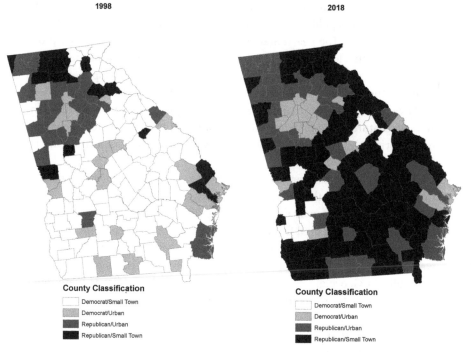

Figure 6.2. County Vote for Georgia Governor, 1998 and 2018

outcomes on the basis of four possible and exclusive categories: (1) Demo-
crat/small-town South (STS), (2) Democrat/urban, (3) Republican/urban, and
(4) Republican/STS.

In the late 1990s, even against a socially conservative Republican opponent, Democrat Roy Barnes gobbled up the vote in the Peach State's rural
counties. Specifically, out of Georgia's prodigious 159 counties (second only
to Texas's 254), in 1998, Barnes won eighty-six percent of the 111 counties classified as STS. Overall, the county-level breakdown of the 1998 Georgia gubernatorial vote was sixty percent Democrat/STS, fourteen percent Democrat/
urban, sixteen percent Republican/urban, and just nine percent Republican/
STS. Contrary to a cluster of Republican/STS counties in northwest Georgia
and a smattering of the same type elsewhere in the state in 1998, in 2018,
Republican Brian Kemp carried eighty-eight percent of the 102 STS counties.
Overall, the county-level distribution of the 2018 vote for Georgia governor
was fifty-seven percent Republican/STS, twenty-five percent Republican/urban,
eleven percent Democrat/urban, and only eight percent Democrat/STS. What
once was a palpable rural-urban factionalism contained within a one-party
Democratic southern state has now become a geographic-based cleavage that

advantages Republicans in the plentiful and sparsely populated counties found throughout the Peach State.[7]

We now move to a set of analyses that demonstrate the Southwide growth in rural support for gubernatorial candidates. As with chapters four and five, Figure 6.3 is based on a simple empirical model that uses county-level data to decompose vote choice by place across time for white southerners. More specifically, the white vote for the GOP in these contests is graphed by decade (1990s, 2000s, 2010s) for urban and STS counties (see Appendix B for model details).[8]

It is interesting to see the lag in rural support, as evident by the higher percentage of Republican voting for governor in urban counties. This said, in more recent decades, rural counties have obviously narrowed the gap. For instance, in the 1990s, the GOP gubernatorial vote cast by whites was 61.4% in urban counties versus 43.5% in rural counties—an eighteen-point difference. In the 2010s, however, the urban-rural margin in Republican gubernatorial voting among southern whites had been reduced to a mere 3.3 points.

County population density is another way to assess changes in white southerners' gubernatorial voting. Here, Figure 6.4 presents the GOP county percentage of the vote cast by southern whites according to density ranging from the tenth percentile (least dense) to the ninetieth percentile (most dense). As in Figure 6.3, the data are plotted by decade; 1990s, 2000s, and 2010s. Partitioning the gubernatorial voting data by decade is revealing of the

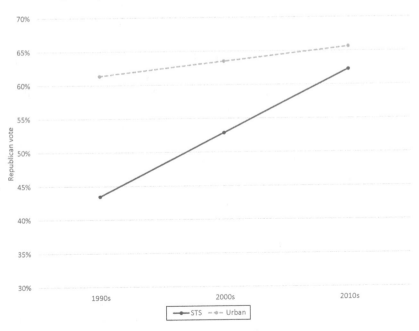

Figure 6.3. White Vote for Governor by Place and Decade

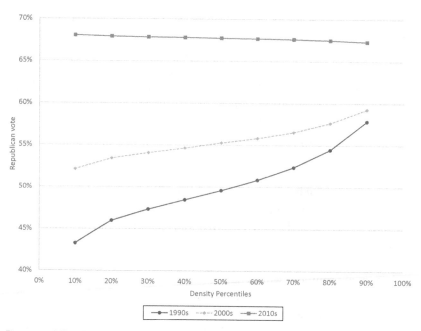

Figure 6.4. White Vote for Governor by Density and Decade

notable changes over the past thirty years in these contests. First, regardless of county density, white southerners have become decidedly more Republican in their voting for governor since the 1990s. Second, the increase in the GOP gubernatorial vote is powered by the surge in rural white support. Consider that, in the 1990s, at the lowest density shown in Figure 6.4 (tenth percentile), the white vote for governor is estimated to be 43.3%, whereas in the densest (ninetieth percentile) counties, the white vote for Republican gubernatorial candidates is a much more substantial 57.8% (a fifteen percentage-point difference). Two decades later, the rural-urban gap in white southerners' gubernatorial voting on the basis of county density has been erased. The plotted data for GOP voting for governor in the 2010s according to county population density is essentially a flat line. In the least dense counties in the 2010s, the white vote cast for Republican gubernatorial contenders is 68.1% versus a 67.3% GOP vote cast for governor among whites in the densest counties.

Cooperative Election Study (CES) Data

Once again, we make use of the CES data, because the CES is a large representative survey with several thousand resident southerners included in any given election cycle. We assess the percentage of the Republican two-party vote cast by whites in southern gubernatorial elections when the county percent STS is set at zero percent, twenty-five percent, fifty percent, seventy-five percent, and one hundred percent. As usual, we split the data according to decade, and because the CES was first administered in 2006, the 2000s consist of 2006 and 2008. This is somewhat incomplete, because three southern states hold their gubernatorial races in odd-year cycles (Louisiana and Mississippi in the odd year following even-year midterms and Virginia in the odd year after the presidential election); hence, there are no CES data for the residents of these states. Also, as mentioned previously, North Carolina is now the only southern state whose elections for governor occur in presidential years. Nonetheless, in the 2000s, this leaves seven southern states holding races for governor in the 2006 midterm (Arkansas, Alabama, Florida, Georgia, South Carolina, Tennessee, and Texas), along with North Carolina in 2008—a very generous sample of white southerners' gubernatorial voting preferences. Similarly, for the 2010s, the CES data include white southerners from the same seven states in 2006 for 2010, 2014, and 2018 and the sample of white North Carolinians for the 2012 and 2016 gubernatorial elections.

On the basis of a fairly simple empirical model of gubernatorial vote choice, Figure 6.5 shows the probability southern whites voted Republican for governor according to the county percent STS, in the 2000s (2006 and 2008) and 2010s (2010–2018).[9] The data for the 2000s reveal no discernible variation in the southern white vote for Republican gubernatorial candidates according to the county percent STS (0.72 Republican at zero percent STS

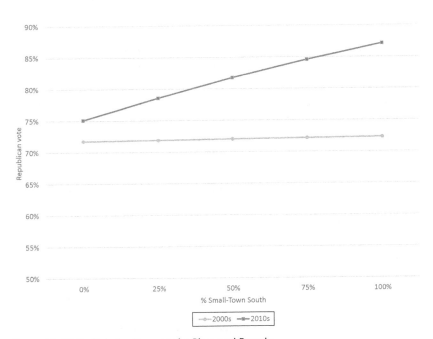

Figure 6.5. White Vote for Governor by Place and Decade

versus 0.72 Republican at one hundred percent STS). The picture drastically changes in the 2010s. In this later decade, there is a clear relationship between more Republican support for governor as the county percent STS increases. At zero percent STS in the 2010s, the likelihood that a white southerner votes Republican for governor was 0.75. Three out of four white southerners selecting the Republican candidate for governor shows, objectively speaking, tremendous support for GOP contenders; but consider that, in one hundred percent STS counties, the white vote for Republican gubernatorial candidates was 0.87. This twelve-point difference in white southerners' support for Republicans running for governor in the 2010s, according to the minimum versus maximum range for county-level percent STS, offers robust evidence of the magnitude and recency of white rural southerners' realignment toward the GOP in America's most salient and important nonfederal office.

Similar to our use of the data displayed in Figure 6.5, we can further verify trends in voting for governor with an examination of the relationship between white support for GOP gubernatorial candidates according to county density. The results shown in Figure 6.6 come from models of the probability that white southerners voted Republican for governor in contested open-seat races, with county density featured as the key explanatory variable. Similar to Figure 6.4, which is based on county-level data, Figure 6.6 shows the propensity of white southerners to cast a Republican vote for governor on the basis of increments in county population density from the tenth percentile (least dense) to the ninetieth percentile (most dense).

Confirming the findings in Figure 6.5, in the 2000s, there was not a relationship regarding the probability of voting for the Republican gubernatorial candidate on the basis of the population density of the county where a white southerner lives. In the least dense counties (tenth percentile) the Republican voting probability is 0.72, as compared with 0.70 in the densest counties (ninetieth percentile). In contrast, the 2010s reveal a pronounced dynamic with respect to the vote for GOP gubernatorial candidates according to county population density. First, the GOP vote for governor in counties at the tenth percentile density goes from 0.72 in the 2000s to 0.84 in the 2010s. This twelve-point increase in support for Republican gubernatorial contenders, found in the least dense counties, is the largest recorded over these two decades. Additionally, in the 2010s, although the GOP gubernatorial vote was always higher compared to what it was in the 2000s, it exhibited an obvious decline as county population density increased. At the highest density (ninetieth percentile) in the 2010s, the 0.71 level of support for the Republican gubernatorial candidate is almost indistinguishable from the number for the corresponding 2000s (0.70 Republican).

In sum, the CES data are illuminating and reliable because of very large representative samples. Despite not having data on residents of the three

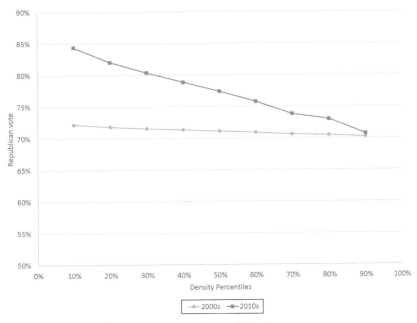

Figure 6.6. White Vote for Governor by Density and Decade

southern states that hold elections for governor in odd years, it remains clear that the strong movement in favor of Republican gubernatorial candidates is being fueled disproportionally by rural white southerners. Many more assumptions have to be made in inferring patterns from county-level data, as we did in the previous section of the chapter. Since we obviously have no need to infer individual behavior with survey data, the findings in Figures 6.5 and 6.6 are more plausible with respect to the changing voting behavior of white southerners according to where they reside. Whether we make the variable of interest (1) the county percent STS or (2) the county population density, our models of white southerners' gubernatorial voting preferences show no variation according to either of these factors in the 2000s. However, in the 2010s, it was true that the percent STS or percent county population density both exhibited a palpable effect on white southerners' likelihood of casting a Republican vote for governor. Support for Republican gubernatorial candidates was much higher in more sparsely populated counties and likewise in those counties with proportionally more STS residents.

Exit Poll Data

We wrap up this chapter with descriptive data on gubernatorial voting from the exit polls conducted nationally and by state. As was the case with the Senate data in the previous chapter, the only state exit polls conducted in the

1990s were for the 1990 elections. Henceforth, there are exit polls for various southern states in every presidential and midterm year from 2004 to 2018. Again, most southern states hold gubernatorial elections in midterm years; North Carolina is the only one with a contest administered in the presidential cycle. Because of their odd-year timing, there are no data for Louisiana, Mississippi, and Virginia. Finally, for the years for which we have exit polls on southern states, only in the 1990 midterm was a poll administered in all seven southern states holding gubernatorial contests.

Table 6.2 shows the percentage of the Republican vote cast by urban and rural/STS whites according to southern state, beginning in 1990 and going up to the 2018 midterm elections.[10] The average of the GOP vote for governor across all states with exit poll data for each election year is provided in the rightmost column in the table. Going back to 1990, for the seven southern states with gubernatorial contests, urban whites voted fifty-five percent Republican versus a sixty percent GOP vote registered by rural/STS whites. Almost thirty years later, in 2018, although the data are from four southern states (Florida, Georgia, Tennessee, and Texas), white support for Republican gubernatorial candidates was much higher: sixty-eight percent in the case of urban whites and seventy-eight percent in the case of rural/STS whites. Further, what also sticks out is that in spite of the elevated support for GOP gubernatorial nominees in 2018, the ten-percentage point difference according to location is the widest margin for the time series. Collectively, southern whites in these four states have never been so inclined to vote Republican for governor, and this is especially true with regard to those residing in rural localities.

In addition to the state exit poll data on gubernatorial voting, we also have data from national exit polls spanning 1990 to 2018. Fortunately, the data are available for every midterm election and all but the 2004 and 2008 presidential elections. Hence, in the case of the Tar Heel State, except for 2004 and 2008, even years in Figure 6.7 show how its white urban and rural/STS electorate voted for governor from 1992 through 2016. For the national exit polls, we simply extracted the subset of voters living in southern states. Another benefit of the national exit polls is the inclusion of voters from all of the seven southern states holding gubernatorial elections in midterm years, which means that, unlike the discussion earlier, here, we can make an apples-to-apples comparison regarding any long-term changes in the pattern of voting in these off-year cycles.

Figure 6.7 displays the percentage of the GOP gubernatorial vote cast by urban and rural/STS white southerners from 1990 to 2018. Singling out North Carolina voters, in 1992, forty-five percent of urban whites voted Republican for governor versus sixty-three percent of rural/STS whites. Almost a quarter century later, in the historic 2016 election of Republican President Donald

Table 6.2. Republican Gubernatorial Vote by State and Location, 1990–2018

Year and location	% Republican share of vote for governor								
	AL	AR	FL	GA	NC	SC	TN	TX	M
1990									
Urban	64	44	41	57	59	86	38	56	55
Rural/STS	62	48	59	52	68	89	44	63	60
2004									
Urban					55				55
Rural/STS					58				58
2006									
Urban			60	74			35	63	58
Rural/STS			66	70			31	70	59
2008									
Urban					62				62
Rural/STS					64				64
2010									
Urban		40	55			71		69	59
Rural/STS		35	68			71		76	63
2012									
Urban					68				68
Rural/STS					76				76
2014									
Urban		65	60	73		78		73	70
Rural/STS		64	70	84		78		84	76
2016									
Urban					61				61
Rural/STS					67				67
2018									
Urban			59	73			66	74	68
Rural/STS			71	83			74	84	78

Note. Entries show the two-party vote for the Republican gubernatorial nominee cast by southern white respondents living in urban or rural places. Source: Exit poll data calculated by authors. *M* = Mean.

Trump, white Tar Heels were markedly more Republican in their gubernatorial preferences. Fully seventy percent of white urban North Carolinians voted Republican for governor in 2016, but this impressive display of GOP support was easily surpassed by rural/STS whites, eighty-one percent of whom backed the losing reelection bid of Republican Governor Pat McCrory.

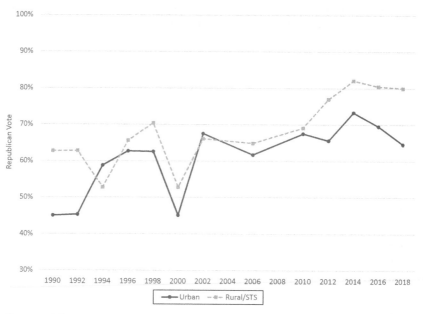

Figure 6.7. White Vote for Governor by Place, 1990–2018

Turning to the data shown for midterm years, growing support for GOP gubernatorial candidates was palpable. The eighteen-percentage point gap favoring greater Republican support among rural/STS voters in 1990 appears to be an outlier until the end of the time series, when again, the difference between urban and rural/STS voting for GOP gubernatorial nominees widened considerably. In fact, in the 1994 and 2002 midterms, white urban voters exhibited greater Republican support for gubernatorial candidates than their white rural/STS counterparts. In 2006 and 2010, versus urban whites, rural/STS whites were only slightly more Republican in their gubernatorial preferences. However, in the past two midterms of 2014 and 2018, the GOP gubernatorial vote disparity according to location was substantial. In 2014, the peak of Republican voting for governor was attained for both rural/STS (eighty-two percent) and urban (seventy-three percent) white southerners. Nevertheless, this place-based gap in Republican voting increased from nine percentage points in 2014 to fifteen points in the 2018 midterms. In 2018, white rural/STS support for GOP gubernatorial contenders was eighty percent, whereas the white urban vote for Republicans seeking the governorship declined eight points since 2014, from seventy-three percent to sixty-five percent.

Our two sources of survey data, the CES and the exit polls, tell a very similar story: regardless of the specific measure of rurality (county percent STS, county population density, or rural/STS setting). In the 2010s, compared with urban whites, rural whites became decidedly more likely to vote Republican in southern gubernatorial elections. This dynamic was evident despite the fact that both groups of voters (rural and urban) substantially increased their overall support for southern GOP gubernatorial candidates in the 2010s relative to the past two decades.

Conclusion

In the 1980s, Black and Black (1987) observed that the Democratic coalition in most of the South was large enough to get their candidates across the finish line in Senate and gubernatorial elections. However, they also voiced a word of caution, because Democratic identification among the white majority electorate was declining; therefore, crossover appeals to independents and a growing Republican constituency had become imperative to stave off the rising GOP. The basic formula for Democratic success was for its candidates to promote a broad mixture of policy positions that included some combination of conservative and progressive views. For instance, Arkansas governor and future President Bill Clinton exemplified this winning Democratic approach: He was tough on crime (e.g., pro–death penalty) but also a proponent of civil rights (appealing to Black voters). The centrist positioning of 1980s Democrats, which cultivated and sustained large biracial voting majorities (Lamis, 1988), has become a liability for the party in more recent election cycles. It is now harder to construct a winning coalition through this centrist approach, because the conservative positioning of the GOP has finally attracted a solid majority of white voters residing in both urban and rural areas.

Speaking of southern Republicans, Black and Black (1987, p. 288) offered a quote by Strong (1971, p. 254), who observed that, "Southern Republicans have a rigid ideology: clean government, sympathy for big business, low taxes, a minimum concern for poor people, and a genteel type of racism . . . they take their ideology seriously. This seriousness prevents them from being flexible enough to broaden their basis of support." In more recent decades, the GOP's positioning has evolved, perhaps mainly with respect to its embrace of populist rhetoric, racial antagonism, and cultural conservatism, which strongly appeals to the values of rural whites, as most vocally promoted by former President Trump. This latest incarnation of the GOP is now a winner throughout most of Dixie. Whereas southern Republicans in the 1980s could not win many gubernatorial contests because of a lack of Black support, the growth of their white base of GOP affiliates is so high now that the absence of Black votes is no longer a hindrance to winning the governorship in most southern states.

Table 6.3 shows the party affiliation of all the governors in the South's eleven states in the immediate aftermath of the 1990 and 2019 elections. The comparison is based on a midterm (1990) and an odd year (2019), because

Table 6.3. The Nationalized Southern Governorship, 1990 versus 2019

| State | Party affiliation of governor | |
	1990	2019
AL	Republican	Republican
AR	Democrat	Republican
FL	Democrat	Republican
GA	Democrat	Republican
LA	Republican	Democrat
MS	Democrat	Republican
NC	Republican	Democrat
SC	Republican	Republican
TN	Democrat	Republican
TX	Democrat	Republican
VA	Democrat	Democrat
South	7 Democrat, 4 Republican	3 Democrat, 8 Republican

Note. The party affiliations of southern governors are presented according to the results of the 1990 and 2019 elections or the party of the current governor in the immediate aftermath of these elections.

most southern gubernatorial elections are held at these times. Almost thirty years apart, there were seven Democratic governors and four Republicans in 1990, compared with three Democrats and eight Republicans in 2019. The prevalence of southern Democrats was, of course, to be expected in 1990, because the party still maintained a considerable advantage with respect to party identification, both in the case of the vast majority of Blacks and a plurality of whites (see chapter eight). In contrast, the altered partisan composition of the South's gubernatorial delegation in 2019 speaks to nationalization; the greater alignment of party on the basis of presidential politics (Hopkins, 2018). In most southern states, because they are deep red at the presidential level, it is assumed that they have Republican governors, and in fact, they do. Likewise, the South currently has one Democratic state, Virginia, which accordingly, had a Democratic governor in 2019. Despite an electoral disadvantage for the party holding the presidency (Prokop, 2021), and not having the advantage of incumbency (the Old Dominion has a one-term limit for governors), Democrats have split the last four gubernatorial contests (2009–2021).

Even in a blue state like Virginia, however, which continues to trend in the Democratic direction, successful Democrats in statewide contests for governor are centrists and, therefore, not nearly as liberal as the party's national brand. The same observation applies to the neighboring state of North Carolina, a political battleground that is shifting in the Democratic direction thanks to substantial demographic changes (e.g., northern in-migration; see Hood and McKee, 2010) that advantage the Democratic Party. The only other state with a Democratic governor in 2019 was Louisiana, which definitely does not track with the partisan changes afoot in the Tar Heel State and in the Old Dominion. No, the Pelican State is now deep red, so one must ask: Why does it have a Democratic governor? There are two reasons that stand out: (1) a tarnished Republican opposition and (2) the importance of performance in a state-level office not as nationalized as a federal position (e.g., Senate and/or House). On the first point, Republican Governor Bobby Jindal was term limited, but his tenure was marred by policymaking that imperiled the health of the Louisiana economy as the state was trying to recover from the Great Recession. Additionally, in the 2015 gubernatorial election, the Democrat John Bel Edwards had the good fortune to find himself in a runoff against Republican David Vitter, who as a US Senator, admitted to extramarital affairs in the DC Madam Scandal. However, after defeating Vitter in 2015, Democratic Governor Edwards managed to win a second term in 2019, principally on the basis of receiving high marks for his performance.

The unusual case of a Democratic governor in deep-red Louisiana speaks to the wider nonpartisan-based leeway afforded governors vis-à-vis senators. For example, in the previous chapter, it was noted that Democratic Senator Doug Jones of Alabama was extremely fortunate to draw as his Republican opponent the scandal-plagued Roy Moore. However, in 2020, facing scandal-free Republican and former Auburn University head football coach Tommy Tuberville meant that Senator Jones was doomed. Let us be clear: We are not claiming that, in Alabama, a Democratic victor in a gubernatorial election thanks to Republican missteps would necessarily go on to win reelection against a scandal-free Republican, but as in Louisiana, the odds of this happening would be greater (ceteris paribus) compared with a Senate contest. Further, we emphasize the importance of performance over partisanship because Democrats have to make greater inroads with a white electorate aligned with the GOP, especially in the case of rural whites, as demonstrated throughout this chapter.

Perhaps two more examples will crystallize why it is now so much easier for Republicans to win gubernatorial elections, even in contexts that are highly competitive and where nominees are not particularly impressive. Referring back to the state exit poll data in Table 6.2, data are shown for the Florida and Georgia gubernatorial elections in 2018. These two contests highlight the built-in advantage that GOP contenders currently have, even though again, both of these states are competitive in statewide elections. To put it bluntly, the two Republican gubernatorial nominees in Florida and

Georgia—Ron DeSantis and Brian Kemp, respectively—were far from out-standing candidates. Indeed, in 2018, they essentially ran as caricatures of President Trump.

In Georgia, Kemp ran a commercial showing him in a pickup truck talking about how he was rounding up undocumented immigrants. In Florida, De-Santis aired an ad showing his wife encouraging their toddler-aged son to "build the wall" with his toy blocks. Unquestionably, this type of unvarnished, ethnically insensitive pandering to anti-immigrant attitudes had a more fa-vorable reception among rural whites than among any other segment of the electorates found in these two neighboring states. Additionally, both Repub-licans drew Black Democratic challengers who were clearly aligned with the more liberal/progressive end of the ideological spectrum. In this context, even with two lackluster GOP gubernatorial nominees, both managed to eke out narrow victories. Of course, more than any other group, Governors DeSantis and Kemp owe their 2018 wins to rural white voters, of whom seventy-one percent backed DeSantis in Florida and a whopping eighty-three percent fa-vored Kemp in Georgia.[11] Just as in V. O. Key's time, the rustics continue to rule, but they now do so on behalf of the Republican Party.

7 Rural Voters in Southern US House Elections

On the eve of the GOP's 1994 takeover of the South's House delegation and, simultaneously, their securing majority control of the US Congress, an article was published in *Social Science Quarterly* titled "The Rise and Stall of Southern Republicans in Congress" (Thielemann, 1992); then, a coauthored book came out with the title *Congress' Permanent Minority? Republicans in the U.S. House* (Connelly and Pitney, 1994). The explanations these authors gave for why Republicans were apparently incapable of becoming the majority party in Congress and also in Dixie, were credible and, in fact, valid at the time. However, the 1994 midterm contests overturned whatever factors had held the GOP in minority status for forty consecutive years in the House of Representatives (Jacobson, 1996) and for an astounding one hundred twenty straight years in the southern states' House contingent (Black and Black, 2002).

Before the 1992 elections, there was indeed scant evidence that southern House Republicans were on the verge of assuming majority status. From 1986 to 1988—three election cycles in a row—the GOP was stalled, holding a third of southern House seats (McKee, 2010); but the electoral playing field was greatly altered in 1992, and a direct reason for this transformation was the disruptive effect of redistricting (Gelman and King, 1994). Among House incumbents seeking reelection, the percentage of redrawn constituents, those new to these Representatives because of redistricting, averaged twenty-five percent, with a median of twenty percent. Hence, most members of Congress (MCs) were seeking another term in 1992 among a substantial district population they had never represented before and with whom they had not, therefore, cultivated a representational relationship. In addition to undermining the incumbency advantage, southern congressional redistricting disadvantaged Democrats in particular, because of the Department of Justice's imperative that line drawers create several majority-minority districts (Bullock, 1995a, 1995b, 2010; Cunningham, 2001), which had the effect of concentrating the most Democratic voters into fewer districts (what is called packing in the redistricting literature) while subsequently making neighboring districts whiter and naturally more Republican on the basis of presidential vote returns (Black and Black, 2002; Hill, 1995; McKee, 2010). In 1990, there were fourteen majority-minority southern congressional districts (twelve percent of 116 districts), and in 1992, there were twenty-six districts in which the white population was under a majority (twenty-one percent of 125 districts).[1]

Starting in 1992, and proceeding for the next two election cycles, southern Republicans netted nine, sixteen, and seven House seats, respectively. In the middle of an ongoing realignment to the GOP (Glaser, 1996), redistricting disproportionally and negatively affected southern Democratic incumbents' re-election bids in 1992 and 1994 (McKee, 2013; Petrocik and Desposato, 1998). Further compounding the problem was that open seats—the most competitive contests, all else being equal (Gaddie and Bullock, 2000)—were much more likely to have been represented by Democrats. Indeed, from 1992 to 1996, there were thirty-nine Democratic open seats versus only fourteen Republican open seats.[2]

Figure 7.1 displays the Republican and Democratic percentages of House seats in the southern congressional delegation from 1992 to 2018. The surge in Republican seat gains between 1992 and 1994 is palpable, and so is the most impressive single-cycle increase over these fourteen elections spanning over a quarter century: the 2010 midterms when Republicans went from fifty-five

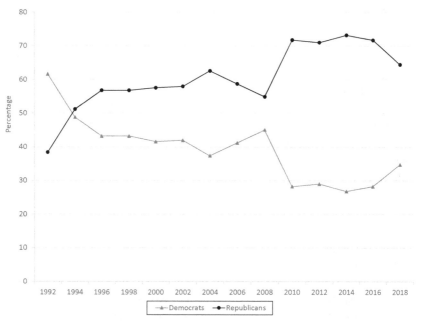

Figure 7.1. Percentage of Republicans and Percentage
of Democrats in Southern House Delegation, 1992–2018

percent to seventy-two percent of the southern House membership. Republican representation in the southern House delegation peaked at seventy-three percent in 2014 and then receded back to a still dominant sixty-four percent in the 2018 elections, when national political conditions clearly broke in favor of the Democratic Party (Jacobson, 2019).

Table 7.1 provides additional detail by showing the number of House Republicans in each southern state delegation from 1992 to 2018. The data indicate, in plain text, a Republican House majority delegation; a Democratic House majority in bold, and an even partisan split where the GOP number appears in brackets. In 1992, Democrats held sixty-two percent of southern congressional districts. Only in the Sunshine State (the most urban in the South) were Republicans the majority, and outside of perfectly balanced bipartisan delegations in Arkansas and South Carolina, the remaining eight southern states had Democratic House majorities. Since 1994, the GOP has held a majority of southern House seats, but the longitudinal changes in partisan composition of individual state delegations exhibit considerable variation. For instance, although the timing of the switch to GOP control varies, five states attaining Republican majorities have remained so ever since (Alabama, Georgia, Louisiana, South Carolina, and Texas). Mississippi, North Carolina, Tennessee, and Virginia have experienced multiple reversals in partisan control from 1992 to 2018. Arkansas goes from an evenly split delegation for the first four election cycles, to majority Democratic for the next five elections and, finally, majority Republican for the last five contests. Nevertheless, widespread Republican dominance is obvious in the later years, including from 2012 through 2016, when all southern House delegations were majority Republican. This streak comes to an end in 2018, when Democrats win seven of Virginia's eleven congressional districts.

So what role have rural whites played in the remarkable ascendancy of southern House Republicans? That is the question addressed at length in this chapter. As documented previously (see chapter three), even for the long period from the 1950s to 1980s when southern Republicanism was fairly equally reflected in rural and urban whites' voting for US Senate and governor, Democrats maintained a stronger grip among rural denizens in House elections where incumbency registered its greatest impact. This dynamic finally unraveled, starting with the 1992 redrawn congressional districts, which unmoored large shares of constituents from their most recent MCs, giving them more incentive to vote for House Republicans within the confines of reconfigured districts that were either open or featured an unfamiliar incumbent (McKee, 2010). As the southern GOP built on its House majority from the mid-1990s through the 2010s, this electoral transformation was, in large part, due to growing and outsized support registered by rural white voters.

Table 7.1. Number of Republicans in the Southern House Delegation, 1992–2018

State	1992	1994	1996	1998	2000	2002	2004	2006	2008	2010	2012	2014	2016	2018
AL	3	3	5	5	5	5	5	5	4	6	6	6	6	6
AR	[2]	[2]	[2]	[2]	**1**	**1**	**1**	**1**	**1**	3	4	4	4	4
FL	13	15	15	15	15	18	18	16	15	19	17	17	16	14
GA	4	7	8	8	8	8	7	7	7	8	9	10	10	9
LA	3	3	5	5	5	4	5	5	6	6	5	5	5	5
MS	0	1	3	**2**	**2**	[2]	[2]	[2]	**1**	3	3	3	3	3
NC	4	8	[6]	7	7	7	7	**6**	5	**6**	9	10	10	9
SC	[3]	4	4	4	4	4	4	4	4	5	6	6	6	5
TN	3	5	5	5	5	4	4	4	4	7	7	7	7	7
TX	9	11	13	13	13	**15**	21	19	20	23	24	25	25	23
VA	4	**5**	**5**	**5**	7	8	8	8	**5**	8	8	8	7	**4**
Total	48	64	71	71	72	76	82	77	72	94	98	101	99	89
Seats	(125)	(125)	(125)	(125)	(125)	(131)	(131)	(131)	(131)	(131)	(138)	(138)	(138)	(138)
Rep %	38	51	57	57	58	58	63	59	55	72	71	73	72	64

Note. Total number of Republican House representatives are displayed for each state's delegation from 1992 to 2018, on the basis of the results in the corresponding year's general election. Numbers in boldface denote a Democratic majority, and bracketed numbers indicate an evenly split delegation (same number of Democrats and Republicans). Rep% = the Republican percentage out of the total number of southern House seats shown in parentheses. Through reapportionment, the southern states gained six House seats in 2002 and seven more in 2012.

Southern House Republican Gains Among
the Rural Electorate: District Data

One of the most striking features of southern politics from the emergence of a GOP presidential opposition in the 1950s up through the 1980s, was the much more gradual electoral success of Republicans in House contests (Black and Black, 1987, 2002; Lublin, 2004; McKee, 2010, 2019; Shafer and Johnston, 2001, 2006; Thielemann, 1992). Simply put, there was a multiple decades-long persistence in white southerners splitting tickets for Republican presidential nominees and Democratic House candidates. Likewise, the abatement of this form of ticket-splitting took years to subside, but it finally has. In the 1990s, white southerners had generally aligned their presidential and House votes under the banner of the same party (Black and Black, 2002; Bullock, Hoffman, and Gaddie, 2005).[3] Nonetheless, because of the South's substantial Black population and a growing non-white electorate, particularly with respect to Hispanics (Odem and Lacy, 2009), the partisan consolidation of white voter preferences did not immediately preclude the presence of split congressional districts. Split districts favor opposite parties for president and House (see chapter three). In the context of southern politics, this has historically meant presidentially Republican districts represented by congressional Democrats. Conversely, same districts refer to those that register election majorities for the same party in presidential and House contests.

Figure 7.2 presents data on the percentage of split districts in the South from 1992 to 2018. Three types of data are displayed: the percentage of all southern congressional districts that are split; the percentage of split Democratic House districts (won by the Republican nominee in the most recent presidential election); and the percentage of split Republican House districts (won by the Democratic nominee in the most recent presidential election). As expected, throughout the time series, split districts held by House Democrats are the most prevalent, peaking at forty-six percent of the Democratic delegation in the 2006 elections. In netting five seats in 2006, southern Democrats were able to score victories in several districts that Republican President George W. Bush carried in 2004. In fact, not only did this kind of partisan overreach, if you will, leave southern Democrats exposed to possibly losing a large share of contests if and when the partisan tide shifted to Republicans (e.g., in 2010), but it also meant that, in 2006, every House Republican represented a district that President Bush also won (no split Republican House districts).

In 2008, another election cycle favoring Democrats (Jacobson, 2009), southern Democrats picked up another five seats. The share of Democratic split districts declined to thirty-four percent, but this remained markedly higher than the eight percent split in Republican House districts. Thus, in 2008, House Democrats had become substantially overexposed, and the reckoning

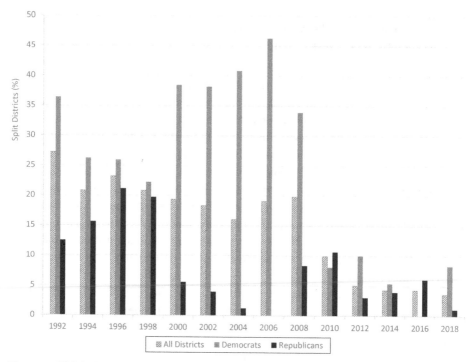

Figure 7.2. All Split Districts and Percentages Held by Democrats and Republicans, 1992–2018

came in the Tea Party–inspired 2010 midterms (Bullock, 2011), when Republicans won back the lion's share of presidentially Republican districts while even managing to net four that the victorious Democratic presidential nominee Barack Obama won in 2008. Clearly though, the 2010 election cycle marked a pivot point, as neither Democratic nor Republican MCs in the South, henceforth, are likely to represent districts favoring the opposite party in presidential elections. In fact, the lowest number of split districts existed in 2018, only five total (under four percent of the southern House delegation): four represented by Democrats and just one held by a Republican.

Figure 7.2 speaks to the nationalization of American politics (Jacobson and Carson, 2020; Sievert and McKee, 2019) in the context of the South. In other words, the long-term process of partisan sorting within the electorate (Abramowitz and Saunders, 1998; Bartels, 2000; Levendusky, 2009) appears to have run its course, so that patterns in voting at the top of the ticket for president are closely mirrored in down-ballot contests such as House elections. This development can be easily and simply confirmed with bivariate correlations of the presidential and House votes. Consider that, in 1992, the correlation between the Republican presidential vote and the Republican

House vote in the South's 125 congressional districts was .684 (p < .001). In 2018, this same relationship among the South's now 138 congressional districts (thanks to reapportionment) was .908 (p < .001).[4]

The rural southern electorate is perhaps the greatest contributor to this nationalization process in House elections (at this point, it should be mentioned that we will be using the Census Bureau's measure of percent rural to draw inferences concerning rurality and southern congressional districts).[5] First, it should be noted that the correlation between the district percent rural and the Republican presidential vote in 1992 was a modest .181 (p < .05). By comparison, the correlation between the district percent rural and the Republican House vote in 1992 was a statistically insignificant (and negative) −.088 (p = .328). Move ahead to 2018, and the correlation between the district percent rural and the Republican presidential vote was .554 (p < .001). Similarly, the correlation between the district percent rural and the Republican House vote in 2018 was now a statistically significant (and positive) .499 (p < .001).[6]

One way to capture the shift of the rural southern electorate in favor of House Republicans is by examining the difference in the percent rural for same and split districts represented by Democrats and Republicans, respectively. The expectation is that, in the case of Democratic MCs, their split (presidentially Republican) districts should be notably more rural than their same districts (presidentially Democratic). With regard to Republican MCs, the reverse is more likely, meaning that their split districts (presidentially Democratic) should be less rural than their same districts (presidentially Republican).

Table 7.2 shows data for the average rural district percent according to split and same, for Democrats and Republicans, and the difference in percent rural among these types of districts for each party.[7] The results are generally in line with expectations: In the case of Democratic House members, from 1992 to 2018, split districts were always more rural than same districts. The greatest rural disparity manifests in 2010, when Democratic MCs lost a whopping twenty-two southern House seats, and their same districts were thirteen percent rural versus fifty-five percent rural in the case of split districts they won. For Republicans, in the first two elections (1992 and 1994), their split districts were actually slightly more rural than their same districts, but this pattern is reversed from 1996 to 2016. In the last election displayed (2018), it appears that the sorting of rural voters is complete, because, regardless of whether the district is same or split, if a Democrat represents it, then the rural percentage is low (an average of eight percent to ten percent rural). In contrast, Republican-held districts are decidedly more rural, whether same or split (thirty percent to thirty-two percent rural). At this point, one caveat is in order: Recall from Figure 7.2 that, beginning in 2010, there are very few Democrats or Republicans who represent split districts.

Table 7.2. Differences in the Rural Percentages for Same and Split Districts by Party, 1992–2018

Party and district	% Rural in year:													
	1992	1994	1996	1998	2000	2002	2004	2006	2008	2010	2012	2014	2016	2018
Democrats														
Same	25	24	21	22	17	13	11	10	14	13	9	9	9	8
Split	46	48	44	45	43	45	44	40	48	55	29	16	None	10
Diff.	-21	-24	-23	-23	-26	-32	-33	-30	-34	-42	-20	-7	N/A	-2
Republicans														
Same	27	31	35	35	35	28	28	28	28	32	29	25	29	30
Split	33	35	31	32	6	9	1	None	16	15	2	5	8	32
Diff.	-6	-4	4	3	29	19	27	N/A	12	17	27	20	21	-2

Note. Diff. = difference; N/A = not applicable.

Just in case Table 7.2 is not sufficient to drive home the point, Figure 7.3 presents the data from the table in graphical form. Displaying the data this way highlights the large differences in the rural composition of Democratic and Republican districts depending on whether they are same or split. Recall that, in 2006 for Republicans and also in 2016 for Democrats, neither respective party had split districts in these years. So, ignoring those two exceptional cases, from 1996 to 2016, the same districts held by Republicans are more rural than their split (presidentially Democratic) districts. Conversely, over these twenty years, the same districts represented by Democrats are much less rural than their split (presidentially Republican) districts. Finally, the last election shown in 2018 reinforces how, despite hardly any split districts held by either party, the few that exist are basically indistinguishable from same districts with respect to the rural percent (less than a two percent rural difference for both Democrats and Republicans).

An additional means to discern the importance of the rural electorate to House Republican gains is documented in Table 7.3. From 1992 to 2018, there were only four election cycles in which southern Republicans experienced a net loss in House seats: 2006, 2008, 2016, and 2018. However, because of substantial redistricting occurring in three states (Florida, North Carolina, and Virginia) for the 2016 House elections, Table 7.3 indicates a net gain of two

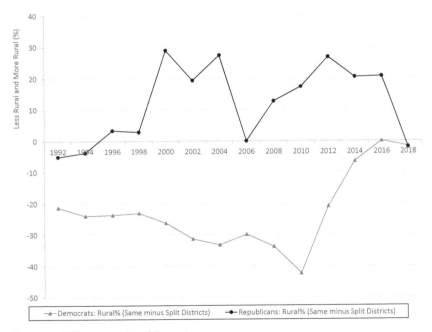

Figure 7.3. Differences in Rural Percentages
in Same and Split Districts by Party, 1992–2018

Table 7.3. Rural Percentages in Republican-Held
versus Newly Won or Lost Districts, 1992–2018

Election year	Republican Held	Newly Won/Lost	Diff.
1992	28 (38)	31 (9)	−3
1994	28 (48)	43 (16)	−15
1996	33 (65)	42 (5)	−9
1998	34 (70)	55 (1)	−21
2000	34 (70)	<1 (1)	33
2002	27 (68)	36 (1)	−9
2004	28 (74)	38 (5)	−10
2006	28 (77)	20 (−5)	8
2008	28 (69)	29 (−8)	−1
2010	28 (72)	39 (22)	−11
2012	27 (88)	48 (5)	−21
2014	24 (97)	34 (4)	−10
2016	28 (96)	26 (2)	2
2018	30 (89)	6 (−9)	24

Note. The displayed rural percentages indicate the average for the total number of districts, which are shown in parentheses. The three election cycles in which Republicans lost seats are shaded gray. Overall, in 2016, House Republicans lost two seats, but a two-seat gain is registered in the table because three states (Florida, North Carolina, and Virginia) were redistricted, and the Democratic gains occurred in newly created open seats. Diff. = difference.

seats for Republicans in 2016 based on the seats the GOP held in 2014. The reason for this discrepancy is that there were three seats in 2016 that were classified as open but newly created through redistricting, and Democrats won two out of three of these contests, which means that in the remaining districts that Republicans held since 2014, they actually picked up victories in two seats that were represented by Democrats in 2014.[8]

Table 7.3 shows (1) the average rural percent in districts Republicans held since the previous election and (2) the rural percent in districts Republicans either won or lost in the current election cycle. For example, in 1992, the average rural percent in districts Republicans won and held before this election cycle was twenty-eight percent. By comparison, in the nine seats Republicans picked up in 1992 (previously held by Democrats), the average rural percent was thirty-one percent. Notice the clear pattern that, with few exceptions, in those election years when Republicans netted seats, the seats they picked up from the Democratic opposition were consistently more rural than the seats Republicans already hold (see the "Difference" column). This was true in

1992, 1994, 1996, 1998, 2002, 2004, 2010, 2012, and 2014. The exceptions to this pattern amount to three districts: In 2000, a Republican won the open contest in heavily urban Virginia District Two (0.6% rural); and in 2016, Republicans won the open seats in Florida Districts Two (forty-nine percent rural) and Eighteen (four percent rural). In contrast, for the three election years in which House Republicans lost seats (2006, 2008, and 2018), on two of these occasions (2006 and 2018) the GOP relinquished fewer rural seats; and on the other occasion (2008), there was essentially no difference in the rural percent for Republican-held districts (twenty-eight percent rural) versus Republican-lost districts (twenty-nine percent rural).

Before we take into account the significance of race with district-level data, Figure 7.4 provides an apt summary of the extent to which the rural southern electorate has migrated in favor of House Republicans. The figure displays the average rural percent at the district level for the entirety of southern House seats for each election from 1992 to 2018 (the dashed line). In addition, the figure shows the average percent rural for all districts held by Democrats and Republicans, respectively, over these fourteen House elections. Nothing short of a partisan sea change has taken place between 1992 and 2018. In 1992, Democrats represented districts with a higher percent rural (thirty-three percent) than those held by Republicans (twenty-eight percent).

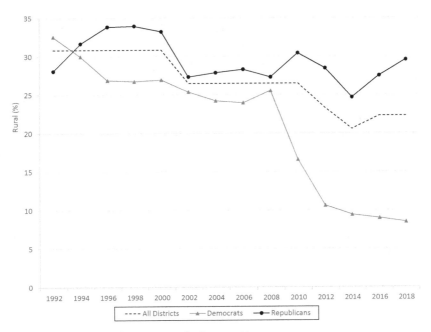

Figure 7.4. Average Rural Percentages for Democratic, Republican, and All Districts, 1992–2018

Over a quarter century later, in 2018, the average rural percent in Democratic districts was eight percent vis-à-vis thirty percent rural in Republican districts. Perhaps most interesting is that even though the average rural percent in southern House districts dropped from thirty-one percent in 1992 to twenty-two percent in 2018, the greatest deviation above the rural average took place in this final election, with Republican-held districts eight percentage points more rural. Conversely, in 2018, the greatest deviation below the southern average district percent rural occurred in Democratic-held districts, which are now fourteen percentage points less rural. Starting in 1994, Republican districts are always more rural than the Southwide average. There is some degree of equilibrium in the rural percentage of Democratic and Republican districts from 1994 through 2000, and then a new stasis held from 2002 to 2008. Then, in 2010, the dam broke as the vast opening of increasingly less rural Democratic-held districts materialized and widened in all subsequent election cycles.

The Newest of the New Southern Politics

In his presidential address to the Southern Political Science Association, Earl Black explained the racial dynamics structuring the outcomes of southern House elections in the 1990s. Black's address was later published in the *Journal of Politics* and titled "The Newest Southern Politics" (1998). With illuminating visual data, later published again and expounded on in similar form in *The Rise of Southern Republicans* (Black and Black, 2002), Black demonstrated, with a series of figures, how the southern House delegation could be delineated on the basis of party and district racial composition. Specifically, by the decade of the 1990s, as southern Republicans secured their majority status in House contests, overwhelmingly white districts (and, hence, white voters) elected Republicans, majority-minority districts elected non-white and usually Black Democrats, and districts with a more even distribution of white and non-white (mainly Black) constituents (biracial coalitions) elected white Democrats.

In 1998, the last election of the decade, the southern House contingent consisted of seventy-one Republicans (sixty-eight whites and three Hispanics) and fifty-four Democrats thirty-three whites, sixteen Blacks, and five Hispanics). White Republicans' districts averaged a seventy-five percent white population. Hispanic Republicans' districts averaged a seventy-one percent Hispanic population. White Democrats' districts averaged a sixty-eight percent white population. Black Democrats' districts averaged a fifty-four percent Black population. Last, Hispanic Democrats' districts averaged a seventy-two percent Hispanic population.[9]

Twenty years later in 2018, the southern House delegation included eighty-nine Republicans (eighty-six whites, two Hispanics, and one Black) and forty-eight Democrats (twenty-two Blacks, seventeen whites, eight Hispanics, and one Asian).[10] It is quite a milestone when the modern southern Democratic Party has a higher number of Black Democrats than white Democrats. White Republicans' districts averaged a sixty-seven percent white population. The two Hispanic Republicans' districts averaged a fifty-one percent Hispanic population. The only Black Republican, Congressman Will Hurd in Texas's Twenty-Third District, had a three percent Black population, but this capacious district, spanning most of the Lone Star State's Mexico border, was also sixty-nine percent Hispanic. White Democrats' districts averaged a fifty-one percent white population. Black Democrats' districts averaged a forty-four percent Black population. Hispanic Democrats' districts averaged a seventy-three percent Hispanic population. The only district represented by an Asian Democrat (Representative Stephanie Murphy's Florida District Seven in the Orlando area) was fifty-eight percent white, twenty-five percent Hispanic, and ten percent Black.

At least on the basis of district racial demographics, the newest southern congressional politics in the late 2010s was more kaleidoscopic than the version analyzed by Black (1998) in the 1990s. With the overall decline in the percentage of non-Hispanic whites, white Republican officeholders now represent districts that are, on average, two-thirds white, which is down from three-fourths white two decades earlier. Representatives who are Hispanic, whether Democratic or Republican, hail from the two southern states with the highest percentage of Hispanics; Texas and Florida. Hispanic Democrats have substantial majority Hispanic districts (averaging over seventy percent Hispanic) primarily located in Texas. In contrast, Hispanic Republicans often win with biracial Anglo (non-Hispanic white) and Hispanic coalitions with relatively lower Hispanic district populations—the small number of these districts are typically located in heavily Cuban American South Florida (the greater Miami area; see Bishin and Klofstad, 2012).[11] White Democrats now represent districts that are, on average, just barely majority white; therefore, these MCs are reliant on the cultivation of multiracial coalitions. Nonetheless, Black Democrats now represent the most multiracial constituencies. As mentioned earlier, not only are Black Democrats' districts plurality Black (average of forty-four percent), but their average district populations are also thirty-one percent white and nineteen percent Hispanic.

Even given the remarkable changes in district demographics cited earlier, it is still possible to simplify the essence of contemporary southern party politics in House contests. In this case, of course, our emphasis is on the rurality of congressional districts. Accounting for race (district percent white) and district percent rural, we can track changes to the southern House delegation. For our purposes, we are interested in parceling southern MCs into three exclusive categories: (1) Republicans, (2) white Democrats, and (3) minority (non-white) Democrats. Taking a page out of Earl and Merle Black's play-book (see Black, 1998; Black and Black, 2002), Figure 7.5 presents four successive snapshots of the southern House delegation as categorized earlier (Republicans, white Democrats, and minority Democrats) for the decennial redistricting elections of 1992, 2002, 2012, and also for the 2018 midterm. Visualization of changes to the southern House contingent is facilitated by superimposing vertical and horizontal bars at the fifty-percent mark for percent white (on the y axis) and percent rural (on the x axis). Recall that, over time, there was a notable decline in the average district percent rural from 1992 to 2018 (see Figure 7.4) and likewise with regard to the district percent non-Hispanic white.[12] This qualification is offered because most southern House districts are not both majority white and majority rural. Nevertheless, the data displayed in Figure 7.5 capture the palpable partisan alterations to the southern House delegation on the basis of party, rurality, and race.

In Figure 7.5, Republicans are denoted by an "x"; white Democrats, with an open circle (○); and minority Democrats, with a solid circle (●). In the 1992 scatterplot, white Democrats are predominant in majority white districts, regardless of the rural percent. Not surprisingly, Republicans are also found in majority white districts, but they are sparse in high-white (more than fifty percent) and high-rural (more than fifty percent) districts, where white Democrats are markedly more prevalent. Most minority (and, specifically, Black) Democrats are located in the lower left, low-white (less than fifty percent) and low-rural (less than fifty percent) quadrant. The outliers are located in the lower right quadrant, which consists of the three Black Democrats who represent high-rural (more than fifty percent) majority Black populations in the southern Black Belt (fifty-five percent rural Mississippi District Two in the Delta; fifty-eight percent rural North Carolina District One in the northeastern part of the state; and fifty-one percent rural South Carolina District Six, encompassing parts of the Midlands, Pee Dee, and tidal Lowcountry).

The 2002 and 2012 scatterplots capture the transition toward rural Republican dominance. For instance, in 2002, it was still the case that a majority of white Democrats (fifty-eight percent: eleven out of nineteen MCs) represent high-white (more than fifty percent) and high-rural (more than fifty percent) districts. However, the growing presence of Republicans in high-white and high-rural districts was evident. By 2012, only one white Democrat held a district in the upper right quadrant: veteran incumbent (first elected in 1996) Mike McIntyre of North Carolina District Seven, situated in the south central part of the state (fifty-two percent rural and sixty-nine percent white).

Finally, by 2018, Republican control of predominantly white and rural southern House districts was overwhelming. In fact, ignoring the district percent white, not a single white Democrat represented a district over thirty percent rural in 2018.[13] And only one white Democrat represented a district

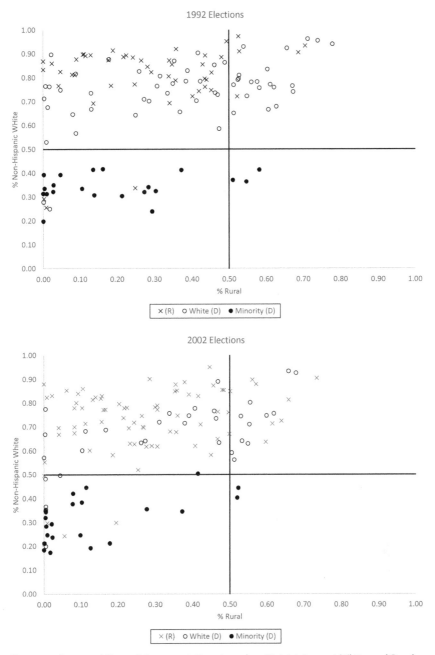

Figure 7.5. Party and Race of Representatives based on District Percent White and Rural

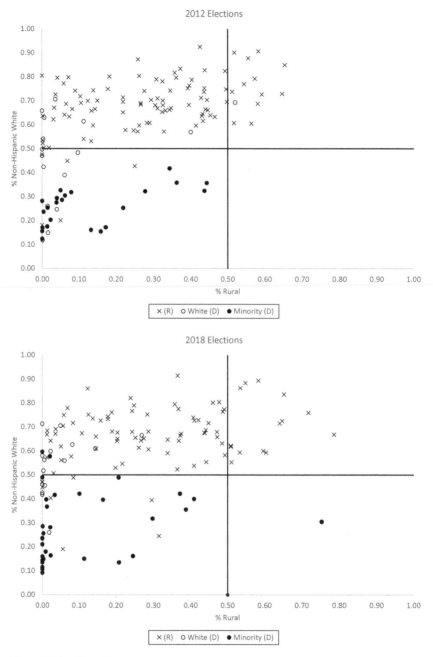

Figure 7.5. (continued)

over twenty-five percent rural: newly elected Abigail Spanberger of Virginia District Seven (twenty-seven percent rural and sixty-seven percent white). In 2020, Congresswoman Spanberger won reelection with fifty-one percent of the two-party vote (rounded up). In the aftermath of the unexpected Republican House gains in the 2020 elections, Representative Spanberger made news for what she said in a leaked Democratic House Caucus call: "If we are classifying Tuesday as a success from a congressional standpoint, we will get [our asses] torn apart in 2022" (Cillizza, 2020).[14] Indeed, from what we have uncovered in this chapter thus far, Congresswoman Spanberger should be thankful to have survived in a southern congressional district that is two-thirds white and has more than one out of four constituents living in a rural area.

Voting Preferences: District Data (1992–2018)

In this section, we present the results of two multivariate models designed to explain voting patterns for GOP House candidates. Unlike the aggregate models in the previous chapters, which relied on counties as the unit of analysis, here, we make use of southern congressional districts from 1992 through 2018. As with the other aggregate-level models already presented, one must exercise caution when making individual-level inferences about white voting behavior. These models, however, do allow us to empirically separate the effects of voting for congressional candidates by time, place, and race. In addition, these models are only one component of our empirical examinations; we also make use of survey data in the remainder of this chapter.[15]

The first model makes use of the district percent rural to assess the role of place in congressional voting behavior. We expect that, over time, the white House vote for Republican candidates should be positively related to the rural composition of congressional districts. The percent rural by district ranges from zero percent to seventy-nine percent. For example, Georgia's Democratic Fifth District located in the heart of Atlanta, and long represented by civil rights hero John Lewis (first elected in 1986) until his passing on July 17, 2020, is zero percent rural. At the other end of the spectrum, Mississippi's Republican First District, situated in the northeast corner of the state and represented by Trent Kelly (since 2015), is seventy-nine percent rural, currently the most rural district in the South. The model results are presented graphically in Figure 7.6. The figure displays the estimated white Republican congressional vote by district type (urban vs. rural) and according to redistricting cycle (1992–2000, 2002–2010, and 2012–2018).

Across the three plotted time periods, the percentage of the GOP House vote in rural districts rose monotonically at a much steeper rate than that found in urban districts. In the first time period from 1992 to 2000, GOP voting in rural and urban southern congressional districts is essentially the same,

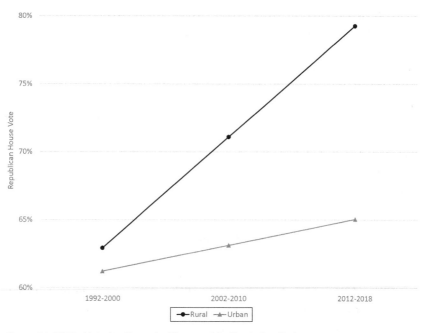

Figure 7.6. White Vote for House by Place and Redistricting Cycle

sixty-three percent and sixty-one percent, respectively. Over time, however, the disparity in the Republican House vote between rural and urban districts continued to widen. In the next time period, 2002 to 2010, the estimated GOP vote share in a rural district rose to seventy-one percent, compared with sixty-three percent for an urban district—an eight-point difference. By the end of the time series, from 2012 to 2018, the rural-urban GOP voting divide stood at fourteen points, with the Republican vote in rural districts at seventy-nine percent, compared with sixty-five percent in urban districts. Looking at things from a different perspective, in just over twenty-five years, Republican voting for US House candidates in rural districts increased by sixteen points. By comparison, over the same period of time, GOP congressional voting in urban districts rose only four points.

The next model substitutes logged population density by district for percent rural as our chief indicator of place. Again, our goal is to study the effects of place, time, and race on congressional voting patterns from 1992 through 2018. The horizontal axis in Figure 7.7 plots logged population density using values from the tenth through the ninetieth percentiles.[16] The three lines graphed across these density values represent the estimated white Republican House vote by congressional redistricting cycle. Unlike the percent rural in a district, population density should be inversely related to the level of Republican voting. In other words, districts with lower density levels should

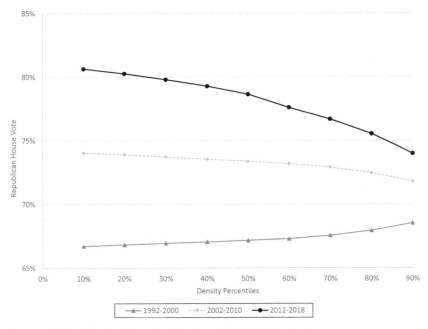

Figure 7.7. White Vote for House by Density and Redistricting Cycle

see more support for the GOP as compared with districts with higher density levels. As an example, Virginia District Seven in the 1992–2000 cycle falls into the tenth percentile for density. This district occupies the southwest corner of the state—a heavily rural area within the Old Dominion. At the other end of the scale, Texas District Eighteen in the 2012–2018 cycle is in the ninetieth percentile. This district is located in Harris County and includes downtown Houston.

Figure 7.7 shows hardly any relationship between district-level population density and voting for GOP House candidates for both 1992–2000 and 2002–2010, as evidenced by the horizontal lines for these time periods. In the 1992–2000 time period, districts in the tenth percentile had an estimated vote share of sixty-seven percent Republican, as compared with sixty-nine percent for districts in the ninetieth percentile. Hence, higher density districts during this time period were actually just slightly more likely to exhibit support for GOP congressional candidates—the opposite of our hypothesized relationship. Nevertheless, the inverse relationship between density and Republican vote share does appear in the next time period (2002–2010). The estimated GOP vote share for districts in the tenth percentile is seventy-four percent, compared with seventy-two percent for those in the ninetieth percentile. Again, however, the two-point difference across the range of the density measure is negligible. For the 2012–2018 time period, the expected relationship finally materializes. In this most recent period, the difference in the estimated share of the Republican vote is now seven points, eighty-one percent for districts in the tenth percentile versus seventy-four percent for districts in the ninetieth percentile.

Finally, another notable finding from Figure 7.7 involves the asymmetric increase in levels of GOP House support over time (comparing the 1992–2000 period with the 2012–2018 period); specifically, the fact that this increase is much more pronounced in lower density districts. For example, in districts at the tenth density percentile, the estimated Republican House vote increased from sixty-seven percent to eighty-one percent—a positive and substantial increase of fourteen points. In contrast, on the other end of the scale, districts in the ninetieth density percentile only saw a five-point increase over this same span of time, with the Republican House vote going from sixty-nine percent to seventy-four percent.

Voting Preferences: CES Data (2006–2018)

We make use of the Cooperative Election Study (CES) to assess white voting preferences in southern House elections from 2006 through 2018. The CES is well suited for this purpose, as each individual respondent can be located within their respective congressional district. Using these survey indicators allows us to add specific contextual data related to place, including the district-level percent rural and logged population density.[17] In this way, we can analyze the behavior of the individual within the district-specific context where they reside.

The analyses are subset to include only non-Hispanic white respondents voting in two-party contested House races. We specify two models that both use a binary dependent variable in which a value of one indicates a vote for a Republican House candidate and a value of zero a vote for the Democratic candidate. One set of models uses percent rural as the place-based contextual measure and a second model uses logged population density. The models also include a variable for decade (2006–2008 for the 2000s and 2010–2018 for the 2010s) and an interactive term to separate the effects of place by time.

The following figures translate the model results into the predicted probability of voting for a Republican House candidate (Hanmer and Kalkan, 2013). Figure 7.8 plots the likelihood of a white southerner voting for a GOP House candidate on the basis of decade and the district percent rural. In this model, voting Republican should be positively associated with higher levels of district ruralism. Looking at the line representing the 2000s (2006–2008 elections), one can see that the probability of voting Republican in a zero percent rural district is 0.59, as compared with 0.63 in a seventy-five percent rural district. The difference between these two extremes is a modest four percentage points. In contrast, the plotted line for the 2010s (2010–2018 elections) is

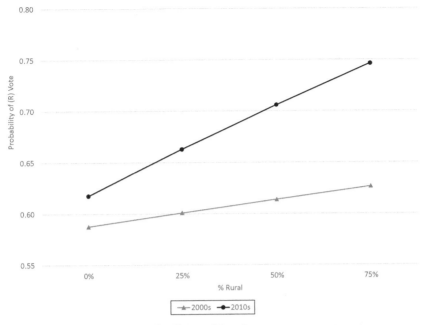

Figure 7.8. White Vote for House by Place and Decade

much steeper, an indication that GOP support among rural voters is more pronounced in this later time period. Now, the probability difference in GOP House voting between a zero percent rural district and a seventy-five percent rural district is thirteen percentage points, 0.62 versus 0.75. Although Republican voting increased across time in both urban and rural districts, this trend was obviously much more pronounced in rural areas. For a wholly urban district (zero percent rural) the increase in GOP House voting amounted to only three percentage points, whereas across the same time period, a maximum rural district (seventy-five percent rural) saw a twelve-point increase in support for Republican congressional candidates.

Figure 7.9 examines white southerners' Republican House voting with respect to district population density. Predicted probabilities are plotted across values of population density ranging from the tenth to the ninetieth percentile for elections occurring in the 2000s (2006–2008) and the 2010s (2010–2018). Here, we expect density to be inversely related to the probability of voting for a Republican congressional candidate. That is, as density increases, which is a proxy for urbanization, GOP House support should decline. Looking at Figure 7.9, one can see that this is exactly what happens. Individuals residing in districts located at the ninetieth percentile in the first time period have a 0.57 probability of voting Republican, compared with a 0.62 probability for individuals located in a district in the tenth percentile. Thus, the

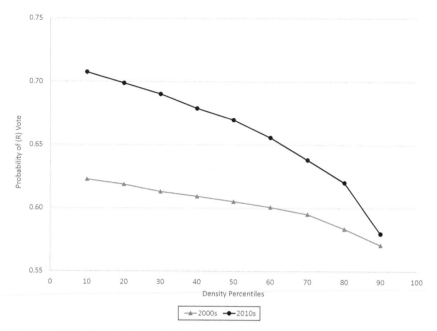

Figure 7.9. White Vote for House by Density and Decade

difference in the probability of voting Republican in House contests across values for density, at 0.05, is modest in the 2000s.

In the 2010s, however, the difference in GOP House voting on the basis of district density becomes quite pronounced. During this decade, an individual in a district in the tenth percentile for density would have a 0.71 probability of voting Republican, compared with a 0.58 probability for an individual residing in a district in the ninetieth density percentile. Visually, the chief pattern of note is the large chasm that opens up across the two time periods with regard to the Republican House preferences of voters in low- and high-density districts. Whereas white voters in districts falling into the ninetieth percentile for density only saw a 0.01 increase in the probability of voting Republican (from 0.57 to 0.58), those in the lowest density districts (tenth percentile) saw a nine-point increase (from 0.62 to 0.71) over the same time span.

Voting Preferences: Exit Poll Data (1992–2018)

In this brief and final section documenting white rural voting preferences in southern House contests, we take a look at exit poll data. Unlike the previous two sections that control for important factors influencing vote choice, here, we examine Republican voting for the US House absent controls, with South-wide exit poll data on urban whites and whites classified as rural/ STS by virtue of living in a rural community or a city with fewer than fifty thousand inhabitants. In short, the descriptive exit poll data should track the pattern of rising rural white support for southern House candidates, even in the absence of routine controls for incumbency and two-party contested races.

Figure 7.10 shows the percentage of the Republican vote cast by rural/STS and urban whites from 1992 to 2018. Again, without any controls for the type of House contest, the long-term pattern of growing white rural support for GOP House candidates is obvious. In 1992, the GOP House vote for rural/STS and urban whites registered in the fifty-percent range (fifty-seven percent for rural/STS whites and fifty-one percent for urban whites). Differences in Republican House voting among rural/STS and urban whites are often minimal and/or ephemeral, until after the 2010 midterms, an election cycle with a commensurate and substantial increase in Republican voting over the 2008 contests (nine percentage points for urban whites and eleven percentage points for STS whites). Since 2010, rural/STS whites are always more Republican in their House vote than urban whites, and the former group's support for GOP House candidates never drops below the seventy-percent range (it did for urban whites in 2018). Despite 2018 being a favorable election cycle for House Democrats, reflected in the decline in Republican House voting exhibited by both rural/STS and urban whites, the nine-point gap in greater GOP House support among rural/STS whites is the largest for the entire time series.

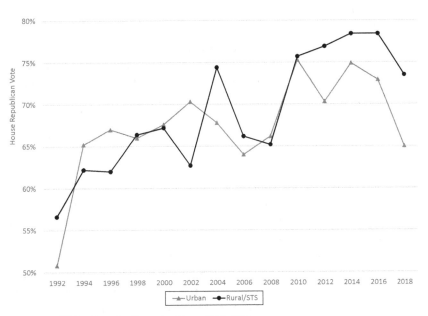

Figure 7.10. White Vote for House by Place, 1992–2018

Conclusion

As we documented in previous chapters, in the most high-profile statewide contests for president, Senate, and governor, from the 1950s through the 1980s, there was not much variation in the voting behavior exhibited by rural and urban white southerners. Both groups were markedly more supportive of Republican presidential nominees than they were of GOP senatorial candidates or Republicans vying for southern governorships. It was not until the 1990s that rural whites' voting for Republicans in these aforementioned contests started to exceed that demonstrated by their urban white counterparts; and as the split-level alignment of presidential Republicanism and "Democratic darn near everything else" narrowed, and then eventually closed (Mc-Kee, 2019), the historical pattern of rural whites' greater fealty to Democratic House incumbents (see chapter three) also withered away.

Beginning in 1992, a confluence of dynamics hastened Republican ascendancy in southern House elections (McKee, 2010) and, in the process, eventually moved rural white southerners firmly into the camp of the GOP. First, redistricting registered an uneven and highly disruptive effect on the electoral status quo. Redrawn congressional boundaries aided minority Democrats running in newly drawn majority-minority districts and also Republicans contesting neighboring districts that were now whiter and consequentially more presidentially Republican. Overall, white Democrats were on the losing end of southern congressional redistricting, because the biracial coalitions that had fueled their victories were broken apart by the creation of majority-minority districts. With lower minority populations as a direct result of redistricting, many of these white Democrats chose retirement, rendering their seats more competitive in open races. Or, these white Democrats sought reelection in more hostile terrain thanks to a high percentage of redrawn constituents more inclined to cast Republican votes for formidable challengers in these reconfigured districts made electorally promising according to the Republican presidential vote.

Further compounding the problem for the Democratic Party in southern House elections was the reality that white southerners had been realigning in favor of the GOP for decades, dating all the way back to Eisenhower's 1950s Republican presidential breakthrough. Hence, by unmooring many of these white constituents from the grip of southern Democratic incumbency, redistricting had become a catalyst for Republican House gains in the early part of the 1990s (Petrocik and Desposato, 1998). Moving beyond the tremendous contribution of redistricting to the rise of southern House Republicans (Black and Black, 2002), like the rest of the nation, the long-term process of partisan sorting further undermined the potency of incumbency as it fell victim to nationalized American politics. As Jacobson (2015) has shown, whereas incumbency was once worth a double-digit advantage over one's opponent, it now yields a paltry electoral dividend of a few percentage points. These days, with minimal deviations, as the presidential vote goes, even accounting for incumbency, so goes the vote for the House.

In this gradual—indeed, multiple generations-long—partisan sorting dynamic (Green, Palmquist, and Schickler, 2002), in the South, rural white southerners are the ones who have moved the farthest yet albeit slowest, in their realignment to the Republican Party. Indeed, even as the GOP consistently registered disproportional gains in more rural districts starting in 1992, it was not until the Republican wave election of 2010 that the permanent division between urban congressional Democrats and rural Republicans was finally consecrated. Since 2010, it has been exceedingly rare to find a southern Democrat who represents a majority white constituency with a rural electorate comprising over twenty-five percent of the district population. Most GOP-held congressional districts now contain an outsized portion of rural constituents, with the white segment of this electorate routinely voting Republican anywhere from the low to high seventy-percent range (depending on the metric for rurality). In sum, contemporary Republican hegemony in southern House elections rests on a bedrock of rural white voters.

8 Survey Says? Rural Whites' Changing Party Identification

It would be nothing short of amazing if the patterns documented and assessed in the previous four chapters did not comport with evidence of palpable gains in Republican affiliation among rural white southerners. It is commonly understood that a generally stable attitude, like the psychological attachment to a political party (Campbell et al., 1960), considerably lags behind the short-term action of casting a vote for a particular candidate (Fiorina, 1981). In the setting of American politics, nowhere has the actual disconnect between party identification and vote choice been more pronounced than in the southern states.

With its characteristic split-level alignment of Republican superiority in presidential politics and Democratic dominance in the remaining contests, lasting from the late 1960s through the 1980s (Black and Black, 1987; Lublin, 2004), southern politics observers often spoke of *Dixiecrats*, voters who preferred Republican nominees for president but remained true (most of the time) to state and local Democrats running in all other down-ballot races (see chapter three). This persistent pattern of voting behavior is all the more impressive, as the term *Dixiecrat* dates back to the single 1948 presidential election, when legions of white southerners voted for the Dixiecrat/States' Rights Democratic Party nominee Strom Thurmond instead of Democratic President Harry Truman because of the latter's embrace and advocacy of Black civil rights (Frederickson, 2001; Key, 1949; see also chapter one). Therefore, for decades, in the minds of most white southerners, the party brands of the national and state/local parties were quite differentiable. In short, many white southerners, particularly those in the rural South, were comfortable voting for more conservative Republican presidential contenders while remaining faithful to their Democratic affiliation in voting for state and local Democratic nominees (who were more conservative than the post-1960 civil rights national Democrats; Rohde, 1991).

The pronounced ticket-splitting pattern of presidential voting for the GOP and Democratic voting in other offices (e.g., president versus House; McKee, 2010) led scholars to investigate whether this behavior meant that some southerners exhibited split partisanship: identifying with one party at the national level and either expressing political independence or an opposite partisan allegiance at the state level. For instance, Hadley (1985) examined the party identification of Louisiana state convention delegates (Democrats in 1982 and Republicans in 1983) and supplemented these data with evidence from five southern states (Alabama, Florida, Louisiana, North Carolina, and Texas) in the mass-level Comparative State Elections Project (CSEP) survey administered in 1968.

Given the prevalence of top-of-the-ticket voting for Republicans and a greater affinity for down-ballot Democrats, in line with expectations, Hadley (1985) discovered that, at an elite level (Louisiana state convention delegates) and among the mass electorate (data from the subset of southerners in the 1968 CSEP), split partisanship was a much more frequent phenomenon among those who identified as national Republicans and as independents or Democrats in state politics. Hadley (1985, p. 259) found that twice as many Democratic delegates to the 1982 Louisiana state convention were split partisans (12.5%) versus the percentage of Republican delegates to the 1983 Louisiana state convention who claimed to be split identifiers (6%). Likewise, with the 1968 CSEP data, among southern respondents who initially identified themselves as Democrats, according to their affiliation at the national and state levels, 13.3% were split Democrats, whereas 4.6% of Republican identifiers were split Republicans on the basis of their affiliation with the major parties at the national and state levels. Among just the Louisiana CSEP sample, there were 15.3% split Democrats and only 2% split Republicans (Hadley, 1985, p. 265).[1]

It is fortuitous, but admittedly coincidental, that Louisiana also happens to be one of three southern states (Florida and North Carolina are the other two) that provides voter registration data according to race and party affiliation. Further, among these three states, Louisiana's data are easily the most publicly accessible. On the other hand, we should note that, according to the 2010 census, at seventy-three percent urban and twenty-seven percent rural, Louisiana was the fifth most urban southern state (McKee, 2019, p. 205). Thankfully, however, within the Pelican State, its sixty-four parishes offer considerable variation on the basis of our frequently utilized urban/small-town South (STS) classification scheme. In the progression of Louisiana maps that follow, we show how the political scene has changed between 2007 and 2019; first, on the basis of the share of whites who register as Republicans as opposed to something else (Democrats or other parties) and, second, according to the electoral success of gubernatorial candidates in parishes that are either urban or STS.

Figure 8.1 displays the percentage of white Republican registration (out of all white registrants) by Louisiana parish in quartiles for 2007. The share of the white Republican registration is based on the following quartiles: first = 0–24.5%, second = 24.6–29.9%, third = 30.0–35.05%, and fourth = 35.06–100%. It is evident that, in 2007, the GOP had more party adherents in terms of

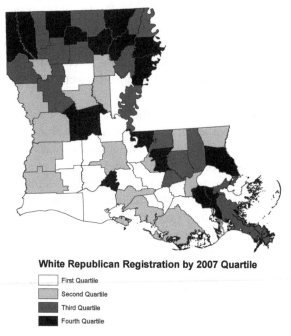

White Republican Registration by 2007 Quartile

☐ First Quartile

▨ Second Quartile

▤ Third Quartile

■ Fourth Quartile

Figure 8.1. Louisiana Parish-Level White
Republican Registration by Party in 2007

voter registration, in the northern part of the state. There are also some high white Republican registration parishes surrounding New Orleans, but it is generally the case that these numbers are much lower in the southwest quadrant of Louisiana, which happens to be Cajun country (Parent, 2006).

Retaining the same quartiles from 2007 for a dozen years later in 2019, Figure 8.2 shows the massive increase in the share of the white Louisiana electorate that is registered as Republican. On the basis of the registration quartiles from twelve years prior, in 2019, there was just one parish (Orleans) with less than twenty-five percent of whites registered with the GOP. In addition, only the neighboring St. Bernard Parish also had a share of white registered voters affiliating with the GOP that was under thirty percent. All of the remaining Louisiana parishes in 2019 had white registered populations that exceeded thirty percent Republican, and fifty-eight out of sixty-two of them are in the highest quartile, on the basis of the 2007 data (>35.05% white Republican registration). Indeed, this means that out of Louisiana's sixty-four parishes, in 2019, over ninety percent were in the highest white Republican registration quartile on the basis of the data from twelve years prior. Remarkably, in 2007, there were zero parishes that had a majority of whites registered as Republican; in 2019, there were twenty parishes whose white population

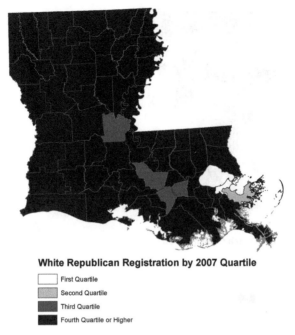

White Republican Registration by 2007 Quartile

☐ First Quartile

▨ Second Quartile

▨ Third Quartile

■ Fourth Quartile or Higher

Figure 8.2. Louisiana Parish-Level White
Republican Registration by Party in 2019

had a majority registered with the GOP. In short, the map in Figure 8.2 tells a powerful story of how far the white population of Louisiana has moved in favor of the GOP, and in a fairly short span of time.

Sticking with 2007 and 2019, which are both years in which gubernatorial elections took place in Louisiana, we take an additional step to examine the distribution of the two-party vote according to whether a parish is urban or STS. In 2007, four years after he lost to the Democrat Kathleen Babineaux Blanco, the Republican and Indian American Bobby Jindal won fifty-four percent of the total votes cast and, hence, avoided a runoff contest in an open primary election with a dozen candidates. Twelve years later, in 2019, the Democratic incumbent Governor John Bel Edwards won a second term, prevailing in a runoff with fifty-one percent of the vote against the Republican Eddie Rispone.[2]

Figure 8.3 presents a map of Louisiana in the 2007 gubernatorial election that classifies each parish into our familiar exhaustive categories: Democrat/ "Small Town South" (STS), Democrat/urban, Republican/urban, and Republican/STS. The shading of the map follows the aforementioned parish classification order from lightest to darkest. When the Republican Bobby Jindal won the Louisiana governorship in 2007, he carried fifty parishes; exactly half were

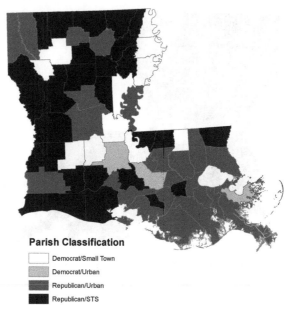

Parish Classification

- Democrat/Small Town
- Democrat/Urban
- Republican/Urban
- Republican/STS

Figure 8.3. Parish Vote for Louisiana
Governor in the 2007 Election

urban (39.1%), and half were STS (39.1%).[3] The Democratic vote attained a majority in fourteen parishes, three of which were urban (4.7%) and eleven were
STS (17.2%). Twelve years later, when Governor Jindal's successor, Democrat
John Bel Edwards, won a second term in 2019, his Republican opponent in the
runoff contest won majorities in forty parishes. The relatively greater con-
centration of Louisiana's larger urban population (e.g., Orleans Parish-New
Orleans, East Baton Rouge Parish-Baton Rouge, and Caddo Parish-Shreveport)
speaks to the fact that Governor Edwards only carried twenty-four parishes
and still won.

Figure 8.4 shows a map of the 2019 gubernatorial runoff election between
the Democrat Edwards and the Republican Rispone. The general partisan
pattern of the vote at the parish-level in 2019 is quite similar to that in the
2007 election. Nevertheless, the pattern of GOP support in rural parishes
comes through in the latter contest. As mentioned previously, in 2007, twenty-
five parishes (39.1%) were Republican/urban, and another twenty-five were
Republican/STS. Although, in percentage terms, there was a slight drop in
the share of Republican/STS parishes in 2019 (twenty-four instead of twenty-
five in 2007), at 37.5%, this was a strong plurality compared with twenty-five
percent Republican/urban (sixteen parishes), 18.8% Democrat/urban, and 18.8%
Democrat/STS (twelve Democratic-won parishes apiece for each location
category).

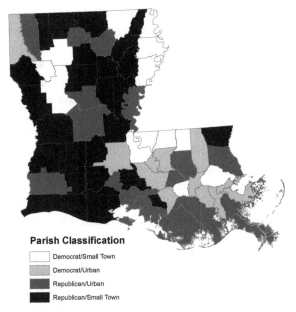

Parish Classification

☐ Democrat/Small Town

▨ Democrat/Urban

▨ Republican/Urban

■ Republican/Small Town

Figure 8.4. Parish Vote for Louisiana
Governor in the 2019 Election

The Louisiana example is an insightful account of the shifting alignment of rural southern whites to the GOP. The availability of detailed registration data on race and party identification made such an examination possible, but for the remainder of the chapter, survey data are evaluated to show South-wide alterations in the partisan allegiance of rural whites. As usual, it warrants displaying the changes among this electorate alongside what has happened to urban whites. Because the previous four chapters covering high-profile elective offices make it apparent that rural whites are most responsible for the contemporary success of Republican candidates, we expect that it is also the case that their rate of affiliation with the GOP has accelerated the most in recent years.

American National Election Studies (ANES) Data

As noted earlier in the book, the ANES Cumulative Data File (CDF) stops providing the place variable data after the 2000 election. However, after 2000, with the exception of 2008, the individual time series studies include place variable data. Hence, the rural/urban variable can be accessed for 2002, 2004, 2012, and 2016. Recall that the ANES no longer conducted surveys in midterm cycles after 2002. Making use of the seven-point party identification scale, as is commonly done because the vote preferences of weak partisans and independent leaners are usually not much different (Keith et al., 1992), the latter group will be classified as partisans in the ANES data presented in the following text. Thus, strong, weak (not so strong), and independent leaners are all treated as partisans.

The long time series allows us to partition the ANES data into decades, starting in the 1950s (1952–1958) and ending in the 2010s (2010–2016). Combining the data according to decade enables us to have samples large enough to have some confidence in long-term changes to party identification. Figure 8.5 shows the percentage of southern Republican identifiers among rural whites and urban whites from the 1950s to 2010s. The general pattern of party identification highlights some significant short-term dynamics unfolding among the broader pattern of Republican ascendancy in the American South. Initially, in the 1950s, the last period that falls under the Democratic Solid South, less than twenty percent of rural and urban whites were Republican adherents.

The next two decades of the 1960s and 1970s are intriguing because of the different identification patterns of rural and urban whites. In the 1960s, the GOP grew mainly because of its appeal to urban whites, thirty percent of whom were identifying as Republicans versus twenty-two percent of rural Republican identifiers. In the 1970s, the pattern of Republican identification reversed so that more rural whites were aligned with the party (thirty-one percent Republican), compared with their urban white counterparts (twenty-five

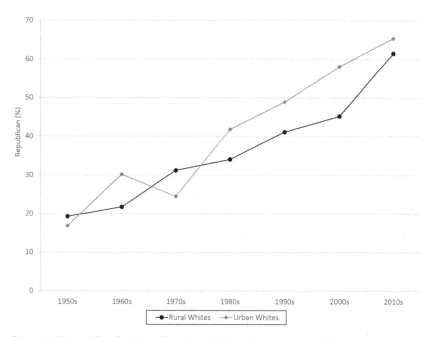

Figure 8.5. Party Identification of Rural and Urban Whites, 1950s–2010s

percent Republican). There seems to be little question that this development reflects the fact that the surging numbers of Black Democratic identifiers after passage of the 1965 Voting Rights Act (Campbell, 1977) made rural whites more uncomfortable in maintaining their ancestral allegiance to the southern Democracy. After the 1970s, however, the rise of Ronald Reagan rebranded the GOP to be more palatable to urban whites, particularly the party's emphasis on upscale conservatism, with its almost unassailable faith in free markets (Black and Black, 1987).[4] From the 1980s through the 2000s, urban whites were notably more Republican than rural whites, but both groups kept increasing in their affiliation with the GOP. Finally, in the 2010s, there was a veritable surge in rural white Republicanism so that the percentage of GOP adherents according to place was no longer statistically distinguishable.

It is useful to illustrate the long-term trends in Republican identification among rural and urban white southerners (as shown in Figure 8.5), but a more complete picture is captured when the other side of the ledger, Democratic identification, is also accounted for. Table 8.1 shows the percentage of rural and urban whites who identified as Republicans and Democrats in the South by decade from the 1950s to 2010s.[5] The data in the table also highlight differences in party identification for the first four decades (1980s versus 1950s) and last three decades (2010s versus 1990s). This distinction is made because urban Republicanism was more prevalent in the first four decades, whereas rural Republicanism has proven comparatively more robust in the last three decades, especially in the 2010s. Finally, the table displays percentage point differences in Republican and Democratic identification, respectively, among rural and urban white southerners ("R-U"), and when these differences are significant, they are denoted by an asterisk indicating $p < .05$.

Rather than repeat the earlier discussion regarding Republican identification in Figure 8.5, we found, instead, that the differences in party identification by place warrant attention in Table 8.1. Hence, as more urban whites were aligned with the GOP in the 1960s, it follows that significantly more rural whites remained Democrats (sixty-nine percent versus fifty-six percent). However, in the 1970s, when southern dealignment (the movement toward political independence) was rising to its highest levels (McKee, 2019), rural whites were now significantly more Republican than urban whites, but there was no significant difference in the percentage of Democratic identifiers. Further, when significantly more urban whites affiliated with the GOP in the 1980s (forty-two percent versus thirty-four percent), it remained true that there was not a significant difference in the share of rural and urban whites aligned with the Democratic Party. Considering the differences in identification patterns by place for the 1980s versus the 1950s, urban whites exhibited a ten-percentage-point greater shift to the GOP (25), compared with their rural white neighbors (15). Conversely, the decline in Democratic identification

Table 8.1. The Remarkable Partisan Transformation of the Southern White Electorate on the Basis of Location, 1950s–2010s

Location	1950s–1980s					1990s–2010s			
	1950s	1960s	1970s	1980s	'80s–'50s	1990s	2000s	2010s	'10s–'90s
Republicans									
Rural	19	22	31	34	15	41	45	62	21
Urban	17	30	25	42	25	49	58	65	16
R-U	2	-8*	6*	-8*		-8*	-13*	-3	
Democrats									
Rural	76	69	52	50	-26	45	42	28	-17
Urban	77	56	55	46	-31	38	32	29	-9
R-U	-1	13*	-3	4		7*	10*	-1	

Note. *The difference between rural and urban white southerners (R-U) is significant at $p < .05$. All data were compiled by the authors from the American National Elections Studies (ANES). Data from 1952 through 2000 are from the ANES Cumulative Data File. Data after the 2000 election are from individual ANES time series studies for 2002, 2004, 2012, and 2016. The ANES has never publicly released data for the place variable for the 2008 election. As for decades, all available data apply to each decade as follows: 1950s = 1952–1958; 1960s = 1960–1968; 1970s = 1970–1978; 1980s = 1980–1988; 1990s = 1990–1998; 2000s = 2000, 2002, and 2004; and 2010s = 2012 and 2016. As noted previously, the ANES terminated midterm election surveys after 2002. In the 1980s, the difference in the percentages of rural and urban Democrats just escapes statistical significance, $p = .0527$ (two-tailed). Independent leaners are classified as partisans according to the party toward which they lean (e.g., independent-leaning Republicans are considered Republicans). Percentages are based on the total number of Democrats (including leaners), Republicans (including leaners), and independents (pure). Percentages were rounded up to the nearest whole number.

was five percentage points greater for urban whites (–31) versus rural whites (–26).

For the next two decades after the 1980s, urban Republicanism was more impressive than the relatively slower rural embrace of the GOP. Specifically, in the 1990s and 2000s, urban white southerners were significantly more Republican than rural white southerners, and the latter were significantly more Democratic. In the first decade of the new millennium, the rural/urban party identification divide peaked, as rural whites were ten percentage points more Democratic (forty-two percent versus thirty-two percent), and urban whites were an impressive thirteen percentage points more Republican (fifty-eight percent versus forty-five percent). However, in the 2010s, rural Republicanism finally caught up, surging from forty-five percent in the previous decade to sixty-two percent. Among urban whites, they also once notched a seventeen-point jump in GOP identification, but it happened between the 1970s and 1980s.

Rural Republicanism is clearly at the forefront of the GOP's most recent success in southern politics. In a comparison of the 2010s with the 1990s, advances in GOP identification have been greater by five percentage points in the case of rural whites (21 versus 16). With respect to the decline in Democratic affiliation between the 2010s and 1990s, it was a notable eight percentage points greater among rural whites (–17 versus –9). In sum, the ANES data, parceled by decade and dating back to the mid-twentieth century, reveal that it is finally the case that rural Republicanism has achieved parity with urban Republicanism. However, just as the passage of time showed that vigorous two-party competition in southern elections was a temporary phase on the way to GOP ascendancy (Bullock, 2017), it also appears that, because rural whites are now stronger supporters of Republican candidates, their alignment with the GOP should continue to outstrip that of urban whites.

Cooperative Election Study (CES) Data

The more recent coverage of the CES surveys, commencing in the 2006 midterms and offering much larger samples, should give us an even better sense of the contemporary patterns in white southerners' party identification on the basis of location. As with the ANES data, we classify the independent leaners in the CES as partisans according to the major party with which they identify more closely. Before turning to possible differences in Republican affiliation among urban and rural whites, Figure 8.6 displays the percentage of Democratic, Republican, and independent identifiers for the CES samples of white southerners from 2006 to 2018. There is not a lot of movement across categories over these dozen years. Nevertheless, in 2006, the share of Republicans was fifty-three percent, and it increased to fifty-nine percent in 2018. The percentage of Democrats went from thirty-five percent in 2006 to twenty-nine

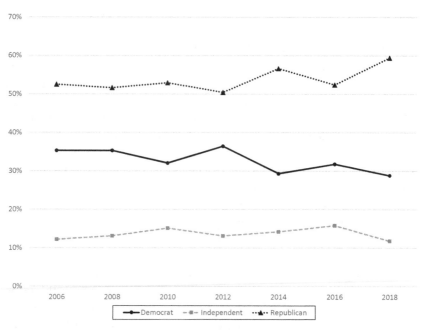

Figure 8.6. Southern Whites' Party Identification, 2006–2018

percent in 2018. Finally, despite some movement in certain election cycles (such as 2016, when sixteen percent of white southerners were independents), in both 2006 (the start of the time series) and 2018 (the end of the time series), independents accounted for twelve percent of white southerners.

Once again, given the uptick in Republican identification at the end of the CES time series and the attendant decline in Democratic affiliates, it is expected that increasing Republicanism among rural white southerners is most responsible for this development. Using the urban and STS binary classification scheme (for details, refer to chapter two), Figure 8.7 confirms this expectation. From 2006 to 2012, there is hardly any difference in the percentage of white southerners identifying as Republicans according to whether they reside in urban or STS settings. After 2012, however, in 2014, 2016, and 2018, respectively, the GOP affiliation gap favors STS white southerners over their urban white neighbors by two, six, and ten percentage points. Furthermore, despite the Republican affiliation difference between STS and urban white southerners being greatest in 2018, the percentage of GOP adherents is highest for both groups in this year: Fifty-eight percent of urban whites are Republicans versus sixty-eight percent of STS whites identifying with the GOP.

Just as we used the CES data in previous chapters to assess Republican voting by decade and with two measures of rurality (county percent STS and county density percentile), we can perform a similar analysis with regard to

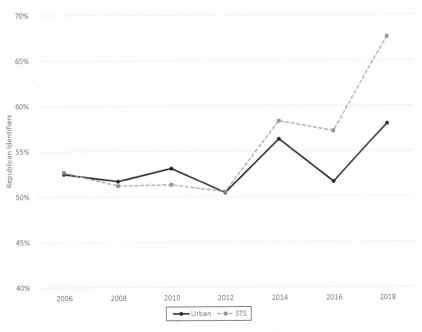

Figure 8.7. Southern White Republicans by Place, 2006–2018

the percentage of Republican identifiers.[6] First, the CES data are partitioned by decade so that 2006 and 2008 represent the 2000s and 2010–2018 comprise the 2010s. On the basis of what Figure 8.7 revealed, we already know that splitting the CES data this way will provide a more conservative estimate of differences in GOP partisanship according to place, as palpable disparities materialize after 2012. Nonetheless, by including the last three election cycles (2014, 2016, and 2018), the 2010s should exhibit more pronounced differences in Republican affiliation, depending on where white southerners reside.

Figure 8.8 arrays the percentage of Republican white southerners in the 2000s and 2010s according to the county percent STS: zero percent, twenty-five percent, fifty percent, seventy-five percent, and one hundred percent STS. Starting with the CES data from the 2000s, going from zero percent STS to one hundred percent STS, the percentage of Republican identifiers increases from a relatively modest 50.9% to 54.5%. In contrast, the 2010s CES data show that GOP affiliation is 51.5% at zero percent STS and increases to 60.5% at one hundred percent STS. Thus, the rise in GOP adherents across the maximum range of percent STS is 3.6 points in the 2000s versus a much more substantial nine points in the 2010s.

Similarly, in Figure 8.9, the two decades of CES data can be presented according to the percentage of white southerners affiliated with the Republican Party based on county population density; ranging from the tenth percentile

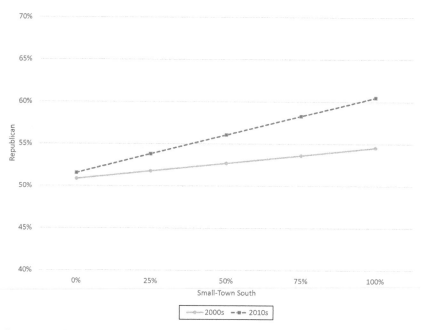

Figure 8.8. White Republican Identification
by Percent Small-Town South (STS) and Decade

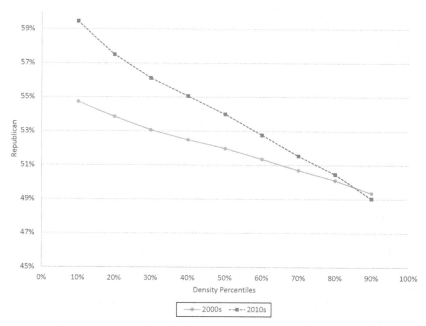

Figure 8.9. White Republican Identification by Density and Decade

to the ninetieth percentile, with the expectation that GOP identification declines as county density increases. In the 2000s, at the tenth-percentile density, Republican identification was 54.7% and dropped to 49.4% in a county at the ninetieth percentile; a 5.3-point disparity. By comparison, in the 2010s, Republican affiliation was 59.5% in a county at tenth-percentile density, but GOP adherents were reduced to forty-nine percent in a county at ninetieth-percentile density. Hence, the difference in the percentage of Republican identifiers across the range of county density (from the tenth to the ninetieth percentile) practically doubled in the 2010s (10.5 points), compared with the 2000s (5.3 points). Using the same measurement of party identification for the CES data, but with much larger samples than the ANES, we find that the most recent election cycles highlighted the disproportionally greater forward movement of rural white southerners to the GOP.

Exit Poll Data

Unlike the CES and ANES, exit polls simply ask whether a voter is a Democrat, Republican, independent, or something else. In other words, many independents probably lean toward one of the major parties, but this cannot be determined. Thus, this simpler three-point[7] party identification scale, which does not account for partisan intensity, undercounts substantial numbers of voters who state they are independents but routinely behave as partisans (e.g., with respect to their vote choice; see Keith et al., 1992). Regardless, we can still make use of exit poll data to determine whether there is any evidence of a trend in the Republican identification of rural/STS white voters. Similar to our findings in previous chapters, there is an unfortunate gap in the administration of state-level exit polls. In 1990, there were eight southern states with exit polls, but it was not until a decade later, in 2000, that state-level exit polls were conducted again and only in three states (Florida, Georgia, and Virginia). However, starting in 2004, at least some of the southern states had exit polls administered from that year through 2018, in midterm and presidential cycles.

Table 8.2 displays the percentage of white voters who claimed to be Republicans in state-level exit polls conducted in southern states, starting in 1990 and ending in 2018. Additionally, the far-right column averages the percentage of Republican identifiers across all of the states with exit poll data shown for a given election year. Going down each column for an individual state makes it evident that Republicanism has consistently grown in most states whether a voter is urban or rural/STS. Indeed, in the most recent elections, for several states (such as Alabama, Florida, South Carolina, Texas, and Virginia), the difference in GOP identification depending on whether a voter is urban or rural/STS is essentially negligible, and in the Palmetto State, urban voters have identified as more Republican by seven percentage points in 2016.

Table 8.2. Republican Identifiers by State and Location, 1990–2018

Election year and place	AL	AR	FL	GA	LA	MS	NC	SC	TN	TX	VA	M
1990												
Urban	36	22	40	44			45	53	40	46		41
Rural/STS	23	20	51	26			40	44	31	32		33
2000												
Urban			45	55							45	48
Rural/STS			57	40							43	47
2004												
Urban	66	41	46	60	55	66	56	60	48	60	54	56
Rural/STS	68	37	47	54	53	72	54	66	47	55	46	55
2006												
Urban			57	57					50	51	49	53
Rural/STS			51	53					37	50	42	47
2008												
Urban		39	41	49	57	73	40	59	33	49	41	48
Rural/STS		39	40	59	57	73	46	57	35	51	53	51
2010												
Urban		37	40		52			63		53		49
Rural/STS		30	52		65			61		50		52
2012												
Urban	60		41			71	45				45	52
Rural/STS	58		51			71	47				40	53
2014												
Urban		40	44	55	57	74	45	65		52	50	54
Rural/STS		43	57	62	62	68	50	56		58	45	56
2016												
Urban			44	56			42	63		55	48	51
Rural/STS			51	62			46	56		67	50	55
2018												
Urban			48	59		72			51	54	43	55
Rural/STS			47	74		75			63	55	41	59

Note. Entries show the percentage of white respondents identifying as Republican in urban or rural places. STS = small-town South. Source: Exit poll data calculated by authors. *M* = Mean.

In contrast, for the most recent election years with available data, other states such as Arkansas, Mississippi, North Carolina, and Louisiana show a modest but real gap indicating that, compared with urban voters, rural/STS voters are more aligned with the Republican Party. Further, in 2018, two states—Tennessee (12 percentage points) and Georgia (15 percentage points)—exhibited double-digit differences in the share of rural/STS voters versus urban voters who identified with the GOP. Finally, in 1990, among the eight southern states with exit poll data, the mean percentage of Republicans was forty-one percent for urban voters and thirty-three percent for rural/STS voters. Almost three decades hence, in the six southern states with exit poll data in 2018, fifty-five percent of urban voters identified with the GOP, and fifty-nine percent of rural/STS voters considered themselves to be Republicans.

Finally, we can extract the subset of southern white voters from the national exit polls dating back to 1990 and terminating in 2018. With the national exit polls, although the sample sizes vary on the basis of the relative population of a state, there are samples of voters from all eleven southern states in midterm and presidential cycles continuously from 1990 to 2018. This means that Figure 8.10 allows for apples-to-apples Southwide comparisons regarding the percentage of Republican affiliated white voters who are urban or rural/STS. Except for 1998, from 1990 to 2002, the percentage of Republican urban voters exceeded the share of Republican rural/STS voters. Admittedly,

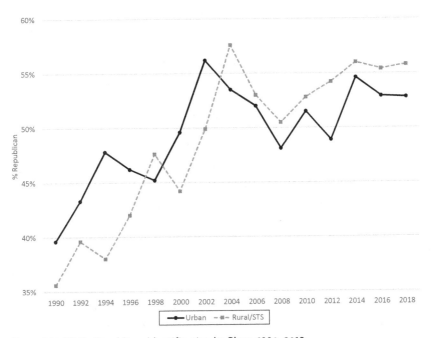

Figure 8.10. White Republican Identification by Place, 1990–2018

the difference in the percentage of Republican identifiers is not very large, but from 2004 to 2018, in every presidential and midterm election, the percentage of rural/STS voters who are Republicans exceeds the corresponding percentage among urban voters.

It is interesting that, on the basis of the three-point party identification scale, Republican affiliation peaks for urban white southern voters (at fifty-six percent) in 2002 and for rural/STS white southern voters (at fifty-eight percent) in 2004. Nonetheless, the overall gains in Republican identification since 1990 are substantial. In the case of urban white voters, forty percent were Republicans in 1990, whereas fifty-three percent of this group affiliated with the GOP in 2018. Likewise, thirty-six percent of white rural/STS voters were Republicans in 1990, whereas in 2018, fifty-six percent of this group identified as Republican. The onward march of southern Republicanism is impressive, particularly in the case of white voters residing in rural/STS communities.

Conclusion

With the exception of Georgia (Springer, 2020), in 1948, every white southerner would have needed to attain the age of twenty-one to vote in the 1948 presidential election. These youngest voters in 1948 would be ninety-three during the 2020 presidential election cycle. Obviously, these nonagenarians constitute a miniscule percentage of the South's current electorate. In other words, there are hardly any Dixiecrats still alive today. They have been replaced by several younger generations of white southerners who are markedly less likely to split their tickets, and even fewer who would still profess being split partisans depending on their affiliation with the major parties at the national versus state level. From the 1980s through the 2000s, most of the leading survey data, regardless of the specific measurement, show that urban white southerners were more aligned with the GOP. However, in the second decade of the latest millennium, there has been a surge in the percentage of rural white southerners who affiliate with the Republican Party. On the basis of the impressive increase in rural whites' Republican voting for president, Congress (House and Senate), and governor, the acceleration of this group's allegiance to the GOP was anticipated.

The current demographic trends in southern politics strongly suggest that Republican identification among urban whites will subside, whereas it should persist and even continue to grow among many, if not most, rural whites. This expectation rests primarily on the policy emphases of the major parties, which are repeatedly reinforced by the slowly churning coalitional makeup of Democratic and Republican supporters (Green, Palmquist, and Schickler, 2002; Grossmann and Hopkins, 2016). In the early days of the 2020s, it is becoming increasingly apparent that the southern GOP is growing its appeal among rural whites by championing racial and social conservatism along with economic populism (Prysby, 2020; also, see chapter twelve for more discussion of this development). With southern Republicans emphasizing policies, beliefs, and values that most closely mesh with the attitudes and opinions held by rural whites, recent election results reflect a widening vote division, as rural whites exhibit the greatest support for GOP candidates, whereas their urban white neighbors are shifting toward the Democratic opposition (Morris, 2021). The next chapter takes another, and perhaps deeper, dive into assessing contemporary changes in the party affiliation of white southerners on the basis of rurality—something we can do thanks to high-quality surveys conducted in a handful of southern states.

9 More Evidence

Rural Voters in Four Southern States

Up to this point, the bulk of the evidence for tracing and assessing the rural Republican realignment in the modern South has been of a systematic and collective kind, with relatively limited emphasis placed on changes transpiring in certain states. Because the Southwide pattern of long-term rural white advancement in favor of the GOP is established and undeniable on the basis of the analyses presented in previous chapters, here, we are able to offer more detailed accounts of political changes in four southern states: Arkansas, Mississippi, Tennessee, and Texas. It is now clear that a regional pattern of secular realignment transpired for most of the multiple-decades-long movement of rural white southerners into the Republican Party, and then this shift hastened in the 2010s. Nevertheless, by looking closer at a handful of southern states, it is possible to discern considerable variation in rates of rural Republicanism.

Sometimes data availability makes choices for you, and this is true with respect to the four states analyzed in this chapter. These states were selected because all four, with Tennessee somewhat of an exception (we will explain), have surveyed their residents for lengthy periods reaching into the 2010s. Specifically, for the purpose of tracking the Republican identification of rural and urban whites, we relied on the Arkansas Poll (1999–2020), the Mississippi Poll (1984–2012), and the University of Texas/Texas Tribune Poll (2008–2020). For Tennessee, our data come from two different surveys with a notable gap in between, the University of Tennessee Poll (1990–1996) and the Vanderbilt Poll (2012–2018).[1]

According to 2010 census data, at the state level, Mississippi (fifty-one percent rural) and Arkansas (forty-four percent rural) are the two most rural states in the South. At the other extreme, Texas (fifteen percent rural) is the second most urban (least rural) southern state after Florida (nine percent rural). Tennessee (thirty-four percent rural), coincidentally, happens to fall in the middle of the pack (ranked six out of the eleven southern states) with respect to its percentage of rural denizens.[2]

In line with previous chapters, we begin this one with a presentation of broader (non-place-based) patterns of recent changes in Republican electoral strength in these four southern states. Next, we offer brief case studies of each state as the electoral context has altered with regard to the political behavior of the rural electorate. Then we display maps in tandem that bookend the earliest gubernatorial election in the 1990s with the latest occurring in the 2010s. Apart from Mississippi, the county-level changes in gubernatorial voting patterns on the basis of place are palpable and transformative. Finally, we show the time series for rural and urban white Republican identifiers on the basis of the survey data sources mentioned earlier. We conclude with some informed speculation about what the latest political changes in these states can tell us about where they are headed with respect to the extent of two-party competition in the 2020s.

David's Index for Arkansas, Mississippi, Tennessee, Texas, and the South

David's Index is an efficient measure for gauging party strength/competitiveness in electoral politics (see David, 1972). There is more than one measure, but we present only the data for what is the Composite B Index: an average of party performance comprising three equal parts for governor, Senate, and House elections. We present data on the percentage of the Republican vote calculated for the averaged combination from these three offices. For instance, for any given election cycle, we computed the mean share of the GOP vote out of all votes cast, in House races, gubernatorial contests, and Senate elections. Next, the GOP portion (out of all votes cast, not just two-party votes) was averaged for each office, and then these three averages were combined to determine the final index.[3] David's Index has been used in various publications, including several that specifically examined long-term changes in southern party politics (e.g., Hood, Kidd, and Morris, 2004, 2014; Lamis, 1988, 1999; McKee, 2010, 2019).

One caveat is worth mentioning before proceeding further with displays of David's Index of GOP electoral competitiveness. Because we computed the Republican index on the basis of all votes cast, not just ballots marked for Republicans and Democrats (if two-party contested), GOP strength is somewhat consistently understated, as there are many instances of third-party contenders siphoning some votes from the major party candidates (e.g., Libertarian nominees in the South are quite prevalent in House races, and they typically draw support from a small segment of otherwise Republican voters). However, there are also instances in which GOP strength is overstated because of the absence of two-party competition, a much more prevalent occurrence in House races than in senatorial or gubernatorial contests.

Figure 9.1 displays David's Index of Republican electoral strength in bar columns from 1990 to 2018 for Arkansas, Mississippi, Tennessee, Texas, and also the entire South as a relevant point of comparison. The state data are arrayed alphabetically and shaded from darkest to lightest gray, starting from left to right with the Arkansas column and ending with the South column.

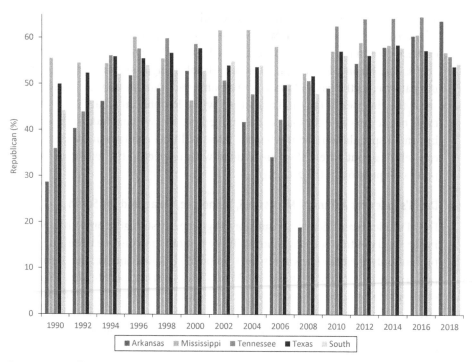

Figure 9.1. David's Index for Arkansas, Mississippi,
Tennessee, Texas, and the Entire South, 1990–2018

The beginning entries for the GOP indices in 1990 demonstrate notable variation in Republican competitiveness across the four states. For instance, Arkansas has an underwhelming GOP electoral presence, with the Republican
index clocking in at less than thirty percent. Tennessee is the next least Republican state, with a GOP index of thirty-six percent. Only Mississippi registers its Republican electoral strength at greater than fifty percent (fifty-six
percent in 1990). Texas is just barely below fifty percent Republican (49.9%),
and in 1990, the Southwide GOP index is forty-four percent.

   After 1992 and through 2008, there was evidence of a cresting pattern, as
Republican electoral strength initially ascends and then curves back downward. Of course, this pattern is variable depending on the state, but given the
favorability of national conditions for the Democratic Party in 2006 and
2008, it is not surprising that the GOP index lost electoral strength in those
cycles. Indeed, the Natural State exhibited this cresting pattern best, as the
GOP index generally made gains from 1992 to 2000 and then endured consistent and considerable decline until bottoming out at nineteen percent in
2008. The feeble electoral performance of the Arkansas GOP in 2008 was due
to the fact that junior Democratic Senator Mark Pryor had no Republican

opponent in his first bid for reelection; the senior senator was Democrat Blanche Lincoln, the governor was Democrat Mike Beebe, three of the state's four House members were Democrats, and none of them drew a Republican challenger.[4] In other words, the data do not deceive; in 2008, the Arkansas GOP constituted a pathetic political opposition.

The Tea Party–fueled GOP electoral tsunami of 2010 certainly lifted all Republican boats, especially those moored in southern waters. From 2008 to 2010, the Arkansas GOP index jumped thirty percentage points, from nineteen percent to forty-nine percent. The Republican index increased from fifty-two percent to fifty-seven percent in Mississippi, fifty-one percent to sixty-three percent in Tennessee, fifty-two percent to fifty-seven percent in Texas, and finally, from forty-eight percent to fifty-six percent for the South. In 2018, the final election year shown in Figure 9.1, there was some decline in Republican electoral strength, and this is to be anticipated, as this was an auspicious election cycle for Democrats during Republican President Trump's first and only midterm. Nevertheless, David's Index of Republican strength still exceeded fifty percent for all four states and Southwide (fifty-four percent). Additionally, in an interesting reversal of a pattern prevailing for most of this time series, Arkansas, usually the least Republican of the featured states, is now the most Republican (sixty-four percent) in 2018. Texas, by comparison, is now the least Republican state of the four, and its GOP index (53.8%) is just slightly below the southern average mentioned earlier.

Another way to visualize and comprehend patterns in David's Index of GOP strength is by applying a ten-year moving average to the data shown in Figure 9.1. Figure 9.2 is a line graph plotting the ten-year moving average of the GOP index for the South, Arkansas, Mississippi, Tennessee, and Texas. By using this ten-year moving average, it is easier to see differences in the GOP index across states and over time. It is also obvious that the moving average serves the purpose of showing a pronounced lag effect in Republican electoral strength. However, this lag is only evident if Republican gains have become markedly more robust in the most recent elections. Once again, this dynamic describes Arkansas better than the other three states.

Because southern Democrats in the early 1990s continued to retain the upper hand in elections for House, Senate, and governor (McKee and Yoshinaka, 2015), this registers with respect to the GOP index at the start of the time series in Figure 9.2. In fact, it was not until 1996 that one state—Mississippi, at fifty-one percent—displayed a GOP index over fifty percent. Then, from 1996 to 2004, except for Mississippi (which peaked at fifty-six percent in 2000), the other three states and the South exhibited an increasingly ascendant Republican growth pattern. After 2004, Arkansas took a deep descent, with its GOP index reaching a nadir for the new millennium at thirty-eight percent in 2012. The GOP index also consistently declined in Texas over the same period,

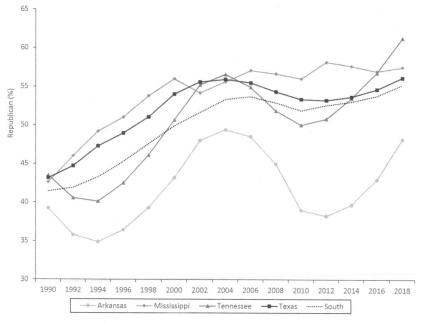

Figure 9.2. David's Index for Arkansas, Mississippi, Tennessee, Texas, and the Entire South, 1990–2018 (Ten-Year Moving Average)

but the decline was less than three percentage points versus eleven points in Arkansas. In contrast, the GOP index already showed a very modest rebound in 2012 for Mississippi and Tennessee. From 2012 to 2018, Mississippi's GOP index shows a fairly flat pattern, whereas Texas and the South displayed incremental increases in GOP strength from 2012 to 2018, with net gains of approximately three points for both. In contrast, the upward tilt in the Republican index for Tennessee and Arkansas over these last four elections is impressive: a net gain of 10.5 points in the Volunteer State (from 50.8% to 61.3%) and 9.9 points in the Natural State (from 38.3% to 48.2%).

In 2018, on the basis of the ten-year moving average, Tennessee was the second most Republican southern state behind Alabama's GOP index of sixty-six percent. Interestingly, according to the ten-year moving average of Republican electoral strength, only Virginia, the most Democratic southern state, had a lower GOP index (at 47.7%) than Arkansas's (noted above). Yet, with respect to the raw GOP index in 2018, at sixty-four percent, not only was Arkansas the most Republican state in the South, but also no other southern state possessed a Republican index cracking the sixtieth percentile. Hence, David's Index is a useful demonstration of the relative competitiveness of the GOP in each southern state, but variation in southern Republicanism is substantial if a moving average is applied to gauge the longer term electoral strength of the GOP in a given state. In other words, Arkansas is the unrivaled laggard regarding the recency of Republican electoral gains, but at least in 2018, it was also the most Republican southern state on the basis of David's Index Composite B, which, once again, is derived from GOP performance in House, Senate, and gubernatorial elections. Last, from 1992 to 2018, the raw GOP index for the South reached its peak at fifty-eight percent in 2014 and an apex of fifty-five percent two cycles later in 2018, according to the ten-year moving average.

As we show in the following sections of this chapter, and have routinely demonstrated thus far in the book, the Republican realignment of rural whites is the principal engine behind the sustained electoral success of the modern southern GOP. This chapter is an opportunity to document the considerable differences in state-level patterns of rural Republicanism among four southern states, including two of the most rural (Mississippi and Arkansas), one of the most urban (Texas), and another (Tennessee) that represents a realistic proximation of the regional median for rurality. Without further ado, we begin with Arkansas.

Arkansas

Arkansas would seem a curious place for fanning the flames of white massive resistance to a budding civil rights movement in the aftermath of the 1954 *Brown v. Board of Education* ruling. Nevertheless, the nation and much of the modern world paid attention as the"Little Rock Nine" courageously integrated Little Rock Central High School in the fall of 1957.[5] But opening the doors of what was a whites-only school to Black students quickly became a tinderbox that ignited wildfires across the South. Arkansas's Democratic Governor Orval Faubus seized on the widely popular and, hence, winning issue of militant segregation (Black, 1976) with his state's overwhelmingly white electorate. Indeed, after first winning the governorship in 1954, Faubus rode a race-baiting platform for five consecutive reelection victories in a period when Arkansas governors had two-year terms with no term limits (Kalb, 2016). Perhaps just as curious as, if not more curious than the racial militance of 1950s Arkansas, was Governor Faubus finally being unseated in 1966 by northeastern Republican carpetbagger Winthrop Rockefeller, who was unquestionably liberal on the race issue. One election cycle later in 1968, showed that the Natural State was truly unique in its schizophrenic voting behavior. Republican Governor Rockefeller won reelection; veteran incumbent Democrat J. William Fulbright prevailed in his Senate race; and the racist populist American Independent Party and former (and soon to be again) Democratic Alabama Governor George Wallace bested Republican Richard Nixon and Democrat Hubert Humphrey with a thirty-nine percent popular presidential vote plurality to capture Arkansas's six electoral votes.

After the 1960s, Arkansas settled into a lengthy period of Democratic dominance. Eventually though, the waning but persistent vestiges of Democratic electoral superiority were extinguished in the early 2010s.[6] To be sure, there were some notable Republican victories during the long period of Democratic control, such as when Republican Frank White scored an upset win over first-term incumbent Democrat Bill Clinton in the 1980 gubernatorial election. Also, populist Republican Mike Huckabee won consecutive gubernatorial terms in 1998 and 2002.

Without question, Arkansas was one of the slowest to have rural whites realign to the GOP. The Natural State has the second lowest percentage of Blacks in the South (second to Texas) and, hence, lacked a relative advantage opportunity for whites to seize the shell of GOP opposition (Hood, Kidd, and Morris, 2014).[7] Stated differently, there was no pressing need for whites to move into the GOP to counter a rising registered Black Democratic electorate because of this group's small size. Without a formidable racial motive to compel Republican realignment, another slowing factor was that Arkansas is one of the poorest southern states; therefore, upscale, economic-based Republicanism that began in the urban South in the 1950s was not appealing to most rural white Arkansans. Also, Arkansas is a small state; currently in the South, only Mississippi has fewer inhabitants. This allowed for charismatic Democratic politicians such as Bill Clinton, Dale Bumpers, and David Pryor to carry out effective retail campaigning throughout the state (Fenno, 1996), successfully cultivating Democratic voters for decades. Also, of course, these politicians were not liberals; they were strategic in blending conservative and progressive issue positions (Black and Black, 1987) that won them the support of majority biracial coalitions. In fact, it was not until Bill Clinton departed the White House that a pronounced break from the Democratic Party emerged in the state.[8]

The Republican takeover of Arkansas politics may have been decades in the making, but now it is hard to contemplate a Democratic comeback. The contemporary Arkansas GOP's mix of economic populism and cultural conservativism would seem to perfectly suit the preferences of the state's large population of rural white voters.[9] Figure 9.3 displays county-level maps of the 1990 (left side) and 2018 (right side) Arkansas gubernatorial elections. The 1990 contest was Democrat Bill Clinton's final gubernatorial victory before winning the White House in 1992. Clinton defeated his Republican challenger, Sheffield Nelson, with more than fifty-seven percent of the two-party vote. In Figure 9.3, as in earlier chapters, counties are designated according to which party won it and whether it is urban or small-town South (STS). Arkansas has seventy-five counties, and in 1990, Clinton carried sixty-four (eighty-five percent) of them; of these Democratic counties, forty-seven (seventy-three percent) were of the STS variety. Of the eleven counties that the hapless

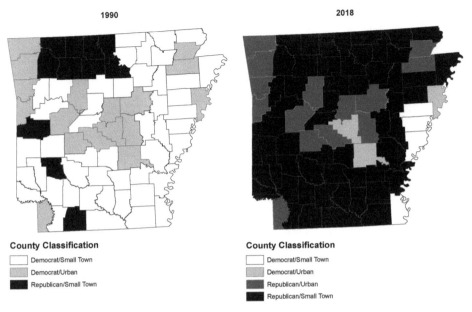

Figure 9.3. County Vote for Arkansas Governor, 1990 and 2018

Republican Sheffield Nelson managed to win, eight constituted a band in the Ozarks region and the other three were located on the western side of the state. All eleven Republican counties were STS.

More than a quarter century later, in the 2018 gubernatorial contest between incumbent Republican Asa Hutchinson and his Democratic challenger, Jared Henderson, the sitting GOP governor amassed sixty-seven percent of the two-party vote and won the most votes in sixty-eight (ninety-one percent) of Arkansas's seventy-five counties.[10] Of the seven counties that the Democrat won, five were located along the Mississippi river and four of these Delta counties had majority Black populations.[11] The other two Democratic counties, Pulaski (Little Rock) and Jefferson, border each other and are urban. Jefferson County has a 56.5% Black population, and Pulaski County's Black population is 36.8%. Of the sixty-eight counties that the Republican Governor Asa Hutchinson won, fifty-four (seventy-two percent) were STS. In modern-day Arkansas, the Republican gubernatorial nominee is competitive everywhere, only losing in the largest and most urban county (Pulaski) and a handful of counties with Black populations markedly larger than the statewide average of 15.3%. Last, even in the seven counties won by the Democratic gubernatorial challenger in 2018, his strongest performance amounted to less than fifty-five percent of the two-party vote: 54.9% in Phillips County.

We conclude this profile of Arkansas with a look at a long time series of survey data from the Arkansas Poll, administered annually since 1999. As is

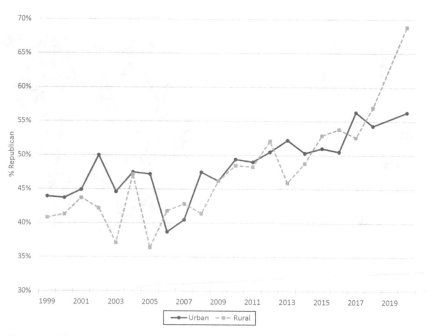

Figure 9.4. Arkansas Partisanship by Place, 1999–2020

the case with the survey data that we present for Mississippi, Tennessee, and Texas, in Figure 9.4, we plot the percentage of white Republican identifiers, urban and rural, with independent Republican leaners considered GOP affiliates.[12] The Arkansas Poll data span 1999 to 2020; there is only one year for which we lack data, and that is 2019. From 1999 to 2005, the percentage of urban white Republicans is higher than the share of rural white Republicans. Then, starting in 2006 and continuing through 2018, like in a competitive basketball game, there were numerous lead changes, with some years showing a higher percentage of rural white Republicans and others showing a greater share of urban white Republicans. It is unfortunate that we lack the data points for 2019; nevertheless, the final numbers for 2020 are striking. In the last and most recent year of the time series, the percentage of rural white Republicans rocketed to sixty-nine percent (they were fifty-seven percent Republican in 2018). In contrast, the share of urban white Republicans increased to fifty-six percent in 2020, a two-percentage-point increase over 2018.

Mississippi

The politics of race has haunted the Magnolia State since its inception (Parker, 1990; Silver, 2012).[13] The most quoted line in V. O. Key's classic, *Southern Politics in State and Nation*, is this one: "Whatever phase of the southern political process one seeks to understand, sooner or later the trail of inquiry leads to the Negro" (1949, p. 5). This observation held best in the case of Mississippi at mid-twentieth century, but it still resonates over seventy years later. According to the 1950 census, forty-five percent of Magnolia State residents were Black, and thirty-one of Mississippi's eighty-two counties were majority Black. What was true in 1950 remains true in present times: Mississippi contains the highest percentage of Black inhabitants in the United States (thirty-eight percent, with twenty-five majority Black counties), and in the South, the Magnolia State is still the most rural; seventy-two percent rural in 1950 and fifty-one percent rural, based on the 2010 census.[14] No other southern state, or any state for that matter, rivals the racially polarized partisan voting exhibited by modern-day Mississippians. Indeed, so stark is the propensity for whites to vote Republican and for Blacks to vote Democratic in general elections that it is not unreasonable to determine racial voting patterns with county-level data alone (McKee, 2015) and thus forego the need to consult the nuances of survey data to capture whatever variation exists with respect to race and vote choice.

Another clear example of race driving Mississippi voting patterns was palpable in 2001, when the state put a referendum before the electorate regarding a vote to change the flag, which prominently featured the Confederate "stars and bars" battle emblem. Voting almost mirrored the racial composition of each county, with the flag remaining unchanged because of white support for keeping it (Klinkner, 2001). However, some notable progress has finally made its way to Mississippi, if primarily in symbolic form. In 2020, the Republican Governor Tate Reeves signed legislation to alter the state flag, and the proposed change was placed on the November ballot, with seventy-three percent of voters approving. Given the Black and white racial makeup of the Mississippi electorate, a nontrivial share of whites opted to place the one-hundred-twenty-six-year-old Confederate version of the flag in the museum and, in its stead, fly a new one with a magnolia blossom in the center and the words "In God We Trust" at the bottom. However, although almost three-quarters of Mississippians voted to expunge their flag of a controversial Confederate symbol, fifty-eight percent chose to reelect Republican President Donald Trump, once again revealing the tight alignment of race and party in candidate preferences.

For decades, two unreconstructed Dixiecrats represented Mississippi in the US Senate: James Eastland (1942–1978) and John Stennis (1947–1988). When these Democrats finally retired, they were replaced by Republicans who both served in the US House (they were first elected in 1972): Congressman Thad Cochran, who won the 1978 open Senate election, and Representative Trent Lott, who was victorious in the 1988 open Senate contest. Unlike their Democratic forbears, neither of these Republican senators cultivated a reputation for being race-baiters, although Senator Lott did step down from his position as majority leader in 2002, after he declared at Strom Thurmond's centennial birthday bash that the country would have been better off if the one-hundred-year-old Dixiecrat had won the presidency back in 1948.[15]

Mississippi Democrats have fared better at holding onto congressional districts. As late as 2008, the four-member House delegation had three Democrats and one Republican.[16] Since the 1982 redistricting, Mississippi has a majority Black district (District Two) covering most of the Delta region in the northwestern section of the state. Nonetheless, because of variation in turnout favoring whites and highly racially polarized voting, white Republican Congressman Webb Franklin managed to represent the fifty-nine percent Black District Two for two terms (1982–1984) before Black Democrat Mike Espy defeated him in 1986. Espy vacated this majority rural district (fifty-five percent rural at the time) to join the Clinton administration as secretary of agriculture, and African American Bennie Thompson has been the District Two congressman since winning the 1993 special House election (Barone and Ujifusa, 1995). Since 2010, the Mississippi House delegation has comprised three Republicans and the aforementioned Democrat.[17] Interestingly, when Senator Cochran stepped down in 2018 (he died in 2019), Mike Espy re-emerged to contest the 2018 special Senate election. In the runoff, Espy lost with forty-six percent of the vote to Republican Cindy Hyde-Smith, who is unabashedly proud of the South's and Mississippi's Confederate heritage. Espy then lost to Hyde-Smith again in the 2020 regularly scheduled Senate race and registered a slightly weaker performance (forty-five percent of the vote), although Hyde-Smith did run behind President Trump.

In 1991, Republican Kirk Fordice became the first of his party to win the Mississippi governorship since Reconstruction, defeating the incumbent Democrat Ray Mabus with fifty-two percent of the two-party vote. In 1999, after Governor Fordice's two terms, Ronnie Musgrove was the last Democrat to be elected governor of Mississippi. Figure 9.5 shows county-level maps of the 1991 (left side) and 2019 (right side) Mississippi gubernatorial elections. In contrast to the sea change in Arkansas gubernatorial elections held over twenty-five years apart, county-level Republican strength was roughly comparable in Mississippi in 1991 and 2019. In 1991, the Republican Fordice won forty-nine of Mississippi's eighty-two counties (sixty-two percent), and of these, forty (eighty-two percent) were of the STS kind. Twenty-eight years later, in the 2019 open gubernatorial election, Republican Lieutenant Governor Tate Reeves bested Mississippi Democratic Attorney General Jim Hood with fifty-three percent of the two-party vote. The Republican Reeves won fifty counties (sixty-one percent), and thirty-nine (seventy-eight percent) of these were of the STS variety.

To be sure, there is some variation in the individual counties that went Republican in 1991 and 2019, but the general patterns for these two gubernatorial

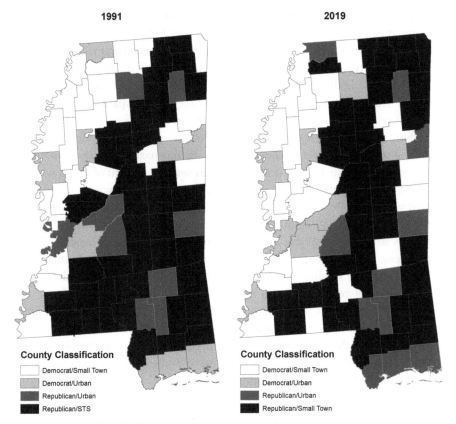

Figure 9.5. County Vote for Mississippi Governor, 1991 and 2019

elections are quite similar, particularly regarding the palpable Democratic strength in the heavily Black Mississippi Delta region. The most plausible explanation for the modest variation in the geographic pattern and overall share of the Republican gubernatorial vote in 1991 versus 2019 boils down to the fact that Mississippi Democrats probably could not have fielded a stronger candidate than Jim Hood. In fact, from 2011 to 2014, before Democrat John Bel Edwards was elected governor of Louisiana in 2015, Mississippi Attorney General Jim Hood (2003–2018) was the only statewide elected Democratic official in the Deep South.

We wrap up this discussion of Magnolia State politics by displaying the percentages of urban and rural whites affiliated with the Republican Party, based on data from the Mississippi Poll starting in 1984 and ending in 2012. The Mississippi Poll was conducted in even years, but unfortunately, we lack data for three consecutive years in the early part of the time series, 1986– 1990. Rural is classified as any place a respondent resides where the population is under ten thousand residents; more than this number and a respondent is classified as urban. Admittedly, this is a conservative estimate of rurality, adopted because Mississippi is such a rural state.[18] As shown in Figure 9.6, a veritable GOP identification chasm separated urban and rural whites in 1984, with fifty percent of the former group affiliating with the Republican Party, compared with thirty-one percent identifying as Republican in the latter group. Through 2012, this nineteen-percentage-point disparity in 1984 is the largest recorded, but it reached fifteen points in 2000.

Since the beginning of the millennium, the gap in GOP identification among urban and rural white Mississippians has narrowed considerably. It was smallest in the final year of 2012, when seventy percent of urban whites identified as Republicans and sixty-seven percent of rural whites also affiliated with the GOP. Again, caution should be taken in expounding on rural-urban differences in Republican affiliation among Mississippi whites, as the state is so racially polarized along partisan lines regardless of location. Nevertheless, longitudinal patterns in GOP identification tied to residential density exhibit the familiar pattern found throughout this book. As shown in Figure 9.6, between 1984 and 2012, there was a twenty percentage-point increase in the Republican affiliation of urban white Mississippians (from fifty percent to seventy percent). In comparison, over this same period, there was an increase of thirty-six percentage points in the GOP identification (from thirty-one percent to sixty-seven percent) of white Mississippians living in the Magnolia State's least populated communities.

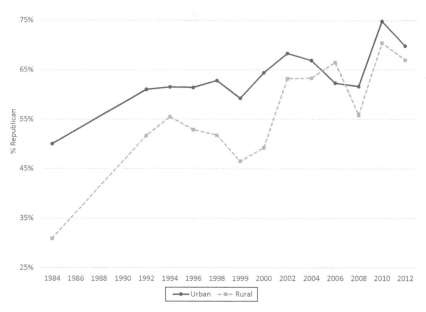

Figure 9.6. Mississippi Partisanship by Place, 1984–2012

Tennessee

The Volunteer State shows a contemporary Republicanism that is robust and, therefore, reminiscent of the GOP's current electoral prowess found in Arkansas and Mississippi. However, the present-day dominance of Tennessee Republicans betrays a political history quite different from that of its aforementioned neighbors to the west and south. In the South, Mountain Republicanism arguably originated in east Tennessee at the time of the Civil War, and it materialized because that section of the state had hardly any slaveholders. The war was a cause better left to the planters more prevalent in the middle and western part of Tennessee. In fact, there were times in the darkest days of southern Republicanism—and, hence, the height of the one-party Democratic Solid South—when Dixie's entire House delegation would have been Democratic if not for the two Republican congressmen representing Tennessee's easternmost congressional districts (Black and Black, 2002; McKee, 2019). And so, as most southern states were building the GOP from scratch, Tennessee had a historic Republican reservoir from which to draw. In 1920, with Jim Crow holding a vise grip over the South, the Volunteer State's ten-member House delegation was evenly split (five Democrats and five Republicans), Republican presidential nominee Warren Harding won Tennessee's twelve electoral votes, and Republican Alfred Taylor won the governorship.[19] In that moment, the Volunteer State was Dixie's unique Republican aberration. However, after 1920, a long period of Democratic dominance set in, and it held until after the 1960s civil rights movement. Still, compared with most southern states, GOP viability returned relatively early in Tennessee, as Republican Howard Baker won an open Senate seat in 1966 and Republican Bill Brock defeated incumbent Democratic Senator Albert Gore Sr. in 1970. Also in 1970, Republican Winfield Dunn was victorious in the gubernatorial election, placing the governor's mansion back in GOP occupancy for the first time since the 1920s.

In presidential politics, Tennessee has been Republican since the end of the Clinton administration. In 2000, former Democratic senator, vice president, and Tennessee native son Al Gore lost the Volunteer State's two-party presidential vote to Republican and Texas Governor George W. Bush by a margin of forty-eight percent to fifty-two percent. Since 2000, the GOP share of the two-party presidential vote in Tennessee has steadily grown, topping out at sixty-four percent in 2016. In his failed reelection bid in 2020, Republican President Donald Trump still captured sixty-two percent of the Volunteer State's presidential votes. Since former attorney, actor, and future presidential hopeful (in 2008) Fred Thompson won the 1994 special Senate election against Democratic Congressman Jim Cooper and, in the same election cycle,

Republican Bill Frist defeated incumbent Democratic Senator Jim Sasser, the GOP has held both of Tennessee's US Senate seats.[20]

In contrast to the Republican Party's lengthy dominance of Senate elections, the Volunteer State's House delegation has seen considerable partisan volatility from the early 1990s until 2010 (see chapter seven), when the nine-member contingent has, henceforth, included seven Republicans and two Democrats. Interestingly, the majority Black District Nine (sixty-six percent Black and zero percent rural) in Memphis has been represented by white and Jewish Democrat Steve Cohen since 2006. The other Democrat, Jim Cooper, returned to the Tennessee House delegation in 2002 and currently represents District Five (two percent rural).[21]

The Tennessee governorship is a curious case. Dating back to 1978, when Republican Lamar Alexander won his first of two consecutive terms (Tennessee has a two-term limit), the Volunteer State's governor's mansion has rotated between the two major parties repeatedly after each incumbent has completed two terms.[22] However, speaking to the current state of GOP electoral hegemony, Tennessee's streak of alternating gubernatorial partisanship was finally snapped in 2018 when term-limited Republican Governor Bill Haslam (2010–2018) was succeeded by Republican Bill Lee. Figure 9.7 displays county-level maps of the 1990 (top) and 2018 (bottom) Tennessee gubernatorial elections. In 1990, incumbent Democratic Governor Ned McWherter coasted to reelection over Republican Dwight Henry, with sixty-two percent of the two-party vote. The overmatched Republican challenger only won five counties (out of ninety-five), and remarkably, Loudon County was a perfect split of 2,171 votes apiece for McWherter and Henry. Of the eighty-nine counties McWherter carried (ninety-four percent), sixty-one (sixty-nine percent) were STS.

In a cycle when national tides were running in a Democratic direction (Jacobson, 2019), the 2018 midterm elections were actually generous to Tennessee Republicans.[23] In the open gubernatorial contest, the Republican Bill Lee amassed sixty-one percent of the two-party vote versus Democrat Karl Dean. As if Democratic Governor McWherter's 1990 performance was not impressive enough, in 2018, the Republican Lee triumphed in ninety-two (ninety-seven percent) of Tennessee's ninety-five counties. Also, as an obvious indication of the completion of the rural Republican realignment, two of the counties that the Democrat Dean captured were urban, including Tennessee's two most populous, Shelby (Memphis) and Davidson (Nashville). In contrast, of the Republican Lee's ninety-two counties, sixty-four (seventy percent) were STS. By 2018, what started with a history of geographically isolated postbellum Mountain Republicanism had finally enveloped the Volunteer State.

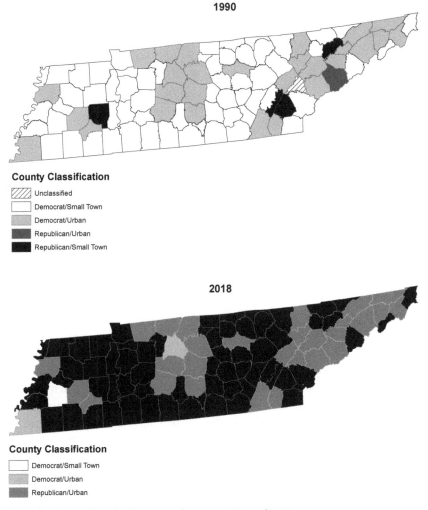

Figure 9.7. County Vote for Tennessee Governor, 1990 and 2018

We end this assessment of Tennessee politics with a presentation of Republican identification based on survey data from the University of Tennessee (1990–1996) and Vanderbilt University (2012–2018). At one time, we intended to fill the interlude after 1996 and before 2012 with survey data from the MTSU (Middle Tennessee State University) Poll, but there were complications with these data; therefore, we decided to simply show the broken time series with the University of Tennessee data in the 1990s and the Vanderbilt data in the 2010s. For the Vanderbilt time series, we are missing data from 2013.

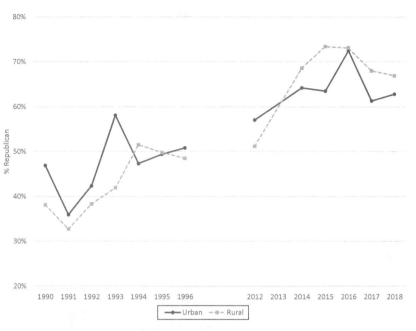

Figure 9.8. Tennessee Partisanship by Place, 1990–96 and 2012–18

Figure 9.8 shows the percentages of urban and rural white Tennesseans identifying with the Republican Party in the 1990s and 2010s.[24] In a way, the decade-and-a-half interlude separating the first time series from the second is illuminating. That is, it is evident how urban and rural Republicanism has grown in more recent years. For most of the earliest years in the 1990s, the percentage of urban white Republicans exceeded that of rural white Republicans (e.g., in 1990, forty-seven percent of urban whites versus thirty-eight percent of rural whites were Republicans). In the 2010s, starting in 2014, the share of rural white GOP identifiers was greater than the percentage of urban white Republicans. Finally, the rate of increase in Republican identification is much larger for rural whites. In a comparison of 2012 to 2018, the percentage of urban white GOP affiliates rose from fifty-seven percent to sixty-three percent. Making this same comparison among rural whites, fifty-one percent were Republicans in 2012 versus sixty-seven percent who identified with the GOP in 2018.

Texas

The sheer size of Texas, both in area and population, dwarfs that of Arkansas, Mississippi, and Tennessee. As mentioned earlier, Texas is the second least rural southern state, and it is the most populous. Two types of population-based comparisons with the three previously covered states are insightful.

First, consider the number of House seats. With four House seats apiece in Arkansas and Mississippi, Texas has nine times as many, a total of thirty-six since 2012. Tennessee has nine congressional districts; hence, Texas has four times as many as the Volunteer State. The total of seventeen congressional districts in Arkansas, Mississippi, and Tennessee amounts to less than half of the Lone Star State's House delegation. Even more compelling is the long-term pattern of seat gains/losses in these four southern states. In 1950, Arkansas and Mississippi both had seven House seats, Tennessee had ten, and Texas had twenty-one. After the 1990 reapportionment (in 1992), Arkansas had four seats, Mississippi had five, Tennessee had nine, and Texas had thirty. In the 2000 reapportionment, slow population growth reduced the Mississippi House delegation to four members (in 2002). Since 1990, the Texas House delegation has increased from twenty-seven to thirty-six. In contrast, the combined House seat total for Arkansas, Mississippi, and Tennessee went from eighteen in 1990 to seventeen before the 2020 reapportionment. Finally, in the latest reapportionment, Texas added two more seats for a total of thirty-eight in 2022, whereas Arkansas, Mississippi, and Tennessee retained their current number of congressional districts.[25]

Second, the number of highly populated counties in Texas is astounding when compared with those in Arkansas, Mississippi, and Tennessee. Of Texas's nation-leading 254 counties, thirty-nine have a population exceeding one hundred thousand inhabitants. The top five counties each include more than one million residents, and the top dozen each contain more than half a million people. Tennessee has thirteen counties with at least one hundred thousand people; not one county contains up to a million residents, and just two counties exceed half a million inhabitants (Shelby and Davidson). Arkansas has seven counties with more than one hundred thousand people, and all of them have under four hundred thousand residents. Mississippi has only six counties exceeding one hundred thousand residents, and all of these counties have less than a quarter-million people. Texas's Harris County (Houston), by itself, has more inhabitants (4,646,630) than Arkansas (2,999,370) and Mississippi (2,984,418) and is sixty-nine percent of Tennessee's total population (6,709,356). The top ten most populous Texas counties encompass over fifty-nine percent of the Lone Star State's residents. In short, with respect to geographic territory and population, Texas is a behemoth.

In the South, only the fast-growing state of Florida approaches Texas in terms of demographic diversity and the aforementioned population statistics. Among the eleven southern states, Texas has the lowest percentage of Blacks (twelve percent) and Anglos (non-Hispanic whites; forty-two percent), the highest share of Latinos (thirty-nine percent), and the second highest percentage of Asians (five percent [behind Virginia]).[26] In fact, Texas is the only majority-minority southern state, with a fifty-eight percent non-Anglo population. Because so much of the Lone Star State's growing population and demographic change is concentrated in its largest cities, over the years, this dynamic has produced one of the most geographically polarized electorates with regard to partisan voting patterns (Myers, 2013). Yes, there are substantial Hispanic populations in rural Texas counties located along the Mexico border and throughout the lesser populated western portion of the state. However, Anglos in these areas are much more participatory (Hood and McKee, 2017b), and along with residents of the rural counties in the eastern half of Texas, these white residents are the reason why, despite the tremendous growth in the largest cities, the Lone Star State remains a Republican redoubt, although one increasingly under Democratic attack.

Aside from the relatively small population of German immigrants who settled in the Texas Hill Country (Key, 1949), the Lone Star State did not possess a sizable Republican constituency to counter the overwhelming number of Democrats from the end of the Civil War through the 1960s. For most of the first half of the twentieth century, Texas politics was Democratic politics, and the principal factional disputes took place among economic liberals versus economic conservatives, with the latter group usually winning the day (Green, 1979). As stated by Key (1949, p. 255), "The confluence of the anxieties of the newly rich and the repercussions of The New Deal in Texas pushed politics into a battle of conservatives versus liberals . . . possibly in portent of the rise of a bipartisan system."

Key (1949) was prescient: Much more so than race, it was class that created a permanent rift in the Texas Democratic Party (Davidson, 1990). In a state with a burgeoning upwardly mobile white urban electorate, 1950s Eisenhower Republicanism found legions of Texas converts, at least at the top of the ticket. However, after carrying Texas twice in the 1952 and 1956 presidential elections, the GOP was shut out for the Kennedy-Johnson 1960s and then easily prevailed in 1972 when Republican President Richard Nixon pummeled his liberal Democratic challenger, George McGovern. In 1976, native rural Georgian Jimmy Carter was the last hurrah for the Democratic Party in Texas presidential elections.[27] Revealing a strong conservative economics-based/free-market connection to 1950s Eisenhower Republicanism, albeit with a much heftier dose of religious conservatism, 1980s Reagan Republicanism found a welcome home in the Lone Star State. In 1980, Reagan bested Carter in Harris County (Houston), Dallas County (Dallas), Tarrant County (Fort Worth), and even in Bexar (San Antonio) and El Paso (El Paso) counties. Carter did manage to eke out a victory in the culturally more liberal Travis County (Austin).

By the 1990s, the Texas Republican Party was clearly ascendant. Since Democrat Lloyd Bentsen left the Senate in 1993 to join the Clinton administration as treasury secretary, only Republicans have occupied Texas's two

Senate seats. Since 1998, no Democrat has won any of Texas's nine statewide elective positions. Republicans took control of the Texas State Senate in 1996 and the Texas State House after the 2002 elections. Neither chamber has flipped back to Democratic control. It was in US House elections where Republican gains took the longest to manifest into a GOP majority. Unlike most of the Democratic-controlled southern states that drew "dummymanders" (see Grofman and Brunell, 2005) in the 1990s, Texas Democrats drew one of the most effective partisan gerrymanders for the 1992 House elections (see Barone and Ujifusa, 1993; Black and Black, 2002). Even with substantial court-ordered changes to Texas's congressional districts for the 1996 elections, it was not until the GOP's enactment of the 2004 "re-redistricted" map that an extremely effective Republican gerrymander produced a GOP House majority (Bickerstaff, 2007; Gaddie, 2004; McKee, 2010; McKee and Shaw, 2005; McKee, Teigen, and Turgeon, 2006).

In spite of the Texas GOP's outstanding track record in electoral politics dating back to the mid-1990s and 1980 in the case of presidential elections, it would appear that Republican hegemony has already peaked. For instance, although the last three presidential contests were never really in doubt (some pundits thought 2020 was, but neither major party nominee campaigned in Texas), the Republican margin of victory in the two-party vote narrowed from sixteen points in 2012 to nine points in 2016, and then to under five points in 2020. Likewise, the 2018 midterm congressional elections were perhaps a canary in the coal mine. Admittedly, Republican Senator Ted Cruz was not that popular; still, Texans and the nation were stunned to see former Democratic Congressman Beto O'Rourke (he represented the eighty percent Hispanic and zero percent rural District Sixteen in El Paso from 2012 to 2016) come within 2.6 percentage points of winning (see the discussion of this contest in the Introduction). Perhaps every bit as compelling and alarming for Texas Republicans were the two Democratic victories against veteran Republican House incumbents: Attorney Lizzie Fletcher defeated John Culberson (first elected in 2000) in Houston-based District Seven (zero percent rural) and former NFL linebacker Colin Allred unseated Pete Sessions (first elected in 1996) in Dallas-based District Thirty-Two (zero percent rural).[28] No Texas House seats changed partisan control in 2020; thus, Fletcher and Allred both won reelection.

The common thread tying together these notable Democratic performances is that they rest on the growing support of urban Texans, including urban Anglos who reside in the Lone Star State's largest cities. The once ruby red and heavily Anglo Texas suburbs are now political battlegrounds, and finally, after decades of movement toward the GOP, Texas's lightly populated rural counties are now Republican fortresses. Driving home this political reality in contemporary Texas politics, Figure 9.9 presents county-level data on the

1990

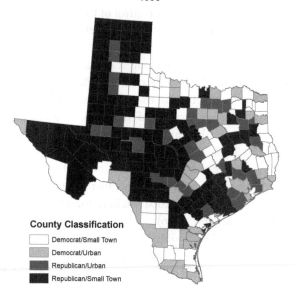

2018

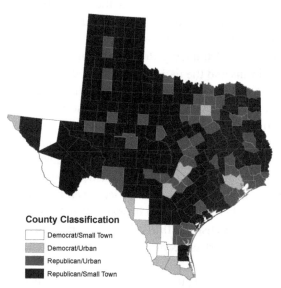

Figure 9.9. County Vote for Texas Governor, 1990 and 2018

1990 (top) and 2018 (bottom) Texas gubernatorial elections. In 1990, Ann Richards was the last Democrat to win the Texas governorship, narrowly defeating Republican Clayton Williams with fifty-one percent of the two-party vote.[29] Richards won 104 counties (forty-one percent), and of these, sixty-nine (sixty-six percent) were STS. Obviously, in capturing well under half of Texas's counties and nonetheless winning, Richards's urban counties were large. Indeed, among her thirty-five urban counties, Richards won Harris, Dallas, Tarrant, Bexar, Travis, and El Paso.

Twenty-eight years later, Republican Governor Greg Abbott defeated his Democratic challenger, Lupe Valdez (Dallas County sheriff from 2005 to 2017) with fifty-seven percent of the two-party vote. However, although Valdez was a weak opponent, among the six urban Texas counties mentioned earlier, Abbott only won Tarrant. In winning the open gubernatorial election in 2014, Abbott faced a better known and better financed opponent than Valdez in Democratic State Senator Wendy Davis.[30] Nevertheless, Abbott captured sixty percent of the two-party vote in this contest and, in the process, carried Harris, Tarrant, and Bexar counties. Perhaps Abbott's reelection performance in 2018 was lackluster because it was a good year for Democrats, and 2014 by comparison was a favorable cycle for Republicans? Another explanation, and not necessarily conflicting with the short-term conditions narrative, is that urban Texans are continuing to move away from the GOP as their rural neighbors are increasingly drawn to the Republican Party. The map of the 2018 gubernatorial election exclaims this. In 2018, Abbott won 234 (ninety-two percent) of Texas's two hundred fifty-four counties, and of this total, 176 (seventy-five percent) counties were of the STS variety.

We close this discussion of Texas with an examination of survey data on the Republican affiliation of white (Anglo) urban and rural Texans. These data, displayed in Figure 9.10, come from the University of Texas/Texas Tribune Poll and span 2008 to 2020.[31] In contrast to the other three states evaluated in this chapter, rural Republicanism is in full bloom in Texas at the start of the time series in 2008, with seventy-four percent of rural white Texans identifying with the GOP versus sixty-five percent of urban white Texans doing the same. Although there is essentially no rural-urban difference in Republican identification in 2009, only in 2010 (and clearly within the margin of error, as in 2009) did the percentage of urban Republicans (sixty-seven percent) exceed that of rural Republicans (sixty-six percent). After 2010, the rural-urban Republican affiliation disparity was the smallest in 2018, with three percentage points separating the two groups. Some of the twenty-three-point rural-urban gap in 2017 might be chalked up to a sampling issue; nevertheless, in 2020, rural whites were thirteen points more Republican (sixty-nine percent) than their urban white neighbors (fifty-six percent).

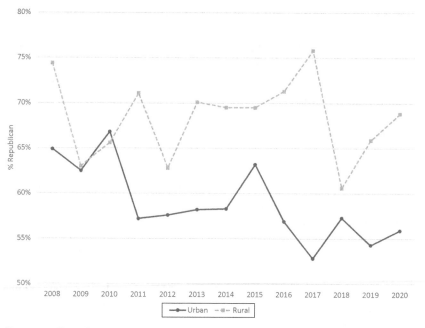

Figure 9.10. Texas Partisanship by Place, 2008–2020

Conclusion

The political future of these four southern states appears to favor continued Republican dominance in Arkansas, Mississippi, and Tennessee, whereas Texas moves in a more competitive direction. In the South, Tennessee (seventy-four percent white) and Arkansas (seventy-two percent white) have the highest percentages of non-Hispanic whites. In fact, no other southern states have Anglo populations in the seventieth percentile. Conversely, Arkansas (fifteen percent Black) and Tennessee (seventeen percent Black) have the second and fourth lowest percentages of Blacks in the southern states. Neither state possesses a bounty of highly populated urban areas, and vis-à-vis rural whites, urban whites in Arkansas and Tennessee also favor the GOP, if not quite as fervently.[32] By comparison, Mississippi will remain a Republican redoubt for a very different reason: The Magnolia State leads the country in its percentage of Blacks (thirty-eight percent), and there is no question that this fact drives the most racially polarized partisan voting patterns in the United States. So long as white Mississippians see their Black neighbors as political opponents, the lily-white Republican Party will rule the state. The absence of any notable rift in white Republican affiliation on the basis of location speaks to the overriding importance of race in sorting whites and Blacks into opposing political parties.

Compared with Arkansas, Mississippi, and Tennessee, like the old advertisement claimed, Texas is "Like A Whole Other Country." The Lone Star State's forty-two percent Anglo population will continue to decline as a percentage of Texas's total population, and Hispanic growth is most responsible for this. With respect to place, the locus of population growth is squarely located in Texas's megacities and their sprawling suburbs in Houston, Dallas, San Antonio, Fort Worth, and now the most recent newcomer, culturally liberal Austin. Anyone who has driven from east (west) to west (east) or from north (south) to south (north) in the Dallas-Fort Worth Metroplex can appreciate the label "Metroplex" for this urban area that seems to stretch on forever. Further endangering extant Texas Republican dominance is that the more rapidly growing urban Anglo population is not nearly as wedded to the GOP as rural Anglos. The partisan polarization of urban and rural Anglos, with the latter group having become decidedly more Republican, has prolonged the Republican advantage, but it is waning.

In party politics, whether the office is for president, senator, governor, House representative, or state legislator, Republican control is a lock in Arkansas, Mississippi, and Tennessee. Indeed, as a telling example of Republican superiority, in 2020, Arkansas Republican US Senator Tom Cotton's only opponent was a Libertarian (Rick Harrington), who garnered a third of the vote. As mentioned, none of these three states will add or lose congressional seats in the 2020 reapportionment; thus, likely minimal district boundary alterations will reinforce the Republican status quo. In contrast, Texas is undergoing considerable political change that has placed it in a state of electoral disequilibrium. Even with Texas Republicans drawing the 2022 congressional map, it will be challenging to craft districts that limit rising Democratic influence.

Of all the aforementioned political offices, Republican anxiety is greatest with respect to presidential politics. The Lone Star State appears to be moving inexorably toward presidential battleground territory. Unlike the double-digit victories Republican President Trump posted in Arkansas, Mississippi, and Tennessee, in 2020, the Lone Star State was comfortably in the competitive single-digit presidential margin of victory states, which also included Georgia, North Carolina, and Florida (in order of competitiveness). Georgia flipped Democratic for the first time since Clinton won it in 1992, and Virginia has been presidentially Democratic since Obama won it in 2008. For Republicans, it is a sobering thought that, on the basis of the 2020 reapportionment, if Texas were to flip Democratic in 2024, along with Georgia, North Carolina, Florida, and Virginia, then this would account for over seventy percent of the South's electoral votes and over forty-two percent of the two hundred seventy needed to win the presidency. In sum, the Lone Star State is on a political path that is very different and substantially bluer than the deep red bucolic ones Arkansas, Mississippi, and Tennessee continue to tread.

10 How Are Rural and Urban Southerners Different?

In the contemporary American South, among the white electorate, the country mouse and the city mouse are in various ways distinct species. In biological parlance, these two types of mice are of the same genus but somewhat distant cousins in taxonomic terms because, on a host of demographics, cultural/racial characteristics and attitudes, policy-based and political dispositions, small-town South (STS) and urban white southerners vary considerably. We make this evident with the use of a large and representative survey of STS and urban white southerners that we administered in the weeks before the world turned upside down because of the onset of the novel coronavirus pandemic in mid-March of 2021.[1]

We present and assess data on STS and urban white southerners who participated in a 2020 survey conducted from a sampling frame provided by the firm Dynata. Thus far, we have emphasized the remarkable changes to the voting behavior and ensuing electoral patterns materializing from the pronounced shift of rural white southerners to the GOP. Also, we have focused on the corresponding changes in party affiliation to this now-core Republican group in chapters eight (Southwide) and nine (in four southern states). In this chapter, we expand on many of the differences between STS and urban whites that we first documented with 2016 Cooperative Election Study data in chapter one (see Table 1.2). Here, we stress variation among STS and urban whites with respect to demographic characteristics, cultural differences, racial attitudes, opinions on divisive issues, and political dispositions. Upfront, we should emphasize that both groups possess profiles that unsurprisingly align better with the Republican Party. Nevertheless, the features of rural white southerners leave no doubt that their fit with the contemporary GOP is a more congruent and cozier one, and this is evidently a reciprocal relationship, as the stronger attachment of these voters to the GOP, in turn, makes the party more responsive to their demands and preferences.

In the next section, we start with a brief exposition of the methodology involved to produce our 2020 survey of STS and urban white southerners. Then, in the following four sections, we present descriptive data on STS and urban whites regarding how these groups differ in demographic characteristics; cultural attributes and racial attitudes; opinions on divisive issues; and, finally, their political dispositions (ideology and party affiliation). In the last section before we conclude, we present the findings of multivariate regressions for the purpose of differentiating STS and urban whites. We end the chapter with a discussion of why the numerous differences between STS and urban whites prolongs the southern GOP's more forceful representation of rural whites' interests, even if this actually makes the Republican Party less competitive in future elections.

Survey Methodology

To better study differences between STS and urban whites in the South, we commissioned our own online survey, which included an oversample of STS respondents.[2] Utilizing an opt-in panel from the survey company Dynata, we queried a total of 3,010 non-Hispanic white southern respondents: fifty percent residing in STS counties and fifty percent living in urban counties.[3]

To ensure that respondents met location criteria, we asked them to provide their county/parish of residence and zip code. Regardless of where they were recorded as living by Dynata, respondents were screened out of the final sample if their self-reported county/parish and zip code were outside the geographic boundaries of the eleven southern states. Our final sample also included only those survey respondents who reported that they were registered to vote.

The survey was in the field for a total of eleven days, beginning on January 31 and concluding on February 10, 2020. Perhaps, in hindsight, we were fortunate that the COVID-19 pandemic had not yet recorded its far-reaching effects on the American population (and so much of the rest of the world), because political attitudes registered among our survey respondents were not colored by this devastating global tragedy.[4] Within their geographic setting (STS or urban), survey respondents were weighted using iterative proportional raking to ensure that the sample was representative in terms of age, gender, and education.[5] Respondents were asked a wide range of questions, including those designed to gather detailed demographic information and questions concerning issues/policies, racial attitudes, and religious and political dispositions (see the Appendix at the end of this chapter for detailed question wording and response options used in the survey). We begin with a discussion of the demographic characteristics of STS and urban white southerners.

Demographics

Table 10.1 presents demographic statistics for STS and urban whites with respect to age and gender, income and education, and nativity and rootedness. As the columns are displayed, the numbers for STS whites are shown first from left to right. The difference in these numbers for STS versus urban whites is shown, and then the last column displays the significance level if there is a

Table 10.1. Demographics for Small-Town South (STS) and Urban Whites

Characteristic	STS	Urban	Difference (STS-urban)	p
Age and gender				
Age (*Mdn*)	55.0	51.0	4.0	<.05
% Male	49.0	48.6	0.4	*ns*
Income and Education				
% >$75,000	19.7	32.3	−12.6	<.001
% With a college degree	17.8	35.9	−18.1	<.001
Nativity and rootedness				
% Southern native	76.6	64.1	12.5	<.001
Years in state (*Mdn*)	30.0	25.0	5.0	<.01
Years in residence (*Mdn*)	10.0	6.0	4.0	<.001

Note. p = significance; *Mdn* = Median; *ns* = not significant.

statistically significant disparity between STS and urban whites. For instance, in median years, an STS white was fifty-five years old in 2020, as compared with fifty-one years old for urban whites. This four-year difference, with STS whites being the older population, is a statistically significant difference with a probability (*p*) value < .05, which means that if we were to obtain one hundred surveys similar to the one we conducted, then we can be certain that in at least ninety-five of them we would find a difference in age between STS and urban whites that was significantly different, as opposed to merely a result of chance.

The only characteristic in Table 10.1 in which STS and urban whites do not differ is gender. Among STS and urban whites, they constitute the same percentage of the male population, which is right around forty-nine percent, obviously making them a smaller population than white women in the American South. The greatest demographic differences register with respect to income and education. Considering higher income white southerners—in this case, as demarcated by respondents in families earning more than seventy-five thousand dollars annually—this amounts to 19.7% of STS whites versus 32.3% of urban whites. To be sure, the cost of living in urban areas is higher, but this income disparity is wide enough to allow a safe assumption that urban whites are employed in jobs that pay more. Affirming this point is that STS whites are not as well educated as their urban counterparts. Specifically, 17.8% of STS whites earned a college degree, whereas 35.9% of urban whites have done the same. At 18.1 percentage points, the education gap among STS and urban whites is the greatest shown in the table.

Finally, regarding nativity and rootedness, with the latter characteristic measured both in terms of years lived in their state and residence, STS whites are clearly the less transient population. Because we asked respondents where they were born, we can determine who are native southerners. More than three out of four STS whites (76.6%) were born in the South and are, therefore, natives to the region. Less than two thirds (64.1%) of urban whites are native southerners. According to the median value, both groups have lived a very long time in their current state of residence: thirty years for STS whites and twenty-five years in the case of urban whites. Last, the median STS white respondent has lived a decade in their current residence, as compared with six years for their urban white neighbors.

Cultural Distinctions and Racial Attitudes

If we consider the cultural conservatism of STS whites, then they certainly do not disappoint on these indicators. The common stereotype of the American South as a land populated by rednecks is not going to fade away any time soon, thanks to media portrayals (Kirby, 2004) and the reality that Dixie persists as a destination where God, guns, and a reverence for place so strongly resonates. Table 10.2 displays data on STS and urban whites for religiosity, gun ownership and gun attitudes, and American and southern identity. Historically, white southerners have been overwhelmingly Protestant (McKee, 2019). Since the mid-twentieth century, the share of white Protestants in the South has declined considerably, and the current STS-urban white disparity is a very substantial 20.2 percentage points. It remains true that a large majority of STS whites (61.7%) identify as Protestants, but this is not the case regarding their urban white neighbors, with well under half of them identifying as Protestants (41.5%).

Almost mirroring the rates of Protestantism found among STS and urban whites is the percentage among these groups who claim to be born-again Christians; that is, having made a deliberate profession to accept Jesus Christ as their Lord and Savior. As noted in the table's footnote, we did not limit the "born-again" question to Protestants, because Catholics may also claim to have undergone this transformative Christian experience. The largest STS-urban white division in the table is found among born-again Christian respondents; a difference of 20.8 percentage points. A clear majority of STS whites (sixty-two percent) were born again, whereas only 41.2% of urban whites expressed having the same religious conversion. White evangelicals are one of the staunchest Republican constituencies ("Two Nations Under God," 2021), and they are disproportionally situated in STS communities.

Table 10.2. Characteristics and Attitudes toward God, Guns, Country, and Regional Identity among Small-Town South (STS) and Urban Whites

Characteristic (%)	STS	Urban	Difference (STS-urban)	p
Religiosity				
Protestant	61.7	41.5	20.2	<.001
Born-again Christian[a]	62.0	41.2	20.8	<.001
Attends church weekly	38.9	34.1	4.8	<.05
Gun owner and gun policy				
Gun owner	62.6	42.2	20.4	<.001
Opposes gun control	53.8	34.2	19.6	<.001
Opposes assault weapons ban	42.1	30.0	12.1	<.001
American and southern identity				
Believes being American is extremely important)	67.1	58.5	8.6	<.001
Southerner	89.8	75.7	14.1	<.001
Native southerner	69.5	49.0	20.5	<.001

[a]Asked of those respondents who self-identified as Protestant or Catholic in terms of religious tradition. p = significance.

Gun ownership and attitudes toward gun control is another domain that manifests clear differences between STS and urban whites. Well over three fifths of STS whites (62.6%) own a gun, whereas only four in ten urban whites (42.2%) own a firearm. It naturally follows that general opposition to gun control measures is higher among STS whites, with 53.8% against restrictions on gun use and ownership, whereas 34.2% of urban whites take the same position. Nationally, there is high support for banning assault weapons; typically, over half of the American public takes the position in favor of making these specific kinds of guns illegal.[6] This is also true in the case of white southerners. Nonetheless, with respect to those opposed to banning assault weapons, the portion holding this view is much higher among STS whites (42.1%) than urban whites (thirty percent).

Gun ownership and gun attitudes tap into a cultural attribute more valued by STS whites, because rural living involves hunting as a livelihood and common recreational activity. As one of the authors of this book will never forget, in discussing a hunting excursion that 2004 Democratic presidential nominee John Kerry took part in while on the campaign trail, a student in a southern politics class remarked that, "John Kerry doesn't hunt right." A damning comment that spoke to the inauthenticity of the Bostonian Democratic contender's attempt to appeal to a demographic (rural whites) that likely would not accept Senator Kerry in this role (Popkin, 1991).

The last set of questions in the table asked about American and regional identity. First, respondents were asked about the importance of being an American. In the table, we report the percentage of respondents who considered being an American as extremely important. Fully 67.1% of STS whites gave this response, whereas 58.5% of urban whites did the same. Next, we posed two questions regarding southern identity. The two listed responses came from one question that asked whether individuals considered themselves to be a nonsoutherner, southerner, or native southerner.[7] Unlike in Table 10.1, which documents the actual percentage of respondents born in the South—and by this definition, they are classified as southern natives—here, we asked respondents how they identify themselves in a regional sense (Cooper and Knotts, 2019). Therefore, a respondent can be a native southerner in the technical sense of having been born in a southern state, but not identify as a southerner and, hence, offer the response "nonsoutherner." The vast majority of STS and urban whites identify as southerners, but to no surprise, this percentage is markedly higher among STS respondents (89.8%) versus urban respondents (75.7%). Finally, whereas 69.5% of STS whites consider themselves to be native southerners, less than half of urban whites (forty-nine percent) view themselves as southern natives.

In Table 10.3, we turn to questions about race and racial attitudes. The data in Table 10.3 come from survey questions presented in Ashley Jardina's influential book *White Identity Politics* (2019). Jardina broke new ground by demonstrating that, much like the reality that many Blacks share a collective group consciousness (Miller et al., 1981), albeit to a lesser degree, many whites also possess the same empowering and motivating view of their race. Thus, the top section of the table shows results from questions asking about white identity. First, respondents were asked how important it was for them to be white. We show the percentage of STS and urban whites who said being white was either extremely or very important. There is hardly any distinction by place with respect to this question: 36.5% of STS whites and thirty-five percent of urban whites agreed that being white was extremely or very important (a statistically insignificant difference). We also posed a question that gauged racial unity/group solidarity. Compared with urban whites (40.9%), a significantly higher share of STS whites (46.8%) believe that it is extremely or very important for whites to work together.

The remainder of Table 10.3 focuses on white attitudes/opinions toward Blacks. An overwhelming majority of STS and urban whites believe that slavery reparations are a bad idea: 88.5% of STS whites think so, and so do 75.9% of urban whites. This 12.6-percentage-point difference in the opinions of STS and urban whites on this question is substantial and statistically significant.

Table 10.3. White Identity and Racial Attitudes
of Small-Town South (STS) and Urban Whites

Belief/characteristic (%)	STS	Urban	Difference (STS-urban)	p
White identity				
Believes being white is extremely/very important	36.5	35.0	1.5	ns
Believes that white unity is extremely/very important	46.8	40.9	5.9	<.01
Reparations and race relations				
Believes slavery reparations are a bad idea	88.5	75.9	12.6	<.001
Believes race relations in the United States are poor	26.4	32.9	−6.5	<.001
Believes race relations in their state are poor	19.5	24.0	−4.5	<.01
Racial resentment				
Preferential treatment for minorities makes whites unable to find a job (agree)	40.2	32.4	7.8	<.001
Blacks should not receive any special favors (agree)	70.3	61.9	8.4	<.001
Blacks have received less than they deserve (disagree)	62.6	48.0	14.6	<.001
The current station of Blacks is a result of a lack of effort (agree)	58.2	47.1	11.1	<.001
Discrimination creates economic difficulty (disagree)	57.3	43.3	14.0	<.001

Note. p = significance; ns = not significant.

The next two questions concerned views toward race relations among whites and Blacks in the national context and also within the state where respondents live. It is notable that, as we show in the bottom of the table, STS whites harbor more racial resentment yet also believe that race relations, whether in the nation or in their state, are not as poor as their urban white counterparts think they are. Specifically, 26.4% of STS whites view race relations nationwide to be poor, whereas 32.9% of urban whites hold this position. Regarding race relations in their state, both groups see interactions with Blacks as better compared with the national condition. In this context, 19.5% of STS whites consider race relations in their state to be poor, and twenty-four percent of urban whites agree.

The bottom of Table 10.3 presents data in response to five questions that all tap into beliefs and attitudes commonly referred to as racial resentment. Here, we display the percentages of STS and urban whites who possess the highest degree of racial resentment on each of the five questions. Notably, for four out of five racial resentment questions regarding attitudes toward Black Americans, a majority of STS whites registered the most racially resentful response option. The exception is the response to the first question, which asked whether preferential treatment for minorities in the hiring process made it difficult for whites to find a job. More STS whites (40.2%) than urban whites (32.4%) agreed with this statement.

Seven out of ten STS whites (70.3%) believe that Blacks should not receive any special favors, and 61.9% of urban whites agree. More than sixty percent (62.6%) of STS whites *disagree* that Blacks have received less than they de-serve, but less than half of urban whites (forty-eight percent) hold this view. The 14.6 percentage-point difference in STS and urban white responses to the aforementioned question is the largest recorded in Table 10.3. With respect to a question examining whether respondents believe that the current station of Blacks is due to their lack of effort, 58.2% of STS whites believe this to be true, whereas 47.1% of urban whites take this position. Finally, we show the percentage of STS and urban whites who *disagree* that racial discrimination faced by Blacks creates economic difficulty. Among STS whites, 57.3% dis-agree with this statement, and 43.3% of urban whites concur.

Opinions on Divisive Issues

There are several issues in American politics that animate the public and do so in a manner that is highly divisive, with entrenched and opposing positions leading to political activism and, at times, violence. In Table 10.4, we present the views of STS and urban whites on a handful of polarizing issues, includ-ing attitudes toward abortion, views on Confederate symbols, and opinions toward immigration. As noted by Stimson (2004), there was a time, before the *Roe v. Wade* (1973) Supreme Court decision legalized abortion, when neither major political party engaged on this issue and upper-middle-class Republi-can white women were the most likely proponents of a pro-choice position. However, the *Roe* ruling led to a countermobilization among religious con-servatives who were emboldened by Republican Ronald Reagan (Nesmith, 1994), who made it clear that he was pro-life when he defeated Democratic President Jimmy Carter in the 1980 presidential election. The issue evolution of abortion attitudes (Adams, 1997) within the context of American politics was a slow process (Carmines and Woods, 2002). Nevertheless, abortion is an issue that disproportionally riles up southern white religious conservatives and was a major contributing factor in this group's pronounced realignment to the Republican Party (McKee, 2019).

Table 10.4. Opinions on Divisive Issues:
Abortion, Confederate Symbols, and Immigration

Belief/characteristic (%)	STS	Urban	Difference (STS-urban)	p
Views on abortion				
It is always illegal	32.0	16.3	15.7	<.001
Views on Confederate symbols				
Leave Confederate monuments as they are	56.9	46.7	10.2	<.001
Confederate flag represents southern pride	65.5	48.8	16.7	<.001
Views on immigration				
Prefer legal immigration decreased a lot	28.0	19.2	8.8	<.001
Immigration takes jobs (extremely/ very likely)	22.8	16.9	5.9	<.001
Favor building border wall	61.4	45.2	16.2	<.001

Note. p = significance.

The staunchest antiabortion/pro-life view is to oppose the medical procedure regardless of the circumstances leading to the pregnancy. Hence, in Table 10.4, we show the percentages of STS and urban whites who believe that abortion should be illegal under any circumstances. There is a substantial place-based difference regarding opinions on abortion according to the absolute pro-life position. Almost one third (thirty-two percent) of STS whites believe that abortion should always be illegal, whereas less than one in six (16.3%) urban whites share this view. With their higher religiosity ratings, as documented in Table 10.2, it was expected that STS whites would be markedly more pro-life than their white metropolitan neighbors. In what is currently the most Republican and second most rural southern state and has the second highest percentage of non-Latino whites (see chapter nine), Arkansas has forced the Supreme Court's hand by passing the nation's most restrictive abortion law in March 2021. According to the legislation, "abortion would only be allowed in cases where it's necessary to save the life or preserve the health of the fetus or mother. The law does not allow any exceptions in situations of rape or incest" (Diaz, 2021).

Despite the Civil War ending more than one hundred fifty years ago, it and the South's Confederate legacy continue to affect all manner of Dixie's public affairs (Goldfield, 2013). In Table 10.4, we have highlighted views toward two of the more controversial Confederate symbols, addressing the perennial question of the Confederate battle flag and the more recent hot-button issue of what to do with Confederate memorials (Cooper et al., 2020). We asked white southerners their opinion of what to do regarding Confederate monuments, with the lion's share of these memorials not surprisingly found throughout Dixie, and especially and particularly in STS settings. With respect to what should be done about Confederate monuments, respondents were given the following four options: (1) leave them as they are, (2) leave them but offer a historical marker for context, (3) place them in a museum, or (4) simply remove them entirely—a solution in line with what conservatives have aggressively opposed as their liberal opponents' advocacy of a "cancel culture." Taking the most conservative view of leaving Confederate monuments as they are is a position embraced by 56.9% of STS whites and a 46.7% minority of urban whites.

Over the decades, a large and multidisciplinary literature has been established to understand attitudes toward the Confederate battle flag (Huffmon, Knotts, and McKee, 2017–2018). An oft-repeated survey question asks respondents if they believe that the Confederate battle flag: (1) is a symbol of southern pride, (2) is a symbol of racial conflict, or (3) equally represents southern pride and racial conflict. Obviously, the most conservative response is option 1; a belief that the Confederate flag is just a symbol of southern pride. As shown in Table 10.4, almost two thirds of STS whites (65.5%) still hold to the opinion that the Confederate flag represents southern pride, whereas under a majority of urban whites (48.8%) share this view. The place-based division over views toward the Confederate flag is the largest found in the table.

During Donald Trump's 2015 campaign for the Republican presidential nomination, word eventually leaked out that his stated desire to build a wall spanning the entirety of America's southern border with Mexico began as an incendiary gimmick.[8] However, primarily because of the rabid responses of Trump's supporters at campaign rallies, the future president's handlers made a point of repeatedly peppering his stump speeches with the sincere pledge to "Build the Wall" and, even better, demand that Mexico pay for it. With the immigration issue sufficiently primed since Trump kicked off his 2015 GOP presidential nomination campaign by declaring that many of the Mexicans crossing the US border were of a criminal element and took jobs from deserving Americans, we have displayed responses to three immigration-related questions at the bottom of Table 10.4. The first question asked respondents of their views toward whether legal immigration should be increased or decreased. On the basis of this ordinal measure, the most conservative response was to prefer that legal immigration be decreased a lot. Among STS whites, twenty-eight percent took this view as compared with 19.2% of urban whites who agreed. Next, 22.8% of STS whites believed it to be extremely or very likely that immigration takes jobs from Americans; 16.9% of urban whites also believed this to be true. Finally, with respect to building the wall, 61.4% of STS whites were in favor of this policy, whereas a 45.2% minority of urban whites were also in favor of this highly divisive action.

Political Differences

Ideology and party identification are, without question, separable concepts (Noel, 2013), but the relationship between these two important political dispositions has tightened over the years. Decades ago, from the 1950s through the 1980s, there was a large percentage of white southern Democrats who also considered themselves to be conservatives (see chapter three). Indeed, among the population of white southerners, conservative self-identification has consistently been the predominant conceptualization among this group (Black and Black, 1987). Also, although over time a large majority of conservatives have come to align with the GOP, the ideological distribution of liberal, moderate, and conservative southerners has changed hardly at all (McKee, 2019). Instead, there has been a growing congruence between party affiliation and ideology, so that majorities of Democrats are also liberals, whereas majorities of Republicans are conservatives. This long-term development is referred to as partisan sorting (Levendusky, 2009), and it is clearly on display among whites in the southern United States.

In our 2020 survey of STS and urban white southerners, we measured ideological self-placement and party identification on the commonly used seven-point scales. Thus, respondents can place themselves as follows along the ideological scale: (1) very liberal, (2) liberal, (3) slightly liberal, (4) moderate, (5) slightly conservative, (6) conservative, and (7) very conservative. For our purposes, and as is typically done, we collapsed these categories so that 1–3 = liberal, 4 = moderate, and 5–7 = conservative. Likewise, for party identification, the scale is as follows: (1) strong Democrat, (2) not-so-strong Democrat, (3) independent-leaning Democrat, (4) independent, (5) independent-leaning Republican, (6) not-so-strong Republican, and (7) strong Republican. We then collapsed the party identification categories so that 1–3 = Democrat, 4 = independent, and 5–7 = Republican.

In the top part of Table 10.5, we show the percentages of STS and urban whites who are liberal, moderate, and conservative. We also display the difference among these three ideological classifications according to place (STS – urban). There are essentially the same shares of STS and urban whites who consider themselves to be moderates, one out of four (twenty-five percent). In contrast, urban whites are substantially more liberal at 30.8% versus 21.2% in the case of STS whites. Conversely, STS whites are notably and significantly more conservative at 53.5%, whereas less than a majority of urban whites (44.7%) place themselves on the conservative end of the ideological scale.

Table 10.5. Ideology, Party Identification, and Partisan Sorting

Ideology	Liberal	Moderate	Conservative
STS	21.2	25.3	53.5
Urban	30.8	24.5	44.7
Difference	−9.6***	0.8	8.8***
Party Identification	Democrat	Independent	Republican
STS	24.9	10.8	64.4
Urban	35.4	7.9	56.7
Difference	−10.5***	2.9*	7.7***
Partisan Sorting (STS/urban)	Liberal	Moderate	Conservative
Democrat	61.3/71.6**	26.1/24.0	12.6/4.4***
Independent	20.1/13.5	52.1/62.2	27.8/24.3
Republican	4.8/8.5**	19.5/15.4*	75.6/76.1

Note. STS = small-town South. Difference (STS − urban) is significant at: $^*p < .05$; $^{**}p < .01$; $^{***}p < .001$.

The middle section of Table 10.5 presents the distribution of STS and urban whites who identify as Democrat, independent, and Republican. Likewise, we show the difference among these party affiliation classifications according to place (STS −urban). A slightly larger and statistically significant portion of STS whites are pure independents, at 10.8% versus 7.9% of urban whites. More than a third (35.4%) of urban whites identify as Democrats, but only a fourth (24.9%) of STS whites also affiliate with the Democratic Party, a substantial and statistically significant difference of 10.5 percentage points. A clear majority of STS and urban whites identify as Republicans, but a higher share of the former group align with the GOP, at 64.4% versus 56.7% in the case of urban whites. This 7.7-percentage-point Republican identification disparity based on place is statistically significant.

The last section of Table 10.5 documents the extent to which STS and urban whites are sorted with respect to ideology and party identification. In each of the nine cells, the value displayed shows the share of party affiliates in each category (Democrat, independent, and Republican) who are liberal, moderate, and conservative. Hence, the summation of each row for each party affiliate (Democrat, independent, and Republican) equals one hundred percent (give or take rounding error). The first entry for each cell is the value for STS whites and the second, after the slash, is the value for urban whites.

Asterisks indicate whether the values for STS and urban whites in each cell are significantly different.

It would appear that the degree of partisan sorting among STS and urban whites is considerable. Nonetheless, there are differences in the extent of partisan sorting for these two groups, depending on party affiliation. For instance, in the case of Democrats, urban whites are more sorted into the liberal category (71.6%) than are STS whites (61.3%). Conversely, close to three times as many STS whites are conservative Democrats (12.6%) versus the percentage of urban white Democrats who are conservatives (4.4%). Among STS and urban whites who are independents, regardless of the ideological classification (liberal, moderate, and conservative), there is no significant difference.

Whereas more STS white conservatives identify as Democrats, which would speak to the historic holdover of this group's allegiance to the Democratic Party, a higher percentage of urban white liberals affiliate with the GOP. The latter finding is also evidence of the fact that southern Republicanism's roots among the urban white electorate meant that the GOP had historically been more successful in securing the allegiance of a relatively more liberal population. Finally, in the case of STS and urban white Republicans, there is no difference regarding the overwhelming share of conservatives aligned with the GOP, more than seventy-five percent for both groups.

We conclude this section with an examination of levels of affective partisan polarization exhibited by STS and urban whites. In line with a classic work on political behavior, which argues Americans are not ideologically sophisticated (Converse, 1964), nor are they terribly informed because of the incentive to be rationally ignorant (Downs, 1957), it is no wonder that increasing partisan polarization among the mass public is tied more to emotional reactions than some elaborate ideologically driven or policy-based motivation. In other words, political tribalism has grown in importance as the descriptive profiles of the major parties' supporters have become more distinguishable (Mason, 2018). For instance, the Democratic Party is now a racially and ethnically diverse coalition, and in the South, its share of white constituents is a minority of this majority-minority electorate (McKee, 2019). In contrast, the southern Republican coalition, despite decades of issue-based changes to the positions advocated by the major political parties (Abramowitz and Saunders, 1998), remains overwhelmingly white (McKee, 2019). In short, the physical appearances of the Democratic and Republican tribes look very different and that seems to matter much more than the finer details of policy- and issue-based disagreements, which take considerably more effort to comprehend.

Because most white southerners affiliate with the Republican Party, we expect that their feelings toward the GOP will be more positive than those registered for the Democratic Party. Furthermore, because we know that STS whites are more Republican than urban whites, we expect that the former group would exhibit higher levels of affective partisan polarization. Affective partisan polarization is computed by taking the difference in feeling thermometer ratings for the two major parties (see Iyengar et al., 2019). Typically, this measure is calculated for partisan groups (e.g., the level of affective partisan polarization exhibited by Republicans and Democrats, respectively). However, because we are not interested in the level of affective partisan polarization according to party identification—but, instead, the level according to place—in Table 10.6, we show levels of affective partisan polarization for STS and urban whites irrespective of their party affiliation.[9]

The feeling thermometer is scaled from a minimum value of 0 to a maximum value of 100. As a gauge of affective assessments of groups, individuals, objects, and/or attitudes/beliefs, lower scores on the feeling thermometer are evidence of emotionally based disapproval. Conversely, higher feeling thermometer scores reflect a warmth/affection/approval of the subject being rated on the scale. With this in mind, Table 10.6 displays the mean and median feeling thermometer ratings of STS and urban whites for the Republican and Democratic parties. As expected, the thermometer scores for the GOP are markedly higher compared with those for the Democratic Party. It is interesting, however, that compared with urban whites, STS whites exhibit substantially different and statistically distinguishable feeling thermometer ratings of the major parties. Specifically, STS whites are markedly more approving of

Table 10.6. Affective Partisan Polarization among Small-Town South (STS) and Urban Whites

Thermometer Rating for:	Republican Party (Rep)	Democratic Party (Dem)	Diff. (Rep – Dem)
M rating			
STS	61.5	31.0	30.5
Urban	51.9	39.8	12.1
Diff. (STS – urban)	9.6	–8.8	18.4
Mdn rating			
STS	71.0	18.0	53.0
Urban	55.0	36.1	18.9
Diff. (STS – urban)	16.0	–18.1	34.1

Note. All differences (Diff.) shown in the table are significant at $p < .001$. Values in gray shading indicate the partisan difference (Rep – Dem) for STS versus urban whites. For example, in the top half of the table, the mean (*M*) thermometer rating partisan difference (Rep – Dem) is 30.5 for STS whites – 12.1 for urban whites, which yields a value of 18.4 points (the similar calculation in the bottom half of the table yields a value of 34.1). *Mdn* = Median.

the GOP by 9.6 points on average and by 16 points with respect to their median rating. Conversely, STS whites are considerably and significantly less approving of the Democratic Party by a difference of 8.8 points on average and by 18.1 points with respect to their median rating.

The last column in Table 10.6 displays the degree of affective partisan polarization registered by STS and urban whites. By a wide margin, STS whites harbor a much higher level of affective partisan polarization in favor of the Republican Party. On the basis of the average feeling thermometer rating, STS whites score the GOP 30.5 points higher than the Democratic Party. Urban whites score the GOP 12.1 points higher than the Democratic Party. As shown in the last row, highlighted in gray, the affective partisan polarization registered by STS whites is 18.4 points greater than that exhibited by urban whites.

On the basis of the median feeling thermometer rating, STS whites score the GOP 53 points higher than the Democratic Party. Urban whites score the GOP 18.9 points higher than the Democratic Party. Also, as shown in the last row highlighted in gray, the affective partisan polarization registered by STS whites is 34.1 points greater than that exhibited by urban whites. All differences in party feeling thermometer ratings assigned by STS and urban whites in Table 10.6 are statistically significant. Both groups express substantially more affection for the GOP, but relatively speaking, STS whites are much more fervent in their feelings for the Republican Party and are considerably more disdainful of the Democratic opposition. In sum, STS whites are decidedly more polarized than urban whites when it comes to the affective form of partisan polarization.

Differentiating STS and Urban Whites

In this penultimate section, we present the results from some simple multivariate statistical models. Multivariate modeling allows one to test the relationship of an explanatory factor while controlling for, or holding constant, other potentially salient factors; and because our survey consists of only southern non-Hispanic white respondents, region and race are not variables. In the initial model, we examine the influence of education, income, age, gender, gun ownership, ideology, party identification, nativity, and evangelicalism on the likelihood of being an STS versus urban resident.[10]

The condensed results of our STS model are found in Table 10.7 (for more detailed model results, please refer to the online Appendix B). The table uses a sign to indicate the direction of the relationship between each characteristic and the probability of being from an STS county as opposed to an urban county (in the table, only statistically significant relationships are shown; significance levels are denoted by asterisks). In Table 10.7, one can see that socioeconomic status is related to type of residency. Education is inversely

Table 10.7. Correlates Related to the Likelihood
of Being a Small-Town South (STS) Resident

Correlate	Relationship
Education	(–)**
Income	(–)**
Age	(+)*
Gender	
Gun owner	(+)**
Ideology	
Party identification	
Native southerner	(+)*
Evangelical	(+)*
No. of cases	2,580

Note. Dependent variable: STS = 1; Urban = 0. Model was estimated using probit. Only statistically significant relationships and direction are shown; $^*p < .05$; $^{**}p < .01$. Full model results are located online in Appendix B.

related to the probability of living in an STS area. In plainer terms, STS residents are characterized by lower education levels, whereas urban dwellers are more likely, on average, to possess more formal education. Likewise, family income level is also negatively related to STS residency. Urban whites are more likely to have higher incomes, compared with STS whites. The typical STS white resident is also more likely to be older, a gun owner, and a native-born southerner, compared with their urban counterparts. Finally, STS whites are more likely to self-identify as evangelicals.

Interestingly, neither partisan affiliation nor ideology are related to the likelihood of residence type. STS whites are no more likely than urban whites in the South to identify as Republicans or conservatives. However, there are sharp demarcation lines between these two groups regarding the other identified characteristics in Table 10.7. Figure 10.1 converts the results from our statistical model into a set of probabilities based on the characteristics that were found to be related to STS residency.[11] Probabilities range from zero to one, with movement toward one in this case an indication of a greater likelihood of STS residency. In the figure, probability estimates are represented by black circles, with ninety-five percent confidence intervals denoted by the left and right bands.

Beginning at the top of Figure 10.1, it is apparent that native-born southerners are more likely to be STS residents, as compared with non-natives (0.46 versus 0.41). Evangelicals have a 0.46 probability of STS residency, compared with 0.42 for nonevangelicals. Gun ownership is a profound dividing

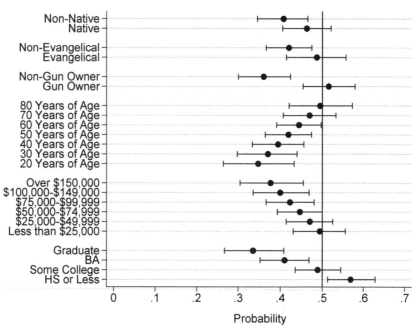

Figure 10.1. Probability of STS Residence

line between rural and urban white southerners. Gun owners have a 0.52 probability of STS residency compared with non–gun owners at 0.36—a 16-point gap. Differences also appear for age (14 points) and income (11 points); however, none of these disparities are as large as that found between education levels. A survey respondent with a high school education or less has a 0.57 probability of STS residency, whereas a respondent with a graduate degree has just a 0.34 likelihood of living in an STS county, a 23-percentage-point difference.

Next, we considered whether STS residency itself is a factor that can be used to explain opinions related to a set of political issues. We did so by including residency along with the other previously identified characteristics in another set of statistical models. In Table 10.8, we present the results from a set of models that examine eight different issues in the following order: gun control; an assault weapons ban; reparations; racial resentment; abortion; the Confederate flag; Confederate monuments; and building a border wall. Except for racial resentment, all the other issues examined are binary in nature, with a value of one representing the conservative position. Racial resentment is an additive scale that ranges from zero to twenty and is constructed from five separate questions. Increasing values on this scale are associated with higher levels of racial resentment (see the Appendix at the end of this chapter for more information on the construction of this index).

Table 10.8. The Effect of Place on Political Issues

Characteristic	Gun control	Assault weapons ban	Reparations	Racial Resentment Scale	Abortion	Confederate flag	Confederate monuments	Border wall
STS	(+)***	(+)*		(+)**	(+)**	(+)*		(+)***
Education				(−)***	(−)**	(−)***	(−)***	(−)***
Income								
Age		(−)***	(+)***	(+)***	(−)**	(+)***	(+)***	(+)***
Gender		(−)**	(−)**		(+)*			
Gun owner	(+)***	(+)***	(+)**	(+)***	(+)**	(+)**		(+)**
Ideology	(+)***	(+)***	(+)***	(+)***	(+)**	(+)***	(+)***	(+)***
Party identification	(+)***	(+)***	(+)***	(+)***	(+)***	(+)***	(+)***	(+)***
Native southerner						(+)**	(+)**	(+)***
Evangelical					(+)***	(−)*		(+)*
No. of cases	2,306	2,340	2,580	2,372	2,458	2,427	2,499	2,544

Note. Dependent variables: gun control (oppose stricter gun control); assault weapons ban (oppose banning assault weapons); reparations (bad idea); racial resentment scale (ranges from zero to twenty, with increasing values indicative of higher levels of racial resentment); abortion (should always be illegal); Confederate flag (symbol of southern heritage/pride); Confederate monuments (leave them as they are); and border wall (in favor of building it). Only statistically significant relationships and direction are shown; * $p < .10$; ** $p < .05$; *** $p < .01$. Full model results are located online in Appendix B.

As with the previous table, Table 10.8 presents a summation of our multivariate model results by displaying the direction of the relationship and its level of statistical significance with each of the eight political issues analyzed.[12] Living in an STS county is associated with opposing gun control and a ban on assault weapons; a belief that abortion should always be illegal; characterizing the Confederate flag as an expression of southern heritage or pride; and support for building a wall on the US-Mexico border. STS residents also score higher on the racial resentment scale as compared with urban white southerners.

There was no discernible statistical effect for STS residency and opinion on reparations or Confederate monuments. On these two political issues, STS and urban whites are no different. It is clear that *place* can have a direct, independent effect on white southerners' opinions even when controlling for a number of other key characteristics such as ideology, partisanship, and socioeconomic factors. Across all models, increasing conservatism (ideology) and Republicanism (party identification) are, not surprisingly, positively related to taking a more conservative position on these eight policy questions. Depending on the specific model, other factors also come into play, including gun ownership with gun control, evangelicalism with abortion, or nativity with Confederate symbols.

For the political issues where STS residency exhibited a statistically significant effect in Table 10.8, we again plotted a set of predicted probabilities in Figure 10.2. The exception is the racial resentment scale, which was analyzed

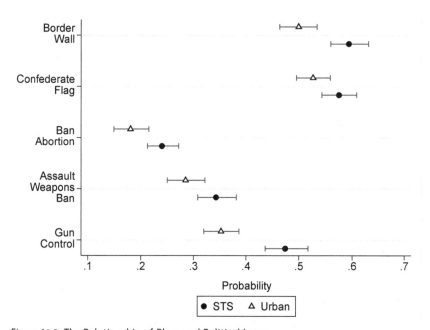

Figure 10.2. The Relationship of Place and Political Issues

using a different statistical technique because it is not binary in nature but rather an ordinal scale. In Figure 10.2, the predicted probability for taking a conservative position on a given political issue was plotted using a black circle to indicate STS residents and a white triangle to indicate urban residents (again, ninety-five percent confidence intervals were also plotted for each point estimate).

Starting at the top of the figure, we can see that STS residents are more likely than their urban counterparts to support building a border wall (0.59 versus 0.50). Next, the probability of an STS resident thinking of the Confederate flag as a symbol of regional heritage or pride is 0.57, as compared with 0.53 for urban residents. There is also a gap of 0.06 between these two groups regarding those who believe that abortion should always be illegal (0.24 for STS residents versus 0.18 for urban residents). Finally, for the issue of gun control, there is a split between rural and urban white southerners, even while controlling for the effects of gun ownership. Slightly more STS residents oppose a ban on assault weapons (0.34) than do urban residents (0.29). On the overall question of gun control, a twelve-point breach manifests. For STS residents, almost half (0.47) are predicted to oppose gun control measures as a general principle, whereas only about a third (0.35) of urban residents take such a position.

Figure 10.3 plots the average values of racial resentment for STS versus urban white southerners. Again, this is an ordinal scale that ranges from zero

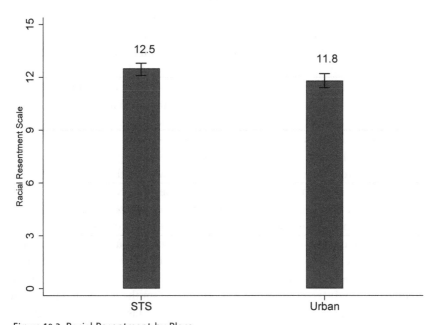

Figure 10.3. Racial Resentment by Place

to twenty, with higher values indicative of increasing levels of racial resentment.[13] For STS white residents, the predicted racial resentment value is 12.5, as compared with 11.8 for urban white residents. Although the relationship between place and racial resentment is statistically significant, the actual difference from these estimates is under a point; a 0.7-point difference to be precise. Therefore, the substantive difference between respondents in urban and rural locales on this subject is quite modest.

Conclusion

Given the numerous differences between rural and urban white southerners—and, more specifically, the nature of these distinctions—the current political posturing of the Republican Party appears considerably more reflective of the profiles, beliefs, and preferences of their STS constituents. This reality may no longer be surprising, but it was decades in the making. In particular, the ongoing culture wars that the southern GOP is often fueling aligns with the social and racial conservatism of rural whites who are significantly more in favor of banning abortion no matter the context, building a wall to keep out interlopers at America's southern border, believe that the Confederate flag is symbolic of southern pride (not racial conflict), and are much more adamant in their embrace and defense of the Second Amendment. This hard-edge approach to hot-button, politically divisive issues was certainly incited over the past four years by Republican President Trump. From what we have systematically shown in this chapter, it should make sense why urban white southerners have not proven as loyal to the GOP at a time when the party under President Trump's tutelage has fanned the flames of division. In short, on a host of salient and controversial issues, urban whites are not nearly as conservative as their STS neighbors.

If southern Republicans continue down the path of expending their political capital on culture war fights to the detriment of addressing pressing issues related to the economy, education, and health care, then expect their urban white constituency to dwindle in size relative to STS voters. This is a growing problem for the GOP in the South (see the expanded discussion in chapter twelve), because, as passionate and stalwart as their rural white base might be, it is declining relative to the rest of the electorate. It is one thing to document the various and significant differences between rural and urban white southerners; it is a whole other endeavor to consider the gulf that separates the characteristics and views of STS whites vis-à-vis the remarkably expanding racial minority electorate in the South, which is decidedly Democratic in affiliation and voting behavior. Because southern Republicans have exhibited little interest in cultivating support from the rising population of minority groups (Latinos, Asians, and Blacks), this fastest growing segment of Dixie's electorate is going to be a metastasizing problem at the ballot box.

If the southern GOP remains disinterested in expanding its appeal to non-whites, then at a minimum, Republicans would be wise to moderate their positions on politically divisive issues or, instead, pay them less attention to reconnect with the expanding and increasingly electorally powerful contingent of urban whites, who at least for now, still favor the Republican Party.

Chapter 10 Appendix

Survey Instrument

The following are original questions with response options shown in parentheses. All questions contained a *don't know* and *prefer not to answer* response option.

Demographic:

Education (1 = high school or less; 2 = some college/vocational degree; 3 = bachelor's degree; 4 = graduate degree)

Income (1 = <$25,000; 2 = $25,000–$49,99; 3 = $50,000–$74,999; 4 = $75,000–$99,999; 5 = $100,000–$149,000; 6 = >$150,000)

Age (in years): 19–98.

Gender (1 = male; 2 = female)

Gun Owner (1 = gun owner; 0 = non–gun owner)

Native Southerner (1 = born in a southern state; 0 = born outside the region)

Evangelical (1 = born-again Christian; 0 = non-Evangelical)

Protestant (1 = Protestant; 0 = Catholic, Jewish, Muslim, secular, other)

Church Attendance (1 = more than once a week; 2 = once a week; 3 = a few times a month; 4 = a few times a year; 5 = never)

Political:

Ideology (1 = very liberal; 2 = liberal; 3 = slightly liberal; 4 = moderate; 5 = slightly conservative; 6 = conservative; 7 = very conservative)

Party Identification (1 = strong Democrat; 2 = weak (not so strong) Democrat; 3 = Independent, leaning Democratic; 4 = Independent; 5 = Independent, leaning Republican; 6 = weak (not so strong) Republican; 7 = strong Republican)

Policy/Political Issues:

Gun Control: Do you favor or oppose stricter gun control laws? (1 = favor; 2 = oppose)

Assault Weapons Ban: Do you support or oppose banning assault weapons like the AR-15 and AK-47? (1 = support; 2 = oppose)

Southern Identity: Which of the following best describes your regional identity? (1 = non-southerner; 2 = converted southerner; 3 = native southerner)

American Identity: How important is being an American to you personally? (1 = extremely important; 2 = very important; 3 = moderately important; 4 = slightly important; 5 = not important at all)

White Identity: How important is being white to your identity? (1 = extremely important; 2 = very important; 3 = moderately important; 4 = slightly important; 5 = not important at all)

White Unity: How important is it that whites work together to change laws that are unfair to whites? (1 = extremely important; 2 = very important; 3 = moderately important; 4 = slightly important; 5 = not at all important)

Slavery Reparations: Do you think providing reparations for slavery is a good idea or a bad idea? (1 = a good idea; 2 = a bad idea)

US Race Relations: Now, we're going to talk about matters of race and race relations for a bit. How would you rate race relations in the UNITED STATES today? (1 = excellent; 2 = good; 3 = only fair; 4 = poor)

State Race Relations: How would you rate race relations in your state today? (1 = excellent; 2 = good; 3 = only fair; 4 = poor)

Abortion: Do you think abortions should be legal under any circumstances, legal only under certain circumstances, or illegal in all circumstances? (1 = always legal; 2 = sometimes legal; 3 = always illegal)

Confederate Monuments: Which of the following comes closest to your opinion about what to do with monuments or memorials to Confederate soldiers who died during the Civil War? (1 = leave them just as they are; 2 = leave them, but add a plaque or marker for context and historical interpretation; 3 = move them to a museum; 4 = remove them completely)

Confederate Flag: Some people say the Confederate battle flag reminds them of white supremacy and racial conflict. Other people say the Confederate battle flag is a symbol of southern heritage and pride. What's your opinion? (1 = racial conflict; 2 = southern pride; 3 = equally both)

Legal Immigration: Do you think the number of immigrants from foreign countries who are permitted to legally come to the United States to live should be? (1 = increased a lot; 2 = increased a little; 3 = left the same as now; 4 = decreased a little; 5 = decreased a lot)

Immigration-Takes Jobs: Now I'd like to ask you about immigration in recent years. How likely is it that recent immigration levels will take jobs away from people already here? (1 = extremely likely; 2 = very likely; 3 = moderately likely; 4 = slightly likely; 5 = not likely at all)

Border Wall: Do you favor, oppose, or neither favor nor oppose building a wall on the US border with Mexico? (1 = favor; 2 = oppose; 3 = neither favor nor oppose)

Trump-Job Approval: Do you strongly approve, approve, disapprove, or strongly disapprove of the way Donald Trump is handling his job as President of the United States? (1 = strongly approve; 2 = approve; 3 = disapprove; 4 = strongly disapprove)

Feeling Thermometers:

I'd like to get your feelings toward some of our political leaders and other groups who are in the news these days by rating them using something we call a feeling thermometer. Ratings between 51 degrees and 100 degrees mean that you feel favorable toward the person or group. Ratings between 0 degrees and 49 degrees mean that you don't feel favorable toward the person or group. You would rate a person or group at the 50-degree mark if you don't feel particularly warm or cold toward them.

Republican Party
Democratic Party
Barack Obama
Donald Trump

Racial Resentment Scale Questions:

No Special Favors: Irish, Italians, Jewish and many other minorities overcame prejudice and worked their way up. Blacks should do the same without any special favors. Do you strongly agree, somewhat agree, neither agree nor disagree, somewhat disagree, or strongly disagree with this statement? (1 = strongly agree; 2 = somewhat agree; 3 = neither agree nor disagree; 4 = somewhat disagree; 5 = strongly disagree)

Less Than Deserved: Over the past few years, Blacks have gotten less than they deserve. Do you strongly agree, somewhat agree, neither agree nor disagree, somewhat disagree, or strongly disagree with this statement? (1 = strongly agree; 2 = somewhat agree; 3 = neither agree nor disagree; 4 = somewhat disagree; 5 = strongly disagree)

Lack of Effort: It's really a matter of some people not trying hard enough; if Blacks would only try harder, they could be just as well off as whites. Do you strongly agree, somewhat agree, neither agree nor disagree, somewhat disagree, or strongly disagree with this statement? (1 = strongly agree; 2 =

somewhat agree; 3 = neither agree nor disagree; 4 = somewhat disagree; 5 = strongly disagree)

History of Discrimination: Generations of slavery and discrimination have created conditions that make it difficult for Blacks to work their way out of the lower class. Do you strongly agree, somewhat agree, neither agree nor disagree, somewhat disagree, or strongly disagree with this statement? (1 = strongly agree; 2 = somewhat agree; 3 = neither agree nor disagree; 4 = somewhat disagree; 5 = strongly disagree)

Whites-Jobs: How likely is it that many whites are unable to find a job because employers are hiring minorities instead? Do you strongly agree, somewhat agree, neither agree nor disagree, somewhat disagree, or strongly disagree with this statement? (1 = strongly agree; 2 = somewhat agree; 3 = neither agree nor disagree; 4 = somewhat disagree; 5 = strongly disagree)

Index Construction. The racial resentment scale was created by coding each of the preceding five questions from 0 to 4, with a value of 4 representing the conservative position that success is due to individual initiative. An index was created by adding these five questions together, producing an ordinal scale ranging from 0 to 20, with higher values denoting greater levels of racial resentment. The Cronbach's alpha for these five questions was 0.83.

11 The 2020 Elections in the South

The 2020 elections in the South did not bring about any drastic shifts in the current alignment of party politics. Dixie remains the GOP's stronghold. Nevertheless, short-term conditions and slower long-term alterations are reflected in the 2020 outcomes. Indeed, Georgia became the pivotal state for determining the majority party in the US Senate, and the Peach State embodied a mix of more immediate and gradual changes that resulted in a Jewish Democrat unseating an incumbent Republican senator and a Black Democratic preacher triumphing over the other Republican senator appointed to the position after Republican Johnny Isakson stepped down because of health concerns. Georgia also went blue in the presidential election, and thus Virginia was not the only Democratic win in the South, which was the case in 2016. North Carolina is the only southern state that still holds its gubernatorial contests in presidential years, and Democratic Governor Roy Cooper was never in jeopardy of losing, despite capturing a modest fifty-two percent of the two-party vote. Finally, a handful of congressional districts flipped partisan control, but on balance, this was a wash, as the total number of Republicans and Democrats in the southern House delegation remained the same as before the 2020 elections.

Table 11.1 offers an informative before-and-after summary of the 2020 elections in the South for presidential, senatorial, gubernatorial, and House elections. The overall takeaway from the table is that 2020 did very little to move the electoral needle in favor of either major party. In presidential elections, in line with the national outcome, Republican President Donald Trump registered a weaker performance in 2020 versus 2016. Florida was the only state where the defeated incumbent president improved on his percentage of the two-party popular vote (1.1 percentage points) since his surprise victory in 2016. Trump's almost three percentage-point deficit in Georgia (−2.8 points) was enough for his Democratic challenger Joe Biden to prevail by 11,779 votes. Trump's second worst performance (compared to 2016) was in the Old Dominion (−2.4 points), showing again that the South's most Democratic state continued to move in a Democratic direction. In the last row of the table, we also present the percentage of the Republican vote in the Electoral College. The 2020 Democratic pickup in Georgia reduced the GOP Southwide

Table 11.1. The Southern Republican Scorecard in the Past Two Election Cycles

State	President % Republican vote			Senators			Governors			House members		
	2020	2016	DIFF.	2020	2018	DIFF.	2020	2018	DIFF.	2020	2018	DIFF.
AL	62.9	64.4	−1.5	2	1	1	1	1	0	6	6	0
AR	64.2	64.3	−0.1	2	2	0	1	1	0	4	4	0
FL	51.7	50.6	1.1	2	2	0	1	1	0	16	14	2
GA	49.9	52.7	−2.8	0	2	−2	1	1	0	8	9	−1
LA	59.5	60.2	−0.7	2	2	0	0	0	0	5	5	0
MS	58.4	59.1	−0.7	2	2	0	1	1	0	3	3	0
NC	50.7	51.9	−1.2	2	2	0	0	0	0	8	10	−2
SC	55.9	57.5	−1.6	2	2	0	1	1	0	6	5	1
TN	61.8	63.6	−1.8	2	2	0	1	1	0	7	7	0
TX	52.8	54.7	−1.9	2	2	0	1	1	0	23	23	0
VA	44.8	47.2	−2.4	0	0	0	0	0	0	4	4	0
South	53.2	54.4	−1.2	18	19	−1	8	8	0	90	90	0
Rep	81.9[a]	90.6[a]	−8.7[a]	81.8[b]	86.4[b]	−4.6[b]	72.7[b]	72.7[b]	0[b]	65.2[b]	65.2[b]	0[b]

Note. The two-party percentage of the Republican (Rep) popular presidential vote is shown for each state and the South, but the Republican percentage in the final row is based on the Electoral College vote total for the Republican presidential nominee. Also, the 2016 Republican electoral vote total is slightly lower than should be the case, because two Texas electors did not vote for Donald Trump. These before-and-after comparisons of Republican representation by elective office are based on the most recent party affiliation of the officeholder before the 2020 elections, even if this person acquired the office after the regularly scheduled 2018/2019 elections (Louisiana and Mississippi had gubernatorial contests in 2019). Diff. = difference. [a]The percentage of the Republican vote in the Electoral College. [b]The other values are the total number of Republicans in each office (Senators, Governors, and House members) in each state.

presidential vote share in the Electoral College by almost nine percentage points compared with the 2016 election.

Besides the two Democratic Senate wins in Georgia, the only other partisan reversal took place in Alabama, where former college football coach and Republican challenger Tommy Tuberville easily defeated freshman incumbent Democrat Doug Jones (sixty percent to forty percent of the two-party vote), who was fortunate to hold the seat because he drew the controversial and scandal-plagued former Alabama Chief Justice Roy Moore in the 2017 special Senate contest.[1] With the North Carolina governorship the only one up for election in 2020, and the incumbent Democrat winning, there was no change to the South's gubernatorial delegation. Republicans held ninety House seats before and after the 2020 elections, but not the same ninety districts. In Florida, President Trump's rants against the Democratic Party's embrace of "socialism" resonated with many Latino voters in two urban Miami-area districts (Twenty-Six and Twenty-Seven) that threw out their first-term Democratic incumbents in favor of two Cuban American Republicans. Reflecting the statewide results and the impressive shift of urban Georgians to the Democratic Party, the Republican-held but zero percent rural Atlanta-area District Seven was captured by a Democrat. The Charleston-based First District of South Carolina (five percent rural) flipped back to Republican after a Democrat scored an upset in 2018. Finally, North Carolina ran its 2020 House elections under a new map that greatly altered several districts, including Districts Two and Six, so that both Republican-held open seats were made substantially more Democratic and urban, which resulted in Democratic victories.

It is worth noting that, in 2020, in the most nationalized offices, president and Senate (Sievert and McKee, 2019), the percentage of the Republican Electoral College vote (eighty-two percent) was almost identical to the Republican share of southern senators; and as the presidential race went, so did the Senate contest(s), with Florida the only southern state not holding a senatorial election in 2020. Republicans in 2020 held eight of the eleven southern governorships (seventy-three percent); proportionally, the GOP's lowest numbers reside in the southern House delegation, constituting a nevertheless very respectable sixty-five percent of the 138 seats.

In this chapter, we offer a recap of the 2020 elections in the South with regard to the presidential, senatorial, and House elections. As per the thrust of this book, our emphasis is firmly placed on the impact of rural white voters in these aforementioned contests. We are interested specifically in the extent to which rural whites' support for Republican candidates vying for these offices may have changed in 2020 compared with the previous election cycle. Additionally, we offer a more detailed examination of rural voting and participation patterns in Georgia's two Senate elections that decided partisan control of Congress's upper chamber. Likewise, in examining House elections, we devote more coverage to the North Carolina contests, because redistricting drastically altered the rural composition of the electorates in the two districts that Democrats gained. In the sections that follow, we go down the political food chain, starting with the presidential election, then moving to Senate contests, and ending with House races. The general upshot of the 2020 elections in the South is one of stasis reinforcing the GOP status quo, principally because although urban white support slightly dropped, this was not true with respect to the robust Republican voting exhibited by rural whites.

The Presidential Election

Barack Obama captured the Electoral College votes in three southern states in 2008 (Florida, North Carolina, and Virginia), but thereafter, Democrats have done no better than win two southern states in presidential elections. The constant has been Virginia, which has remained Democratic since 2008. The Old Dominion was only joined by Florida in 2012, and was by itself in the Democratic win column in 2016; then, in 2020, Georgia unexpectedly went blue for the first time since 1992. In Table 11.2, the county-level (two-party) percentage of the Republican presidential vote is displayed for every southern state in the last two elections (2016 and 2020). The vote is partitioned according to whether counties are small-town South (STS) or urban. By making comparisons across these county types and with the Republican presidential nominee held constant, the data provide a good sense of place-based contemporary voting patterns across the South.

As Table 11.2 shows, from 2016 to 2020 there was no overall decline in the GOP share of the presidential vote in the South among STS counties. In fact, the Republican vote actually ticked up 1.1 percentage points. In comparison, the urban Republican presidential vote in Dixie declined nine tenths of a percentage point between 2016 and 2020. In the aggregate, the rural-urban county-level difference in the southern GOP share of the presidential vote expanded from 17.7 points in 2016 to 19.7 points in 2020. In 2016 and 2020, South Carolina was the only southern state in which the GOP presidential vote in urban counties exceeded that found in STS counties. However, with the single exception of Florida, where the rural-urban gap in Republican presidential voting was reduced in 2020, in the remaining ten southern states this disparity grew. In some of these southern states the Republican presidential advantage in STS counties in 2020 was extraordinary: over 27 points in Texas; over twenty-five points in Georgia; over twenty-three points in Virginia; and over twenty-one points in Tennessee. Whatever political baggage President Trump carried nationally in 2020, it certainly did not weigh him down among Dixie's numerous STS counties.

Table 11.2. Republican Presidential Vote in the South by County Type, 2016 and 2020

| | % Republican presidential vote in: | | | | | |
| | 2016 | | | 2020 | | |
State	STS	URBAN	DIFF.	STS	URBAN	DIFF.
AL	71.3	61.1	10.2	72.6	59.9	12.7
AR	70.8	61.0	9.8	73.0	59.9	13.1
FL	70.7	49.9	20.8	70.6	51.2	19.4
GA	73.2	47.8	25.4	71.5	45.7	25.8
LA	68.6	58.1	10.5	70.4	56.9	13.5
MS	60.4	58.0	2.4	61.1	56.3	4.8
NC	62.2	49.7	12.5	64.2	48.7	15.5
SC	52.2	58.5	−6.3	52.6	56.4	−3.8
TN	77.1	58.8	18.3	78.3	56.7	21.6
TX	76.7	51.3	25.4	77.6	49.8	27.8
VA	65.1	56.3	8.8	64.8	41.1	23.7
Total	69.2	51.5	17.7	70.3	50.6	19.7

Note. Data were calculated by the authors from *Congressional Quarterly* for the 2016 election and *Dave Leip's Atlas of U.S. Presidential Elections* for 2020. The Republican percentage of the presidential vote is based on the two-party vote cast in each southern county. Diff. = difference.

The drawback regarding the data in Table 11.2 is that there is no distinction in the vote with respect to race. Although the state exit polls were limited to six of the same southern state electorates surveyed for 2016 and 2020, these data allow us to confine presidential preferences to white voters.[2] The half-dozen states with exit polls conducted for 2016 and 2020 were Florida, Georgia, North Carolina, South Carolina, Texas, and Virginia. As usual, with the exit poll data, we bifurcated white southerners as either rural/STS (cities with under fifty thousand people) or urban (suburban residents and those living in cities with more than fifty thousand inhabitants). By isolating white voters, it is apparent from the data in Table 11.3 that the rural white South in 2020 remained steadfast in its presidential Republicanism.

In the six southern states in Table 11.3, collectively, the GOP presidential vote cast by rural/STS whites dipped 1.3 percentage points in 2020 versus 2016. In contrast, the aggregate 2020 Republican presidential vote registered among urban whites dropped 5.4 percentage points since 2016. Hence in the South, Trump's slippage in support was considerably more notable with

Table 11.3. The Republican Presidential Vote Cast by White Southerners, 2016 and 2020

	% Republican vote for presidential election in:					
	2016			2020		
State	RURAL/STS	URBAN	DIFF.	RURAL/STS	URBAN	DIFF.
FL	72.7	65.3	7.4	72.9	61.1	11.8
GA	90.0	73.2	16.8	82.9	66.1	16.8
NC	72.9	64.3	8.6	80.1	61.2	18.9
SC	65.9	74.7	−8.8	78.1	70.4	7.7
TX	87.2	70.5	16.7	82.1	64.4	17.7
VA	72.2	59.9	12.3	63.1	51.9	11.2
Total	77.4	66.6	10.8	76.1	61.2	14.9

Note. Data were calculated by the authors from the exit poll for each listed state in 2016 and from the 2020 exit poll for each listed state available on the *CNN* website: https://www.cnn.com/election/2020/exit-polls/president/national-results/5. STS = small-town South; Diff. = difference.

respect to white urban voters. Further, because the decline in the GOP presidential vote cast by urban whites far exceeded that of rural/STS whites, from 2016 to 2020, this rural-urban difference in the southern Republican presidential vote increased from 10.8 points in 2016 to 14.9 points in 2020.

Only in Virginia, where President Trump's support was substantially reduced among both rural/STS and urban whites, did the rural-urban disparity narrow in 2020 (from 12.3 points in 2016 to 11.2 points in 2020). All six southern states exhibited a decline in the urban white percentage of the GOP presidential vote in 2020. In the Palmetto State, where the county-level 2020 Republican presidential vote was higher in urban counties (see Table 11.2), at least among white South Carolinians, an 8.8-point urban GOP presidential vote advantage in 2016 was reversed to favor rural/STS whites by 7.7 percentage points in 2020. Admittedly, the six southern states included in Table 11.3 are some of Dixie's most urban (e.g., Florida, Texas, Virginia, and Georgia are the four most urban southern states in that order); but, given the county-level patterns revealed in Table 11.2, it is likely that most rural/STS whites in the five southern states omitted from the table (Alabama, Arkansas, Louisiana, Mississippi, and Tennessee) were just as supportive, if not even more so, of President Trump in 2020. Conversely, it would seem credible that most urban whites in these same five excluded southern states registered a drop in support for President Trump in 2020. Regardless, among the most Republican segment of the electorate in the South—white voters—it is the subset of rural/ STS residents who remained most supportive of the embattled and ultimately defeated Republican president in 2020.

Senate Elections

Data on southern Senate contests in 2020 further confirm the solid support of rural white voters for GOP nominees in these high-profile offices. What Republican electoral slippage exists in 2020 is generally due to a reduction in urban whites' support of GOP Senate candidates compared with the most recent previous elections for these seats. Similar to Table 11.2 for the 2020 presidential election, Table 11.4 displays the Republican share (two-party) of the Senate vote in STS and urban counties for every southern state but Florida, which had no Senate election in 2020, and Arkansas, because no Democrat challenged incumbent Republican Senator Tom Cotton. Also, the special Senate election in Georgia is omitted, because Republican Kelly Loeffler was originally appointed to the office and first stood for election in 2020 under the format of an open contest that allowed for multiple candidates to run under the same party label (the two Georgia Senate contests are examined in greater detail in the latter half of this section).

Because, in most cases, the 2020 Senate contest is for a seat last up for election in 2014, this midterm cycle is the comparison year in Table 11.4. There are however, two exceptions, the comparison case for Alabama is the 2017 special Senate contest in which Democratic incumbent Doug Jones was first

Table 11.4. The Republican Senate Vote in the South by County Type

	% Republican vote for Senate in:					
	2014			2020		
State	STS	URBAN	DIFF.	STS	URBAN	DIFF.
AL[a]	60.3	46.0	14.3	70.0	57.2	12.8
GA	67.0	51.3	15.7	72.2	46.8	25.4
LA	62.7	54.2	8.5	84.1	73.6	10.5
MS[b]	55.3	52.3	3.0	57.6	53.2	4.4
NC	57.4	49.7	7.7	62.9	49.1	13.8
SC	47.3	60.0	−12.7	50.6	55.7	−5.1
TN	70.8	64.5	6.3	79.6	59.1	20.5
TX	80.2	61.8	18.4	78.3	52.1	26.2
VA	59.4	47.7	11.7	61.5	40.7	20.8
Total	64.3	54.7	9.6	70.0	51.6	18.4

Note. [a]2017 Alabama special election. [b]2018 Mississippi special election runoff. STS = small-town South; Diff. = difference.

elected. Similarly, rather than show data from the regularly scheduled 2018 Mississippi Senate election because the seat would next be up for election in 2024, we show data from the Mississippi 2018 special Senate election because the winner had to stand for reelection in 2020.

Thus, Table 11.4 includes nine two-party contested southern Senate elections in 2020. Two incumbent Democrats sought reelection in 2020 (Alabama's Doug Jones and Virginia's Mark Warner), and so did six Republicans: David Perdue (GA), Bill Cassidy (LA), Cindy Hyde-Smith (MS), Thom Tillis (NC), Lindsey Graham (SC), and John Cornyn (TX). Finally, Republican Senator Lamar Alexander chose to retire rather than seek reelection in 2020; therefore, Tennessee had an open-seat contest that was won by Republican Bill Hagerty (with sixty-four percent of the two-party vote). Two of these Senate seats changed partisan hands: Alabama Democratic Senator Doug Jones was defeated by Republican challenger Tommy Tuberville, and Georgia Republican David Perdue lost to Democratic challenger Jon Ossoff in the runoff on January 5, 2021.

In the nine southern Senate contests in 2020 (summarized in Table 11.4), the STS county share of the Republican vote increased by 5.7 percentage points (from 64.3% to 70.0%) over the last election held for the seat. In contrast, with respect to urban southern counties, the GOP share of the Senate vote in 2020 dropped 3.1 percentage points (from 54.7% to 51.6%). Overall, these contrary dynamics resulted in a rural-urban county-level Republican Senate vote difference that went from 9.6 percentage points to 18.4 percentage points in 2020. With respect to individual states, only in Texas was the GOP percentage of the 2020 Senate vote lower in STS counties (going from 80.2% in 2014 to 78.3% in 2020), and only in Alabama was the rural-urban gap in the 2020 Senate Republican vote lower than in the previous election. Reflecting the presidential returns in Table 11.2, South Carolina is again the only southern state where the rural-urban GOP vote gap favors urban counties. Nevertheless, the Palmetto State shows a 7.6-percentage-point narrowing of this rural-urban Republican Senate vote difference in 2020 (going from −12.7 points in 2014 to −5.1 points in 2020). The aberrant case of South Carolina highlights the need for data limited to white voters, and we are fortunate to have exit poll data on Palmetto State voters in 2014 and 2020.

Similar to the presidential data presented in Table 11.3, Table 11.5 shows exit poll data on the six southern states with 2020 Senate elections that can be compared with the previous Senate contest for this seat. The row for Alabama is highlighted in gray because this is the one contest for which we lack data limited to white voters in the previous Senate election (in this case, the 2017 special election).[3] Thus, to make an apples-to-apples comparison, for Alabama, the data include all voters residing in rural/STS settings and urban locations. Additionally, and perhaps coincidentally, all six Senate contests in

**Table 11.5. The White Republican Senate Vote in Contests
with an Incumbent Seeking Reelection**

| | | % Republican vote for Senate in: | | | | | |
| | | 2014 | | | 2020 | | |
State	Incumbent	RURAL/STS	URBAN	DIFF.	RURAL/STS	URBAN	DIFF.
AL (2017)	Jones (D)	63.3	39.0	24.3	60.0	60.3	−0.3
GA	Perdue (R)	84.4	73.5	10.9	85.4	67.7	17.8
NC	Tillis (R)	71.6	63.1	8.5	78.5	62.8	15.7
SC	Graham (R)	77.5	80.0	−2.5	77.8	70.0	7.8
TX	Cornyn (R)	85.2	76.4	8.8	83.8	67.6	16.2
VA	Warner (D)	65.0	60.9	4.1	64.0	52.3	11.7
Total		71.1	64.2	6.9	75.3	62.6	12.7

Note. Data were calculated by the authors from the exit poll for each listed state in 2014; 2017 data for Alabama are from the *Washington Post*, at https://www.wash ingtonpost.com/graphics/2017/politics/alabama-exit-polls/, and these Alabama data (including for 2020) are not limited to white voters (so that 2017 and 2020 are properly compared); the 2020 exit poll data for each listed state are available on the *CNN* website, at https://www.cnn.com/election/2020/exit-polls/senate/alabama. STS = small-town South; Diff. = difference; D = Democrat; R = Republican.

2020 include incumbents seeking reelection (see the names and party affiliations of these senators in the "Incumbent" column in Table 11.5).

Starting with the anomalous case of Alabama, in which we cannot confine comparisons to white voters, it is readily apparent that in the 2017 special Senate election, urban Alabamians were notably turned off by the Republican candidacy of former Alabama Chief Justice Roy Moore, who received a paltry thirty-nine percent of their votes. To be sure, Roy Moore was doomed when multiple allegations surfaced about his dating and courting the affection of teenaged girls while in his thirties, but the urban repulsion may have also reflected the country bumpkin image of a man who, with his wife by his side, both rode horses to cast their votes on the day of the 2017 special election. In the absence of a scandal-plagued Republican in 2020, Democratic incumbent Doug Jones's luck ran out, as sixty percent of rural/STS and urban voters alike favored his Republican challenger.

In the remaining five Senate contests in Table 11.5, a clear pattern emerges. In 2020, the urban white Republican Senate vote drops in *every one* of these contests; by a substantial ten percentage points among urban white South Carolinians. Likewise, in two Senate contests in 2020 (Texas and Virginia), the white rural/STS Republican vote declined, but in both instances, these reductions were modest (less than two percentage points apiece). Also, whereas

South Carolina Republican Senator Graham did better among urban whites in 2014 (by 2.5 percentage points), that was no longer true in 2020, when rural/STS whites favored him by 7.8 percentage points. In all five of these Senate contests in 2020, the rural-urban GOP vote gap expanded over the previous election. For all six Senate contests in Table 11.5, in spite of the meager urban support for Republican Roy Moore in 2017, the aggregate urban Republican Senate vote was lower in 2020 by 1.6 percentage points (62.6%) versus the previous Senate election (64.2%). The 2020 rural/STS Republican Senate vote for these six elections in 2020 was 4.2 percentage points higher (75.3%) than in the previous Senate contest (71.1%). Finally, in 2020, the rural-urban GOP Senate vote margin was 12.7 percentage points, compared with 6.9 percentage points in the previous elections for these six Senate seats.

After the media declared Joe Biden the winner of the 2020 presidential election on the Saturday (November 7) after Election Day, all eyes figuratively turned to the two Georgia Senate runoff elections slated for January 5, 2021. In Georgia, if no candidate wins a simple vote majority in the general election, then there must be a runoff among the top two vote getters. Senator David Perdue led Democrat Jon Ossoff in the initial contest, with 49.7% of the total votes cast. Ossoff captured forty-eight percent of the Senate ballots, but the presence of a Libertarian candidate took 2.3% of the Senate vote total away from the major party candidates and, hence, triggered the runoff in early January. In the special Senate election, appointed Republican Senator Kelly Loeffler was one candidate among a total of twenty who ran in this open general contest, which included a half-dozen Republicans (including Congressman Doug Collins of Georgia District Nine) and eight Democrats (including Matt Lieberman, the son of former Connecticut Senator and 2000 Democratic vice-presidential nominee Joe Lieberman). Democrat Raphael Warnock, the pastor of Atlanta's historic Ebenezer Baptist Church, once led by Martin Luther King Jr., finished first in the special election, with 32.9% of the Senate votes. Senator Loeffler took second place, with 25.9% of the Senate vote total.

In the lead up to the two Georgia Senate runoffs, President Trump's behavior was becoming increasingly erratic as he insisted, through his favorite medium of Twitter, that the 2020 presidential election was stolen from him. Although Trump went down to Georgia to campaign for the two Republican Senators (as did President-elect Joe Biden on behalf of the two Democratic challengers), a bizarre dynamic unfolded, which cost both Republicans their Senate seats: Trump and some of his allies, including lawyers Lin Wood and Sydney Powell, actually admonished supporters to not participate in the January 5th runoff, because they claimed that, like the outcome of the 2020 presidential election, the outcomes were rigged in favor of the Democrats. Indeed, President Trump's escalating and politically desperate feud with Republican

Georgia election officials (including Secretary of State Brad Raffensperger and his aide Gabriel Sterling) and Republican Governor Brian Kemp had jettisoned any chance of mobilizing a united and winning GOP coalition of Trump supporters and urban Republicans. In the Georgia Senate runoffs, the Democrat Ossoff unseated the Republican Perdue with 50.6% of the vote (a 1.2-percentage-point margin) and the Democrat Warnock defeated the Republican Loeffler with fifty-one percent of the vote (a two-percentage-point margin).

In Figure 11.1, we have used scatterplots to array county-level turnout among registered white (top) and Black (bottom) voters in the November 3, 2020, general election (on the horizontal axis) and the January 5, 2021, Georgia Senate runoff contests (on the vertical axis). Additionally, we have indicated STS counties with gray triangles and urban counties with solid circles. These data are the actual county turnout percentages for all individuals in the Georgia voter registration database who claim their race to be either white or Black. A forty-five-degree line is included in both scatterplots to show the extent to which turnout declined in the 2021 Senate runoff vis-à-vis the 2020 general election. Simply, the farther below the forty-five-degree line on the y axis, the greater is the drop in runoff turnout versus general election participation. Comparing white turnout in the top scatterplot to Black turnout in the bottom scatterplot makes it evident, even to the naked eye, that the white dropoff in participation at the Senate runoff stage exceeds that of Black turnout. In other words, it is apparent that the plotted registered Black turnout is relatively closer to the forty-five-degree line. However, what is not certain from Figure 11.1 is whether there is much difference among whites and Blacks with respect to county type: STS versus urban.

We turn to Table 11.6 to further investigate differences in county-level registered turnout patterns for white and Black Georgians in the 2020 general election and the 2021 Senate runoffs. As per the usual pattern documented in this chapter, the top half of the table shows the breakdown in the Republican share of the Senate vote for STS counties versus urban counties in the general election and then in the Senate runoff contests. For the special Senate contest, in the general election, we summed up all of the Republican votes cast as opposed to those only for Senator Loeffler. It is interesting that, in both STS and urban counties, the GOP share of the vote slightly declined in the Georgia runoff elections, and because this modest reduction is just a bit greater in urban counties, the rural-urban Republican Senate vote gap expanded ever so slightly in both contests.

Because the changes to the Republican Senate vote at the runoff stage were so minimal with regard to STS versus urban counties, the bottom half of Table 11.6 offers a more plausible explanation for why two Democrats prevailed in the 2021 Georgia Senate runoff races: a turnout disparity in favor of

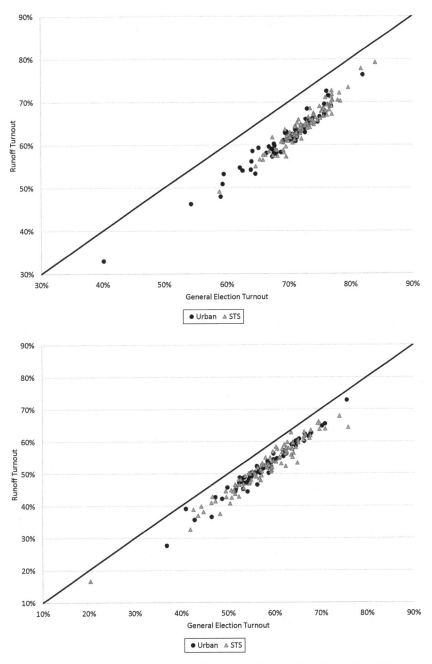

Figure 11.1. White (top) and Black (bottom) Turnout in Georgia Counties, 2020–2021

Table 11.6. The Republican Senate Vote and Registered Turnout in Georgia Counties

| | % Republican vote for Senate in: | | | | | |
| | 2020 General election | | | 2021 Runoff election | | |
Variable	STS	URBAN	DIFF.	STS	URBAN	DIFF.
Regular (Perdue)	72.2	46.8	25.4	71.0	45.3	25.7
Special (Loeffler)	72.0	46.4	25.6	70.8	44.8	26.0
% Registered turnout						
All	66.9	64.3	2.6	59.2	57.7	1.5
Whites	71.9	71.5	0.4	63.7	64.2	−0.5
Blacks	59.1	58.9	0.2	53.5	54.3	−0.8

Note. Results were calculated by authors using election returns and state voter registration and history files. The 2020 Senate special election included the vote totals for all Republican and Democratic candidates in the race. STS = small-town South; Diff. = difference.

urban voters, white and Black. In the Senate runoffs, overall turnout (regardless of race) declined by 6.7 points (from 64.7% to 58.0%); white turnout declined by 7.5 points (from 71.6% to 64.1%); and Black turnout declined by 4.7 points (from 58.9% to 54.2%). Hence, among the most Democratic segment of the Georgia electorate, Black turnout did not decline to the extent that it did among the markedly more Republican white Georgia electorate (with a turnout decline 2.8 percentage points higher among whites in the Georgia Senate runoff contests).

Also, all things constant, urban Georgians are notably less Republican (more Democratic) than their STS counterparts (again, this is palpable in the top half of the table). However, whether one looks at all voters, white voters, or Black voters, in every instance, the decline in Georgia Senate runoff participation is greater among STS residents.[4] In fact, among white and Black Georgians, STS turnout was slightly higher than urban turnout in the general election, but in the Senate runoffs, STS turnout is now lower. In these two razor-thin Georgia Senate runoff contests, which decided partisan control of the US Senate, a relatively greater decline in white and STS participation produced what were once thought to be two improbable Democratic victories (see Niesse and Peebles, 2021).

House Elections

Unfortunately, 2020 exit poll data for the South or for individual southern states are not available at the time of this writing. However, these data would not provide much insight simply because the 2020 House elections offered more of the same when compared with the partisan balance registered in the 2018 midterm contests. In the last two cycles, competition has been on the upswing with respect to two-party contested House races in the South; eighty-eight percent contested elections in 2018 (sixteen uncontested seats) and ninety-two percent contested elections in 2020 (only eleven uncontested seats in 2020).[5] With regard to incumbents seeking reelection, eighty-six percent ran in the 2018 House elections (twenty open seats), and eighty-five percent sought another term in 2020 (twenty-one open seats).[6] As mentioned earlier, the total number of Republicans and Democrats in the southern House delegation remained the same in 2020, despite six seats changing partisan control. In 2018—a midterm cycle very favorable to Democrats (Jacobson, 2019)—every Democratic seat (whether open or with an incumbent running) was retained by the party, as Democrats defeated seven Republican incumbents and picked up two Republican-held open seats. Most of the nine districts that Democrats flipped in 2018 were heavily urban, with these districts averaging a six percent rural population. In 2020, the three Democratic pickups all came from Republican-held open seats, whereas all three Republican gains were in contests against Democratic incumbents. As shown later, none of the districts in 2020 that switched parties had proportionally large rural populations.

Table 11.7 summarizes some key indicators for southern House elections in 2018 and 2020. In 2020 and 2018, the mean rural population in southern House districts was twenty-two percent.[7] Although a half-dozen seats flipped partisan control (see the bottom section of the table), this registered almost no effect on the average (and median) percent rural population in districts held by Republicans (twenty-nine percent rural) and Democrats (nine percent rural). In the next part of the Table 11.7, the bivariate correlations are shown for the Republican share of the House vote and the percent rural in House districts. In 2018, this correlation was positively related and statistically significant ($p < .01$). In 2020, the correlation was even stronger at 0.54 and statistically significant ($p < .01$). In short, the higher the House district percent rural, the higher the GOP (two-party) percentage of the southern House vote.

The last section of Table 11.7 displays the six House districts that flipped partisan control in 2020. The district percent rural and the two-party share of the 2020 presidential vote are presented so that they correspond with the party of the winning House candidate. The first three listed House districts—Florida Districts Twenty-Six and Twenty-Seven and South Carolina District One—went from Democratic in 2018 to Republican in 2020. All of these districts are heavily urban, with the rural percent topping out at five in South Carolina District One, which covers most of Charleston and the coastal Lowcountry down to Hilton Head at the Georgia border. Districts Twenty-Six and

Table 11.7. Rurality and the Southern House Vote in 2018 and 2020

Variable	2018 Elections	2020 Elections
Average (and median) % rural population		
Districts held by Rep.	29.6 (28.6)	29.1 (28.0)
Districts held by Dem.	8.5 (1.0)	9.3 (1.1)
Bivariate correlation	0.499 (*p* < .01)	0.535 (*p* < .01)
Rural/presidential % vote in 2020		
Districts that flipped control in the 2020 House elections	Rep.	Dem.
FL District Twenty-Six	2.3/52.8	
FL District Twenty-Seven	0.0/48.4	
SC District One	5.0/53.0	
GA District Seven		0.0/53.2
NC District Two		3.5/65.4
NC District Six		9.2/62.3

Note. Data were compiled by the authors. Data on the 2020 presidential vote are based on the two-party percentage. The districts in Florida and South Carolina flipped partisan control from Democrat to Republican; the districts in Georgia and North Carolina flipped from Republican to Democrat. Rep. = Republican; Dem. = Democrat.

Twenty-Seven in Florida are the southernmost in the state. Fittingly, Cuban American Republicans won both of these seats in 2020 (Campo-Flores and Findell, 2020). Zero percent rural, District Twenty-Seven is much more geographically compact than neighboring District Twenty-Six, with the former surrounding most of the southern half of greater Miami. District Twenty-Six takes in the remainder of Miami-Dade County and all of Monroe County, which borders Miami-Dade to the west and then drops south to encompass the Florida Keys. District Twenty-Six covers a lot of territory (all the way down to Key West) but is only 2.3% rural, because most of the population resides in urban areas, not the Everglades. In 2020, Florida District Twenty-Seven was the only one of the six southern seats that switched partisan control where the opposing party's presidential nominee won it (Democrat Joe Biden, with fifty-two percent).[8]

Among the three House districts that flipped in favor of Democrats in 2020, the most urban is Georgia District Seven, zero percent rural and located in northeast greater Atlanta. Republican Congressman Rob Woodall represented District Seven since 2010 and vacated it after the 2018 midterm when he beat Democratic challenger Carolyn Bourdeaux by 433 votes (Cohen and

Cook, 2019, p. 524). Bourdeaux then prevailed in the open seat in 2020. Whereas the three districts that flipped to Republicans in 2020 were all captured by defeating freshman incumbents, these three districts that turned to Democrats were all open seats in 2020.[9] Additionally, North Carolina's 3.5% rural District Two and 9.2% rural District Six were vastly altered through court-ordered redistricting. In fact, the prior incarnations of these two districts were heavily rural and Republican; therefore, in the remainder of this section, we will focus on the changes made to these North Carolina seats.

As a brief backstory, after the 2010 reapportionment, North Carolina Republicans drew an extremely effective partisan gerrymander for the 2012 House elections (Barone and McCutcheon, 2013, pp. 1233–1234; McGann et al., 2016). Through legal wrangling in federal court, the congressional district lines were redrawn for the 2016 House elections,[10] but as in 2014, the new map once again yielded ten Republicans and three Democrats. In the 2018 midterm, no seats changed party control again, but the results for North Carolina District Nine were thrown out because of rampant election fraud involving a Republican operative helping to elect the GOP House nominee. In the later special election for District Nine, held in September of 2019, the Republican candidate Dan Bishop prevailed; hence, heading into the 2020 election cycle, the North Carolina House delegation still comprised ten Republicans and three Democrats.[11] However, before the 2020 elections, another court case resulted in the directive to redraw North Carolina's congressional map,[12] and under the new plan, Democrats netted two seats in Districts Two and Six.

Figure 11.2 presents maps of North Carolina's congressional districts as they were drawn for the 2018 and 2020 elections. The maps highlight Districts Two and Six as they were configured for the 2018 and 2020 House contests. In 2018, District Two contained parts of six counties, whereas District Six was constructed from eight counties.[13] In 2018, the lower portions of these districts bordered each other. District Two was thirty-seven percent rural, whereas District Six was forty-seven percent rural. Furthermore, in 2016, Republican presidential nominee Donald Trump won fifty-five percent of the (two-party) vote in District Two, and fifty-eight percent of the vote in District Six. In 2018, Republicans George Holding (first elected in 2012) and Mark Walker (first elected in 2014) were victorious with fifty-three percent and fifty-seven percent, respectively, of the major party vote in these House districts.

As evident in the 2020 North Carolina congressional map, Districts Two and Six were vastly altered. Specifically, District Two was reduced in size to cover most of one county, Wake, capturing the bulk of its largest two cities, Raleigh and Cary. District Six was geographically reduced to cover all of Guilford County (Greensboro) and added most of the city of Winston-Salem

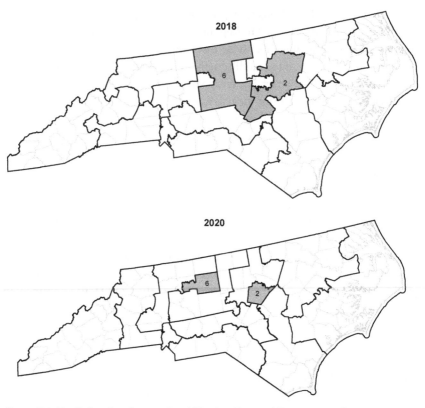

Figure 11.2. North Carolina Congressional Districts Two and Six in 2018 and 2020

to the west in neighboring Forsyth County.[14] With the substantial changes to these districts, as documented in Table 11.7, District Two was now 3.5% rural and sixty-five percent Democratic according to the 2020 presidential vote, and District Six was now 9.2% rural and sixty-two percent Democratic with regard to the 2020 presidential vote. Thus, the marked alterations to these districts made them inhospitable to Republicans. Because the remaining eleven North Carolina districts did not upset the political status quo, this was a textbook case of redistricting-induced incumbent displacement (Cain, 1984), meaning that neither GOP representative had a place to go; hence, both decided to retire.[15] In the 2020 open-seat contests for Districts Two and Six, the newly elected Democrats (Deborah Ross in District Two and Kathy Manning in District Six) won sixty-four percent and sixty-two percent of the major party vote, respectively.[16]

Conclusion

In the South, the 2020 elections for president, senator, governor, and US House served to reinforce the current state of party politics, especially with respect to the voting behavior of rural and urban whites. If anything, across all of these offices, the evidence indicates that the rural-urban division in support of Republican candidates has grown since 2016/2018 and also since the last elections were held (in 2014) for most 2020 Senate contests. At the county level, without limiting the data to southern whites, there is a consistent increase in the rural-urban vote gap that shows Republican candidates are now receiving even more of their support in small-town South settings. Although the national decline in support for President Trump registered in the South too, the rural-urban difference in the vote for the controversial Republican, whether measured with county-level data or exit poll data limited to white southerners in select southern states, expanded in 2020.

The examination of southern Senate contests reveals that President Trump was a bit of a drag on the Republican ticket because rural support for GOP Senate candidates was relatively more robust. With the increase in rural whites' support for GOP Senate candidates in 2020, coupled with the decline in urban whites' support of Republican Senate nominees, the increase in this rural-urban GOP vote gap has expanded to a greater degree than that exhibited at the presidential level. In the case of the two Georgia runoff contests, which determined partisan control of the US Senate, the data leave no doubt that two factors worked against the Republican senators: a relatively greater decline in white turnout and a relatively greater decline in rural/STS turnout. In these pivotal elections, President Trump proved a critical distraction. By fanning the flames with his false narrative of a stolen presidential election, Trump offered the perverse motivation for his supporters to sit out the Georgia Senate runoffs, and when all the votes were counted, the Democratic challengers prevailed with embarrassingly slim margins.

In the lone southern gubernatorial election in North Carolina, sitting Governor Roy Cooper was reelected with a margin of less than five percentage points. Although no one expected Cooper to lose, the wrongheaded prognostications of a 2020 blue wave manifested in this unexpectedly close contest. So what might explain the competitiveness of the Tar Heel State's 2020 gubernatorial election? There is no need to look any further than the rural-urban division in the white vote cast for governor. Consider that, in 2016, when Democrat Roy Cooper defeated Republican Governor Pat McCrory with 50.1% of the two-party vote, sixty-seven percent of rural/STS whites backed McCrory, whereas sixty-one percent of urban whites did the same. This six-point rural-urban GOP vote gap pales beside what transpired in 2020. In the 2020 gubernatorial contest, seventy-seven percent of rural/STS whites backed Republican Lieutenant Governor Dan Forest, but only fifty-eight percent of urban whites followed suit. Hence, in 2020, the rural/STS Republican gubernatorial vote cast by white North Carolinians surged ten points, whereas it declined three points among urban white Tar Heels. This voting dynamic resulted in a nineteen-point rural-urban Republican vote chasm among white North Carolinians, and thus substantially narrowed the reelection margin of a capable Democratic chief executive.

To be sure, the favorable short-term political conditions for Democrats in the 2018 midterm House elections registered in the South. However, with few exceptions, the nine House seats that southern Democrats wrested from Republicans were heavily urban and perhaps a more natural fit for Democratic representation. Nevertheless, three of these newly elected Democrats in disproportionally urban House districts ended up losing in 2020. Conversely, in 2020, Democrats flipped three Republican-held open seats that were also heavily urban. One district (Georgia District Seven) was hurtling toward the Democratic column, as witnessed by the GOP incumbent's close call in 2018, which prompted his retirement in 2020 and subsequent victory of his former Democratic challenger in the open seat. The other two Democratic-turned House districts were in North Carolina, and it was apparent that both would be won by Democrats, because redistricting for the 2020 elections made them deep blue bastions with markedly diminished rural electorates.

The 2020 elections in the South have reaffirmed the impressive loyalty of rural whites to the GOP. In comparison, these contests have also raised new questions regarding the extent to which urban white southerners will continue to move in favor of the Democratic opposition. In the concluding chapter, we consider long-term changes to the size and composition of the rural and urban southern electorate and what this may portend for party politics.

12 Too Little, Too Late?

In this final chapter, we make the connection between the contemporary rural Republican realignment in the South and the larger demographic patterns in the region that are clearly registering an electoral effect in favor of the Democratic opposition (Bullock, 2021; Bullock et al., 2019; McKee, 2019; Morris, 2021). Thus, the chapter title plays on the size of the rural white electorate: Although substantial, it is relatively small and declining and, we think, will ultimately be overwhelmed by the growing and increasingly formidable Democratic coalition of younger, more racially/ethnically diverse, female, and nonnative voters. At this moment in southern politics, despite the present state of Republican electoral dominance, each passing election cycle reveals net gains for the currently outmatched Democrats. In this light, the rural whites aligned with the GOP appear to be the final resistance to the modernization of Dixie and, with it, a rising coalition of voters aligned with the Democratic Party who better reflect the demographic profile of the region's current residents and those to come.

In this concluding chapter, we postulate about what the rural Republican realignment of white southerners can tell us about the status of party politics in historical terms. Specifically, the conversion of rural whites to the GOP, a group that was the backbone of the southern Democracy, once again reinforces why the long history of racial differences and division, along with the importance of culturally conservative beliefs and values, continues to stymie the emergence of a colorblind class-based politics with the coalitional heft to topple today's ruling Republicans. Rather, it would appear that compositional changes to the southern electorate are doing more of the work in undermining the GOP's electoral advantage. Rural whites, as the core segment of the modern southern GOP, do not exhibit any inclinations to weaken their attachment to a party that suits their preferences increasingly well. No, it is the decline in this group's numbers (albeit an uneven pattern of decline) that accounts for the growing viability of Democratic challenges. As we mentioned at the outset of this book, unlike the presidentially heavy top-down 1950s-to-1980s version of the southern GOP, which thrived in metropolitan areas, the latest incarnation of the Republican Party traces its most well-worn and thus entrenched paths back to the one-party Democratic Solid South, and this is evident in the profiles of rural white supporters (see chapter ten). In contrast, there is really no regional predecessor to the modern southern Democratic Party. Its fundamental elements are a diverse group of supporters who, in the Old South, would almost all have been disfranchised, played only a limited political role, or would not have resided in the region at all. This coalition includes northern in-migrants, Blacks, women, a growing Latino and Asian population, and a host of young people.

Specifically, we make the case for a weakening southern Republican Party principally with respect to documenting the declining size of the rural white population over the last twenty years and also by providing some insightful data on northern in-migration patterns from 2010 to 2019. We then consider in more detail the remarkable demographic changes to Virginia, which have contributed to the Old Dominion being Dixie's most Democratic state. Many of the demographic changes taking place in Virginia are present in other southern states; hence, a focus on this state gives us a clearer view of why other states, such as Georgia of late, are now yielding critical victories for a recently politically inconsequential Democratic Party.

We frame our final substantive discussion around the significance of President Donald Trump in maintaining—and, in many cases, strengthening—the GOP's grip on the political loyalties of rural white southerners. Clearly, as one man, Trump has a political influence that is transitory, but his impact and imprint on the rural white southern electorate appears to be enduring. Last, we conclude with some informed speculation regarding our expectations of an increasingly politically fractured South. The incredibly persistent cultural cohesion across Dixie (Reed, 1982) is fraying like it never has before. Population changes from within and without, occurring at varying rates depending on the state, make for a more kaleidoscopic, multicultural setting in which the major parties will find alternatively promising and discouraging electoral opportunities in more places than were possible until the last decade or so. This political balkanization of the South makes it more important than ever for election scholars to pay careful attention to the goings-on in Dixie.

The Political Significance of a Rural
White Republican Southern Electorate

In the long run, the removal of segregationist authoritarian enclaves throughout the South by the end of the 1970s—particularly in sections of the Deep South, these so-called *Paths Out of Dixie* (Mickey, 2015)—have proven to be a mirage for the representational advances of most Blacks. To be sure, the biracial coalitions that emerged in the 1970s and held strong through the 1980s (Lamis, 1988) empowered southern Blacks, giving them a significant say in the selection of Democrats who more often than not won their elections for the House, Senate, and governor. However, these biracial coalitions have been replaced by racially polarized voting coalitions with rural southern white Republicans at the forefront of opposing the interests of most of their Black counterparts who have been firmly aligned with the Democratic Party since the mid-1960s. The latest version of contemporary southern politics reaffirms a region of white rule (Black and Black, 1987), as it has been, harkening all the way back to the end of Reconstruction and solidifying white governance under the Democratic banner in the last decade of the 1800s when Democrats put down the Populist revolt (Key, 1949; Kousser, 1974).

There is no question that Black influence is considerable in various pockets of the South where their numbers overwhelm that of their white neighbors (Bullock and Gaddie, 2009). Otherwise, the end of Jim Crow, followed by the re-enfranchisement of a substantial share of southern Blacks disproportionally affiliated with the Democratic Party, the impressive and ongoing gains in Latino populations, and the recent shift of urban whites away from the Republican Party, has generally not been enough, yet, to successfully counteract the remarkable political influence of a rural white electorate that is now the base of Dixie's GOP.

However, as we have argued in several places throughout the book, the resulting electoral dominance tied to the realignment of rural whites to the Republican Party is, in many parts of the South, on borrowed time. It is not necessarily that demography is destiny; rather, destiny lies in the marginal, incremental changes in many localities where the rural-led brand of Republican politics appears increasingly antiquated to the modern beliefs of Dixie's voters and those found throughout most of the United States. If the southern GOP retains an outsized rural influence over policy positions, core principles, and style of campaigning and governing, then expect the Republican Party to eventually recede in political strength to those redoubts where very little demographic diversity occurs to effectively alter the composition of these electorates (e.g., Arkansas, Alabama, Louisiana, Mississippi, and Tennessee). In the remainder of the southern states, dubbed "growth states" by Bullock et al. (2019), the impressive churning of these electorates is to the political detriment of rural white voters who hold decidedly different political views and values vis-à-vis more recent arrivals who disproportionally settle in urban areas (Morris, 2021).[1]

In the 1970s and 1980s, the ideological distribution of the southern congressional delegation reflected the power of the biracial coalitions responsible for electing a majority contingent of white Democrats. Since then, the breathtaking partisan sorting of southern Senate and House members in Congress has removed the moderate middle, where no Democrats or Republicans reside because the major parties have polarized toward their respective liberal and conservative ends of the ideological spectrum (Fleisher and Bond, 2004; Theriault, 2008). More than any other factor, this state of affairs is due to the rural Republican realignment of white southerners. As discussed, southern Blacks have been staunchly loyal to the Democratic Party since the 1964 Johnson-versus-Goldwater presidential election that took place only a few months after Democratic President Johnson spearheaded passage of the 1964 Civil Rights Act. Because urban white southerners were the group most responsible for the rise of southern Republicans from the 1950s until the 1990s, it was the slower shift of rural white southerners to the GOP that explains best why there is no longer a political center. Rural whites have pulled the southern GOP farther from the ideological middle. With rural voters now the base of the Republican Party, rather than cater to the more socially moderate but economically conservative preferences of urban whites, the southern GOP now vigorously promotes the more populist, culturally and racially conservative views of their most loyal rural constituents.

It is interesting that, after Reconstruction ended in the 1877 political compromise that awarded Republican Rutherford B. Hayes the presidency, there have arguably been only two periods in which southern party politics came close to reflecting the views of a racially heterogeneous and ideologically diverse governing coalition: the ephemeral Populist movement in the 1890s and the post–civil rights era that lasted from roughly the 1970s to the early 1990s. Apart from these moments in southern political history, an overwhelmingly white, rural, and racially conservative Democratic Party called the shots in Dixie. This Democratic Solid South regime was toppled by the 1960s civil rights movement, but decades hence, from around the mid-1990s to current times, a lopsidedly white; increasingly rural; and racially, religiously, and socially conservative GOP has held the advantage in shaping the South's public affairs.

We find it curious that, despite the widespread and generally accurate accounts of how the growing rural-urban divide in contemporary American politics is a fundamental factor in deciding elections (e.g., Hopkins, 2017; Johnston et al., 2020; Lang and Pearson-Merkowitz, 2015; Scala and Johnson, 2017), this is the first book-length account that tackles its most politically consequential development: the rural Republican realignment (RRR) of white southerners. Instead, scholars are increasingly focusing on the changing South and how, in many parts of the region, high-growth urban areas are fostering Democratic competitiveness. We, however, focused on the reason why Republicans have become so politically formidable and why the strong GOP affiliation of rural whites makes Democratic efforts to become a more viable opposition a generally slow and painstaking process. Put differently, we have emphasized how partisan changes within the native white population in the South have proven capable of prolonging Republican electoral dominance as Republicanism has begun to wane among urban whites and is admittedly under siege with regard to Dixie's latest newcomers. It took a long time for the white rural Democratic South to morph into the contemporary white rural

Republican South (McKee, 2008), and we suspect that a return to a very different Democratic South will be years in the making, just as it has been where such a development has come to fruition: in Virginia. In the next two sections, we consider demographic changes that do not augur favorably for continued rural southern Republican hegemony.

The Size of the Rural White Electorate

Most of this book has been devoted to documenting the recent realignment of rural whites into stalwart GOP identifiers. In this last chapter, we also want to examine this group in terms of its compositional contribution to the southern Republican Party. Rural whites are one of the chief building blocks of the Republican coalition in the region. As contended, it is unlikely these individuals will be changing party affiliations any time soon. The issue then, from a structural perspective, is centered on the fact that demographically the population of the rural South is contracting over time. This includes whites within these geographies—the strongest component of the GOP base. This noted decline is occurring in both nominal (raw numbers) and relative terms (in comparison with urban areas).

This inquiry begins with an exploration of the size of the non-Hispanic white voting-age population in small-town South (STS) areas versus urban areas. Demographic growth of white urban dwellers, as has been demonstrated previously, is more likely to benefit the Democratic Party. This statement is, in part, explained by in-migration from outside the South. Such movement often brings voters into the region with a proclivity to vote Democratic. One need look no further than the suburban Atlanta-metro counties of Cobb and Gwinnett, which were once firmly GOP strongholds but now have transformed into blue bastions. To be sure, much of this partisan transformation is due to the influx of minorities into these areas. However, the relocation of whites for job opportunities to the economic hub of Atlanta has also had a decided effect. Using US Census figures over the past decade (2010–2019) it is estimated that about a quarter of the non-Hispanic white population in these two counties arrived from outside the state; 26.8% in Cobb and 24.6% in Gwinnett.[2]

There are several ways to explore changes in the size of the rural white population in the South. In line with our analyses presented in previous chapters, we will rely on our categorization of STS counties to examine the nominal size of the non-Hispanic white voting-age population in the region. Using US Census data from 2000, 2010, and 2019, we compare the relative size of the white population in these areas to that in urban counties. By definition, residents live in either urban counties or STS counties, so if the proportion of the white population living in STS areas is contracting, then the proportion of urban areas will be growing.

Table 12.1 segments the non-Hispanic white voting-age population by state and place over time. It is evident from the table that the relative STS-urban balance across all eleven states in the region is shifting in favor of urban areas. The sole exception to this rule is Virginia, which saw literally no shift across this time period.[3] In 2000, 19.3% of the white voting-age population in Virginia lived in STS areas. Twenty years later, in 2019, that percentage remained unchanged. Although the pattern uncovered in the Old Dominion is neutral in that the STS-urban distribution for whites remains unchanged, this has not been enough to offset the ascendancy of Virginia Democrats. As documented later in this chapter, Virginia is the one southern state which has transformed from red to purple, and now to blue over the past several decades.

Florida and Louisiana saw only slight shifts in the STS-urban balance of the white voting-age populations within their states: −0.8 for Florida and −0.4 for Louisiana. Florida is the most urban state in the South, with only 3.4% of the white population residing in STS counties in 2019. There is simply less room for population shifts to occur within the Sunshine State. Comparatively, Louisiana is much less urban, but its population growth has been dormant. From 2000 to 2019, the white voting-age population in the state grew by only 2.1%.

The remaining eight states all saw the percentage of non-Hispanic whites residing in STS areas falling at a more decided pace. Figures ranged from −2.9 in Mississippi to a high of −6.8 in Arkansas. Finally, Table 2.1 also provides a regionwide calculation for the STS-urban split for the white voting-age population. In 2000, a fifth (20.1%) of this population lived in STS areas. By 2019, this figure had fallen to 16.8 percent, producing a net difference of −3.3 percentage points. At this point, it has certainly been established that the balance of the white voting-age population in the South is shifting from STS areas to urban locales.

We next move to a comparison of raw population numbers by place over time. Figure 12.1 presents a set of boxplots organized by groups of STS and urban counties.[4] Plotted is the rate of change in the raw number of non-Hispanic white voting-age residents during the following time periods: 1990–2000; 2000–2010; and 2010–2019.[5] A positive rate of change means that the population count increased over the time period under analysis; a value of zero indicates no change, and a negative value denotes a reduced population. For example, from 2010 to 2019, Darlington County, South Carolina, had a value of −.024. One can translate this finding as follows: The count of non-Hispanic white voting-age residents in Darlington County fell by 2.4% from 2010 to 2019.

A boxplot graphically displays the distribution of a variable; in this case, the rate of change for the white population count. The top of the box represents

Table 12.1. Distribution of the Non-Hispanic White Voting-Age Population by State, 2000–2019

State and location	2000	2010	2019	Change
AL				
Urban	66.0	73.8	74.6	
STS	34.0	26.2	25.4	−5.1
AR				
Urban	60.6	61.9	63.8	
STS	39.4	38.1	32.6	−6.8
FL				
Urban	95.8	96.4	96.6	
STS	4.2	3.6	3.4	−0.8
GA				
Urban	74.8	78.1	78.6	
STS	25.2	21.9	21.4	−3.9
LA				
Urban	79.7	78.5	79.1	
STS	21.3	21.5	20.9	−0.4
MS				
Urban	55.6	57.5	58.5	
STS	44.4	42.5	41.5	−2.9
NC				
Urban	79.0	84.5	85.2	
STS	21.0	15.5	14.8	−6.2
SC				
Urban	84.3	89.7	90.2	
STS	15.7	10.9	9.8	−5.9
TN				
Urban	67.7	70.4	71.6	
STS	32.3	29.6	28.4	−3.9
TX				
Urban	82.2	84.3	85.2	
STS	17.8	15.7	14.8	−3.0
VA				
Urban	80.7	80.4	80.7	
STS	19.3	19.6	19.3	0.0
South				
Urban	79.9	81.7	83.2	
STS	20.1	18.3	16.8	−3.3

Source: Data were compiled by the authors from US Census Bureau data, 2000, 2010, and 2019.

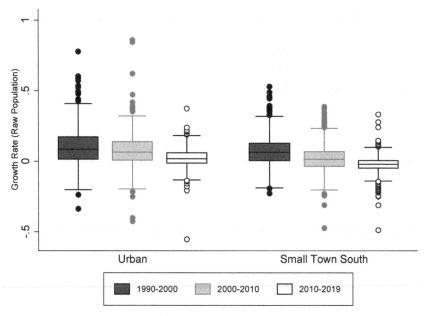

Figure 12.1. Southern Non-Hispanic White Voting-Age Population

the seventy-fifth percentile, and the bottom of the box represents the twenty-fifth percentile; the horizontal line inside the box indicates the median, dividing the distribution in half, with fifty percent of observations (counties) falling below and fifty percent located above. The whiskers on the plot represent values that fall within ±1.5 times the interquartile range, with observations falling outside that range considered outliers (appearing as circles).[6]

The growth rates for the non-Hispanic white voting-age population are declining over time in both urban and STS counties. For example, the median value for urban counties over the last thirty years fell from 11.2 (1990–2000) to 8.2 (2000–2010), and finally to only 2.3 (2010–2019). For STS counties, however, the declining growth rates are even more pronounced. Median values fell from 8.5 from 1990–2000 to 1.9 from 2000–2010, to −2.6 in the last time period (2010–2019). In fact, sixty-eight percent of STS counties in this last time period showed a negative rate of population change (as compared with thirty-six percent of urban counties).

Evidence has been presented that demonstrates that the non-Hispanic white voting-age population of the rural South is declining, both in comparison with urban areas as well as in the actual counts for this group within STS counties. Thus, the demographic group that has become one of the most reliable components of the southern GOP is clearly contracting. Non-Latino whites in urban areas, on the other hand, are not shrinking at the same rate. In some urban and suburban counties, this demographic is even on the increase.

For example, Travis County, Texas—where the state capital, Austin, is located—saw an increase in the non-Hispanic white population of 74,530 from 2010 to 2019, which translates into a seventeen percent growth rate. Travis County, however, is a dark blue outpost in Central Texas. In 2020, Biden won seventy-two percent of the vote, up from Clinton's sixty-six percent share in 2016.

As detailed in previous chapters, STS whites have become the backbone of the GOP coalition in the South over the past several decades. Although this pattern is unlikely to be altered in the near future, the fact that the size of this group is also contracting is not an encouraging harbinger for the future success of the Republican Party in Dixie. We will circle back to this finding and its implication for party politics in the South near the end of the chapter.

Northern In-Migration

At the turn of the twenty-first century, population growth in the United States has been most robust in the South (Hillygus, McKee, and Young, 2017), where a market-friendly economic environment has prompted the relocation of substantial numbers of businesses and lured the employment of thousands of domestic in-migrants and foreign immigrants. Additionally, the South is a leading retirement destination by virtue of its mild winters. The massive increase in the southern population has forever altered the composition of the electorate, and these changes continue apace. As mentioned earlier, scholars now look at the disparities in population gains because they are highly correlated with the competitiveness of party politics (Bullock, 2021).

Recent research indicates that it is generally the case that movers in the southern states tend to be more Democratic than residents who stay put, and this dynamic prevails regardless of whether movers are native to the South or in-migrants (Morris, 2021). Nonetheless, as several studies have shown (Hillygus, McKee, and Young, 2017; Hood and McKee, 2010; McKee and Teigen, 2016), the most recent northern newcomers to Dixie are generally more Democratic in affiliation and voting preferences than are southern natives, and this distinction is even more pronounced depending on the region these migrants come from. For instance, in partitioning the United States into five regions (Midwest, Mountains/Plains, Northeast, Pacific Coast, and South), Black and Black (2007) make it apparent that two sections strongly favor the Democratic Party (Northeast and Pacific Coast), two are dominated by the Republican Party (Mountains/Plains and South), and one acts as essentially America's battleground in calibrating the closely divided balance in national politics (Midwest).

Table 12.2 displays data on northern in-migration to the southern states from 2010 to 2019. Each state's estimated population in 2019 is listed (Population column), as well as the percentage of non-South in-migrants accounting for each state's total population (Migrants column). Next, out of the total

Table 12.2. Northern In-Migration Statistics for the South, 2010–2019

State	Population	% Migrants	% White	% Black	% Northeast	% White NE	% Black NE
AL	4,903,185	7.8	71.0	17.5	21.3	63.9	24.3
AR	3,017,804	13.4	75.2	11.1	9.4	70.9	11.4
FL	21,477,737	17.2	71.2	8.0	48.3	65.7	9.7
GA	10,617,423	11.6	48.7	28.8	35.1	40.2	35.5
LA	4,648,794	7.1	65.5	17.0	19.2	63.5	15.5
MS	2,976,149	8.1	55.3	29.2	15.6	55.7	24.0
NC	10,488,084	15.1	64.7	15.3	47.9	60.1	20.6
SC	5,148,714	15.3	71.3	13.5	46.1	70.3	15.8
TN	6,829,174	13.1	74.6	12.3	18.9	74.3	10.3
TX	28,995,881	12.6	54.5	11.1	17.2	52.7	11.1
VA	8,535,519	19.9	63.7	14.6	51.6	60.3	18.3
South	107,638,464	13.8	63.7	13.4	35.1	60.9	15.9

Note. Data were compiled by the authors from the US Census Bureau. The Migrants column shows the percentage of non-southern in-migrants from 2010 to 2019. The next two columns list the percentages of the non-South migrant population who are white and Black. The Northeast column lists the percentage of non-South migrants who are from the northeast region of the United States. The White NE and Black NE columns list the percentages of White and Black migrants, respectively, from the northeast region of the United States.

non-South in-migrant population, the percentages of white and Black arrivals are provided. Because the largest percentage and also most Democratic component of northern in-migrants hail from the Northeast, we present the percentage of the non-South in-migrant population that is from this region.[7] Finally, within the northeastern immigrant population to the South, we display the percentages of whites and Blacks (White NE and Black NE, respectively).

In the last row of the table, all of the data are aggregated to determine the regionwide numbers. By 2019, well over one hundred million people reside in the American South, which amounts to 32.8% of the US population. Almost fourteen percent of the South's population consists of domestic in-migrants who relocated to the region from 2010 to 2019. There is considerable variation in the proportion of these in-migrants across the southern states. Non-South migrants are less than ten percent of the state population in Louisiana, Alabama, and Mississippi. Not surprisingly, these three states with the lowest percentage of new residents from outside the South are now some of the most Republican, and we see scant likelihood of Democrats mounting many successful political challenges in statewide elections for years to come, despite the fact that John Bel Edwards is the twice-elected Democratic governor of Louisiana. On the high end, Virginia, Florida, South Carolina, and North Carolina have populations that are more than fifteen percent non-South migrants.

Among the region's northern in-migrant population, it is notable that the Black percentage (13.4%) is significantly lower than Dixie's total percentage of Blacks, which is twenty percent. Nevertheless, depending on the state, this number exhibits marked variability. Only Florida has a percentage of Black non-South in-migrants under double digits (eight percent), but its neighbor to the north, Georgia, has the second highest percentage of Black migrants from outside the South at 28.8%. There is no question that this relatively high share of Black migrants to the Peach State is a major contributor to Georgia flipping Democratic in the 2020 presidential election and the 2021 Senate runoffs.

The northeastern United States has solidified into a Democratic bastion since Bill Clinton won the 1992 presidential election (McKee and Teigen, 2016). Not only is this section of the United States one of the most Democratic, but also, given its greater proximity to the South (e.g., as compared with the heavily Democratic Pacific Coast; see Black and Black, 2007), the largest portion of non-South in-migrants come from the Northeast, currently accounting for thirty-five percent of Dixie's domestic migrant population. Once again, there is a wide range of variation in southern states' percentage of non-South migrants who come from the Northeast. Only 9.4% of in-migrants to Arkansas arrive from the Northeast, which is intuitive, as the migrant stream to the Natural State is much stronger among Midwesterners, given its geographic location. Indeed, the northeastern migration pattern is predominantly one that points directly south, which explains why the southern states along the Eastern Seaboard receive the highest share of these in-migrants (Virginia, Florida, North Carolina, South Carolina, and Georgia). With respect to the Black percentage of northeastern in-migrants, Georgia leads the way at 35.5%. Finally, Virginia, the South's most Democratic state has become so, in no small degree because of northeastern in-migrants. Not only does the Old Dominion contain the South's highest share of northern in-migrants (19.9%), but among this population, over half relocated from the Northeast (51.6%).

The Old Dominion Reverses Course:
What Virginia Tells Us About a Changing South

There was a long period when Virginia was one of the most presidentially Republican southern states. The Old Dominion was the only southern state Democratic presidential nominee Jimmy Carter failed to win in 1976. In fact, until Democrat Barack Obama won Virginia in 2008, the last Democrat to win the Old Dominion's electoral votes was President Johnson back in 1964. However, since Obama won Virginia in 2008, no Republican presidential nominee has recaptured the state. In the 2021 elections, Republicans narrowly swept the three statewide offices for governor, lieutenant governor, and attorney general. Also, in House of Delegates elections (state house contests), Republicans won fifty-two of the one hundred seats. Nevertheless, these odd-year contests coming after the presidential election have historically gone poorly for the party in the White House, in this case the Democrats.[8] So, we do not make too much of short-term political conditions that turned in favor of Virginia Republicans. Indeed, one election cycle cannot constitute a trend and we know this dynamic in favor of the out-party in the off-year is typical in Virginia (Prokop, 2021).[9]

In contrast, before the 2021 elections, there has unquestionably been a long-term Democratic trend in the Old Dominion, and it is not confined to presidential contests. Prior to the Republican Party's strong performance in 2021, the last victorious Republican for Virginia governor was Bob McDonnell in 2009, all three statewide elected positions were held by Democrats (governor, lieutenant governor, and attorney general), and both legislative chambers were under Democratic control. In addition, heading into the 2022 midterm elections, both Virginia US Senators are Democrats (Tim Kaine and Mark Warner) and the US House delegation is majority Democratic (seven Democrats and four Republicans). In fact, even accounting for the 2021 elections, versus the other ten southern states, none come close to the blue hue of present-day Virginia.

So why did the Old Dominion become the most Democratic southern state? There is no simple answer, but Table 12.2 serves as a partial explanation. The large northern in-migrant population, coupled with the majority of these newcomers arriving from the most Democratic section of the United States (the Northeast), has certainly elevated the competitiveness of Virginia Democrats. In other words, compositional change by means of in-migration has, on net, produced a more Democratic electorate. As this partisan transformation has been underway, like the rest of the rural South, Virginia's rural electorate has moved in the Republican direction. As documented in Table 12.1, at least among the white (non-Latino) voting-age population, Virginia is the sole southern state in which its STS counties have not experienced population decline for 2019 versus 2000.

Nevertheless, this has not been enough for Virginia Republicans to prevent a Democratic takeover. First, Virginia's white voting-age population currently splits eighty-one percent to nineteen percent urban/STS (see Table 12.1), the fifth highest ratio favoring urban whites over STS whites in the eleven southern states. Second, urban whites in Virginia are notably more Democratic than the rank-and-file urban white southerner; this is due in part to in-migration patterns. Finally, population growth (regardless of race/ethnicity) in the Old Dominion has been very uneven, with urban areas growing at a faster rate than rural settings. By default, this means that larger Democratic minority populations are settling in urban parts of Virginia.

Figure 12.2 displays a county-level map of population change rates in Virginia spanning 2010 to 2019. The counties indicated in cross-hatched gray have registered negative growth over those ten years on the order of negative five percent to negative eleven percent. The counties indicated as clear/white are next lowest in terms of population growth, at zero percent to negative five percent. The remaining shades in the figure become darker for counties experiencing the highest rate of population growth. The counties indicated with the darkest shades saw their populations from 2010 to 2019 increase upwards of fifteen percent to thirty-five percent. Having a sense of Virginia geography, it is evident from Figure 12.2 that the counties with the slowest growth rates are more likely to be rural. In contrast, several of the counties undergoing the highest population growth are located in northern Virginia.

Separating the Old Dominion into STS and urban counties, the average rate of population growth in STS counties is −0.6%, and this translates into a net increase of 7,223 residents in the aggregate (summing all of the population numbers from 2010–2019 in the STS counties). In comparison, in the more prevalent urban counties, from 2010 to 2019, the net population change amounts to a 6.5% increase and a total gain of 605,486 inhabitants. Among the core and suburban counties (and corresponding independent cities) that constitute Virginia's portion of the Washington, DC, metropolitan statistical area,

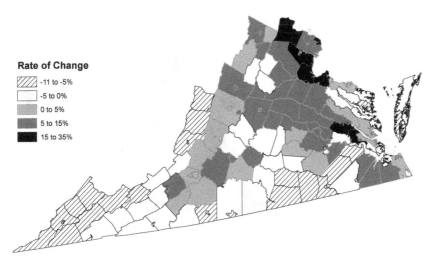

Rate of Change
- -11 to -5%
- -5 to 0%
- 0 to 5%
- 5 to 15%
- 15 to 35%

Figure 12.2. Population Change in Virginia Counties, 2010–2019

from 2010–2019, the population growth was 16.7%, which is an increase of 355,794 residents (or fifty-eight percent) of the Old Dominion's total population growth. This area is commonly referred to as northern Virginia, or NOVA, and it is overwhelmingly urban and heavily Democratic; but this is a fairly recent political development.[10]

Figures 12.3 and 12.4 display county-level maps of the US Senate vote in Virginia for the 1996 and 2020 elections. As we have done throughout the book, we use different shades to distinguish among four possible types of counties on the basis of the party of the winner (Democratic or Republican) and whether the county is classified as urban or STS. The two lightest shades (clear and light gray) designate Democratic/STS and Democratic/urban counties, respectively. The two darkest shades denote Republican/urban and Republican/STS counties, respectively. Unique to Virginia among the southern states, there are several independent cities that are essentially treated as county-equivalent governing units; therefore, as in Figure 12.2, Figures 12.3 and 12.4 display smaller geographic areas within counties that represent these independent cities.

The 1996 county-level Senate returns shown in Figure 12.3 are for the "Warner versus Warner" contest. Veteran Republican incumbent Senator John Warner (first elected in 1978) was challenged by Democratic political upstart Mark Warner. The election was competitive, with John beating Mark by fifty-three percent versus forty-seven percent of the two-party vote. Senator Warner won fifty-five percent of Virginia's counties/independent cities (73 out of 133); among the counties won by the Republican incumbent, fifty-eight percent (forty-two) were urban, and forty-two percent (thirty-one)

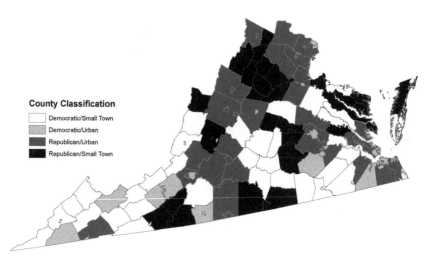

Figure 12.3. County Vote in Virginia for US Senate, 1996

Figure 12.4. County Vote in Virginia for US Senate, 2020

were STS. In comparison, among the forty-five percent of Virginia counties/ independent cities (60 out of 133) that favored the Democrat Mark Warner, sixty-five percent were STS, and thirty-five percent were urban. In other words, the Republican Warner's support was greater in urban areas. In 1996, it was still the case that rural Virginia was more Democratic than Republican, and urban Republicanism was more important for delivering GOP victories. In NOVA, Republican Senator Warner won fifty-five percent of the major party vote.

After a thirty-year career in the US Senate, Republican John Warner finally retired in 2008. By this time, Mark Warner had established himself as a political heavyweight, having served as governor from 2002 to 2006 (Virginia governors have a one-term limit). Mark Warner won the 2008 open Senate seat by trouncing the Republican Jim Gilmore, who preceded Warner in the governor's mansion (1998–2002). The two-party vote split sixty-six percent to thirty-four percent in favor of Warner. In 2020, Senator Warner was seeking his third term and faced Republican challenger and US Army veteran Daniel Gade. This election was not very competitive, as Democratic Senator Warner defeated the Republican Gade with fifty-six percent to forty-four percent of the two-party vote. However, what had changed remarkably since the 1996 US Senate race was the geographic distribution of the major party vote. In his losing bid in 2020, Gade actually won sixty-three percent of Virginia's counties/ independent cities (84 out of 133), and sixty-eight percent (57) were STS, whereas thirty-two percent (27) were urban. In the thirty-seven percent of Virginia's counties/independent cities (49 out of 133) that delivered Democratic Senator Warner a third term, seventy-three percent (36) were urban, and twenty-seven percent (thirteen) were STS. Consummating the sea change in Virginia politics, in NOVA, Democratic Senator Warner captured sixty-nine percent of the two-party vote.

The political transformation of Virginia speaks to changes occurring in several other states. Rural Republican realignment (RRR) has placed an unshakable grip on the Virginia GOP, but this has come at a significant electoral cost. Because in-migration favors Democrats and so does the expanding electorate in urban areas, a more diverse and larger Democratic coalition consistently outvotes their Republican neighbors who are more prevalent in the less populated countryside. In some ways, this dynamic has parallels with contemporary California. In the Golden State, a racially and ethnically diverse and growing electorate overwhelmed the Republican opposition around the mid-1990s. Since then, with rare exceptions, the California GOP has proven to be a routine loser in statewide and district-based elections. Similar to rural Virginia, the Republican redoubts found in certain pockets of inland California no longer come close to offsetting the electoral heft of the larger urban and coastal Democratic coalition.

Likewise, in the southern states of Georgia, North Carolina, and Texas, compositional changes to these electorates are substantial, and they favor the Democratic Party. Georgia, in particular, stands out for its large in-migration of Blacks. The Tar Heel State has a very high percentage of northern in-migrants who favor the Democratic Party (Hood and McKee, 2010). And in Texas, despite the short-term pivot of thousands of Hispanics toward Trump in the 2020 election, it remains true that the booming Latino electorate favors Democrats, whereas the most rapidly growing and largest metropolitan centers are moving in the Democratic direction (see chapter nine). Finally, as is the case in Virginia, the white rural electorates in Georgia, North Carolina, and Texas are deep red, but at the state level, these constituencies are ceding electoral ground to an expanding, markedly urban, and increasingly Democratic opposition.

Postscript: Trump and the Future of the Southern GOP

The political realignment of rural southern whites, to borrow a term from V. O. Key (1959), can be described as a secular process. In this case, the term *secular* references a transformation occurring slowly, over a very long period of time. Hopefully, this fact been well established by the pages that preceded this chapter. President Trump, therefore, was not the precipitating agent of this shift. Nevertheless, Trump's populist message acted as an accelerant, which sped up the conversion of rural whites to the GOP and/or made previous Republican converts even more committed (Jacobson, 2021). Legions of the former president's most die-hard supporters are white southerners living in rural/STS settings.

If there remain doubts regarding the deep well of affection that rural white southerners had (and probably still have) for Republican President Donald Trump, the following figures should put these to rest. For decades, the American National Election Studies (ANES) has made use of feeling thermometers to gauge the degree of emotional satisfaction or displeasure/disapproval that respondents express toward certain groups, objects, or political figures. Not surprisingly, these thermometer scales are highly correlated with vote choice. Simply put, those politicians/candidates given high ratings on the feeling thermometer scale ranging from zero to one hundred (the lower the rating, the less the rater approves; the higher the rating, the more affection the rater has) are overwhelmingly the beneficiaries at the ballot box.

We can capture the robustness of these thermometer scales by showing data from two different sources: (1) the 2019 ANES Pilot Study, which includes a large sample of rural and urban white southerners; and (2) the survey of urban and STS whites that we conducted in the late winter of 2020 (see chapter ten). For purposes of comparison, we present feeling thermometer data on Barack Obama and Donald Trump. We make use of boxplots because this is an intuitive and visually instructive means to show the distribution of opinions. Figure 12.5 displays the feeling thermometer data on Obama and Trump from the 2019 ANES Pilot Study.

The left side of Figure 12.5 pairs the Trump and Obama boxplots next to each other as determined by the responses of urban white southerners.

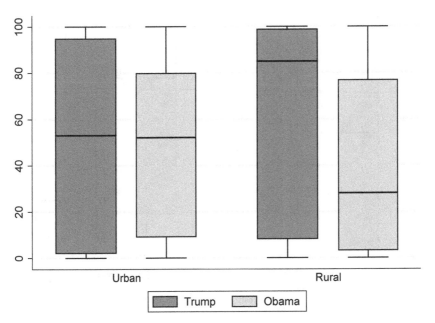

Figure 12.5. Feeling Thermometers by Place for White Southerners, 2019

Unexpectedly, the values for the middle of the distribution (the median) for urban whites' feelings toward Trump and Obama are almost equivalent: fifty-three for Trump and fifty-two for Obama. This said, urban whites generally register greater affection for Trump than for Obama, and this is evident on the basis of the higher third quartile numbers (ninety-five for Trump and eighty for Obama).[11] The data on rural white southerners tell a much different story. It is fair to say that a disproportionate share of rural white southerners loathed Obama and adored Trump. Not surprisingly, neither president fared well regarding responses at the first quartile (eight for Trump and three for Obama), but the separation favoring Trump at the median is impressive: the middle rural white southern respondent placed Trump at eighty-five on the feeling thermometer scale and Obama at twenty-eight; a fifty-seven-point chasm favoring the Republican president. Also notable is the disparity in the Trump and Obama ratings at the third quartile. At the seventy-fifth percentile, rural whites gave Trump a rating of ninety-nine on the feeling thermometer, one point short of the one-hundred-point maximum. In comparison, Obama notched a rating of seventy-seven at the third quartile.

Figure 12.6 shows similar data based on the 2020 survey that we administered to a sample of urban and STS whites. What is immediately striking is how congruent these data are with the ANES 2019 Pilot Study. Even with a slightly different measure of rurality (see chapter two), the general distribution of the numbers hardly differ in any of the four boxplots. Once again,

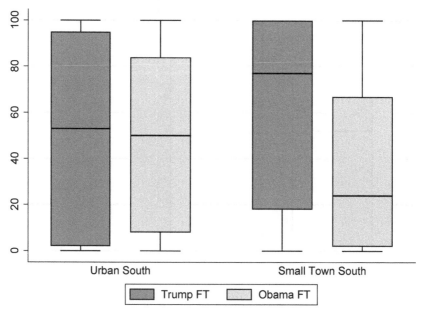

Figure 12.6. Feeling Thermometers by Place for White Southerners, 2020

among urban whites, the middle respondent shows little distinction in his/ her affection toward Trump (with a rating of fifty-three) versus Obama (with a rating of fifty). It is the third quartile in which Trump is notably more favored than Obama, receiving a rating of ninety-five on the one-hundred-point scale as compared with a rating of eighty-four for Obama.[12] Also, as was true in Figure 12.5, a goodly portion of STS whites view Obama as the Antichrist and Trump as the Second Coming. Remarkably, among STS whites, the first quartile for Trump (rating of eighteen) is not much lower than the median thermometer rating for Obama (rating of twenty-four). The disparity in the respective median thermometer ratings for Trump (rating of seventy-seven) and Obama (rating of twenty-four) registers a fifty-three-point canyon favoring the Republican president. Last, in the third quartile, STS whites have Trump maxed out with a one-hundred-point rating on the feeling thermometer, whereas Obama registers a sixty-seven.

We have discussed the boxplot data by first considering urban whites' feelings toward Presidents Obama and Trump and then doing the same for rural/STS whites' feelings toward these presidents. It is also the case that if the assessment was instead made by comparing feelings toward Trump among rural/STS whites versus urban whites, and then repeating the comparison with respect to Obama, these differences would be obvious too, because urban whites are not nearly as disapproving of Obama or as smitten with Trump as are their rural/STS neighbors. Narrowing the scope to just President Trump, a common approval question also reveals a substantial difference in the views of urban and STS whites. Relying on the same 2020 survey used to produce Figure 12.6, we asked white southerners for their approval of President Trump. We did not offer a neutral response option (e.g., neither approve nor disapprove). Rather, the response options were either favorable or unfavorable, as follows: (1) strongly disapprove, (2) disapprove, (3) approve, and (4) strongly approve. Among urban whites, one out of three (33.3%) strongly disapproved of Trump, compared with one out of four STS whites (24.6%). At the other end of the distribution, 40.2% of STS whites strongly approved of Trump versus 31.9% of urban whites. Finally, if we collapse the two approving categories (approve and strongly approve), then Trump's approval among STS whites was sixty-eight percent as compared with fifty-seven percent among urban whites, an eleven-percentage-point difference that is statistically significant.[13]

At the time of this writing, the national Republican Party is still in the throes of a postelection civil war between the Trump base and GOP establishment factions. At the 2021 Conservative Political Action Conference, or CPAC, in Orlando, Florida (February 25–28), Trump was the keynote speaker and made an attempt to reassure the Republican faithful that he was committed to uniting the Republican Party rather than working to lead a breakaway faction under a new label.[14] Of course, as was a routine feature of Trump's erratic presidency, mixed messaging was on full display in Trump's ninety-minute speech. While averring the GOP was united except for a small group of Republican "hacks" inside the beltway, he also uttered the names of every Republican member of Congress who voted to impeach/remove him from office in the wake of the Trump-inspired January 6, 2021 attack on the US Capitol. As Republican campaign strategist Karl Rove (2021) pointed out, it is difficult to mobilize a unified GOP against the ruling Democratic Party when Trump is fixated on perpetuating the "Big Lie" of a stolen 2020 presidential election while aggressively seeking to oust the small number of Republicans who dared cross him during the ex-president's second impeachment.[15]

The GOP's current disarray is something that must be fixed for Republicans to optimize their electoral performance in the 2022 midterm elections. Hence, a pressing question is what will happen to Trump's most ardent supporters, of whom so many are rural white southerners? We suspect that, given the characteristics associated with this group (e.g., conservative, less educated, and evangelical Christian), they would appear the least likely to abandon the GOP ship and swim toward the Democratic Party. Nonetheless, Trump proved a historically galvanizing force in getting his supporters to the polls; therefore, it is probable that his absence from elective office will demobilize many rural white southerners.

Therefore, a very likely post–Trump-era scenario might be the withdrawal of numerous white small-town southerners from the political arena. For instance, as covered in chapter eleven, with many Trump voters believing that the 2020 presidential election was stolen in Georgia, 2021 Senate runoff turnout among white voters in STS counties showed a decided dropoff. Of course, this Senate runoff election is not necessarily indicative of where Trump supporters may be in the future. It is also clear that, Trump aside, the realignment of rural whites in the South to the Republican Party is now an established and enduring feature of politics in the region.

Final Thoughts

The relative decline of the rural white population in the South, combined with the possibility that some subset of this group (Trump loyalists) may withdraw from the body politic, does not bode well for the GOP's future electoral prospects. In fact, one might say that, long term, this is certainly a losing formula. To stay viable, the southern GOP must alter its composition. Southern Republicans cannot continue to assemble electoral coalitions with an overreliance of votes cast by rural whites.

Given demographic realities, the Republican Party must make inroads in recovering some share of white voters in urban settings that have been lost over the last few decades.[16] As discussed in chapter ten, in many respects, urban white southerners are a different political species than their rural white neighbors. Cultural and other socioeconomic differences are present between these two groups, and whites in urban areas are not as ideologically conservative as STS whites. In our 2020 survey, fifty-four percent of STS whites self-identified as conservative, compared with less than a majority (forty-five percent) of urban whites. Hence, it appears that the southern GOP needs to retool its appeal (and messaging) to these more moderate urban residents without losing the support of rural dwellers in the process.

Second, the southern GOP's political tent will also need to make room for racial/ethnic minorities. As the rural white population shrinks, it is being replaced by an ever-growing number of minorities. At least in the short term, there is no evidence that Black southerners, who as a group are almost monolithic in their support of the Democratic Party, will be defecting to the GOP. Another group, however, may present a better possibility: Latinos. Although decidedly tilting Democratic, Latinos do show some proclivity to support Republican candidates. For example, Latinos helped Trump win both Texas and Florida in 2020 (Hood and McKee, 2021; Lewis and Fagenson, 2020). In Florida, forty-six percent of Latinos voted for Trump, and in Texas, forty-one percent did so.[17] As with urban whites, the GOP need not win huge majorities (or even a majority) of Latino voters; only a large enough percentage to produce a winning electoral coalition.

Latinos, as a group, are growing faster than the Black population in the South and are already a large share of the Texas and Florida electorates. Their settlement patterns are also different from those of whites and Blacks, with a higher rate of Latinos relocating to rural areas (McKee, 2019). Also, a large majority of Latinos are Catholic, and a growing number are evangelical Protestants, making this overall demographic more susceptible to the culturally conservative appeals of the Republican Party on social issues. Conversely, Latinos tend to be more liberal on economic/social welfare issues—a potential draw for the Democratic Party.[18] If, as has been the case since the end of the civil rights movement, the southern GOP continues to shun the cultivation of Black support (Black and Black, 2002), then the growing Latino electorate is the most obvious and untapped segment of the electorate allowing for a new approach to Republican party-building in the region.

Some political operatives viewing the ongoing demographic changes in the South make the case that it is only a matter of time before Democratic majorities emerge (e.g., Judis and Teixeira, 2002). There is no question one has to acknowledge that current trends do not currently favor the GOP. However, for the "demographics is destiny" hypothesis to come to fruition, one must also hold all current political relationships constant while projecting into the future (Hood, 2016). No one, including us, can be certain of what the future holds for the status of party politics in Dixie. For example, who could have predicted Donald Trump's substantial and lasting effect on the state of party politics since 2016? He has pushed the GOP in an even more racially and culturally conservative direction (Sides, Tesler, and Vavreck, 2018) and at the same time moved elected Republicans toward the interests of the economically downscale populist views of their white rural base (Miller and Schofield, 2008; Prysby, 2020). In the immediate term, this development is not problematic in many southern states such as Alabama, Arkansas, Louisiana, Mississippi, and Tennessee. However, in the remainder of southern states, an overemphasis on the preferences, beliefs/values, and concerns of the white rural electorate is repelling urban whites, whose votes are desperately needed for the GOP to stay in control.

Not long ago, and for decades, scholars made common use of a Deep versus Rim/Peripheral South subregional dichotomy (see Black and Black, 1987, 2002, 2012; Key, 1949; Matthews and Prothro, 1966; McKee, 2010, 2017), because it proved empirically useful for explaining different electoral dynamics. For example, collectively, the five Deep South states with proportionally larger Black electorates, are significantly more Republican (Black and Black, 2012; McKee and Springer, 2015). However, as we saw in the 2020 presidential election and then in the January 2021 Senate runoffs, the Deep South state of Georgia has emerged as one of the most competitive. In contrast, two Rim South states, Arkansas and Tennessee, are now unquestionably two of the most Republican in the region (see chapter nine). In short, this subregional distinction has lost its empirical usefulness (Knuckey, 2017), because there are now too many exceptions to the rule of a more Republican Deep South. Instead, as we have alluded to on many occasions, in the most current version of southern politics, what is driving the relative political strength of the major parties is the degree to which their electorates are being demographically altered.

Therefore, in taking in the big picture, there are many places in the South where Republican dominance should persist for years to come, and this arguably entails the five aforementioned states of Alabama, Arkansas, Louisiana, Mississippi, and Tennessee. The common thread among these states is the minimal changes to their electorates as a consequence of modest population growth and in-migration patterns that generally reinforce the Republican ruling status quo (McKee and Teigen, 2016). Additionally, there simply is not a critical mass of urban white voters in any of these states that has shifted toward the Democratic Party in any meaningful degree to undermine the GOP hegemony built on a foundation of rural whites. Simply put, the RRR of southern whites in these states should be able to sustain the GOP's political dominance for the foreseeable future.

In contrast, Florida, Georgia, North Carolina, South Carolina, Texas, and Virginia (Bullock, 2021; Bullock et al., 2019) all show varying and pronounced degrees of political change that are closely tied to the alteration of their electorates through high population growth, with much of it due to the arrival of a racially and ethnically diverse stream of northern and international immigrants. In all of these states, on net, these changes to the voting population undermine the clout of rural whites, who are decidedly more Republican. Further, the population growth occurring in these states is overwhelmingly taking place in urban centers (Morris, 2021), which already tilt Democratic. If demographic changes in these states are viewed as a political arms race, then the white rural Republican electorate is losing. In this context, it is imperative that Republicans find a way to diversify and broaden their appeal to capture a greater segment of the urban electorate.

Perhaps more than at any time in southern history, the eleven ex-Confederate states have balkanized to an extent that scholarly attention needs to be paid to them individually. As mentioned, in the United States, the South leads the way in population growth, and because much of this growth is a consequence of new arrivals, the region is changing at a faster rate than ever before. Often, these newcomers do not share the political views and affiliations of the native populations where they settle (Hood and McKee, 2010). Indeed, all across Dixie, there are local settings in which the changing electorate has reached the tipping point at which heretofore Republican control switches in favor of Democrats. In an important work, Frymer (2010) demonstrated that because Blacks are so wedded to the Democratic Party, they have become a captive electorate. In other words, Democratic politicians have taken Black interests for granted, because there is no fear of them defecting to the Republican opposition. Similarly, white rural Republicanism in the South may have reached the point where these voters are now captives of the GOP.[19] As the majority party in most of the region, unlike in the case of Black Democrats, it seems that elected southern Republicans are now equally captive to their rural white constituents. In other words, sometimes the tail wags the dog. If this is true, then the inability of the GOP to respond to the political demands of a burgeoning urban electorate may eventually render Republicans the minority party in most of a remarkably changing South.

Appendices A and B

Appendix A: Detailed List of Data Sources by Chapter

 Available online at: https://uscpress.com/files/galleries/Hood-McKee _Appendix_A.pdf.

Appendix B: Empirical Model Results by Chapter

 Available online at: https://uscpress.com/files/galleries/Hood-McKee _Appendix_B.pdf.

Notes

Introduction: Texas: Thirty Years Apart

1. Throughout this book, unless stated otherwise, we define the American South as the eleven states that seceded from the Union during the Civil War: Alabama, Arkansas, Florida, Georgia, Louisiana, Mississippi, North Carolina, South Carolina, Tennessee, Texas, and Virginia.

2. The election return data are from *Dave Leip's Atlas of U.S. Presidential Elections*: https://uselectionatlas.org/.

3. Sulphur Springs, Texas, is located in 59.6% rural Hopkins County (2010 census data).

4. The relevant portions of the 1988 vice presidential debate transcript can be found here: https://www.npr.org/templates/story/story.php?storyId=5425248.

5. Our geographic county classification system is discussed in detail in chapter two. The small-town South (STS) definition used in Figure I1 is based on the 2010 census data and then applied to Texas counties for 2018 and 1988, so the classification scheme remains constant for this thirty-year span. If we did not apply this methodology, then in 1988, there would be many more STS counties in Texas at that time, because the state has become increasingly urban/metropolitan since then.

6. For the first time since Bentsen in 1988, the Democratic Party in 2018, with Beto O'Rourke as its nominee, won a majority of the US Senate votes in the Lone Star State's six counties housing its largest cities (Harris, City of Houston; Bexar, City of San Antonio; Dallas, City of Dallas; Travis, City of Austin; Tarrant, City of Fort Worth; and El Paso, City of El Paso). Note as well that most of the small-town counties won by O'Rourke in 2018 were in heavily Hispanic South and West Texas.

7. As a point of comparison to presidential elections, sixty-nine percent of Bush's majority-vote counties were small town in 1988, whereas more than three out of four (seventy-six percent) of Trump's majority-vote counties in 2016 were classified as small town.

Chapter 1: America's Longest and Deepest Realignment

1. We mentioned the Deep South states in the body of the chapter; hence, the Peripheral or Rim South states comprise Arkansas, Florida, North Carolina, Tennessee, Texas, and Virginia. After chapter one, we do not emphasize this common subregional division of the South terribly much because of a growing consistency in rural political behavior regardless of southern state/subregion.

2. The equal population standard elucidated in *Baker v. Carr* (1962) came from state legislative malapportionment complaints in Tennessee; *Gray v. Sanders* (1963) ended the county unit system in Georgia (see chapter six); *Reynolds v. Sims* (1964) ruled in favor of an equal population standard applied to state legislative elections in a case that originated from Alabama; and *Wesberry v. Sanders* (1964) was another case from Georgia that established equal population in congressional districts.

3. Lest the reader get confused, although the core of the southern Democracy, its Black Belt counties, were perhaps the worst fit for a Roman Catholic candidate because of such a high percentage of Southern Baptists, this section of Dixie aligned with Al

Smith regarding his antiprohibitionist sentiments (see footnote 3 in Key, 1949, p. 319). It is also true that, in several instances in which the Republican vote exceeded what was expected in accordance with the percentage of Black county inhabitants, this was due to a Populist past where defections from the southern Democracy in the late 1800s connected with GOP presidential support in 1928.

4. The overriding legal defense of the white Democratic primary was that the party amounted to a private club and, therefore, its leaders could determine who participated in these elections. Black and Black (1987, p. 84) had this to say about such a legal strategy: "The proposition that southern Democratic parties were simply private organizations with no implicit state functions was so preposterous that only small children believed it and only constitutional lawyers debated it."

5. Truman won eleven of Tennessee's twelve electoral votes. Thanks to a faithless elector, Thurmond secured one electoral vote in the Volunteer State, even though he finished third, behind Dewey in the popular vote.

6. Key (1949, p. 333) quotes one of Thurmond's most notorious statements: "All the laws of Washington, and all the bayonets of the Army cannot force the negroes into their (southerners) homes, their schools, their churches and their places of recreation and amusement." In a radio address, and with a somewhat more genteel tone, Governor Wright of Mississippi had this to say to his state's Black citizens: "If any of you have become so deluded as to want to enter our hotels and cafes, enjoy social equality with the whites, then kindness and true sympathy requires me to advise you to make your home in some state other than Mississippi" (Key, 1949, p. 334).

7. The entire States' Rights Democratic Party platform is available online, thanks to The American Presidency Project, and it can be found at this link: https://www.presidency .ucsb.edu/documents/platform-the-states-rights-democratic-party.

8. Thus, the economic views of States' Rights Democrats were clearly more in keeping with those promulgated by national Republicans; the latter were reluctant to embrace Dixie's racial conservatism, which was enough to maintain rural southern whites' fealty to the Democratic Party for years to come.

9. The ANES samples are small; therefore, the 1952 and 1956 data have been combined so that urban white southerners equal 125 respondents and rural white southerners equal 254 respondents.

10. In the counties mentioned in the text, with much greater Black participation in 2020 and the pronounced movement of urban whites away from the GOP, the Democratic presidential nominee Joe Biden only lost to Trump in Knox County (home to the city of Knoxville and the University of Tennessee) in deep red Tennessee. Virginia is unique among the southern states for having several cities like Richmond, designated as county equivalents. In 2020, Joe Biden won almost eighty-five percent of the two-party vote in Richmond City. Pinellas County, FL, one of four in the Sunshine State that flipped to Trump in 2016 (McKee and Smith, 2019), flipped back to the Democrats and Joe Biden, who won 50.1% of the two-party vote.

11. The difference in this split-ticket voting (Republican for president and Democratic for House) for urban white southerners (n = 101) versus rural white southerners (n = 207) is significant at $p < .01$.

12. Briefly (for eight months), Republican Ben H. Guill represented District Eighteen in Texas (Amarillo area) in 1950 but was then defeated by the Democrat in the regularly scheduled 1950 contest (Kalb, 2016, p. 1290).

13. Recent scholarship suggests that 1960 actually included notable attempts by Republicans in the South to elevate Nixon's candidacy as the more conservative candidate,

and particularly with respect to racial issues; offering an early window into the GOP's "Southern Strategy," which took full bloom under Goldwater in the 1964 presidential election (see Galsworthy, 2021).

14. The 1964 ANES sample included fifty-nine urban whites and 118 rural whites. Despite these small samples, the sixty-three percent urban white vote for Goldwater, compared with his thirty-one percent share garnered among rural whites, is a difference significant at $p < .001$.

15. It is uncanny that the popular vote percentage cast by Mississippians for the blatantly racist Dixiecrat Thurmond in his three-way race (Thurmond, Truman, and Dewey; the Progressive Henry Wallace did get 225 Mississippi votes) in 1948 (87.17%) is almost exactly the same as the percentage Goldwater took versus Johnson in 1964 (87.14%).

16. There were thirty-three Republican senators voting on the 1964 Civil Rights Act; twenty-seven voted yes, and six voted no (details are available online here: https://www.govtrack.us/congress/votes/88-1964/s409).

17. Alabama Democratic Governor George Wallace and other leading Democrats in his state supported Goldwater and therefore played an active role in making sure Lyndon B. Johnson was excluded from the 1964 ballot. After the 1964 election, President Johnson and Governor Wallace would, of course, end up playing two of the lead roles over the struggle for Black civil rights, as so many of the major turning points took place in Alabama: For instance, predating Wallace's tenure as governor was arguably the start of the mass movement phase of civil rights protest, with Rosa Parks igniting the Montgomery bus boycott in December 1955; the unrest in Birmingham in 1963 catalyzing Johnson's successful push for the 1964 Civil Rights Act the following summer; and, finally, the 1965 Selma campaign that is credited with galvanizing support for passage of the 1965 Voting Rights Act.

18. The difference between these two correlations is significant at $p < .001$.

19. Nationally, Nixon's two-party popular vote percentage over Humphrey was 50.4%. In the South, the 1968 popular presidential vote split thirty-five percent for Nixon, thirty-four percent for Wallace, and thirty-one percent for Humphrey (McKee, 2019, pp. 83–84).

20. Goldwater flipped five out of eight seats in Alabama, netted one seat in the ten-member Georgia delegation, and picked up a seat in Mississippi's five-member delegation. It is important to note that Howard "Bo" Callaway was the victorious Republican in Georgia's Third District and came very close to winning the governorship two years later (see chapter six). The Louisiana and South Carolina House delegations remained one hundred percent Democratic. Goldwater had no coattails in the Rim South, and facing Johnson, the two Republicans in the Texas House delegation (Bruce Alger in District Five and Ed Foreman in District Sixteen) both lost reelection in 1964 (Kalb, 2016, p. 1323).

21. As noted by Lloyd (2012, p. 490), "The constituents for Southern demagogues like George Wallace were drawn mainly from rural landowners and members of the white poor and working classes, who could not easily pivot to new strategies of de facto segregation."

22. The difference between these two correlations is significant at $p < .001$.

23. George Wallace was born in the little town of Clio, located in Barbour County, Alabama. According to the 2015–2019 American Community Survey data, Clio had 1,015 residents.

24. Who can forget Trump brandishing a Bible in front of St. John's Episcopal Church in Washington, DC, while a few blocks away, military force dispersed peaceful protestors (Forgey, 2020)?

25. The original quote by Black and Black (2002, p. 119) is italicized.

26. Specifically, we code as urban those white southern respondents who live in a city or suburb, whereas rural white southern respondents are those who live in a town or rural setting. All of the SFPs are publicly available through the University of North Carolina's Odum Institute data archive: https://dataverse.unc.edu/. Incidentally, in the fall 1994 SFP, there were more Republican identifiers among urban whites than rural whites, which was to be expected at this time, and also comports with the ANES data reported in the chapter.

27. Unrelated to the data shown in Table 1.2 but once again speaking to the increase in rural white southerners aligned with the GOP, in the 2016 CES, there was a question asking respondents whether they voted in the Republican or Democratic presidential primaries. Among STS whites who reported voting in the 2016 presidential primary, seventy-six percent claimed they participated in the Republican contest. In contrast, among urban white southerners who said they participated in the 2016 presidential primary, sixty-two percent reported voting in the GOP contest. Not surprisingly, this fourteen-point rural/urban 2016 GOP presidential primary voting participation difference is significant ($p < .001$).

28. Speaking to the dynamics we have uncovered in this section, Kitschelt and Rehm (2019) make a convincing case that over the long term in American politics (since the mid-twentieth century), at least in the case of white voters, low-income/low-education voters have shifted toward the GOP because of its embrace of the authoritarian pole on a noneconomic ideological dimension. In contrast, high-income/high-education whites have shifted toward the Democratic Party because of its embrace of the libertarian pole on the same noneconomic ideological dimension. Conversely, high-income/low-education whites have become the most solid Republican group, because they agree with the GOP's conservative position on the economic dimension and authoritarianism on the noneconomic dimension, whereas low-income/high-education whites are the most aligned with the Democratic Party because of its relatively more progressive stance on the economic dimension and libertarian positions on the noneconomic dimension. These changing positions of voters with respect to party alignment in contemporary times have upended the old structure of party politics during the New Deal era (circa 1932–1969). Whereas low-income/low-education whites were the core of the Democratic Party, they are now a swing group. Likewise, whereas high-income/high-education whites were the core of the GOP, they are now a swing group. For both of these groups, they align better with the party positioned closer to them on the noneconomic ideological dimension (e.g., low-income/low-education whites prefer authoritarianism over libertarianism, whereas high-income/high-education whites prefer libertarianism over authoritarianism).

29. Key's 1959 article was not an examination of southern politics; it was focused on electoral realignment in various northern (primarily New England) towns from the late 1800s up to the 1952 election.

Chapter 2: Measuring Place and the Data Associated with It

1. There are many ways to define and subsequently measure rurality. Throughout the book, we make use of several measures of rurality as outlined in this chapter. Unlike our approach, Scala and Johnson (2017) used a county-level rural-urban continuum to assess differences in the presidential vote from 2000 to 2016. Nevertheless, the rural-urban continuum used by Scala and Johnson (2017) is similar to a population density measure and clearly shows that the least populated nonmetropolitan US counties are substantially and consistently the most Republican in presidential elections.

2. There are occasions in the book where we utilize other definitions of place outside of the three discussed in this chapter. For example, the American National Election Studies has long categorized survey respondents by the type and size of place in which they were interviewed with a variable that we recode as binary for rural and urban (urban combines large cities and suburban areas).

3. There is a wealth of information from the US Census Bureau on the urban/rural topic. For a general overview, see the US Census Bureau's webpage "Urban and Rural" at: https://www.census.gov/programs-surveys/geography/guidance/geo-areas/urban-rural.html. Other helpful documents include Ratcliffe (2016); Ratcliffe et al. (2016); and the Urban Area Criteria for the 2010 US Census, 76 Fed. Reg. 53030–53043 (August 24, 2011).

4. For an excellent and not overly technical description of the changing methodology used by the Census Bureau to characterize urban/rural population and territory, see Ratcliffe (2016).

5. Currently, blocks are classified as being geographically situated either wholly within an urban area (i.e., urban area or urban cluster) or wholly within a rural area.

6. One should not confuse the discussion of the US Census Bureau's definitions of urban and rural areas with metropolitan and micropolitan statistical areas as defined by the US Office of Management and Budget. Although correlated, these constructs are not synonymous/equivalent. See Ratcliffe et al. (2016) for a more detailed discussion on this matter.

7. See pages 53031–53033 of "Urban Area Criteria for the 2010 Census," 76 Fed. Reg. 53030–53043 (August 24, 2011) for a detailed discussion of the changes that were implemented beginning with the 2000 census for defining urban areas and urban clusters.

8. There were some minor changes made to the criteria used by the US Census Bureau in classifying urban areas between the 2000 census and the 2010 census. These changes do not affect the urban/rural measure for our purposes. The Census Bureau document "Differences Between Urbanized Area Criteria from the 1990 Census and Census 2000" explains these changes in detail (https://www2.census.gov/geo/pdfs/reference/ua/1990_2000uadif.pdf).

9. As of this writing, data from the 2020 census to produce rural/urban calculations are not available.

10. As discussed previously, the US Census Bureau made changes to its definition of urban between the 1990 census and the 2000 census. As such, the calculations for our STS measure differ slightly from those for 2000 and 2010. See the Appendix at the end of this chapter for specific details.

11. The map in Figure 2.1 displays the binary coding discussed earlier where any county/parish with ninety-five percent or more of its population classified as STS is coded as STS. All other counties/parishes, by definition, are urban.

12. Independent cities in Virginia have the same status as counties and are included in our classification scheme.

13. STS population segments can be found in what we classify as urban counties. The computation here only includes the population for counties that are ninety-five percent (or greater) STS. As such, the region's overall STS composition in 2010 was 29.3% (Table 2.2), but the 714 STS counties segmented alone account for just 14.9% of the South's total population.

14. Population density values can be extremely skewed on the upper end (i.e., highly populated and geographically compact urban areas), with heavy clustering for smaller values also present. Using the logged value of population density creates a more

symmetrical distribution which aids statistical analysis. See pp. 108–121 of Tufte (1974) for a lengthier discussion on this topic.

15. In terms of land mass, Brewster County is larger than Rhode Island, Connecticut, or Delaware.

16. More than a majority of Brewster County's population lives in the county seat of Alpine, which, at 5,982 people, is above the US Census threshold for an urban area. As a consequence, this sprawling and extremely remote county is classified as a majority urban area. Outside of Alpine, one is more likely to see a jackrabbit than another human being.

17. As a comparison, Brewster County would be classified as one hundred percent STS, while Dallas County is 0.7% STS.

18. As shown in chapter nine, we present Mississippi Poll data up to 2012.

Chapter 2: Appendix

1. In the case of an Urban Cluster (UC) that spans multiple counties: If the UC is greater than 20,000 people, then this territory will be counted as urban, even if the population of the UC in any given county is less than 20,000.

2. A county may contain more than one UC and still be classified as small-town as long as these UCs individually do not contain more than 20,000 persons.

3. Requires visual confirmation.

4. Source: https://ipums.org.

5. The STS calculation for 1990 is more conservative than the 2000–2010 definition because some urban population residing outside of UAs that should be classified as STS are instead classified as urban.

Chapter 3: Presidential Republicanism and Democratic Darn Near Everything Else

1. Data on the timing/scheduling of southern gubernatorial elections are from Kalb (2016). Arkansas (up to 1986) used to hold biennial gubernatorial elections, and Texas did the same until 1972. Before 1952, Alabama, Georgia, and South Carolina already held their gubernatorial contests in midterm even years, whereas Mississippi and Virginia contests are held in odd years (the year after the midterm even year in Mississippi and the year after the presidential election in Virginia). After 1972, Louisiana moved its contest to the odd year after midterm even years. Tennessee (after 1952), Florida (after 1964), and Texas (after 1972) all hold their contests in midterm even years.

2. There were four Republican senators in the southern delegation in 1968, and three of them won elections in 1966: Strom Thurmond (South Carolina; Democratic incumbent who switched to the GOP in 1964), Howard Baker (Tennessee; newly elected), and John Tower (Texas; reelected). In 1968, Republican Edward Gurney defeated former Democratic Governor Leroy Collins in an open Senate seat in Florida.

3. The lengthy note under variable VCF0902 of the ANES CDF Codebook makes it clear that classifications for the type of House seat in the 1970s are suspect. Additionally, one part of the same "General Note" states that "ANES samples are not designed to be representative at the Congressional district level. Samples include cases from only some US Congressional districts; for most congressional districts in which interviewing actually takes place, only a small number of interviews are taken" (ANES CDF [1948–2016] Codebook, p. 431).

4. The remaining distribution for rural and urban whites by district type was: twenty percent of rural whites in Republican incumbent districts and five percent of rural whites

in open seats; forty-two percent of urban whites in Republican incumbent districts and eleven percent of urban whites in open seats.

5. We cannot separate rural voters from those located in small cities of 10,000 to 49,999 people because these categories were already combined in the 1984 exit poll raw dataset. There are separate categories for rural/small-town and cities of 10K to < 50K after 1984, but for the sake of consistency, throughout the book we rely on this binary classification of rural/STS and urban voters for all data reported from the exit polls.

6. In 1984, omitting Louisiana's so-called Cajun/jungle/open primary contest, which the national exit poll did not include, every remaining southern state except for Florida had a Senate contest. In 1986, seven southern states (Alabama, Arkansas, Florida, Georgia, Louisiana, North Carolina, and South Carolina) held Senate elections, and the Democrats swept them, contributing to the end of a national Republican Senate majority first obtained in the 1980 elections. In 1988, only five states (Florida, Mississippi, Tennessee, Texas, and Virginia) had Senate elections, and none of these involved a Republican incumbent seeking reelection.

7. Unless it isn't clear from the text, because the total share of rural and urban white voters is not equally distributed in the national exit polls (there are more urban voters: sixty-two percent of the total sample for 1984–1988), these comparisons are performed on the basis of the distribution of rural voters among all rural voters and, likewise, the corresponding distribution of urban voters among all urban voters. These same computations were performed with regard to the ANES data displayed in Figure 3.2 (there are more classified rural whites than urban whites in the ANES).

8. For similar reasons, urban whites are much more likely to vote a straight Republican ticket for president and House (Same-RR), because they are relatively more prevalent in House districts won by Republicans (admittedly, this statement comes across a bit tautological). For instance, in all House elections (opposed and unopposed) in 1984 and 1988, fifty-seven percent of urban whites voted Republican for president and House versus forty-eight percent of rural whites who did the same (a difference significant at $p < .001$).

9. With respect to the median percent rural in 1988 southern House seats, it is forty-two percent for Split-RD districts; twenty-eight percent for Same-RR districts; and just two percent for Same-DD districts. These data on the percent rural come from David Lublin's publicly available dataset ("Congressional District Demographic and Political Data, 1972–1994"), which can be found here: http://davidlublin.com/sample-page /data/.

10. According to the ANES, in the 1980s, eighty-three percent of rural white southerners had grown up in the South, whereas seventy-two percent of urban whites grew up in the region (a statistically significant difference, $p < .001$).

Chapter 4: Voting for the Biggest Prize: Presidential Elections

1. The two county-level models are estimated using OLS regression where the percentage of the Republican presidential vote is the dependent variable. Independent variables include a time variable organized by decade (1990s, 2000s, and 2010s), the percentage of non-Hispanic whites by county, the percentage of STS by county or the logged population density by county, a dummy variable for open-seat election cycles, and a dummy variable for election cycles featuring a Republican incumbent. To decompose effects by time, place, and race, we also include a set of requisite interactive terms. Finally, to account for unmeasured differences that exist across counties, we include

county fixed effects (a set of *n* – 1 county indicators). As the size of counties varies tremendously, both models are weighted by the total two-party presidential vote cast in each county. Once specified, OLS model interpretations are straightforward. For Figure 4.1, the STS indicator is set to either zero (one hundred percent urban) or one (one hundred percent STS). For Figure 4.2, the tenth percentile through ninetieth percentile values for logged density are used. In both models, the variable measuring race is set to one (one hundred percent non-Hispanic white), the value of the time variable is set to represent various decades, and the election type is specified as an open-seat contest. The effects for a county representing the mean value for STS or density are also included when interpreting the effects of the models presented. Finally, through manipulation of the interactive terms, we can estimate the white GOP presidential vote by decade and place. Detailed model results can be found in Appendix B online.

2. Using the tenth through the ninetieth county-level population-density percentiles allows us to examine the range on this indicator while eliminating the most extreme values at both ends of the spectrum.

3. We should clarify that, although the ANES Cumulative Data File blocks access to the place variable after the 2000 election, it is possible to get data on the ANES place variable from the individual election time series after 2000, with the exception of the 2008 contest. Thus, in chapter eight, we present ANES data that run through the 2016 election.

4. Perot amassed just under nineteen percent of the national popular presidential vote in 1992, which declined to less than nine percent of the national popular presidential vote in 1996. In the South, Perot's best 1992 performance was in his native Texas (winning twenty-two percent of the popular vote), and his worst performance was in Mississippi (under nine percent). In regional terms, Perot was decidedly less popular in Dixie in 1996, winning a region-best nine percent of the popular vote in Florida while being held to under eight percent in the rest of the southern states (with a low of 5.59% of the popular vote in Tennessee).

5. The two specified models are estimated using probit and include the following predictors: either the STS indicator or logged population density; time (decade); and a requisite interactive term. The dependent variable is binary and is coded one to represent a Republican presidential vote or zero to represent a vote for a Democratic presidential candidate. Cases are limited to include non-Hispanic white respondents, and models are weighted using the included CES cumulative weight variable. Full model results can be found in Appendix B online.

6. As with all probability models presented throughout this book, predicted values are generated using the Hanmer and Kalkan (2013) observed values method.

7. See endnote 2.

8. Unfortunately, the size of place variable was not included in the state exit polls for the 1990s.

9. We subset the national exit poll data to include only the eleven southern states.

10. In more recent surveys, the ANES no longer publicly discloses a respondent's county of residence.

11. A state-level exit poll was not administered in every state in a given election year.

12. Starting with Bill Clinton in 1992, every subsequent president has come into office under unified government in both chambers of Congress (put differently, the newly elected president has come into office with copartisan majorities in the House and Senate) and then, at some point, lost his party majority in either one or both congressional chambers. Likewise, Joe Biden came into office in 2020 with party majorities in Congress

but having a Senate majority only because Vice President Kamala Harris is the tie-breaking vote. Hence, it is very likely that President Biden will lose one or both congressional chambers in the 2022 midterm elections.

13. The South actually had 160 total electoral votes in 2016, but two Texas electors (out of thirty-eight) did not vote for Trump (one voted for John Kasich, and one voted for Ron Paul).

14. For the purposes of the two maps presented, a county is classified as STS if it is at least ninety-five percent on our STS measure. Urban counties are any that are less than ninety-five percent STS. This classification of an STS county is, therefore, a very conservative one.

15. In 2016, most of the Democrat/STS strongholds consist of heavily minority (Black and/or Latino) rural counties located in the Black Belt region (especially the Mississippi Delta), and several Texas counties near or along the Mexico border.

Chapter 5: US Senate Elections: Republicans' Most-Promising and Attainable Seats

1. In the 1961 Texas special Senate election runoff, the vote went 50.6% in favor of Republican John Tower (Kalb, 2016).

2. These are the eighteen counties that constitute Alabama's Black Belt: Barbour, Bullock, Butler, Choctaw, Crenshaw, Dallas, Greene, Hale, Lowndes, Macon, Marengo, Montgomery, Perry, Pickens, Pike, Russell, Sumter, and Wilcox.

3. The two county-level models are estimated using OLS regression when the percentage of the Republican Senate vote is the dependent variable. Independent variables include a time variable organized by decade (1990s, 2000s, and 2010s); the percentage of non-Hispanic whites by county; the percentage of STS by county or the logged population density by county; a dummy variable for open-seat election cycles; and a dummy variable for election cycles featuring a Republican incumbent. To decompose effects by time, place, and race, we also included a set of requisite interactive terms. Finally, to account for unmeasured differences that exist across counties we include county fixed effects (a set of $n-1$ county indicators). As the size of counties varies tremendously, both models are weighted by the total two-party Senate vote cast in each county. Once specified, OLS model interpretations are straightforward. For Figure 5.3, the STS indicator is set to either zero (one hundred percent urban) or one (one hundred percent STS). For Figure 5.4, the tenth-percentile through the ninetieth-percentile values for logged density are used. In both models, the variable measuring race is set to one (one hundred percent non-Hispanic white), the value of the time variable is set to represent various decades, and the election type is specified as an open-seat contest. The effects for a county representing the mean value for STS or density are also included when interpreting the effects of the models presented. Finally, through manipulation of the interactive terms, we can estimate the white GOP Senate vote by decade and place. Detailed model results can be found in Appendix B online.

4. The two specified models are estimated using probit and include the following predictors: either the STS indicator or logged population density; time (decade); race type (open seat; Republican incumbent); a set of $n-1$ state dummies with Virginia used as the excluded category; and requisite interactive terms. The dependent variable is binary and is coded one to represent a Republican Senate vote and zero to represent a vote for a Democratic Senate candidate. Cases are limited to include non-Hispanic white respondents in states featuring a contested Senate contest. Models are weighted using the included CES cumulative weight variable. Full model results can be found in Appendix B online.

5. The 2004 and 2008 national exit polls asked about the Senate vote but did not include a place indicator; hence, for our purposes, that is why data for these two elections are excluded from Figure 5.7.

6. Doug Jones's best performance was in the Black Belt and rural Macon County, where he captured 88.4% of the two-party vote. We should note that, given the extreme racial polarization in the contemporary partisan loyalties of Alabamians and throughout the Deep South (Black and Black, 2012; McKee and Springer, 2015), it should come as no surprise that Macon County contains the highest percentage of Blacks in Alabama, at 82.6% (according to the five-year 2014–2018 American Community Survey estimate available here: http://mcdc.missouri.edu/applications/acs/profiles/report.php?p=37&g=05000US01087&s=Demographic).

Chapter 6: The Rural Transformation in Southern Gubernatorial Elections

1. One telling example of how nationalized politics benefited a southern Republican senator comes from North Carolina. The 1984 Senate election was one of the most anticipated and competitive in the history of the Tar Heel State. Democratic Governor Jim Hunt was term limited and decided to run against Republican Senator Jesse Helms, who first won his seat in 1972. This was a clash of political titans, and true to form, Senator Helms touted his socially conservative credentials, which brought him another of what would be several, close victories. Senator Helms prevailed with fifty-two percent of the two-party vote and served in the Senate for another eighteen years (Kalb, 2016). Governor Hunt's career was not over; he served two more terms in the 1990s (elected in 1992 and reelected in 1996). As the southern GOP continued to move in a more conservative direction with regard to racial and social issues, Senator Helms was very adept at garnering the support of traditionally Democratic voters in rural eastern North Carolina. Because most white voters in the eastern part of the state were affiliated with the Democratic Party, but exhibited strong support for Republican Senator Helms, they came to be known as "Jessecrats."

2. Cooper won 10,263 more votes than McCrory, out of a total of 4,608,117 cast for these major party gubernatorial candidates (Cohen and Barnes, 2017, p. 1386).

3. Eugene Talmadge was a true southern rabblerouser. Key (1949, p. 106) called him "Georgia's demagogue . . . a candidate in every state-wide Democratic primary save one between 1926 and 1946."

4. Fittingly, the two southern states containing the most viable GOP opposition, North Carolina and Tennessee, with their formidable Republican strongholds in the mountainous sections of these states (Heard, 1952), last had Republican governors serve in office in 1900 and 1922, respectively.

5. The two-party 1966 Georgia gubernatorial vote split 453,665 (50.2%) for the Republican Callaway and 450,626 (49.8%) for the Democrat Maddox (Kalb, 2016, p. 1688).

6. Maddox defeated Jimmy Carter in the 1966 Democratic gubernatorial primary, but Carter won Georgia's governorship in 1970. At that time, Carter clearly benefited from the "strange-bedfellows" biracial coalition of Blacks and racially conservative rural whites. As stated by Alter (2020, p. C4), Carter "used dog whistles and code words . . . to signal to conservative rural voters that he was on their side . . . [and] even proposed inviting George Wallace . . . to speak in the Georgia state capitol."

7. In the 2018 map (right side of Figure 6.2), notice the band of counties running roughly across the middle of Georgia, but in a diagonal pattern from northeast to southwest. This is Georgia's Black Belt region; thus, most of the counties located in this band

are rural but heavily Democratic, because they contain the highest percentage of Black residents.

8. The two county-level models are estimated using OLS regression where the percentage of the Republican gubernatorial vote is the dependent variable. Independent variables include a time variable organized by decade (1990s, 2000s, and 2010s), the percentage of non-Hispanic whites by county, the percentage of STS by county or the logged population density by county, a dummy variable for open-seat election cycles, and a dummy variable for election cycles featuring a Republican incumbent. To decompose effects by time, place, and race, we also include a set of requisite interactive terms. Finally, to account for unmeasured differences that exist across counties we include county fixed effects (a set of $n - 1$ county indicators). As the size of counties varies tremendously, both models are weighted by the total two-party gubernatorial vote cast in each county. Once specified, OLS model interpretations are straightforward. For Figure 6.3, the STS indicator is set to either zero (one hundred percent urban) or one (one hundred percent STS). For Figure 6.4, the tenth percentile through ninetieth percentile values for logged density are used. In both models, the variable measuring race is set to one (one hundred percent non-Hispanic white), the value of the time variable is set to represent various decades, and the election type is specified as an open-seat contest. The effects for a county representing the mean value for STS or density are also included when interpreting these models. Finally, through manipulation of the interactive terms, we can estimate the white GOP gubernatorial vote by decade and place. Detailed model results can be found in Appendix B online.

9. The two specified models are estimated using probit and include the following predictors: either the STS indicator or logged population density; time (decade); race type (open seat; Republican incumbent); a set of $n - 1$ state dummies with Virginia used as the excluded category; and requisite interactive terms. The dependent variable is binary and is coded one to represent a Republican gubernatorial vote or zero to represent a vote for a Democratic gubernatorial candidate. Cases are limited to include non-Hispanic white respondents in states featuring a contested gubernatorial contest. Models are weighted using the included CES cumulative weight variable. Full model results can be found in Appendix B online.

10. As always with the exit poll data, rural/STS whites consist of those voters classified as rural or residing in a city of fewer than fifty thousand residents; all other voters are classified as urban.

11. Once it became clear that President Trump lost Georgia in the 2020 contest, he has been relentless in his efforts to weaken Governor Kemp for not backing Trump's false claim of the election being stolen. In contrast, Governor DeSantis is on better terms with Trump, and there is some evidence (voting for DeSantis as a presidential hopeful at the 2021 Conservative Political Action Conference, or CPAC, in Orlando, FL), along with plenty of talk, of DeSantis being a possible contender for the 2024 Republican presidential nomination. This development has produced tension between Trump and DeSantis.

Chapter 7: Rural Voters in Southern US House Elections

1. Grofman and Brunell (2005) assessed the prevalence of the "dummymander" in several southern states in the 1990s, so called because these maps were usually drawn by Democrats but had the effect of producing Republican gains. Under the preclearance provision in Section 5 of the Voting Rights Act (which gave the Department of Justice oversight in most southern states' election administration, including redistricting), the Department of Justice was adamant about pressing a "maximum [B]lack" policy

(Cunningham, 2001), meaning that wherever possible, majority-minority districts should be drawn. Hence, in states such as Georgia, two new majority Black districts were created in addition to the one already represented by civil rights icon John Lewis, which was compact and covered inner-city Atlanta. In neighboring North Carolina, a state without a majority-minority district before 1992, two majority Black districts were added to its twelve-member House delegation; and like the new districts in the Peach State, North Carolina's were anything but compact. These districts had tortured shapes and were spatial works of abstract art (see McKee, 2019, pp. 98–99; Monmonier, 2001) because the Democratic line drawers did their best to satisfy the Department of Justice while also mistakenly hoping to salvage the reelection bids of white incumbents residing in substantially redrawn bordering districts. These plans manifested into dummymanders because of the faulty assumption that white voting behavior would essentially remain constant before and after redistricting (Petrocik and Desposato, 1998). It did not. As discussed in the text, redrawn voters shifted strongly in favor of Republican candidates (McKee, 2010, 2013) and were the principal reason why many white Democratic incumbents became casualties of Democratic-drawn maps. Starting with the Supreme Court case *Shaw v. Reno* (1993), which concerned the North Carolina congressional plan, many of these majority-minority districts in the South were struck down as racial gerrymanders because race was the overriding reason for their creation. Hence, throughout the 1990s, several southern states were tied up in litigation related to their congressional plans. In fact, Florida, Georgia, Louisiana, North Carolina, South Carolina, Texas, and Virginia all held House elections under multiple congressional plans in the 1990s because of constitutional issues regarding the drawing of their district boundaries starting in 1992. The 2000s was comparably a much quieter decade with respect to redistricting litigation and the implementation of multiple redistricting plans in the southern states. After the 2002 elections, Texas Republicans finally captured their first trifecta (control of the governorship and both chambers of the state legislature) since Reconstruction and then implemented a new congressional map for 2004 that performed impressively (and ruthlessly) in the objective of defeating several Anglo Democratic incumbents (Bickerstaff, 2007; Gaddie, 2004; McKee, 2010; McKee and Shaw, 2005; McKee, Teigen, and Turgeon, 2006). Texas then performed another redistricting that altered the boundaries of five congressional districts for the 2006 elections (McKee and McKenzie, 2013) and registered its greatest effect in altering the partisan outcome in Texas District Twenty-Three (see the later endnote about this). Georgia was the only other southern state holding House elections under multiple redistricting maps in the 2000s' redistricting cycle. Georgia Republicans attained the trifecta after the 2004 elections and then implemented a new congressional map for the 2006 midterms. This plan emphasized cleaning up the tortured boundaries drawn by Democrats under the previous map and, therefore, actually made knocking off incumbent Democrats a secondary priority (see Hood and McKee, 2009). Nevertheless, the redrawn districts served as a slow bleed that did eventually unseat a targeted white Democratic incumbent, Jim Marshall (of Georgia District Eight), in the Republican tsunami of 2010. In the 2010s' redistricting cycle, Florida, North Carolina, and Virginia held House elections under new maps in 2016 because of legal rulings. Finally, North Carolina, which would have easily won the most effective partisan gerrymander award of 2012 (see McGann et al., 2016), if such a thing existed (with a Republican-drawn map), had to hold its 2020 House elections under a new court-mandated plan, which advantaged Democrats (more on this in chapter eleven).

2. From 1992 to 1996, Republicans won nineteen of the thirty-nine Democratic-held open seats (forty-nine percent), while Democrats only gained one of the fourteen

Republican-held open seats. From 1992 to 1996, there were another seventeen open seats that we designate as newly created as a direct result of redistricting and, therefore, were not previously represented by a Democratic or Republican incumbent. Most of these districts were of the majority-minority kind designed to elect minority (Democratic) Representatives (thirty-eight percent average Black district populations and fifty percent median Black district populations); hence, Republicans only prevailed in two of these contests.

3. In the 1980s (1980, 1984, and 1988 elections combined), the American National Election Studies (ANES) data had thirty-four percent of rural white southerners voting Republican for president and Democratic for House and twenty-five percent of urban white southerners splitting their votes in the same fashion. The difference across groups is not statistically significant. In comparison, the ANES data from 1992 to 2000 show a decided decline in this type of split-ticket voting: ten percent of urban white southern-ers and thirteen percent of rural white southerners (the difference across groups is not statistically significant). The difference in the rate of Republican president/Democratic House ticket-splitting in the 1980s compared with 1992–2000 (twenty-one percentage points) is significant for rural white southerners ($p < .001$), and this difference of fifteen percentage points across the same time periods (1980s vs. 1992–2000) for urban white southerners is also significant ($p < .001$).

4. In case the reader expected to see the Republican president/Republican House vote correlation in a more recent presidential year (since 1992 was one), the correlation is actually slightly weaker in 2016 versus the 2018 midterm: .890 ($p < .001$).

5. Unfortunately, we are unable to replicate our small-town South (STS) measure at the congressional district level. As congressional districts are created using block-level data, one can rely on the US Census Bureau's urban/rural block-level classification scheme to calculate the percent rural/urban at the district level. Our other chief aggregate-level measure of rurality, population density, is available for use at the congressional district level.

6. We can also use district density to demonstrate a similar relationship with the presidential and House vote. In 1992, the correlation between district density (district population per square mile of land area) and Republican presidential vote was −.236 ($p < .01$). The corresponding correlation in 1992 for density and Republican House vote was −.042 ($p = .640$). By 2018, the correlation between district density and Republican presidential vote was −.577 ($p < .001$). Finally, the correlation between district density and Republican House vote was −.516 ($p < .001$). So, just like the correlations in the text based on district percent rural, in 1992, there was no relationship between this variable and the Republican House vote. In 2018, the relationship is now statistically significant and not much different from the corresponding relationship based on the district presidential vote.

7. An example from Table 7.2 might be helpful for clarity's sake; in the case of Dem-ocrats in 1992, the average rural percent in their same (presidentially Democratic) districts was twenty-five percent versus an average of forty-six percent rural in their split (presidentially Republican) districts, which is a rural district population difference (twenty-five percent minus forty-six percent) equal to negative twenty-one percentage points.

8. In 2016, out of a total of fifty-one districts in Florida, North Carolina, and Virginia, there were thirty-nine with incumbents seeking reelection in redrawn districts. The average percent of redrawn constituents for these incumbents was twenty-eight, with a redrawn median of twenty-five percent. The three districts that were altered so much that we could not designate a previous incumbent, were Florida District Ten (won by a

Democrat), North Carolina District Thirteen (won by a Republican), and Virginia District Four (won by a Democrat). The two seats the Republicans picked up in 2016 that were represented by Democrats in 2014 were the open contests in Florida Districts Two and Eighteen. Another discrepancy regarding the newly won Republican seats is that there have been several sitting Democrats who switched to the Republican Party before winning reelection (see McKee et al., 2016; Yoshinaka, 2016). For instance, the net seat pickup for 1996 is five, but we already mentioned that Republicans gained six seats since 1994. This can be explained by Georgia Democratic Congressman Nathan Deal's switch to the GOP in 1995 and subsequent reelection as a Republican. In our dataset, the past party affiliation of Congressman Deal in the 1996 House elections is Republican because he made the switch in 1995.

9. For these data, the Hispanic district percent of the population can be of any race, but the white and Black district population percentages are non-Hispanic.

10. We exclude District Nine in North Carolina because the 2018 general election results were invalidated because of fraud. In a special election held in 2019, the open seat was won by a white Republican (Dan Bishop), and it was previously won by a white Republican, Robert Pittenger, who was first elected in 2012.

11. For example, Hispanic Republican Henry Bonilla represented majority Hispanic Texas District Twenty-Three from 1992 to 2006 when he lost reelection in a special run-off to Hispanic Democrat Ciro Rodriguez (Barone and Cohen, 2007). During his tenure, Congressman Bonilla had cultivated strong support among his district's Anglo population in the western parts of San Antonio. Texas District Twenty-Three was subjected to three consecutive redrawings, starting in 2002 (very minimal changes in 2002 and much more substantial alterations in 2004 and 2006). In the 2006 reconfiguration of Texas District Twenty-Three, the Anglo population declined from forty-one percent to twenty-nine percent, and the Hispanic population rose from fifty-five percent to sixty-six percent.

12. Southwide, in 1992, the average House district percent white was seventy percent; it was sixty-four percent in 2002, fifty-eight percent in 2012, and fifty-six percent in 2018. These data were computed from the National Historical GIS (NHGIS) website: https://data2.nhgis.org/main.

13. In 2018, the only minority Democrat to represent a majority rural and minority white district (the solid dot in the lower right quadrant for the 2018 scatterplot) was Black Congressman Bennie Thompson (seventy-five percent rural and thirty-one percent white).

14. In the spirit of Earl and Merle Black, we reinserted the expletive that the journalist Chris Cillizza had removed.

15. The two district-level models are estimated using OLS regression where the percentage of the two-party Republican House vote is the dependent variable. Independent variables include a time variable organized by congressional redistricting cycle (1992–2000, 2002–2010, and 2012–2018), the percentage of the population for each congressional district composed of non-Hispanic whites, the percentage rural by district or the logged population density by district, a dummy variable for open seats, and a dummy variable for Republican incumbents. Only contested elections are included in the model estimates shown in the figures. To decompose effects by time, place, and race, we also include a set of requisite interactive terms. Finally, to account for unmeasured differences that exist across counties, we include district fixed effects (a set of n − 1 indicators). Once specified, OLS model interpretations are straightforward. For Figure 7.6, the rural indicator is set to either zero (one hundred percent urban) or .786 (78.6% being the

maximum value for rural). For Figure 7.7, the tenth percentile through the ninetieth percentile values for logged density are used. In both models, the variable measuring race is set to one (one hundred percent non-Hispanic white), the value of the time variable is set to represent the three redistricting cycles, and the election type is specified as an open-seat contest. The fixed effect for a district representing the mean value for rural or density is also included when interpreting the models. Finally, through manipulation of the interactive terms, we can estimate the white GOP House vote by time period and place. Full model results can be found online in Appendix B.

16. Using the tenth through the ninetieth county-level population density percentiles allow us to examine the range on this indicator while eliminating the most extreme values at both ends of the spectrum.

17. The two specified CES models are estimated using probit and include the following district-level predictors: either the percent rural indicator or logged population density; time (decade); race type (open seat; Republican incumbent); and requisite interactive terms. The dependent variable is binary and is coded one to represent a Republican House vote or zero to represent a vote for a Democratic congressional candidate. Cases are limited to include non-Hispanic white respondents residing in congressional districts featuring a contested race. Models are weighted using the included CES cumulative weight variable. Full model results can be found in Appendix B online.

Chapter 8: Survey Says? Rural Whites' Changing Party Identification

1. The last publication we are aware of that considered split party identification in the American South was a book chapter by Clark and Lockerbie (1998). These authors made use of data from the 1991–1992 Southern Grassroots Party Activists project, which was a survey of local party activists (county-level party committee members and their chairs as well as some 1992 national convention delegates) residing in the eleven ex-Confederate states.

2. The elections data on Louisiana gubernatorial contests are from the Louisiana Secretary of State's website.

3. Because Bobby Jindal won a majority of the vote in an open primary but was the only Republican candidate, the Democratic vote is aggregated from the votes cast for a total of five Democratic candidates.

4. Critics of Reagan's economic philosophy chided it as "trickle-down" economics because of its focus on large tax cuts for the wealthy. The belief that cutting taxes could lead to a balanced budget without commensurately cutting spending led Reagan's future vice president to refer to Reaganomics as "voodoo economics" when George H. W. Bush was running against his future boss in the 1980 Iowa caucuses.

5. In Table 8.1, the percentage of Republican and Democratic identifiers among rural and urban whites never sum to one hundred percent for any decade, because these party percentages include the total number of pure independents in the denominator.

6. The two specified models are estimated using probit and include the following predictors: either the STS indicator or logged population density, time (decade), and a requisite interactive term. The dependent variable is binary and is coded one to represent a Republican Party identifier or zero to represent a Democratic or an independent identifier. Cases are limited to include non-Hispanic white respondents. Models are weighted using the included CES cumulative weight variable. Full model results can be found online in Appendix B.

7. The sliver of voters who answer "something else" are excluded from the exit poll data displayed in this section of the chapter.

Chapter 9: More Evidence: Rural Voters in Four Southern States

1. North Carolina and South Carolina were the only other potential candidates with long-running surveys continuing into the 2010s. In South Carolina, the Winthrop Poll dates back to the mid-2000s, but the data typically do not include a county indicator and do not include variables for place (e.g., rural, urban, and suburban). In North Carolina, the Elon University Poll has been administered since 2001 and contains a place variable; however, despite repeated requests for access to these data, we were not able to procure them.

2. Tennessee's 2010 percentage of rural inhabitants (33.6%) clusters with the rural percentages found in two other southern states: North Carolina (33.9% rural) and South Carolina (33.7% rural).

3. If there is no senatorial or gubernatorial contest in that cycle, then this number is averaged from the most recent previous contest, or if there is an election after the one of interest for computing the index, then the GOP percentage of the votes in those senatorial or gubernatorial contests occurring immediately before and after the specific election cycle are averaged together.

4. In 2008, Republican Congressman John Boozman of District Three, and now Arkansas's senior senator, also did not face a major party (Democratic) opponent but rather a Green Party nominee (Abel Tomlinson).

5. In the next school year, rather than prolong the tense standoff with white segregationists while ensuring the safety of the Little Rock Nine, Governor Faubus closed Little Rock Central High School.

6. Arkansas's state legislative chambers (House and Senate) did not flip in favor of Republican majorities until the 2012 elections (Barone and McCutcheon, 2013). Taking these Republican state legislative majorities in tandem (House and Senate) made Arkansas the last southern state to cede Democratic control to the Republican opposition (McKee and Yoshinaka, 2015).

7. Arkansas and Tennessee are the only two southern states not covered by the Section 5 preclearance provision of the Voting Rights Act. Further, after the large-scale increase in majority-minority congressional districts drawn in the southern states for the 1992 elections, Arkansas is the only one to have never created a majority-minority US House district.

8. Even with the presence of H. Ross Perot in 1992 and 1996, the Democrat Bill Clinton won over fifty-three percent of the total number of presidential votes cast in his home state of Arkansas. Clinton also carried all but five Arkansas counties in 1992 and all but nine in 1996. Arkansas has been presidentially Republican ever since Clinton was term limited in 2000, and the Republican share of the two-party vote has increased in every cycle from 2000 to 2016 (ranging from fifty-three percent to sixty-four percent). President Trump's share of Arkansas's two-party vote in 2020 hardly changed from 2016 (64.2% compared with 64.3% in 2016).

9. Veteran Arkansas politician Mike Huckabee (Arkansas lieutenant governor from 1993 to 1996; Arkansas governor from 1996 to 2007; and GOP presidential contender in 2008 and 2016) is perhaps the quintessential example of the winning Republican formula in the state, because he is the clearest case of an economic populist and cultural conservative (serving as an ordained Southern Baptist preacher before getting into politics).

10. Hutchinson previously served in the Arkansas US House delegation, representing District Three from 1996 to 2001, when he vacated the seat to serve in the George W.

Bush administration. A Republican has represented Arkansas's District Three since 1966, when John Paul Hammerschmidt won it. Congressman Hammerschmidt held the seat until he retired in 1992. Interestingly, the open-seat contest in 1992 was won by Asa Hutchinson's brother Tim, who then vacated the seat in a successful run for the 1996 open Senate election. Until the 2012 districts were established, Arkansas District Three covered much of the northwest corner of the state. Because of greater population growth in this section of Arkansas, District Three has been decidedly reduced in geographic territory, with the slower growing District Four appropriating many of District Three's pre-2012 inhabitants.

11. Crittenden County, the northernmost Delta county that the Democrat won, has a forty-eight percent Black population and is majority-minority if the 2.6% Hispanic population is factored in. All of the racial data discussed in this section are based on the 2015–2019 American Community Survey (ACS) five-year estimate.

12. For the data displayed in Figure 9.4, based on the Arkansas Poll survey categories, we have recoded respondents so that "City" and "Suburb" = urban and "Small Town" and "Rural" = rural.

13. On the eve of the Civil War, only South Carolina had a higher percent slave population (fifty-seven percent) than Mississippi's (fifty-five percent), and the Magnolia State was the second to secede after the Palmetto State (McKee, 2019, p. 7).

14. Contemporary data on percent Black, statewide and at the county level, are from the 2015–2019 ACS five-year estimate.

15. State senator Chris McDaniel, known for his racial conservatism, primaried Thad Cochran in 2014, and the contest went to a runoff. Under Mississippi law, if a voter did not participate in the first primary, then he/she could vote in the runoff, whereas voters who participated in the Democratic primary were not supposed to be allowed to participate in the Republican runoff contest. There were multiple precincts in the heavily Black Mississippi Delta that registered no Republican participation in the first primary but then cast votes in the Republican runoff principally because African Americans were motivated to vote against McDaniel (see Hood and McKee, 2017a).

16. In 1950, both Mississippi and Arkansas had seven congressional districts, one more than Florida. In the 2000 reapportionment, because of sluggish population growth, Mississippi's five House seats were reduced to four. As often happens when a state loses House seats, two incumbents ran against each other (Ashton, Crespin, and McKee, 2021); Democrat Ronnie Shows versus Republican Chip Pickering in the redrawn District Three in the 2002 election. In this sixty percent rural district, Pickering defeated Shows with sixty-four percent of the two-party vote. The 2000 Republican percentage of the presidential vote was sixty-five percent in District Three, and whereas the Republican Pickering retained sixty-one percent of his old constituency in the redrawn District Three, the Democrat Shows kept thirty-eight percent of his same constituency. In *The Hand of the Past in Contemporary Southern Politics* (2005), James Glaser provides an insightful account of Democrat Ronnie Shows's successful campaign against Republican Delbert Hosemann in the District Four (forty-seven percent rural) open-seat contest in the 1998 election.

17. Similar to Arkansas, Mississippi was the next slowest to have both of its state legislative chambers flip to Republican control, which finally happened after 2011.

18. Recall that, with the exit poll data, we classify rural/STS voters as those living in a rural community or in a city with fewer than fifty thousand residents. Jackson, Mississippi's largest city, contained 166,383 residents, a number based on the 2015–2019 ACS five-year estimate. Similarly, Arkansas's largest city, Little Rock, contained 197,958

inhabitants according to the same ACS five-year estimate. Thus, neither of the South's two smallest states in terms of population had a city with a population over two hundred thousand; further, both states had just one city with over one hundred thousand residents. As argued by recent research on southern politics (see Bullock, 2021; Bullock et al., 2019; Morris, 2021), a division of states into slow growth (also called stagnant) and high growth is an apt way to distinguish between those that are more Republican (slow-growth states) versus those in which the Democratic Party is growing in electoral strength (high-growth states). We weigh in on this development in the final chapter.

19. In 1920, both of Tennessee's senators were Democrats. In 1920, outside of Tennessee there were only two other Republicans in the southern House delegation: Harry Wurzbach in Texas District Fourteen and C. Bascom Slemp in Virginia District Nine (Kalb, 2016, p. 1215).

20. Democrat Al Gore vacated his Senate seat to become Bill Clinton's vice president in 1992, and Democrat Harlan Matthews served as a placeholder until the 1994 special election (he was appointed by Democratic Governor Ned McWherter).

21. Jim Cooper is a member of the Blue Dog Coalition; hence, he is a moderate Democrat by national standards. In his previous congressional stint, Cooper represented Tennessee District Four from 1982 to 1994. In 1992, Tennessee District Four was seventy-four percent rural.

22. Specifically, the progression of Tennessee governors from 1978 to 2018 was as follows: Republican Lamar Alexander (1978–1986), Democrat Ned McWherter (1986–1994), Republican Don Sundquist (1994–2002), Democrat Phil Bredesen (2002–2010), and Republican Bill Haslam (2010–2018).

23. In the 2018 open Senate race to replace retiring Republican Bob Corker, Republican Congresswoman Marsha Blackburn (District Seven) defeated former Democratic Governor Phil Bredesen, with fifty-five percent of the two-party vote.

24. In the University of Tennessee Poll, *urban* and *rural* are based on community size as follows: urban = "Large, Small City," whereas rural = "Town, Small Town, Rural, Farm." In the Vanderbilt University Poll, *urban* and *rural* are place descriptions as follows: urban = "Urban, Suburban," and rural = "Rural."

25. See the following link for the reapportionment of the US House of Representatives based on the 2020 census: https://www.census.gov/library/visualizations/2021/dec/2020-apportionment-map.html.

26. All of these data on population size and racial demographics are according to the 2015–2019 ACS five-year estimates.

27. The 1976 presidential election was also the last time a Democrat won Mississippi.

28. Congressman Pete Sessions epitomizes the political survivor. In the incumbent-friendly 2002 Texas congressional redistricting, Sessions thought it prudent to vacate his then-current District Five in favor of District Thirty-Two, which contained only sixteen percent of his old constituency. After losing to Allred in 2018, in 2020, Sessions reemerged as the winner in the open-seat contest in District Seventeen, which is located south of the Dallas-Fort Worth Metroplex, is twenty-two percent rural, and contains an electorate wholly new to once-again freshman Congressman Sessions.

29. In 1994, Republican George W. Bush defeated Richards with fifty-four percent of the two-party vote. After Bush won the presidency in 2000, Republican Lieutenant Governor Rick Perry assumed the governorship and, in the absence of term limits, became Texas's longest serving governor, finally stepping down in 2014.

30. Wendy Davis received national recognition for filibustering an antiabortion bill in the Texas Legislature.

31. In the University of Texas/Texas Tribune Poll, the terms *urban* and *rural* are based on the respondent's self-description as follows: urban = "Urban, Suburban" and rural = "Rural."

32. In the South, combining the total number of state legislators in both chambers, after the 2020 elections, only Arkansas (twenty-one percent Democratic) and Tennessee (twenty-four percent Democratic) had state legislative delegations under twenty-five percent Democratic (these data come from the National Conference of State Legislatures: https://www.ncsl.org/).

Chapter 10: How Are Rural and Urban Southerners Different?

1. In addition to a once-in-a-century worldwide pandemic, 2020 was also characterized by a summer of racial unrest and protest across the country as George Floyd, a Black man, was killed by a white Minneapolis police officer, Derek Chauvin, on May 25th.

2. The population of those surveyed was limited to the eleven-state South. Postsurvey analysis indicated that the distribution of completed surveys closely approximates the share of the non-Hispanic (NH) white population by state. For reference, the distribution of completed surveys by state is provided below:

State	NH white population (%)	Survey distribution (%)	Survey *N*
AL	5.5	5.4	164
AR	3.8	4.1	125
FL	19.2	16.4	494
GA	9.5	8.9	267
LA	4.8	2.6	77
MS	2.9	3.4	101
NC	11.1	13.6	410
SC	5.4	3.9	118
TN	8.5	11.4	342
TX	20.3	21.3	643
VA	9.1	9.0	272

3. Respondents were screened to include only those who self-identified as non-Hispanic white in racial terms and reported that they were registered to vote.

4. For instance, it was later revealed in an excerpt from Bob Woodward's book *Rage* (2020) that President Trump was briefed on the likely devastating effects of the novel coronavirus and purposely chose to downplay the impact in his public comments. Trump's irresponsible and foolhardy decision unquestionably depressed his approval rating and ultimately contributed to his defeat by Joe Biden in the 2020 presidential election (Jacobson, 2021).

5. The 2017 American Community Survey (five-year) was used as the population data source for weighting. Education, age, and gender distributions were tabulated for the citizen voting-age population of non-Hispanic whites residing in the combined group of STS counties (and the combined group of urban counties) across the region.

6. See the results of recent public opinion polls asking respondents about an assault-weapons ban at the PollingReport.com website: https://www.pollingreport.com/guns.htm.

7. Based on how the question was constructed, native southerners are a subset of all the respondents who identified as southerners.

8. Because there was such a strong embrace among Trump's core supporters to build the wall along the border with Mexico, it ultimately became a leading administration policy. Billions of dollars were put into building the wall, and the Trump administration diverted close to four billion dollars in congressional allocations for this purpose (Booker, 2020).

9. Once party identification is taken into account, there is no significant difference in levels of affective partisan polarization. Stated differently, among Republicans, whether they are STS or urban whites, they will register statistically insignificant differences with respect to affective partisan polarization, because their shared party affiliation is doing most of the work in explaining disparities in feeling thermometer ratings for the Republican and Democratic parties.

10. The model presented in Table 10.7 is estimated using the probit procedure in Stata. A set of $N-1$ dummy variables for the eleven states surveyed are also included (Florida is used as the excluded comparison category), in addition to the explanatory variables detailed in the text. Significance tests for model coefficients are based on robust standard errors clustered by county FIPS (Federal Information Processing Standards) code. As a value of one on the dependent variable is coded to represent STS residents (and zero to represent urban residents), the model examines the likelihood that a specific correlate (factor) is related to STS residency. The coding for independent variables is as follows: education (1 = high school or less; 2 = some college/vocational degree; 3 = bachelor's degree; 4 = graduate degree); income (1 = under $25,000; 2 = $25,000–$49,999; 3 = $50,000–$74,999; 4 = $75,000–$99,999; 5 = $100,000–$149,000; 6 = over $150,000); age (in years): nineteen to ninety-eight; gender (1 = male; 2 = female); gun owner (1 = gun owner; 0 = non–gun owner); ideology (1 = very liberal; 2 = liberal; 3 = slightly liberal; 4 = moderate; 5 = slightly conservative; 6 = conservative; 7 = very conservative); party identification (1 = strong Democrat; 2 = weak Democrat; 3 = independent leaning Democratic; 4 = independent; 5 = independent leaning Republican; 6 = weak Republican; 7 = strong Republican); native southerner (1 = born in a southern state; 0 = born outside the region); and evangelical (1 = born-again Christian; 0 = nonevangelical).

11. Predicted probabilities displayed in Figures 10.1 and 10.2 are generated using the Hanmer and Kalkan (2013) observed values method.

12. The models presented in Table 10.8 are estimated using the probit procedure (in Stata), except for the model results presented for the racial resentment scale, which were estimated using OLS regression. Dependent variables, with the exception of the racial resentment scale, are all coded where one represents the conservative issue position. See Endnote 10 for an explanation of the coding for the independent variables (explanatory characteristics). A set of $n-1$ dummy variables for the eleven states surveyed are also included in each model (Florida is used as the excluded comparison category) in addition to the explanatory variables detailed in the text. Significance tests for model coefficients are based on robust standard errors clustered by county FIPS code. Specific coding for the eight dependent variables on political issues are as follows: gun control (1 = oppose stricter gun control; 0 = favor); assault weapons ban (1 = oppose banning assault weapons; 0 = favor); reparations for slavery (1 = bad idea; 0 = good idea); racial resentment scale (ranges from zero to twenty, with higher values representative of increasing levels of racial resentment); abortion (1 = illegal in all circumstances; 0 = always legal/sometimes legal); Confederate flag (1 = symbol of southern heritage and pride; 0 = symbol of white supremacy and racial conflict/equally both [southern heritage/pride and white supremacy/racial conflict]); Confederate monuments (1 = leave them just as they

are; o = leave them, but add context/move to a museum/remove them completely); and border wall (1 = favor building border wall; o = neither favor nor oppose/oppose).

13. Average effects by place presented in Figure 10.3 were estimated using the margins command in Stata.

Chapter 11: The 2020 Elections in the South

1. On his way to winning the 2020 Republican Senate primary, Tuberville clobbered former Alabama Senator Jeff Sessions (sixty-one percent to thirty-nine percent) in the runoff. Sessions was disgraced by President Trump after he, in his role as US Attorney General, recused himself from the investigation of Russian interference in the 2016 presidential election.

2. An exit poll for Alabama was added in 2020, most likely because of the Senate contest, despite the reality that neither the Senate race nor the presidential contest would be competitive. Interestingly, compared with the rest of the South, Alabama whites do not appear as polarized on the basis of location. In the 2020 presidential race, for instance, the white urban vote for Trump was 77.9%, and it was 77.3% for rural/STS white Alabamians.

3. We are not aware of the raw data for the exit poll in the 2017 Alabama special Senate contest ever being made publicly available, and because news organizations have never shown the geographic breakdown of the vote with respect to race, we do not know how white Alabamians voted in this contest with regard to rural/STS and urban locations. On the basis of the Alabama 2020 Senate exit poll data made available from CNN, which allows one to filter the data by race, seventy-six percent of urban whites and seventy-six percent of rural/STS whites both voted for the Republican challenger Tommy Tuberville.

4. Nonetheless, it is true that among all voters, despite the relatively greater decline in rural/STS turnout in the Georgia Senate runoffs, rural/STS participation was marginally higher (59.2% versus 57.7%).

5. In the 2014 midterm elections, there were forty-two uncontested southern House seats (twenty-five seats with Republican incumbents, two Republican-held open seats, and fifteen seats with Democratic incumbents). In the 2016 elections, there were twenty-six uncontested southern House seats (seventeen seats with Republican incumbents, two Republican-held open seats, and seven seats with Democratic incumbents). Of the sixteen uncontested southern House seats in 2018, there were two with Republican incumbents seeking reelection and fourteen with Democratic incumbents running for another term. Of the eleven uncontested southern House seats in 2020, there were seven with Republican incumbents seeking reelection, three with Democratic incumbents running for another term, and one Republican-held open seat (Louisiana District Five). Technically, there were only ten uncontested southern House seats in 2020, but Louisiana District Five is classified as uncontested only because the election went to a runoff with the top two vote getters from the initial open primary (which included four Democratic candidates) both being Republicans. Luke Letlow, the winner of the House election in Louisiana District Five died of complications from COVID-19, and another southern congressman, Ronald Wright of Texas District Six, also died from an illness related to COVID-19.

6. Because 2018 was expected to be a banner year for Democrats nationally (and it was), of the twenty open southern House seats, only two were vacated by Democrats (Gene Green retired from Houston-based District Twenty-Nine, and Beto O'Rourke

vacated El Paso–based Texas District Sixteen to run against Republican Senator Ted Cruz). The 2020 House elections were expected to advantage Democrats again, but this was not true. However, because politicians have to make plans in advance (Jacobson and Kernell, 1983), early in the 2020 election cycle, with short-term conditions favoring Democrats, this most likely explains why of the twenty-one open southern House seats, the only one held by a Democrat was Georgia District Five, which civil rights icon John Lewis represented from 1986 until his passing on July 17, 2020.

7. Because of North Carolina's extensive redistricting, the median rural district percent in southern House districts went from nineteen percent in 2018 to eighteen percent in 2020.

8. Nationalization was at historic levels in 2020, as it was in 2018. In 2018, the bivariate correlation of the 2018 Republican House vote and the 2016 Republican presidential vote (two-party) in southern House districts was .908 (p < .01). In 2020, the bivariate correlation of the 2020 Republican House vote and the 2020 Republican presidential vote in southern House districts was also .908 (p < .01).

9. In South Carolina District One, Democratic Congressman Joe Cunningham lost to Republican and first female graduate of The Citadel, Nancy Mace; in Florida District Twenty-Six, Democratic Representative and Ecuadorian American Debbie Mucarsel-Powell lost to Republican and former Miami-Dade Mayor Carlos Giménez; and in a rematch from 2018, Florida District Twenty-Seven Congresswoman Donna Shalala (former University of Miami president and Department of Health and Human Services secretary in the Clinton administration) lost to Republican and Spanish television news reporter Maria Elvira Salazar.

10. North Carolina Districts One and Twelve were ruled unconstitutional racial gerrymanders (Cooper v. Harris, 581 US ___ (2017), necessitating a mid-decade remap.

11. There were actually two special North Carolina House elections that took place on September 10, 2019: the aforementioned District Nine contest and also a special contest in District Three, which was open because of the death of Republican Congressman Walter Jones. Republican Greg Murphy won the special election in District Three.

12. In 2019, a three-judge panel of the Wake County Superior Court ruled in Common Cause v. Lewis (18-CVS-014001, Wake County Superior Court) that, in violation of the North Carolina Constitution, the state's congressional districts were an unconstitutional partisan gerrymander. The state court ordered the General Assembly to redraw congressional districts before the 2020 election.

13. In 2018, the six counties making up District Two were: Franklin, Harnett, Johnston (partial), Nash, Wake (partial), and Wilson (partial). In 2018, the eight counties making up District Six were: Alamance, Caswell, Chatham, Guilford (partial), Lee, Person, Randolph, and Rockingham.

14. In District Two, the cities of Cary (133,812) and Raleigh (342,530) constituted sixty-five percent of the district population (733,499). In District Six, the cities of Greensboro (269,666) and Winston-Salem (202,317) constituted over sixty-four percent of the district population (733,498). These data were retrieved from the North Carolina General Assembly Redistricting website: https://www.ncleg.gov/Redistricting.

15. In the remaining districts, all ten incumbents won reelection, and in District Eleven, which was open because Republican Congressman Mark Meadows became President Trump's chief of staff, twenty-five-year-old Republican Madison Cawthorn won the 2020 election, with fifty-six percent of the two-party vote.

16. Congresswoman Deborah Ross was a civil rights lawyer and former North Carolina State House representative (https://ross.house.gov/about). Before winning her House

seat in 2020, Congresswoman Kathy Manning was an attorney who founded an immigration law firm (https://manning.house.gov/about).

Chapter 12: Too Little, Too Late?

1. Bullock et al. (2019) split the southern states into "stagnant" (slow-growth) and "growth" states. Stagnant states are Alabama, Arkansas, Louisiana, Mississippi, and Tennessee. Hence, the growth states are Florida, Georgia, North Carolina, South Carolina, Texas, and Virginia.

2. Source: 2010–2019 American Community Surveys (five-year estimates); "Geographical Mobility in the Past Year for Current Residence in the United States." Table B07004H.

3. In Virginia, the non-Hispanic white voting-age population loss/gain experienced in STS and urban areas from 2000 to 2019 was almost identical in percentage terms. As a consequence, the population balance between these geographic areas remained unchanged.

4. For continuity, we use counties categorized as STS and urban in 2010 and compare population shifts for these groups back in time (1990 and 2000) and forward in time (2019).

5. Rate of change was calculated as: (count of non-Hispanic white VAPt – count of non-Hispanic white VAPt – 1)/count of non-Hispanic white VAPt – 1. VAP = voting-age population and t = time (year).

6. The interquartile range is the value that represents the difference between the seventy-fifth and twenty-fifth percentile values.

7. The Northeast includes the New England states of Connecticut, Maine, Massachusetts, New Hampshire, Rhode Island, and Vermont; the Mid-Atlantic states of Delaware, Maryland, New Jersey, New York, and Pennsylvania; and Washington, DC.

8. There was a uniform shift toward the GOP in the 2021 Virginia elections. For instance, in the gubernatorial election pitting former Democratic governor Terry McAuliffe against Republican Glenn Youngkin, the two-party vote split fifty-one percent in favor of the GOP, while every single Virginia county and independent city (133) tilted more Republican compared to the Republican presidential vote registered in 2020 (an average shift of 5.2 percentage points in the Republican direction). In small-town South counties/independent cities, the 2020 presidential vote was 64.8 percent, and the 2021 gubernatorial vote was 69.6 percent. Likewise, in urban counties/independent cities, the 2020 presidential vote was 41.1 percent, and the 2021 gubernatorial vote was 47.6 percent. Before the 2021 state house contests, Virginia Democrats held fifty-five of the one hundred seats. The most recent elections for state senate took place in 2019, and the next cycle is 2023. Virginia Democrats have a twenty-one-to-nineteen-seat state senate majority. There is every reason to believe that southern Republicans' good fortune will extend into the 2022 midterms, as short-term political conditions favor the GOP, and President Biden's low approval rating is a drag on the Democratic Party. Also, in the 2021 Virginia elections, compared to 2020, Republican voters turned out at a considerably higher rate than their Democratic counterparts (Zitner, 2021). This voter enthusiasm gap (based on mobilization patterns) will likely favor Republicans in the 2022 midterm elections. The 2021 elections data discussed in this note are publicly available from the Virginia Department of Elections: https://results.elections.virginia.gov/vaelections/2021 %20November%20General/Site/Statewide.html.

9. As noted by Prokop (2021), "The incumbent president's party has lost 11 of the past 12 Virginia governor's races. That isn't just a coincidence. It fits a long-running national pattern of backlash against the president's party in the midterms."

10. Specifically, NOVA as we define it includes: Arlington County, Fairfax County, Loudon County, Prince William County, Alexandria City, Fairfax City, Falls Church City, Manassas City, and Manassas Park City.

11. It is worth noting that, among urban white southerners, the first quartile number is higher for Obama (a value of nine) than for Trump (a value of two). Of course, both of these numbers are extremely low.

12. As was true in Figure 12.5, at the first quartile, urban whites place Obama a little higher (a value of eight) than Trump (a value of two).

13. Significance level: $p < .0001$.

14. In his subsequent summer 2021 rallies (in various states such as Florida, North Carolina, Ohio, and Wisconsin), Trump continued to beat the drum regarding his false claim that the 2020 presidential election was stolen from him (Maass, 2021). Additionally, rather than fade from the political scene, Trump has currently left the door open for a 2024 presidential run while actively seeking out and offering his weighty endorsement to 2022 midterm GOP hopefuls who keenly recognize that Trump remains the party's single most influential kingmaker (Bender, 2021) because of his enduring popularity among rank-and-file Republican voters (Jacobson, 2021).

15. Nevertheless, at least on the $1.9 trillion "American Rescue Plan" pushed by President Biden and congressional Democrats in the spring of 2021, united congressional Republican opposition was impressive. In comparison, the more recently passed Infrastructure Bill (signed by President Biden on November 15, 2021) saw considerable bipartisan support in this time of hyperpolarization. Thirteen Republicans in the House voted yes (six Democrats voted no; see Broadwater and Montague, 2021) and so did nineteen Republican senators (Farrington, 2021).

16. For an interesting overview of suburban areas and party support, see "Laboratories of Democracy: The 2020 Presidential Election Will Be Decided in the Suburbs" (*The Economist*, January 4, 2020; https://www.economist.com/united-states/2020/01/04/the-2020-presidential-election-will-be-decided-in-the-suburbs).

17. Source: Data from the 2020 *CNN* Exit Poll (https://www.cnn.com/election/2020/exit-polls/).

18. For a lengthier discussion of the future role of Hispanics in southern politics, see Hood, Kidd, and Morris (2014, pp. 183–187).

19. An interesting example of the lack of pushback from white rural voters was the 2017 tax reform legislation, which, by all accounts, was a boon for the upper-middle-class and wealthy, whereas it did very little by way of assisting those on the lower end of the income scale. President Trump appeared to cave to the GOP establishment and monied interests in promoting this legislation, whereas the more recent passage of the $1.9 trillion "American Rescue Plan" would appear markedly more responsive to the interests and needs of downscale white rural southerners of a populist bent.

Bibliography

Abramowitz, Alan I. "Issue Evolution Reconsidered: Racial Attitudes and Partisanship in the U.S. Electorate." *American Journal of Political Science* 38, no. 1 (February 1994): 1–24.

———. *The Disappearing Center: Engaged Citizens, Polarization, and American Democracy*. New Haven, CT: Yale University Press, 2010.

Abramowitz, Alan I., and Kyle L. Saunders. "Ideological Realignment in the U.S. Electorate." *Journal of Politics* 60, no. 3 (August 1998): 634–652.

Abramson, Paul R. "Generational Change and the Decline of Party Identification in America, 1952–1974." *American Political Science Review* 70, no. 2 (June 1976): 469–478.

———. "Developing Party Identification: A Further Examination of Life-Cycle, Generational, and Period Effects." *American Journal of Political Science* 23, no. 1 (February 1979): 78–96.

Acharya, Avidit, Matthew Blackwell, and Maya Sen. *Deep Roots: How Slavery Still Shapes Southern Politics*. Princeton, NJ: Princeton University Press, 2018.

Adams, Greg D. "Abortion: Evidence of an Issue Evolution." *American Journal of Political Science* 41, no. 3 (July 1997): 718–737.

Aistrup, Joseph A. *The Southern Strategy Revisited: Republican Top-Down Advancement in the South*. Lexington: University Press of Kentucky, 1996.

Alter, Jonathan. "When Jimmy Carter Was Silent on Civil Rights." *Wall Street Journal*, September 19–20, 2020, C4.

Ansolabehere, Stephen, and James M. Snyder, Jr. *The End of Inequality: One Person, One Vote and the Transformation of American Politics*. New York: W. W. Norton & Co., 2008.

Ash, Kathleen, Wesley Johnson, Gracie Lagadinos, Sarah Simon, Jared Thomas, Evan Wright, and Jason Gainous. "Southern Accents and Partisan Stereotypes: Evaluating Political Candidates." *Social Science Quarterly* 101, no. 5 (September 2020): 1951–1968.

Ashton, Bennie, Michael Crespin, and Seth C. McKee. "Dueling Incumbent U.S. House Elections, 1843–2018." Paper presented at the annual meeting of the Midwest Political Science Association, Chicago, April 2021.

Barone, Michael, and Richard E. Cohen. *The Almanac of American Politics 2008*. Washington, DC: National Journal, 2007.

Barone, Michael, and Grant Ujifusa. *The Almanac of American Politics 1994*. Washington, DC: National Journal, 1992.

———. *The Almanac of American Politics 1996*. Washington, DC: National Journal, 1995.

Barone, Michael, and Chuck McCutcheon. *The Almanac of American Politics 2014*. Chicago: University of Chicago Press, 2013.

Bartels, Larry M. "Partisanship and Voting Behavior, 1952–1996." *American Journal of Political Science* 44, no. 1 (January 2000): 35–50.

Bartley, Numan V., and Hugh D. Graham. *Southern Politics and the Second Reconstruction*. Baltimore: Johns Hopkins University Press, 1975.

Bass, Jack, and Walter De Vries. *The Transformation of Southern Politics: Social Change and Political Consequence Since 1945*. Athens: University of Georgia Press, 1995.

Beck, Paul Allen. "Partisan Dealignment in the Postwar South." *American Political Science Review* 71, no. 2 (June 1977): 477–496.

Bender, Michael C. "The Unquiet Exit of Donald Trump." *Wall Street Journal*, July 10–11, 2021, C1–C2.

Bickerstaff, Steve. *Lines in the Sand: Congressional Redistricting in Texas and the Downfall of Tom DeLay.* Austin: University of Texas Press, 2007.

Bishin, Benjamin G., and Casey A. Klofstad. "The Political Incorporation of Cuban Americans: Why Won't Little Havana Turn Blue?" *Political Research Quarterly* 65, no. 3 (September 2012), 586–599.

Bishop, Bill, and Robert G. Cushing. *The Big Sort: Why the Clustering of Like-Minded America is Tearing Us Apart.* Boston: Houghton Mifflin, 2008.

Black, Earl. *Southern Governors and Civil Rights: Racial Segregation as a Campaign Issue in the Second Reconstruction.* Cambridge, MA: Harvard University Press, 1976.

———. 1998. "Presidential Address: The Newest Southern Politics." *Journal of Politics* 60, no. 3 (August 1998): 591–612.

Black, Earl, and Merle Black. *Politics and Society in the South.* Cambridge, MA: Harvard University Press, 1987.

———. *The Vital South: How Presidents are Elected.* Cambridge, MA: Harvard University Press, 1992.

———. *The Rise of Southern Republicans.* Cambridge, MA: Harvard University Press, 2002.

———. *Divided America: The Ferocious Power Struggle in American Politics.* New York: Simon & Schuster, 2007.

———. "Deep South Politics: The Enduring Racial Divide in National Elections," in *The Oxford Handbook of Southern Politics*, eds. Charles S. Bullock III and Mark J. Rozell (New York: Oxford University Press, 2021), 401–423.

Booker, Brakkton. "Trump Administration Diverts $3.8 Billion in Pentagon Funding to Border Wall." *National Public Radio*, February 13, 2020. https://www.npr.org/2020/02/13/805796618/trump-administration-diverts-3-8-billion-in-pentagon-funding-to-border-wall.

Broadwater, Luke, and Zach Montague. "In Infrastructure Votes, 19 Members Broke With Their Party." *New York Times*, November 6, 2021. https://www.nytimes.com/2021/11/06/us/politics/defectors-infrastructure-bill-squad.html.

Buchanan, Scott E. "The Effects of the Abolition of the Georgia County-Unit System on the 1962 Gubernatorial Election." *Politics & Policy* 25, no. 4 (December 1997): 687–704.

Bullock, Charles S., III. "Affirmative Action Districts: In Whose Faces Will They Blow Up?" *Campaigns & Elections* 16, no. 4 (April 1995a): 22–23.

———. "Comment: The Gift that Keeps on Giving? Consequences of Affirmative Action Gerrymandering." *American Review of Politics* 16 (Spring 1995b): 33–39.

———. *Redistricting: The Most Political Activity in America.* Lanham, MD: Rowman & Littlefield, 2010.

———, ed. *Key States, High Stakes: Sarah Palin, the Tea Party, and the 2010 Elections.* Lanham, MD: Rowman & Littlefield, 2011.

———. "Politics in the South: Out of Step with the Nation Again," in *The New Politics of the Old South, 6th ed.*, eds. Charles S. Bullock III and Mark J. Rozell (Lanham, MD: Rowman & Littlefield, 2017).

———. "Growth Versus Stagnation and a New Realignment," in *The New Politics of the Old South, 7th ed.*, eds. Charles S. Bullock III and Mark J. Rozell (Lanham, MD: Rowman & Littlefield, 2021).

Bullock, Charles S., III, Donna R. Hoffman, and Ronald Keith Gaddie. "The Consolidation of the White Southern Congressional Vote." *Political Research Quarterly* 58, no. 2 (June 2005): 231–243.

Bullock, Charles S., III, and M.V. Hood III. "The Damnedest Mess: An Empirical Evaluation of the 1966 Georgia Gubernatorial Election." *Social Science Quarterly* 96, no. 1 (March 2015): 104–118.

Bullock, Charles S., III, and Ronald Keith Gaddie. *The Triumph of Voting Rights in the South.* Norman: University of Oklahoma Press, 2009.

Bullock, Charles S., III, Susan A. MacManus, Jeremy D. Mayer, and Mark J. Rozell. *The South and the Transformation of U.S. Politics.* New York: Oxford University Press, 2019.

Burden, Barry C., and David C. Kimball. *Why Americans Split Their Tickets: Campaigns, Competition, and Divided Government.* Ann Arbor: University of Michigan Press, 2002.

Cain, Bruce E. *The Reapportionment Puzzle.* Berkeley: University of California Press, 1984.

Campbell, Angus, Philip E. Converse, Warren E. Miller, and Donald E. Stokes. *The American Voter.* Chicago: University of Chicago Press, 1960.

Campbell, Bruce A. "Patterns of Change in the Partisan Loyalties of Native Southerners: 1952–1972." *Journal of Politics* 39, no. 3 (August 1977): 730–761.

Campo-Flores, Arian, and Elizabeth Findell. "Latino Voters Move Toward Trump." *Wall Street Journal,* November 6, 2020, A6.

Canon, David T., and David J. Sousa. "Party System Change and Political Career Structures in the U.S. Congress." *Legislative Studies Quarterly* 17, no. 3 (August 1992): 347–363.

Carmines, Edward G., and James A. Stimson. *Issue Evolution: Race and the Transformation of American Politics.* Princeton, NJ: Princeton University Press, 1989.

Carmines, Edward G., and James Woods. "The Role of Party Activists in the Evolution of the Abortion Issue." *Political Behavior* 24, no. 4 (December 2002): 361–377.

Carter, Dan T. *The Politics of Rage: George Wallace, the Origins of the New Conservatism, and the Transformation of American Politics.* New York: Simon & Schuster, 1995.

——. *From George Wallace to Newt Gingrich: Race in the Conservative Counterrevolution, 1963–1994.* Baton Rouge: Louisiana State University Press, 1996.

Caughey, Devin. *The Unsolid South: Mass Politics and National Representation in a One-Party Enclave.* Princeton, NJ: Princeton University Press, 2018.

Choi, Eunjung, and Seth C. McKee. "Campaign Strategies and Campaign Effects in the Sunshine State." *Florida Political Chronicle* 19 (Winter 2009): 1–19.

Cillizza, Chris. "This Democratic Congresswoman Just Spoke Some Hard Truth to her Party." *CNN,* November 6, 2020. https://www.npr.org/templates/story/story.php?story Id=5425248.

Clark, John A., and Brad Lockerbie. "Split-Partisan Identification," in *Party Activists in Southern Politics: Mirrors and Makers of Change,* eds. Charles D. Hadley and Lewis Bowman (Knoxville: University of Tennessee Press, 1998), 111–128.

Cohen, Richard E., and James A. Barnes. *The Almanac of American Politics 2018.* Bethesda, MD: Columbia Books & Information Services, 2017.

Cohen, Richard, and Charlie Cook. *The Almanac of American Politics 2020.* Bethesda, MD: Columbia Books & Information Services, 2019.

Connelly, William F., Jr., and John J. Pitney, Jr. *Congress' Permanent Minority? Republicans in the U.S. House.* Lanham, MD: Rowman & Littlefield, 1994.

Converse, Philip E. "The Nature of Belief Systems in Mass Publics," in *Ideology and Discontent,* ed. David E. Apter (New York: The Free Press of Glencoe, 1964), 206–261.

Cooper, Christopher A., M.V. Hood III, Scott Huffmon, Quentin Kidd, H. Gibbs Knotts, and Seth C. McKee. "Switching Sides but still Fighting the Civil War in Southern Politics." *Politics, Groups, and Identities* 10, no. 1 (2022): 100–116.

Cooper, Christopher A., and H. Gibbs Knotts. *The Resilience of Southern Identity: Why the South Still Matters in the Minds of Its People.* Chapel Hill: University of North Carolina Press, 2019.

Cosman, Bernard. *Five States for Goldwater: Continuity and Change in Southern Presidential Voting Patterns.* Tuscaloosa: University of Alabama Press, 1966.

Cover, Albert D. "One Good Term Deserves Another: The Advantage of Incumbency in Congressional Elections." *American Journal of Political Science* 21, no. 3 (August 1977): 523–541.

Cox, Gary W., and Jonathan N. Katz. "Why Did the Incumbency Advantage in U.S. House Elections Grow?" *American Journal of Political Science* 40, no. 2 (May 1996): 478–497.

———. *Elbridge Gerry's Salamander: The Electoral Consequences of the Reapportionment Revolution.* Cambridge: Cambridge University Press, 2002.

Cramer, Katherine J. *The Politics of Resentment: Rural Consciousness in Wisconsin and the Rise of Scott Walker.* Chicago: University of Chicago Press, 2016.

Cunningham, Maurice T. *Maximization, Whatever the Cost: Race, Redistricting and the Department of Justice.* Westport, CT: Praeger, 2001.

David, Paul T. *Party Strength in the United States: 1872–1970.* Charlottesville: University Press of Virginia, 1972.

Davidson, Chandler. *Race and Class in Texas Politics.* Princeton, NJ: Princeton University Press, 1990.

Diaz, Jaclyn. "Arkansas Passes Near-Total Abortion Ban-And A Possible 'Roe V. Wade' Test." *National Public Radio*, March 10, 2021. https://www.npr.org/2021/03/10/975 546070/arkansas-passes-near-total-abortion-ban-as-lawmakers-push-for-supreme -court-case.

Dotray, Matt. "Thank or Blame West Texas for Keeping the State Red." *Lubbock Avalanche-Journal*, November 10, 2016. https://www.lubbockonline.com/news/20181110 /thank-or-blame-west-texas-for-keeping-state-red.

Downs, Anthony. *An Economic Theory of Democracy.* New York: Harper & Row, 1957.

Farrington, Dana. "Here Are the Republicans Who Voted for the Infrastructure Bill in the Senate." *National Public Radio*, August 10, 2021. https://www.npr.org/2021/08/10 /1026486578/senate-republican-votes-infrastructure-bill.

Feinstein, Brian D., and Eric Schickler. "Platforms and Partners: The Civil Rights Realignment Reconsidered." *Studies in American Political Development* 22 (Spring 2008), 1–31.

Fenno, Richard F., Jr. *Senators on the Campaign Trail: The Politics of Representation.* Norman: University of Oklahoma Press, 1996.

———. *Congress at the Grassroots: Representational Change in the South, 1970–1998.* Chapel Hill: University of North Carolina Press, 2000.

Fiorina, Morris P. *Retrospective Voting in American National Elections.* New Haven, CT: Yale University Press, 1981.

Fleisher, Richard, and John R. Bond. "The Shrinking Middle in the US Congress." *British Journal of Political Science* 34, no.3 (July 2004), 429–451.

Forgey, Quint. "D.C. Faith Leaders Blast Trump's Bible Photo-Op." *Politico*, June 2, 2020. https://cutt.ly/zzoxpML.

Frady, Marshall. *Wallace.* New York: Random House, 1996.

Frederickson, Kari. *The Dixiecrat Revolt and the End of the Solid South, 1932–1968.* Chapel Hill: University of North Carolina Press, 2001.

Frymer, Paul. *Uneasy Alliances: Race and Party Competition in America.* Princeton, NJ: Princeton University Press, 2010.

Gaddie, Ronald Keith. "The Texas Redistricting, Measure for Measure." *Extensions: A Journal of the Carl Albert Congressional Research and Studies Center.* Fall (2004), 19–24.

Gaddie, Ronald Keith, and Charles S. Bullock III. *Elections to Open Seats in the U.S. House: Where the Action Is.* Lanham, MD: Rowman & Littlefield, 2000.

Galsworthy, Tim. "Carpetbaggers, Confederates, and Richard Nixon: The 1960 Presidential Election, Historical Memory, and the Republican Southern Strategy." *Presidential Studies Quarterly,* November 19, 2021. https://onlinelibrary.wiley.com/doi/10.1111/psq .12760.

Gelman, Andrew, and Gary King. "Enhancing Democracy Through Legislative Redistricting." *American Political Science Review* 88, no. 3 (September 1994), 541–559.

Gelman, Andrew, David Park, Boris Shor, Joseph Bafumi, and Jeronimo Cortina. *Red State, Blue State, Rich State, Poor State: Why Americans Vote the Way They Do.* Princeton, NJ: Princeton University Press, 2008.

Gervais, Bryan T., and Irwin L. Morris. *Reactionary Republicanism: How the Tea Party in the House Paved the Way for Trump's Victory.* New York: Oxford University Press, 2018.

Glaser, James M. *Race, Campaign Politics, and the Realignment in the South.* New Haven, CT: Yale University Press, 1996.

———. *The Hand of the Past in Contemporary Southern Politics.* New Haven, CT: Yale University Press, 2005.

Goldfield, David. *Still Fighting the Civil War: The American South and Southern History.* Baton Rouge: Louisiana State University Press, 2013.

Green, George Norris. *The Establishment in Texas Politics: The Primitive Years, 1938–1957.* Norman: University of Oklahoma Press, 1979.

Green, Donald, Bradley Palmquist, and Eric Schickler. *Partisan Hearts and Minds: Political Parties and the Social Identities of Voters.* New Haven, CT: Yale University Press, 2002.

Greenwood, Michael J. "Research on Internal Migration in the United States: A Survey." *Journal of Economic Literature* 13, no. 2 (June 1975), 397–433.

Grofman, Bernard, and Thomas L. Brunell. "The Art of the Dummymander: The Impact of Recent Redistrictings on the Partisan Makeup of Southern House Seats," in *Redistricting in the New Millennium,* ed. Peter F. Galderisi (Lanham, MD: Lexington Books, 2005), 183–199.

Grossmann, Matthew, and David A. Hopkins. *Asymmetric Politics: Ideological Republicans and Group Interest Democrats.* New York: Oxford University Press, 2016.

Hadley, Charles D. "Dual Partisan Identification in the South." *Journal of Politics* 47, no. 1 (February 1985), 254–268.

Haney-López, Ian. *Dog Whistle Politics: How Coded Racial Appeals have Reinvented Racism and Wrecked the Middle Class.* Oxford: Oxford University Press, 2014.

Hanmer, Michael J., and Kerem Ozan Kalkan. "Behind the Curve: Clarifying the Best Approach to Calculating Predicted Probabilities and Marginal Effects from Limited Dependent Variable Models." *American Journal of Political Science* 57, no. 1 (January 2013), 263–277.

Hayes, Danny, and Seth C. McKee. "Booting Barnes: Explaining the Historic Upset in the 2002 Georgia Gubernatorial Election." *Politics & Policy* 32, no. 4 (December 2004), 708–739.

Heard, Alexander. *A Two-Party South?* Chapel Hill: University of North Carolina Press, 1952.

Hetherington, Marc J. "Resurgent Mass Partisanship: The Role of Elite Polarization." *American Political Science Review* 95, no. 3 (September 2001), 619–631.

Hicks, William D., Seth C. McKee, and Daniel A. Smith. "Contemporary Views of Liberal Democracy and the 2016 Presidential Election." *PS: Political Science & Politics* 54, no. 1 (January 2021), 33–40.

Hill, Kevin A. "Does the Creation of Majority Black Districts Aid Republicans? An Analysis of the 1992 Congressional Elections in Eight Southern States." *Journal of Politics* 57, no. 2 (May 1995), 384–401.

Hillygus, D. Sunshine, Seth C. McKee, and McKenzie Young. "Reversal of Fortune: The Political Behavior of White Migrants to the South." *Presidential Studies Quarterly* 47, no. 2 (April 2017), 354–364.

Hillygus, D. Sunshine, and Todd G. Shields. *The Persuadable Voter: Wedge Issues in Presidential Campaigns*. Princeton, NJ: Princeton University Press, 2009.

Hitt, Homer L. "Population Movements in the Southern United States." *The Scientific Monthly* 82, no. 5 (May 1956), 241–246.

Hood, M.V., III. "Race, Class, Religion and the Southern Party System: A Field Report from Dixie." *The Forum: A Journal of Applied Research in Contemporary Politics* 14, no. 1 (2016), 83–96.

Hood, M.V., III, Quentin Kidd, and Irwin L. Morris. "The Reintroduction of the *Elephas Maximus* to the Southern United States: The Rise of Republican State Parties, 1960–2000." *American Politics Research* 32, no. 1 (January 2004), 68–101.

——. *The Rational Southerner: Black Mobilization, Republican Growth, and the Partisan Transformation of the American South*. New York: Oxford University Press, 2014.

Hood, M.V., III, and Seth C. McKee. "Trying to Thread the Needle: The Effects of Redistricting in a Georgia Congressional District." *PS: Political Science and Politics* 42, no. 4 (October 2009), 679–687.

——. "What Made Carolina Blue? In-Migration and the 2008 North Carolina Presidential Vote." *American Politics Research* 38, no. 2 (March 2010), 266–302.

——. "Black Votes Count: The 2014 Republican Senate Nomination in Mississippi." *Social Science Quarterly* 98, no. 1 (March 2017a), 89–106.

——. "Texas: Big Red Rides On," in *The New Politics of the Old South: An Introduction to Southern Politics*, 6th ed., eds. Charles S. Bullock III and Mark J. Rozell (Lanham, MD: Rowman & Littlefield, 2017b), 302–337.

——. "Texas: A Shifting Republican Terrain," in *The New Politics of the Old South: An Introduction to Southern Politics*, 7th ed., eds. Charles S. Bullock III and Mark J. Rozell (Lanham, MD: Rowman & Littlefield, 2021), 147–178.

Hopkins, Daniel J. *The Increasingly United States: How and Why American Political Behavior Nationalized*. Chicago: University of Chicago Press, 2018.

Hopkins, David A. *Red Fighting Blue: How Geography and Electoral Rules Polarize American Politics*. Cambridge: Cambridge University Press, 2017.

Huffmon, Scott H., H. Gibbs Knotts, and Seth C. McKee. "Down with the Southern Cross: Opinions on the Confederate Battle Flag in South Carolina." *Political Science Quarterly* 132, no. 4 (Winter 2017–2018) 719–741.

Iyengar, Shanto, Yphtach Lelkes, Matthew Levendusky, Neil Malhotra, and Sean J. West-wood. "The Origins and Consequences of Affective Polarization in the United States." *Annual Review of Political Science* 22 (May 2019), 129–146.

Jacobson, Gary C. "The 1994 House Elections in Perspective." *Political Science Quarterly* 111, no. 2 (Summer 1996), 203–223.

———. *A Divider, Not a Uniter: George W. Bush and the American People.* New York: Pearson/Longman, 2007.

———. "The 2008 Presidential and Congressional Elections: Anti-Bush Referendum and Prospects for the Democratic Majority." *Political Science Quarterly* 124, no. 1 (Spring 2009), 1–30.

———. "The Republican Resurgence in 2010." *Political Science Quarterly* 126, no. 1 (Spring 2011), 27–52.

———. "It's Nothing Personal: The Decline of the Incumbency Advantage in U.S. House Elections." *Journal of Politics* 77, no. 3 (July 2015), 861–873.

———. "Extreme Referendum: Donald Trump and the 2018 Midterm Elections." *Political Science Quarterly* 134, no. 1 (Spring 2019), 9–38.

———. "The Presidential and Congressional Elections of 2020: A National Referendum on the Trump Presidency." *Political Science Quarterly* 136, no. 1 (2021), 11–45.

Jacobson, Gary C., and Jamie L. Carson. *The Politics of Congressional Elections.* Lanham, MD: Rowman & Littlefield, 2020.

Jacobson, Gary C., and Samuel Kernell. *Strategy and Choice in Congressional Elections.* New Haven, CT: Yale University Press, 1983.

Jardina, Ashley. *White Identity Politics.* Cambridge: Cambridge University Press, 2019.

Jewell, Katherine Rye. *Dollars for Dixie: Business and the Transformation of Conservatism in the Twentieth Century.* Cambridge: Cambridge University Press, 2017.

Johnston, Ron, David Manley, Kelvyn Jones, and Ryne Rohla. "The Geographical Polar-ization of the American Electorate: A Country of Increasing Electoral Landslides?" *GeoJournal* 85, no. 1 (February 2020), 187–204.

Judis, John B., and Ruy Teixeira. *The Emerging Democratic Majority.* New York: Simon & Schuster, 2002.

Kalb, Deborah, ed. *Guide to U.S. Elections: Volume II. Seventh Edition.* Los Angeles: SAGE/CQ Press, 2016.

Keith, Bruce E., David B. Magleby, Candice J. Nelson, Elizabeth Orr, Mark C. Westlye, and Raymond E. Wolfinger. *The Myth of the Independent Voter.* Berkeley: University of California Press, 1992.

Key, V. O., Jr. *Southern Politics in State and Nation.* New York: Alfred A. Knopf, 1949.

———. "A Theory of Critical Elections." *Journal of Politics* 17, no. 1 (February 1955), 3–18.

———. "Secular Realignment and the Party System." *Journal of Politics* 21, no. 2 (May 1959), 198–210.

Kirby, Jack Temple. *Media-Made Dixie: The South in the American Imagination.* Athens: University of Georgia Press, 2004.

Kitschelt, Herbert P., and Philipp Rehm. "Secular Partisan Realignment in the United States: The Socioeconomic Reconfiguration of White Partisan Support since the New Deal Era." *Politics & Society* 47, no. 3 (September 2019), 425–479.

Klinkner, Philip A. "Waving the 'White' Flag: Racial Voting Patterns in the 2001 Missis-sippi Flag Referendum." *PS: Political Science and Politics* 34, no. 3 (September 2001), 647.

Knuckey, Jonathan. "The Myth of the 'Two Souths?' Racial Resentment and White Party Identification in the Deep South and Rim South." *Social Science Quarterly* 98, no. 2 (June 2017), 728–749.

Kousser, J. Morgan. *The Shaping of Southern Politics: Suffrage Restriction and the Establishment of the One-Party South, 1880–1910.* New Haven, CT: Yale University Press, 1974.

Kuziemko, Ilyana, and Ebonya Washington. "Why Did the Democrats Lose the South? Bringing New Data to an Old Debate." *American Economic Review* 108, no. 10 (October 2018), 2830–2867.

"Laboratories of Democracy: The 2020 Presidential Election Will Be Decided in the Suburbs" (*The Economist*, January 4, 2020, 16–17. https://www.economist.com/united-states/2020/01/04/the-2020-presidential-election-will-be-decided-in-the-suburbs.

Ladewig, Jeffrey W., and Seth C. McKee. "The Devil's in the Details: Evaluating the One Person, One Vote Principle in American Politics." *Politics and Governance* 2, no. 1 (April 14, 2014): 4–31.

Lamis, Alexander P. *The Two-Party South.* Oxford: Oxford University Press, 1988.

——, ed. *Southern Politics in the 1990s.* Baton Rouge: Louisiana State University Press, 1999).

Lang, Corey, and Shanna Pearson-Merkowitz. "Partisan Sorting in the United States, 1972–2012: New Evidence from a Dynamic Analysis." *Political Geography* 48 (September 2015), 119–129.

Layman, Geoffrey. *The Great Divide: Religious and Cultural Conflict in American Party Politics.* New York: Columbia University Press, 2001.

Levendusky, Matthew. *The Partisan Sort: How Liberals Became Democrats and Conservatives Became Republicans.* Chicago: University of Chicago Press, 2009.

Lewis, Simon, and Zachary Fagenson. "Florida Latinos Boost Trump's Margin of Victory in Battleground State." *Reuters*, November 4, 2020. https://cutt.ly/Fzoz4j2.

Lloyd, Richard. "Urbanization and the Southern United States." *Annual Review of Sociology* 38 (August 2012), 483–506.

Lublin, David. *The Republican South: Democratization and Partisan Change.* Princeton, NJ: Princeton University Press, 2004.

Lupton, Robert N., and Seth C. McKee. "Dixie's Drivers: Core Values and the Southern Republican Realignment." *Journal of Politics* 82, no. 3 (July 2020), 921–936.

Maass, Harold. "The Return of the Trump Rally." *The Week,* June 14, 2021. https://the week.com/donald-trump/1001167/trumps-rally-revival.

Mason, Lilliana. *Uncivil Agreement: How Politics Became Our Identity.* Chicago: University of Chicago Press, 2018.

Matthews, Donald R., and James W. Prothro. *Negroes and the New Southern Politics.* New York: Harcourt, Brace & World, 1966.

Maxwell, Angie, and Todd Shields. *The Long Southern Strategy: How Chasing White Voters in the South Changed American Politics.* New York: Oxford University Press, 2019.

Mayhew, David R. *Congress: The Electoral Connection.* New Haven, CT: Yale University Press, 1974.

McGann, Anthony J., Charles Anthony Smith, Michael Latner, and Alex Keena. *Gerrymandering in America: The House of Representatives, the Supreme Court, and the Future of Popular Sovereignty.* New York: Cambridge University Press, 2016.

McGinniss, Joe. *The Selling of the President, 1968.* New York: Pocket Books, 1969.

McKee, Seth C. "Rural Voters in Presidential Elections, 1992–2004." *The Forum: A Journal of Applied Research in Contemporary Politics* 5, no. 2 (January 2007), Article 2.

———. "Rural Voters and the Polarization of American Presidential Elections." *PS: Political Science & Politics* 41, no. 1 (January 2008), 101–108.

———. *Republican Ascendancy in Southern U.S. House Elections.* New York: Routledge, 2010.

———. "Political Conditions and the Electoral Effects of Redistricting." *American Politics Research* 41, no. 4 (July 2013), 623–650.

———. "Politics in Black and White: The Mississippi Delta," in *Defining the Delta: Interdisciplinary Perspectives on the Lower Mississippi River Delta*, ed. Janelle Collins (Fayetteville: University of Arkansas Press, 2015), 133–144.

———. "Race and Subregional Persistence in a Changing South." *Southern Cultures* 23, no. 2 (Summer 2017), 134–159.

———. *The Dynamics of Southern Politics: Causes and Consequences.* Thousand Oaks, CA: CQ Press, 2019.

McKee, Seth C., and Stephen C. Craig. "A Political History of Florida Elections, 1866–2016." *Florida Political Chronicle* 25, no. 2 (Fall 2017–Spring 2018), 93–122.

McKee, Seth C., and Danny Hayes. "Polls and Elections: Dixie's Kingmakers: Stability and Change in Southern Presidential Primary Electorates." *Presidential Studies Quarterly* 39, no. 2 (June 2009), 400–417.

———. "The Transformation of Southern Presidential Primaries." In *Presidential Elections in the South: Putting 2008 in Political Context*, eds. Branwell DuBose Kapeluck, Robert P. Steed, and Laurence W. Moreland (Boulder, CO: Lynne Rienner Publishers, 2010), 39–69.

McKee, Seth C., and Mark J. McKenzie. "Analyzing Redistricting Outcomes," in *Rotten Boroughs, Political Thickets, and Legislative Donnybrooks: Redistricting in Texas*, ed. Gary A. Keith (Austin: University of Texas Press, 2013), 95–146.

McKee, Seth C., and Daron R. Shaw. "Redistricting in Texas: Institutionalizing Republican Ascendancy," in *Redistricting in the New Millennium*, ed. Peter F. Galderisi (Lanham, MD: Lexington Books, 2005), 275–311.

McKee, Seth C., and Daniel A. Smith. "Trump Territory," in *Florida and the 2016 Election of Donald J. Trump*, eds. Matthew T. Corrigan and Michael Binder. (Gainesville: University Press of Florida, 2019), 49–75.

McKee, Seth C., and Melanie J. Springer. "A Tale of 'Two Souths': White Voting Behavior in Contemporary Southern Elections." *Social Science Quarterly* 96, no. 2 (June 2015), 588–607.

McKee, Seth C., and Jeremy M. Teigen. "Probing the Reds and Blues: Sectionalism and Voter Location in the 2000 and 2004 U.S. Presidential Elections." *Political Geography* 28, no. 8 (November 2009), 484–495.

———. "The New Blue: Northern In-Migration in Southern Presidential Elections." *PS: Political Science and Politics* 49, no. 2 (April 2016), 228–233.

McKee, Seth C., Jeremy M. Teigen, and Mathieu Turgeon. "The Partisan Impact of Congressional Redistricting: The Case of Texas, 2001–2003." *Social Science Quarterly* 87, no. 2 (June 2006), 308–317.

McKee, Seth C., and Antoine Yoshinaka. "Late to the Parade: Party Switchers in Contemporary US Southern Legislatures." *Party Politics* 21, no. 6 (November 2015), 957–969.

McKee, Seth C., Antoine Yoshinaka, Keith E. Lee, Jr., and Richard McKenzie. "Party Switchers and Reelection: A Precinct-Level Analysis." *American Review of Politics* 35, no. 2 (December 6, 2016), 1–26.

Mendelberg, Tali. *The Race Card: Campaign Strategy, Implicit Messages, and the Norm of Equality.* Princeton, NJ: Princeton University Press, 2001.

Mickey, Robert. *Paths Out of Dixie: The Democratization of Authoritarian Enclaves in America's Deep South, 1944–1972.* Princeton, NJ: Princeton University Press, 2015.

Miller, Arthur H., Patricia Gurin, Gerald Gurin, and Oksana Malanchuk. "Group Consciousness and Political Participation." *American Journal of Political Science* 25, no. 3 (August 1981), 494–511.

Miller, Gary, and Norman Schofield. "The Transformation of the Republican and Democratic Party Coalitions in the U.S." *Perspectives on Politics* 6, no. 3 (September 2008), 433–450.

Monmonier, Mark S. *Bushmanders and Bullwinkles: How Politicians Manipulate Electronic Maps and Census Data to Win Elections.* Chicago: University of Chicago Press, 2001.

Morris, Irwin L. *Movers and Stayers: The Partisan Transformation of 21st Century Southern Politics.* New York: Oxford University Press, 2021.

Muravchik, Stephanie, and Jon A. Shields. *Trump's Democrats.* Washington, DC: Brookings Institution Press, 2020.

Murphy, Reg, and Hal Gulliver. *The Southern Strategy.* New York: Scribner, 1971.

Myers, Adam. "Secular Geographical Polarization in the American South: The Case of Texas, 1996–2010." *Electoral Studies* 32, no. 1 (2013) 48–62.

Nadeau, Richard, Richard G. Niemi, Harold W. Stanley, and Jean-Francois Godbout. "Class, Party, and South/Non-South Differences: An Update." *American Politics Research* 32, no. 1 (January 2004), 52–67.

Nadeau, Richard, and Harold W. Stanley. "Class Polarization in Partisanship among Native Southern Whites, 1952–90." *American Journal of Political Science* 37, no. 3 (August 1993), 900–919.

Nelson, Michael. *Resilient America: Electing Nixon in 1968, Channeling Dissent, and Dividing Government.* Lawrence: University Press of Kansas, 2014.

Nesmith, Bruce. *The New Republican Coalition: The Reagan Campaigns and White Evangelicals.* New York: Peter Lang, 1994.

Niesse, Mark, and Jennifer Peebles. "Turnout dip among Georgia Republicans flipped U.S. Senate." *Atlanta-Journal Constitution,* February 2, 2021. https://cutt.ly/tzoPXgX.

Nixon, H. C. "The Southern Legislature and Legislation." *Journal of Politics* 10, no. 2 (May 1948), 410–417.

Noel, Hans. *Political Ideologies and Political Parties in America.* New York: Cambridge University Press, 2013.

NPR. "Senator, You're No Jack Kennedy." *National Public Radio,* May 23, 2006. https://www.npr.org/templates/story/story.php?storyId=5425248.

Odem, Mary E., and Elaine Lacy, eds. *Latino Immigrants and the Transformation of the U.S. South.* Athens: University of Georgia Press, 2009.

Parent, Wayne. *Inside the Carnival: Unmasking Louisiana Politics.* Baton Rouge: Louisiana State University Press, 2006.

Parker, Frank R. *Black Votes Count: Political Empowerment in Mississippi After 1965.* Chapel Hill: University of North Carolina Press, 1990.

Petrocik, John R. *Party Coalitions: Realignment and the Decline of the New Deal Party System.* Chicago: University of Chicago Press, 1981.

———. "Realignment: New Party Coalitions and the Nationalization of the South." *Journal of Politics* 49, no. 2 (May 1987), 347–375.

Petrocik, John R., and Scott W. Desposato. "The Partisan Consequences of Majority-Minority Redistricting in the South, 1992 and 1994." *Journal of Politics* 60, no. 3 (August 1998), 613–633.

Phillips, Kevin P. *The Emerging Republican Majority.* New Rochelle, NY: Arlington House, 1969.

Popkin, Samuel L. *The Reasoning Voter: Communication and Persuasion in Presidential Campaigns.* Chicago: University of Chicago Press, 1991.

Prokop. Andrew. "What Glenn Youngkin's Virginia win means for Democrats." *Vox,* November 3, 2021. https://www.vox.com/2021/11/3/22752593/virginia-governor-results-youngkin-wins.

Prysby, Charles. *Rich Voter, Poor Voter, Red Voter, Blue Voter: Social Class and Voting Behavior in Contemporary America.* New York: Routledge, 2020.

Ratcliffe, Michael. "A Century of Delineating a Changing Landscape: The Census Bureau's Urban and Rural Classification, 1910 to 2010." Washington, DC: US Census Bureau, 2016). Accessed at https://www2.census.gov/geo/pdfs/reference/ua/Century_of_Defining_Urban.pdf.

Ratcliffe, Michael, Charlynn Burd, Kelly Holder, and Alison Fields. "Defining Rural at the U.S. Census Bureau" (Washington, DC: US Census Bureau, December 8, 2016). https://www.census.gov/library/publications/2016/acs/acsgeo-1.html.

Reed, John Shelton. *One South: An Ethnic Approach to Regional Culture.* Baton Rouge: Louisiana State University Press, 1982.

Reiter, Howard L., and Jeffrey M. Stonecash. *Counter Realignment: Political Change in the Northeastern United States.* Cambridge: Cambridge University Press, 2011.

Rodden, Jonathan A. *Why Cities Lose: The Deep Roots of the Urban-Rural Political Divide.* New York: Basic Books, 2019.

Rohde, David W. *Parties and Leaders in the Postreform House.* Chicago: University of Chicago Press, 1991.

Rove, Karl. "Trump's Appeal Rings Hollow at CPAC." *Wall Street Journal,* March 4, 2021, A17.

Salts, James D. *The Man from Missouri.* New York: Authors Co-operative Publishing Co., 1916.

Scala, Dante J., and Kenneth M. Johnson. "Political Polarization along the Rural-Urban Continuum? The Geography of the Presidential Vote, 2000–2016." *ANNALS of the American Academy of Political and Social Science* 672, no. 1 (July 2017), 162–184.

Schaller, Thomas F. *Whistling Past Dixie: How Democrats Can Win Without the South.* New York: Simon and Schuster, 2008.

Schickler, Eric. *Racial Realignment: The Transformation of American Liberalism, 1932–1965.* Princeton, NJ: Princeton University Press, 2016.

Seagull, Louis M. *Southern Republicanism.* New York: John Wiley and Sons, 1975.

Shafer, Byron E. *The American Political Pattern: Stability and Change, 1932–2016.* Lawrence: University Press of Kansas, 2016.

Shafer, Byron E., and Richard G. C. Johnston. "The Transformation of Southern Politics Revisited: The House of Representatives as a Window." *British Journal of Political Science* 31, no. 4 (October 2001), 601–625.

Shafer, Byron E., and Richard Johnston. *The End of Southern Exceptionalism: Class, Race, and Partisan Change in the Postwar South.* Cambridge, MA: Harvard University Press, 2006.

Sides, John, Daron Shaw, Matt Grossmann, and Keena Lipsitz. *Campaigns and Elections: Rules, Reality, Strategy, Choice.* New York: W. W. Norton and Co., 2018.

Sides, John, Michael Tesler, and Lynn Vavreck. "The 2016 U.S. Election: How Trump Lost and Won." *Journal of Democracy* 28, no. 2 (April 2017). 34–44.

———. *Identity Crisis: The 2016 Presidential Campaign and the Battle for the Meaning of America.* Princeton, NJ: Princeton University Press, 2018.

Sievert, Joel, and Seth C. McKee. "Nationalization in U.S. Senate and Gubernatorial Elections." *American Politics Research* 47, no. 5 (September 2019), 1055–1080.

Silver, James W. *Mississippi: The Closed Society.* Jackson: University Press of Mississippi, 2012.

Springer, Melanie Jean. "Why Georgia? A Curious and Unappreciated Pioneer on the Road to Early Youth Enfranchisement in the United States." *Journal of Policy History* 32, no. 3 (July 2020), 273–324.

Stanley, Harold W. "Southern Partisan Changes: Dealignment, Realignment or Both?" *Journal of Politics* 50, no. 1 (February 1988), 64–88.

——. "Presidential Elections and the South," in *Writing Southern Politics: Contemporary Interpretations and Future Directions,* eds. Robert P. Steed and Laurence W. Moreland (Lexington: University Press of Kentucky, 2006), 219–239.

Stimson, James A. *Tides of Consent: How Public Opinion Shapes American Politics.* Cambridge: Cambridge University Press, 2004.

Stonecash, Jeffrey M. *Class and Party in American Politics.* New York: Routledge, 2000.

——. *Reassessing the Incumbency Effect.* New York: Cambridge University Press, 2008.

Stonecash, Jeffrey M., Mark D. Brewer, and Mack Mariani. *Diverging Parties: Social Change, Realignment, and Party Polarization.* New York: Routledge, 2003.

Strong, Donald S. *Urban Republicanism in the South.* Tuscaloosa: University of Alabama Bureau of Public Administration, 1960.

——. "Further Reflections on Southern Politics." *Journal of Politics* 33, no. 2 (May 1971), 239–256.

Taeuber, Conrad. "Rural-Urban Migration." *Agricultural History* 15, no. 3 (July 1941), 151–160.

Teigen, Jeremy M. Daron R. Shaw, and Seth C. McKee. "Density, Race, and Vote Choice in the 2008 and 2012 Presidential Elections." *Research & Politics* (April–June 2017), 1–6.

Theriault, Sean M. *Party Polarization in Congress.* Cambridge: Cambridge University Press, 2008.

Thielemann, Gregory S. "The Rise and Stall of Southern Republicans in Congress." *Social Science Quarterly* 73, no. 1 (March 1992), 123–135.

Tilove, Jonathan. "Why Beto O'Rourke's 254-County Strategy Flopped." *Austin American-Statesman*, December 31, 2018. https://www.statesman.com/news/20181214/why-beto-orourkes-254-county-strategy-flopped.

Timpone, Richard J. "Mass Mobilization or Government Intervention? The Growth of Black Registration in the South." *Journal of Politics* 57, no. 2 (May 1995), 425–442.

Tufte, Edward R. *Data Analysis for Politics and Policy.* Englewood Cliffs, NJ: Prentice-Hall, 1974.

"Two Nations Under God." *The Economist*, March 6, 2021, 28–29.

Wang, Elbert, Darla Cameron, and Chris Essig. "More than 4,884,528 Texans Voted Early in the Midterm Election." *Texas Tribune*, November 3, 2018. https://apps.texastribune.org/features/2018/general-election-early-voting/.

Wattenberg, Martin P. *The Decline of American Political Parties, 1952–1996.* Cambridge, MA: Harvard University Press, 1998.

Whalen, Charles, and Barbara Whalen. *The Longest Debate: A Legislative History of the 1964 Civil Rights Act.* Cabin John, MD: Seven Locks Press, 1985.

Wilkerson, Isabel. *The Warmth of Other Suns: The Epic Story of America's Great Migration.* New York: Random House, 2010.

Woodward, Bob. *Rage.* New York: Simon & Schuster, 2020.

Woodward, C. Vann. *The Strange Career of Jim Crow.* Oxford: Oxford University Press, 2002.

Wright, Gavin. *Sharing the Prize: The Economics of the Civil Rights Revolution in the American South.* Cambridge, MA: Belknap Press of Harvard University Press, 2013.

Yoshinaka, Antoine. *Crossing the Aisle: Party Switching by U.S. Legislators in the Postwar Era.* New York: Cambridge University Press, 2016.

Zitner, Aaron. "Votes Offer Road Map to GOP And a Warning for Democrats." *Wall Street Journal,* November 4, 2021, A1, A4.

Index

Abbott, Greg, 195

abortion, 34–35, 205–6, 214–18, 286n30, 288–89n12

Abramowitz, Alan I., 28, 78, 136, 210

Abrams, Stacey, 117

Abramson, Paul R., 23, 65

Acharya, Avidit, 102

Adams, Greg D., 205

Aistrup, Joseph A., 18, 53

Alabama: 55, 157, 245, 269n1,2, 291n1; Black Belt counties, 2–3, 8, 277n2, 278n6; Black voters, 25–26, 67, 102–3; Democrats & congressional elections, 99, 102, 110–12, 129, 230, 231–32, 275n6, 289n1,2,3; Democrats & gubernatorial elections, 26–27, 101, 121, 274n1; Democrats & presidential elections, 13, 21, 179; civil rights issues, 13, 17, 271n17; in-migrant voters, 252; mountain Republicanism, 8; race/racism, 179; Republicans & congressional elections, 99, 100–103, 111–12, 129, 133, 226, 275n6, 289n1,2,3; Republicans & gubernatorial elections, 27, 121, 231–32, 274n1; Republicans & presidential elections, 19, 23–26, 92, 100, 179, 264, 271n17,20; Republican self-identification, 169, 178; small-town South (STS) voters, 229, 231

Alexander, Lamar, 188, 231, 286n22

Allred, Colin, 193, 286n28

American Community Survey, 46, 271n23, 278n6, 285n11, 287n5

American National Election Studies (ANES): 47–48, 83, 276n10; 2019 Pilot Study, 259, 260; Cumulative Data File (CDF), 32–33, 61, 79, 87, 161, 274n3, 276n3; Democratic strength in the South, 69; and Republican strength in South, 2, 65, 67–68, 162, 259; and presidential voting patterns, 15–16, 18–19, 22, 86–87, 91, 271n14; and rural white southerners, 22, 28–29, 32–33, 40, 53, 61, 64, 71–75, 77, 162, 164–65, 169, 270n9, 271n14, 272n26, 275n7,10, 281n3; split-ticket voting, 69–71; and urban white southerners, 22, 29, 65, 69, 71–72, 74–75, 165, 270n9, 271n14, 272n26, 275n7,10, 281n3

Ansolabehere, Stephen, 10

Arkansas Poll, 48, 174, 181–82

Arkansas: 206, 269n1, 284n6,7, 285n17, 291n1; Black voters, 21; Democrats & congressional elections, 107, 112, 133, 191; Democrats & gubernatorial elections, 55, 121, 127, 180, 184, 274n1, 285n16; Democrats & presidential elections, 8, 27, 87, 284n8; in-migrant voters, 253; reapportionment/redistricting, 191; Republicans & congressional elections, 107–8, 112, 191, 230, 275n6, 284–85n10, 285n16; Republicans & gubernatorial elections, 55, 113, 121, 180, 184, 274n1, 284n9; Republicans & presidential elections, 25–26; Republican strength, 187, 196–97, 245, 264, 287n32; rural white voters/rurality, 40, 44, 171, 174, 179, 180, 229–30, 248, 264, 285–86n18; self-identified Republicans, 175–77, 178–79; white supremacy, 13, 179

Ash, Kathleen, 32

authoritarianism, 272n28

Bafumi, Joseph, 35

Barnes, Roy, 117–18

Barone, Michael, 101, 184, 193, 239, 282n11, 284n6

Bartels, Larry M., 28, 65, 136

Bartley, Numan V., 6, 19, 53, 92, 114

Bass, Jack, 59, 113

Beck, Paul Allen, 23, 65

Bentsen, Lloyd, 1–3, 6–7, 192, 269n6

Bickerstaff, Steve, 193, 279–80n1

Biden, Joe, 224, 233, 238, 251, 270n10, 276–77n12, 287n4, 291n8, 292n15

bifactionalism, 116

birtherism, 95